Christian Science Today

Power, Policy, Practice

Christian Science Today

POWER, POLICY, PRACTICE

Charles S. Braden

1958
SOUTHERN METHODIST UNIVERSITY PRESS: DALLAS

By Charles S. Braden

RELIGIOUS ASPECTS OF THE CONQUEST OF MEXICO

MODERN TENDENCIES IN WORLD RELIGIONS

VARIETIES OF AMERICA RELIGION, *Editor*

PROCESSION OF THE GODS, *with Gaius G. Atkins*

THE WORLD'S RELIGIONS

MAN'S QUEST FOR SALVATION

THESE ALSO BELIEVE

THE SCRIPTURES OF MANKIND

WAR, COMMUNISM, AND WORLD RELIGIONS

JESUS COMPARED

TO MY WIFE

Preface

IT IS NOW nearly half a century since Mary Baker Eddy died. Both she and her movement have been written about a great deal during these years, but not one really full-length treatment, either of the founder or of the movement, has been produced on the basis of objective scholarship. Nearly everything that has been written has been either pro or contra, and often violently so. Perhaps it is still too early for any book on the subject to be regarded as non-partisan, since feeling still runs high. If the objective scholar, weighing his evidence ever so carefully, comes forward with conclusions that run counter to the claims of those who are emotionally partisan in their attitude toward Christian Science, his findings will be regarded as an attack upon the movement. If, on the other hand, there appears something favorable to Christian Science, it will at once be claimed that the author has sold out to the Christian Scientists, or that he has been afraid to print the facts lest his book might not sell, or that for some other scarcely more noble reason has obscured the truth.

When, for example, Lyman Powell wrote a scathingly critical book about Christian Science, it was deprecated by Scientists as untrue and malicious, but accepted by non–Christian Scientists as a good and reasonable statement. When, later, Powell was granted limited access to the archives of the Mother Church, and finally issued a book which has almost taken its place alongside the official *Life of Mrs. Eddy* by Sibyl Wilbur, the cry went up that Lyman Powell had been bought off, or that for some reason he had gone over to the camp of the enemy.

From the standpoint of objective scholarship neither of Powell's books can claim high standing. In the one case he wrote from evidence, or supposed evidence, on the one side—the contra—and in his later book he apparently used only evidence supplied by the other side. Why Powell in his second book chose to do that, this writer has no means of knowing; but the fact is that he seems not to have considered seriously a great deal of very valuable source material which surely would have modified his presentation substantially had he taken it into account. Possibly he weighed this material and decided against its use; but in so controversial a field he ought by all means to have stated the grounds on which he rejected these sources. Perhaps the basis for a clear-cut decision was lacking—but in such a case true scholarship requires a presentation of the conflicting sources, thus permitting the reader to know that he must make up his own mind as to how the conflicting evidence is to be evaluated. If he is then still swayed to one side or the other by his own emotional or traditional bias, there is nothing the writer can do about it. But at least the writer has performed a service by bringing to light materials on the basis of which decisions can and should be made.

Though this is the essence of objectivity, much is being said against such a position today. Scholars do have opinions and convictions; they should state them with vigor, it is asserted. There is truth and there is falsehood, and the truth must be declared. Perhaps it is the task of scholarship in an age of propaganda to keep insisting, in the fields of history and religion and politics and economics, that conclusions are not so easily come by as the convinced are wont to claim they are; that there is a considerable area in all these fields where there is not a clear distinction between white and black, light and darkness, but a great deal of gray, darker or lighter, in which the scholar is obliged to move while seeking for truth.

It may properly be asked whether complete objectivity is ever possible even among the most distinguished scholars, for every scholar is first of all human, and as a product of his social environment has unconsciously absorbed ideas and an emotional bent on most subjects of primary concern to man. This is notably true in the field of religion. Even if one stands completely outside the stream of religion—and who does?—might he not still have unconscious biases against all religion and be incapable therefore of understanding what religion is about essentially?

The present writer believes that it is possible to have a very profound regard for religion personally and still to be relatively objective in the treatment of a faith not his own, but he does not expect to arrive at a complete lack of bias. He believes, as he has stated elsewhere, that every writer ought to declare what his general point of view is so that readers may look for the outcropping of his biases and seek a corrective of such as they find. Be it known, then, that the author of this book is an ordained clergyman of the Methodist church; that he regards himself as a liberal in religion, as well as in the social and economic areas. He confesses to a prejudice in favor of democracy as over against autocracy of any kind, either fascist or communist, of freedom as over against authoritarian control, in religion as well as in these other fields—with the implied right to think for himself and to change his mind in any of these areas if there appears to be good reason to do so. Perhaps some of these biases may emerge in the course of the book, but it will be the writer's studied purpose to present as adequately as possible the facts that must be the basis of value judgments regarding Mrs. Eddy and the movement which she founded, and then to let the reader draw his own conclusions.

The writer has had before him practically everything that has been published and freely circulated of primary source material, and has carefully canvassed most of the secondary sources. He has sought the unrestricted use of the rich body of material in the archives of the Mother Church, beyond the official publications open to all—with no success whatsoever, it must be regretfully added. Overtures were made several years ago to Christian Science officials, first through the Illinois Committee on Publication, and the writer has been in frequent communication not only with this official but also with the Manager of Committees on Publication or members of his staff. He has even sought the aid of the Board of Directors of the Mother Church. These efforts have largely been in vain.

But fortunately he has had access to an enormous body of material not yet published, or circulated among only a very few persons. This included memoirs and diary records of persons closely associated with Mrs. Eddy in the intimacy of her own home, the class notes of students of Mrs. Eddy and some of the more prominent teachers of Christian Science, and scores of letters that passed between Mrs. Eddy and other individuals, or between leaders of the movement. All this has been invaluable not merely in supplying the necessary facts, but in giving the feel of an enthusiastic new movement.

Likewise, he has had the benefit of numerous interviews with Christian Science church members and leaders, as well as with some who either have withdrawn from or were excommunicated by the church for one reason or another; and he has read mountains of letters that they have received or written. That there is a dissatisfied minority in Christian Science is not surprising. Most groups have the same situation. The writer holds no brief for either the majority view or that of the minority, but he has sought to understand the points at which these differ and to set forth both views fairly. As an objective historian, there is nothing else for him to do.

Accepting full responsibility for all the conclusions reached and set forth in this study, the writer is enormously grateful to all those who have in any way aided in his search for pertinent material. For obvious reasons, the names of some who have contributed to the study have had to be withheld. But the writer has in his possession or available to him either the originals or photostatic copies of letters and other materials cited in the course of the study. He will welcome inquiry concerning any point from responsible scholars.

⋆The main purpose of this study is to see what has happened and is happening in Christian Science since Mrs. Eddy's time, with reference both to its organization and its teaching, or thought, and its practice. The writer is not interested here in turning out another biography of Mrs. Eddy, nor in the attempt to settle the dispute as to her originality versus her dependence upon Quimby or Hinduism or Hegel or any other previous source. Although the final word may not have been said in these matters, they lie for the most part outside the scope of this particular book.

Here Christian Science is taken for granted. It is a movement that came into being historically through the teaching and organizational activity of Mary Baker Eddy. At her death in 1910 it had a definite body of doctrine, or teaching, and a quite definite organization. This will necessarily have to be stated, and something of the growth of the church organization will have to be reviewed as a basis for an understanding of Christian Science today. Incidentally, Mrs. Eddy's ideas, and to some extent her person, will have to be discussed too, since she *was* so much the movement herself.

But the chief interest will be in seeing what has happened since her death. Has the essential nature of her teaching been modified? At least attempts have been made to go beyond her teachings in some respects. Are there any trends in Christian Science thought today that are new, or that have appeared in the half-century since her passing? If so, how has the church regarded them?

Has there been any development on the organizational side? Have there been any sectarian offshoots? What has become of them? How has the church dealt with them? How is the church dealing currently with those who hold views supposedly at variance with the official views?

It is to be hoped that this study will throw some light on the nature of religious institutions, by serving as a case study of a rather typical recent religious institutional development.

CHARLES S. BRADEN

Dallas, Texas
April 17, 1958

Acknowledgments

IN THE WRITING of a book, the author is always in some measure indebted to the work of others. Sometimes this indebtedness is quite unconscious; sometimes he can specify at exactly what points he has been influenced, and can name the person to whom he is indebted. Quite often he knows that he is in debt to someone, but cannot say to whom. In his research for this book the writer has read almost everything pertinent that has been published, and a great deal of unpublished matter. Where he has quoted directly, and usually where he has only paraphrased or employed in some other way facts or ideas taken from the work of others, he has indicated the source in a parenthesis inserted in the text.

Comparatively few quotes from copyrighted publications used herein are of sufficient length to require formal permission to quote from copyright owners. Some of the longer quotes are from formerly copyrighted material which is now in the public domain, and may therefore be freely used without formal permission. This is true of all quotations from *Science and Health,* and most of those from others of Mrs. Eddy's writings. Unless otherwise indicated all references are to the final editions, currently in use, of *Science and Health* and the *Manual.*

To all who have given their formal permission to quote, and to all from whom no permission was required, the author is grateful. He desires to express appreciation also to all those whose work has contributed materially to this study—for example, Altman K. Swihart, whose *Since Mrs. Eddy* supplied the major basis for what he wrote concerning Annie C. Bill and her movement, though without direct quotation at any length. To all who furnished materials through personal interview or through correspondence, or through the gift of books, pamphlets, letters, photostats, newspaper clippings, magazines, etc., whether they were used directly or not, he tenders thanks: in particular to the *Christian Century* for permission to reprint passages from correspondence between the author and George Channing, published in that magazine in 1952.

To librarians in a dozen cities, universities, and colleges across the country—from Boston to Berkeley, from Harvard to Huntington, and from Chicago to Dallas—who have brought out "of their treasure what is new and what is old," for his scrutiny, the author is grateful.

To all the friends within and outside Christian Science who have offered counsel and encouragement during the years in which the study has been carried on, he owes a debt of real gratitude. And finally to the Southern Methodist University Press and its kindly editors and staff, he is most thankful. What a lot of people and of human effort it takes to produce a book! The author can only hope that the reader of this particular volume will say as he finishes it: "Well, it was worth it!"

Contents

PLATES

PART I

Origins of the Movement

1

Christian Science Today

CHRISTIAN SCIENTISTS are found in almost all American cities of any size. They are neighbors to many of us. We meet them socially, in business, at school. We see their churches—often, in larger cities, magnificent structures, always neat and dignified. Their reading rooms are familiar to us, from the outside at least. Always there is an open Bible on display, and the textbook, *Science and Health*. The quiet elegance of many of these rooms makes one hesitate as an outsider to wander in and read the literature available, though outsiders are always welcome.

Everybody knows the *Christian Science Monitor*, which is found on many of the newsstands; and if the current number is not readily available, older copies of this excellent daily, along with the *Christian Science Journal* and *Sentinel*, are to be found in almost any railroad or bus station—indeed, anywhere that people are likely to find themselves obliged to spend time waiting. Many take advantage of this free literature and become acquainted with the faith that produces it.

Even so, by and large, most people do not know much about Christian Science except that it is a healing movement. They have heard stories about someone in their community who claimed to have been healed through this means. Sometimes they have heard of a Christian Scientist who, in fidelity to his convictions, has refused medical assistance and died. Such stories abound.

Who are these people? What do they believe? What do they get out of their faith? Why do they become Christian Scientists? Are they Christians?

I sat one morning in my club in Evanston with a friend and fellow-resident. He was a businessman, an insurance broker, going every day to Chicago for his day's work. In the course of the conversation some familiar mention was made by him of Methodism. "Oh, are you a Methodist?" I asked, for that happened to be my own religious affiliation.

"No," he replied, "not now, but I used to be. Now I am a Christian Scientist."

"Indeed," I replied. "As one Methodist to one who was once of that persuasion, would you mind telling me why you left the Methodist church for Christian Science?"

"Gladly," he answered, for Christian Scientists are generally eager to witness to their faith. The livest and most effective public meetings they hold are the Wednesday night testimony meetings where one after another rises to witness as to what his faith has done for him.

"Ten years ago," he told me, "I was a cripple. Arthritis had developed to the point where I was almost immobilized. I had to give up my work. I could no longer go to my office daily. I had sought the best medical help available. They had treated me with all the medicines known at that time. They seemed quite unable to help me. My condition grew steadily worse.

"One day a relative who was a Christian Scientist came to visit me. 'Why don't you try Christian Science?' she asked.

" 'But I don't believe in it,' I replied.

" 'Well, why don't you try it anyway, it can't hurt you,' she countered.

"I hesitated. I shared the average popular prejudice against it and its claims.

" 'Do you mean,' I said, 'that it might possibly help me even if I don't believe?—for I certainly don't.'

" 'Regardless of how you think of it, let me call a practitioner,' she said.

"What did I have to lose? I thought. Then I said, 'All right, but I don't think it will do any good.'

"A practitioner came. He gave me a treatment. I let him come again. Slowly, though not at once, I began to feel better. The treatments continued. To my amazement I began to be able to move more freely and without pain, then to walk, and finally I was enabled to undertake my work again and begin going back to the office.

"Which, by the way, I should be doing right now. Will you excuse me, please?" he said, rising to go.

And off he went with a light step to catch his train for a hot day's work in the city. No wonder he became a Christian Scientist.

Here was one answer. People are led into Christian Science through having themselves been healed, or through the healing of someone very dear and close to them. I recall a colleague in the academic world, who later became an important leader in the movement, telling me how it was the healing of his wife that first brought him into it.

Clearly this is not the only answer. But if one reads widely in the literature of the movement, periodical or book, he is likely to reach the conclusion that it is the most important answer of all. Every *Journal* and every *Sentinel* contains testimonies as to the healing wrought through the faith, and so do most of the books. The radio, which is increasingly employed as a propaganda medium by the church, constantly throws out testimonies of practical healing, and television shows, now bringing Christian Science to the screens of American homes all the way across the continent, feature healing as a primary offering of the Christian Science faith. The very name of the textbook, which contains what Christian Scientists believe is an inspired message from God vouchsafed to Mary Baker Eddy, stresses healing: *Science and Health*. Mrs. Eddy herself declared that her church was designed to "reinstate primitive Christianity and its lost element of healing" (*Manual*, p. 17), that she regarded "healing [as] better than teaching" (*Manual*, p. 92), that the individual's ability to heal "shows [his] position as a Christian Scientist" (*Science and Health*, p. 182). Persons who have been disciplined for some purported lapse in their loyalty to the continuing movement complain bitterly that this was despite an exemplary record of healing which they understood Mrs. Eddy to teach was the crucial test of a Christian Scientist. Unquestionably, healing will always be a primary concern of the movement.

A prominent Christian Science official wrote in a personal letter to me the other day what I think represents the general Christian Scientist view: "Our Church would cease to have a reason for existing if it should cease to heal."

But healing is not the sole interest which draws people into Christian Science. It has a definite philosophy which appeals to some minds as more tenable than any other. This metaphysics is a profound idealism, a belief that Mind alone is real—Mind being synonymous for Christian Scientists with God. In a time of strong emphasis upon either a materialistic philosophy or the denial of any need, or even possibility, of finding an ultimate answer as to the nature of the universe, not a few people have been attracted to the idealistic presuppositions of Christian Science.

Of course Mrs. Eddy's doctrine is not the only absolute idealism. There are formal schools of idealistic thought, as for example that of Bishop Berkeley. The discoveries of modern physicists tend to probe beyond the material world, to dissolve it into force, energy, and to eat away steadily at the claims of material existence as separate and distinct from mind. And Christian Science, primarily a religion but also a philosophy, builds upon these premises a healing system and claims that the healing which its adherents are able to mediate results as a direct corollary of the fact of the nonmaterial nature of the universe. The healing, they believe, tends to confirm the philosophy. It is thus proven true experimentally, they claim. The proof of the pudding is in the eating.

But I suspect that the number of those who come into Christian Science for the satisfaction of their philosophical questions, apart from healing, is relatively small. For most people, probably, healing is primary, the philosophy underlying it secondary—chiefly credible perhaps because it is alleged as the underlying basis of their healing. Had they not been healed they would not have accepted the philosophy.

Then there are many who are in Christian Science because they were born into Christian Scientist families and grew up in the faith

—absorbed it in the home and learned it in the Sunday school (which the church maintains for those under twenty years of age). They learn to expect healings to take place, and I have talked to many young people who have been confirmed in the faith either by a personal healing or by healings observed within their family groups. Of course, like all other forms of religious faith, Christian Science loses some of its young people because they find in their environment other ideas which appeal to them as more tenable. So far as I know no study has been made to see whether young people of this faith weather the adolescent years and exposure to radically different ideas any better or any worse than those of other faiths. I think it safe to say that more of those who grow up in Christian Science are held to it by what is regarded by them as a satisfying philosophy than are attracted to it initially by this consideration.

But Christian Science is more than just a means of keeping well. General well-being is a definite concern, and this includes not only bodily health but what is spoken of as "supply." Christian Science practitioners not only treat people for what the world regards as sickness, but seek also to aid them, through treatment, in the effort to assure abundance in their economic life. I know personally one case of a young bond salesman who was getting nowhere in his business until he took treatments from a practitioner, but who from that time forward began to prosper until he had become, when I met him, a great success in his field. I happened to be present at the home of a practitioner when a telephone call came through from one who sought his aid in a business venture, and I heard the counsel he gave.

It is a commonly held belief concerning Christian Scientists that they come from the wealthy and advantaged classes mostly. This is not true. While the movement has always attracted some people of wealth and position, who because of their prominence receive much public attention, it appears that the majority of Christian Scientists are from what might be called the upper middle class, economically; and there are obviously a great many of very moderate means. But holding as they do to the conviction that they must emphasize the positive, manifest prosperity as well as health, they express in every possible way their faith in the availability of supply. They dress well. They build solidly. They are optimists as to the future. Observed by outsiders, the resulting picture is impressive.

On the basis of this philosophy they do exhibit a calmness and serenity which many a modern wishes he could acquire. Christian Scientists definitely believe in the necessity of following a discipline. This includes the unremitting study of their textbook and other writings by Mrs. Eddy. Almost unfailingly every Christian Scientist opens his day with a study of the "lesson sermon"—a collection of citations from *Science and Health* and the Bible, prepared in Boston and assigned to the field through the official *Quarterly*. It is this regimen which accounts, in considerable part, for the apparent calm and serenity of the average Christian Scientist. He takes time to be alone, to read, to reflect, to pray. This is the secret of poise and serenity in any faith. Christian Scientists seem to be more successful in getting their people to follow the discipline than are most other faiths.

Some have suggested—and of course these were outsiders—that one of the appeals of Christian Science is the fact that it denies the reality of evil and that it thus escapes from the real world into one of imagined security. It is said that this tendency to *escapism* is deep within many for whom the real world is too much, and that they seize upon this philosophic justification for withdrawing themselves from the world. The characteristic serenity of Christian Scientists generally is sometimes attributed to a resultant insularity.

Nevertheless Christian Scientists as individual citizens may become responsible and influential members of their communities. The late Lord Lothian, British ambassador to the United States, was an outstanding example of this. But there are definite limitations, for while they are enjoined to "promote peace on earth and good will toward men," they are at the same time forbidden to participate in the activities of organizations or societies outside those of the Mother Church. (*Manual*, pp. 44-45) As a church, they do not engage largely in eleemosynary projects as do other churches. But by and large Christian Scientists are regarded as estimable citizens in most communities.

A testimony which appeared in the *Sentinel* (LVII, 1670) expressed very well the various values Christian Scientists find in their faith. During the three and a half years he had been studying Mrs. Eddy's teaching, the writer said, it had had a regenerating influence on his life, and a great deal of good had come into his experience. The thing for which he was most grateful was a greater consciousness of the presence of good. He was surprised to find how much more time he spends than before doing good in one way or another, and with greater cheerfulness and optimism. Before studying "Science," he had seldom thought to help others or to appreciate the good they were doing. And there is now a joy in doing this that he did not formerly experience. This he regards as a proof of progress, and he is grateful. The Bible has been illuminated for him, and has become a meaningful book. Before, he had seldom bothered to look at it; now it is an absorbing book. It has brought a lessening of fear in his affairs and much greater happiness, even while his problems are being worked out. The book is so full of kindness and helpful counsel that he can't help loving it. It has become thrilling reading since his discovery that those healings which took place centuries ago are taking place today, and that even a little understanding brings some degree of harmony. No wonder he is grateful to Mrs. Eddy, he writes, since without Christian Science his understanding of Truth would have been impossible.

Are they Christian? Of course they are. Traced historically, Christian Science is an offshoot of Protestant Christianity. Its basis is the Bible. It purports to be a recovery of the lost emphasis of primitive Christianity, especially in healing. There is a good deal of evidence to prove that Mrs. Eddy never desired to form a separate church, but only to restore to Christianity in her own day the lost emphasis on healing. She was a loyal New England Congregationalist in her earlier years. To be sure, doctrinally she departs at a number of points from the theological beliefs of orthodox Protestant Christianity. In her insistence upon the oneness of God, she follows Unitarian thought—though she professes belief in the Trinity as she defines it (a definition quite different from the orthodox). Her conception of Christ differs from that of ordinary Protestant thought.

She draws a sharp distinction between the historical Jesus and the Christ, but in this she has ample precedent within historic Christianity at various times. It will be recalled that Nestorius, Bishop of Byzantium, was deposed in 431 A.D. over this very issue.

Let us say, then, that Christian Science is not typical orthodox Protestantism, but that it is linked historically with that branch of the Christian faith. It is definitely a part of the vast and varied proliferation of the movement which arose as a result of the historic appearance of Jesus. The majority of Christians, the orthodox, may reject the Christian Science interpretation of Christ and his teaching, but that does not make it non-Christian. It is only to declare that the interpretation is different from their own, which they assume to be the right one.

Surely, in a day of relative religious freedom, it is anyone's right to interpret and to express his faith in his own way. Certainly this is the very heart of the Protestant contention. Any group which makes the Bible the basis of its faith and makes Christ so central as Christian Scientists do can hardly be refused the name Christian. Christianity in its historic development has been interpreted from many angles. Here is simply one more.

Christian Science is a modern restatement of the Christian faith developed by Mary Baker Eddy. Eventually it took organized form as one of the numerous Christian denominations of American life. It has encountered bitter antagonism on the part of orthodox religionists, both Catholic and Protestant, as well as on the part of the orthodox medical fraternity. But gradually religious opposition has lessened. The church has come to be respected and almost, if not quite, fully accepted by her sister churches. The quiet Christian character of so many of those who hold to the Christian Science faith, the exemplary lives they live in the community, and the serenity and calm which many of them have achieved through their faith have been important factors in winning this acceptance.

2

The Founder

MARY BAKER EDDY, founder of Christian Science, was one of the most remarkable women to appear on the American scene during the nineteenth century. She was also one of the most controversial figures of the period. Judged according to generally accepted standards of success in our culture, she was an almost complete failure at fifty years of age, yet at eighty-nine she died surrounded by every evidence of wealth, comfort, and power, mourned by many thousands of devoted followers, and acclaimed as an unusually successful person even by those who make material possessions a measure of success.

At fifty Mrs. Eddy was regarded by most people as an impractical, aspiring author of a book which she could get no publisher to accept and which she lacked funds to publish privately. At the time of her death thirty-nine years later the printing presses were kept busy printing not only this often-rejected book but dozens of other books, pamphlets, and periodicals she had written or inspired. Profits from the distribution of all these had made her a woman of wealth.

At the half-century mark she was almost alone, with not more than a small handful of followers who believed in her. Yet at her passing thousands whom she had taught, or who attributed their healing to her, mourned her as Mother. That massive pile of masonry, the great Mother Church in Boston, was filled to overflowing with worshiping converts to her faith when the announcement was made from the pulpit that she had passed away, and in churches all over the United States and in many distant parts of the world she was mourned as the beloved Founder and Leader of their faith.

It is difficult to read the story of her years of struggle and final triumph without a feeling of profound admiration for her resourcefulness, her undaunted courage, her indefatigable labors, her persistence in the face of opposition, her skill in handling people, and her ability to win almost fanatical loyalty from her followers—even when one may disagree with the substance of her teaching and cherish sincere questions as to the methods she used or as to the nature of the organization which through her efforts was brought into being.

Mary Baker Eddy *was* Christian Science for so many years that to tell the story of its development, even after her death, imposes upon the writer the obligation to give at least a brief sketch of her life and the influences that acted upon her to produce the amazing results she achieved during her later years. For Mrs. Eddy, though no longer present in the flesh, has cast a long shadow, and her influence in respect to Christian Science thought, practice, and organization must be considered in any history of the movement since her death.

Many full-length lives of Mrs. Eddy have been written. There is *The Life of Mary Baker Eddy* by Sibyl Wilbur, officially approved and published by the Christian Science Publishing Society. There are also the approved, but less popular, *Mary Baker Eddy* by Lyman Powell, and more recently *The Cross and the Crown* by Norman Beasley, which has been warmly received by the Christian Science church people. These are all highly laudatory treatments of the Founder. The two latter books are advertised as being by non-Christian Scientists, although it must be said of *The Cross and the Crown*, as reviewer Perry Miller pointed out in the *New York Times*, that it "presents a point of view which must be termed, for lack of a better phrase, pro-Scientist." Then there is *Mrs. Eddy* by Hugh A. Studdert-Kennedy, one of the most sincere of Christian Scientists, who however had resigned from the church before he wrote his book. It is a reverent, eminently appreciative work, but failed to win official approval. It has been praised by some leading Christian

Scientists as an unusually penetrating treatment of Mrs. Eddy's life, and in no sense derogatory of her.

Mary Baker Eddy: The Truth and the Tradition was written by Ernest Sutherland Bates with the collaboration of a onetime member of the Mother Church Board of Directors, John Valentine Dittemore. It contains a great deal of material not ordinarily available which Dittemore was able to furnish, and, although the material has been privately authenticated by the church's official historian, Clifford P. Smith, the book is regarded by orthodox Scientists as anathema. Finally, the Edwin Dakin book, *Mrs. Eddy: The Biography of a Virginal Mind,* an unusually comprehensive treatment which makes use of probably the widest range of source materials employed by any writer, has been roundly condemned by the church authorities as prejudiced and unfair. One who attempts, as the present author does, to take an objective approach to the subject, may properly regret the spirit in which the book was written, and still admit that it is probably the best and most thoroughly documented biography that has yet appeared.

The bare facts relating to the life of Mary Baker Eddy may be simply given. She was born at Bow, New Hampshire, July 16, 1821, the youngest of six children. Mark and Abigail Baker, her parents, were devoutly religious New Englanders. Mark Baker was a rather stern Calvinist, unyielding in his convictions. Mary was later to write of him that his relentless theology emphasized the final judgment day, the peril of endless punishment, and a God devoid of mercy toward unbelievers. (*Retrospection and Introspection,* p. 13) To that faith he sought to win her, but to no avail. She was often in disagreement with her father, and in time his urgent insistence may have had some effect upon her health. She became anxious and worried. Finally the doctor advised her parents to take her out of school, and so her formal education was early interrupted. She did attend school for a brief period later; but most of her education was gained through her own efforts and the help of her brothers and sisters, particularly her brother Albert, who was a student at Dartmouth and later studied law in the office of Franklin Pierce. This accounts readily enough for the fact that her literary style left much to be desired, and that many years later, after she had established the Christian Science movement, the Rev. James Henry Wiggin was employed to assist her in the revision of *Science and Health*, not from the standpoint of doctrine, but from that of its expression in readable and correct English.

Mary early showed a disposition to write, contributing poems and articles to the local press. She wrote a good deal of verse during her adolescent years. Some of it bears the earmark of youthful writing, being neither better nor worse than many another youthful effort. In later years she was to produce a number of hymns that were of a high order.

For years she was a semi-invalid. It was said that she was sometimes hysterical and had to be held or carried about by her father. Often the physician was in attendance upon her. But at other times she appeared well and happy and full of life.

The removal of the family from Bow to Sanbornton Bridge, when she was nearing fifteen, improved their economic position, but for Mary it meant the breaking of ties of friendship which she was loath to sever. One of her youthful poems was called forth by this loss. If it does not reveal poetic ability of the highest order, it does reveal Mary Baker as a very normal young lady whose heart could become involved in young romance.

According to parish records, at the age of seventeen Mary joined the Congregational church at Tilton, New Hampshire. Her recollection half a century later was that she was twelve at the time. In her autobiography, written when she was seventy, she asserts that she refused to accept the somewhat morbid theology pressed upon her by the examining committee of the congregation, since hers was not a religion of fear lived under the shadow of divine judgment, but one of love, joy, and peace. As she recalls it, she was accepted into membership despite her refusal to subscribe to the rigorous faith of the church's elders. Hers was more nearly the faith of her mother, who often found it necessary to restrain her husband in his vigorous efforts to bring Mary to an acceptance of his rigid Calvinism. There was a close bond between Mary and her mother.

Life at Sanbornton, a village since renamed Tilton, was more exciting than at Bow. For a while she studied again, this time at the Holmes Academy at Plymouth. Letters preserved from that period reveal her entering into ardent friendship with others of her age, and her evident enjoyment of parties. They also show that she read rather extensively. She was fond of poetry; Milton was her favorite, and a notebook still preserved contains much of his verse and that of others. She kept up a lively correspondence with her brothers, particularly Albert, who had become a law partner of Franklin Pierce. Albert had also become a state legislator; shortly before his death in 1841 he was elected to the United States House of Representatives. Their letters refer often to the ill health that each suffered from time to time. But Mary was to recall this as one of the happiest periods of her life.

It was as a friend of her older brother, Samuel, that George Glover first came into her life. When George was just past twenty-one, his sister married Samuel Baker, and Mary met him at the ceremony. She was then a girl of twelve, and George, playfully taking her upon his knee, told her he would return some day and marry her. The promise made in jest was fulfilled when he returned in 1843, to find Mary an attractive young lady.

George Glover's business was building and selling houses in Charleston, South Carolina, and so it was there that he took his bride. About the time of their marriage he had undertaken to build a cathedral in Haiti and was assembling materials for shipment to the island. Their marriage, which she later described as a happy one, did not long endure. They were together little more than half a year when he was stricken with a fever and was gone in a few days, leaving her with an as yet unborn child in a relatively strange place to go on alone. The record of their life in the South is scanty, and some controversy has arisen over George Glover, about whom little appears to be known. Was he the rich, slave-holding promoter he was sometimes represented to be, a well-known, highly esteemed, solid citizen? Or was he rather a struggling young businessman, never out of debt, trying to get ahead? For our purposes here it does not greatly matter.

Mary was crushed by her loss. She returned to her family in the

North shortly after the funeral, and on September 11, 1844, gave birth to a son whom she named George after his father. Her constitution, seemingly never robust, suffered from the shock of her loss and the weariness of the long journey home. For a while there was grave concern about her recovery, but slowly she was nursed back to health and was able to see and to be with her child.

Perhaps it was because of her illness that George Glover's widow found it difficult to care for her little boy. She surrendered his care largely to a former servant of the family, Mahala Sanborn. She was never really to know the close association with her son that most mothers have with their children, and he grew away from her, becoming more deeply attached to Mahala than to her. Later, after Mahala Sanborn married, George moved with his adopted family to Minnesota. Thereafter he came into his mother's life only now and again for brief periods, none of them very happy ones. She who was to become "Mother" to thousands was never really mother to her own child.

From this time on Mary Baker Glover was apparently never free from pain. What she described as an early spinal trouble was aggravated by her trying experiences, and she was in great discomfort much of the time. There is little wonder that she became preoccupied, as her letters show, with the question of health. Although she was almost constantly under the care of physicians, she found no lasting relief.

Meanwhile she did not a little writing—poetry, stories, essays, even a novelette—which was published mostly in local periodicals, though she did get one poem accepted by the famous *Godey's Lady's Book*. She was courted for a time by a young minister, a widower. But nothing came of this. There were other suitors too. One young lawyer seems to have interested her more than the others, but he went to the West Coast to practice law and soon afterward died. A note in Mary's own handwriting, beneath a picture of him pasted in a scrapbook, says that they were engaged to be married before he left New Hampshire. To the sorrow occasioned by his death was added soon after the grief of her mother's passing, which occurred in 1849.

Her father, Mark Baker, remarried, and after this Mary felt obliged to find a new home. Her sister Abigail offered her domicile, but was unwilling to take her child also. Little George had already gone to live with Mahala and her husband at Groton, New Hampshire. Now Mary gave up any prospect of having him with her and joined Abigail.

The successful suitor was handsome Daniel Patterson, a dentist, who practiced homeopathy to some extent. The hope was held out that through this agency Mary might be restored to health. Certain it is that Mary Baker Patterson did experiment with homeopathic remedies, but her health did not improve appreciably. What she described as "spinal inflammation, and its train of sufferings, gastric and bilious," remained unhealed, and she still had periods of deep depression and hysteria.

This second marriage proved an unhappy one. Dr. Patterson was not a good provider. The couple fell into debt and had to have help from her relatives. The doctor spent a good deal of time practicing in other towns, often leaving Mary alone. It is said that he also became interested in other women. Seldom free of entanglements of one sort or another, Dr. Patterson was captured by the Grays during the Civil War while he was on a sightseeing drive outside the city of Washington, D.C. He spent some months in Confederate prisons, then made his escape and returned to his wife in the North.

During this period Spiritualism was popular in New England. Mrs. Patterson became interested and is known to have experimented with seances for a while, passing into trance on occasion, according to the testimony of her friend Sarah Crosby and others. Mesmerism, as hypnotism was then called, was also a matter of considerable interest at the time, and some healings of disease were being attributed to this agency. Mary was interested in healing, if only because she was herself an inveterate sufferer. According to her own written statements, she dabbled in what was then popularly known as "animal magnetism." It should be observed in passing that such interests were not necessarily abnormal, for this was a period when "the best people" discussed these subjects and not infrequently experimented with what have since become known as "psychical phenomena."

When reports spread throughout the countryside that in Portland, Maine, a man named Phineas P. Quimby was effecting remarkable cures without resort to medicine, hope was awakened in Mary that here at last she might gain health. She wrote Quimby to ask if he would come to heal her. When this was not possible, she resolved to go to him. Dependent upon Abigail, who had acquired some little wealth through marriage, she turned to her sister to help her make the trip. Abigail was willing to send Mary to a health resort in Hill, New Hampshire, where the fashionable water-cure was provided, but would have nothing to do with a healer like Quimby, whom she regarded as a charlatan. Mary, however, saved out part of the money sent her by Abigail and went to Portland.

The extremely controversial subject of Mary's relationship with Quimby and possible indebtedness to him for much she later thought and taught has been discussed often and somewhat fruitlessly. For our purposes it does not greatly matter whether she did or did not borrow from Quimby in the process of developing her own thought and practice. The record shows indisputably that she believed herself healed through contact with him, and that from then on she pursued not only her own health but the health of others. Healing became her major preoccupation, and her life was given over largely to her efforts to bring to the world in effective form the gospel of healing.

In those days titles were casually assumed, and Phineas Quimby was known as "Doctor." Mrs. Patterson first saw Dr. Quimby on October 10, 1862, when she was forty-one years of age. For a considerable period she was an enthusiastic disciple of Quimby, accepting his belief that he had rediscovered the secret of healing practiced by Jesus. It was Quimby's contention that the Bible embodied a science to solve all life's problems; and as a deeply religious person who read her Bible constantly Mary was impressed by the gospel emphasis on healing. From her correspondence with Quimby, fortunately preserved, it is evident that she sought to follow his methods, not only in respect to her own health but also in the treatment of others.

From their letters, it appears that Quimby believed he took his patients' ills upon himself and then, drawing spiritual strength from Wisdom (God), "threw them off." At one point Mary writes Quimby that, in trying to help her nephew to get rid of his smoking habit, she feels in herself a "constant desire to smoke." She urges Quimby to help her rid herself of this feeling. Also, she is beginning again to have pains in her back and stomach. She calls this "suffering somewhat from old habits," and seeks his aid in overcoming the condition.

By this time Mrs. Patterson was already endeavoring to help Quimby with some of his patients. She went to Warren, Maine, to aid two of them, and while there delivered a public lecture "on P. P. Quimby's spiritual Science healing disease as opposed to Deism or Rochester-Rapping Spiritualism." This may be said to mark the beginning of her public ministry.

In one letter she told Quimby of her fear of not being able to throw off the "griefs" that she took upon herself in her healing activity. She tells how when a Miss Jarvis came to her bed with a cough it always set her coughing. One of her biographers wrote later: "This strange doctrine of transference was to cling stubbornly throughout many years to come." (Studdert-Kennedy, *Mrs. Eddy*, p. 123)

Separated now from Dr. Patterson and having no home of her own, Mary went to live at Albion, Maine, with a Mrs. Crosby whom she had met at Quimby's office. Destitute and terribly unhappy, Mary was suffering from the return of her old illness. She might have taken refuge in her sister's home, but she and Abigail had become permanently estranged. Abigail, convinced by Mary's healing at Quimby's hands, had sought his help in healing her son Albert of certain undesirable habits. When he was unsuccessful in his effort she accused the old gentleman of being a fraud, and Mary's loyalty to her friend and teacher led to a break between the sisters that was never mended. Though for the next few years Mary suffered from poverty and illness, she never again asked a cent from her sister—nor, so far as is known, did her sister offer any help.

About this time their father died. Although he was then a man of substantial means, he left Mary nothing in his will. Had she broken with him also? After a few months with Mrs. Crosby, she returned once more to Lynn, where she had lived with Dr. Patterson, and made a last effort to salvage her marriage with the dentist. Physically, she seemed to have improved. She entered into community activities and wrote poetry and some news items for the local paper. Outwardly she appeared more serene and happy than ever before, but inwardly she was not, as her letters show.

Then, in January, 1866, Dr. Quimby died. Her strongest support was gone. She mourned his loss in a poem published in the *Lynn Advertiser* under the title: "On the Death of P. P. Quimby, Who Healed with the Truth that Christ Taught."

Mary Baker Patterson was now forty-five years old. Half of her life was already spent. Anyone attempting to evaluate it at this point would have to write that thus far she had done nothing of any great consequence, and there seemed little promise that she would do anything really unusual. Certainly her life looked more like a failure than a success. She was still an attractive woman. She had a flair for writing. But she was in poor health, she was unhappily married, and she was faced with an economically and socially precarious future.

Yet the year 1866 was to be the turning point in her life. On the first day of February, scarcely a fortnight after Quimby's death, she fell on an icy pavement and was painfully injured. As she told her story many years later, when she was an elderly woman, the injury was "pronounced fatal by the physicians." But on the third day afterward, she relates, she opened her Bible to Matthew 9:2, and "as I read, the healing Truth dawned upon my sense; and the result was that I rose, dressed myself, and ever after was in better health than I had before enjoyed." (*Miscellaneous Writings*, p. 24) Eventually she was to describe Christian Science as a discovery made in February, 1866. This date is officially regarded as the beginning of Christian Science.

An examination of all the documented sources bearing upon the

famous accident and its outcome throws more than a shadow of
doubt on the accuracy of Mrs. Eddy's recollections. The physician
who attended her, Dr. Alvin M. Cushing of Springfield, Massachusetts, quoting from notes taken at the time, made affidavit many
years afterward that he had never pronounced her case hopeless
or even critical. Reading from his professional record made at the
scene, he testified under oath that he had attended the patient twice
on the day of her fall, twice the next day, once on the third, and
again on the fifth, giving her medicine during his visits and seeing
her finally on February 13, at which time she appeared to have
recovered "from the disturbance caused by the accident." She had
not intimated at any time that she had been miraculously healed
on the third day, but had complimented him on his skill in selecting
remedies. His notes showed that he attended her once more, six
months later, this time to prescribe for a bad cough.

Sibyl Wilbur, in the official biography, says that she interviewed
Dr. Cushing in 1907, at which time he told her that he had given
Mrs. Patterson a remedy, and that when he called again she had
walked across the room to show that she was healed. He did not
recall their having spoken of a healing by prayer. Miss Wilbur does
not quote Dr. Cushing directly, nor does she mention his subsequent visits to Mrs. Patterson.

Then there is the letter in Mrs. Patterson's own handwriting
to Julius A. Dresser, who had also been a patient of Dr. Quimby.
Dated February 14, 1866, it reads:

Two weeks ago I fell on the sidewalk and struck my back on the ice, and
was taken up for dead, came to consciousness amid a storm of vapors
from cologne, chloroform, ether, camphor, etc., but to find myself the
helpless cripple I was before I saw Dr. Quimby. The physician attending
said I had taken the last step I ever should, but in two days I got out of
my bed *alone* and *will* walk; but yet I confess I am frightened, and out of
that nervous heat my friends are forming, spite of me, the terrible spinal
affection from which I have suffered so long and hopelessly. . . . Now
can't *you* help me? I believe you can. I write this with this feeling:
I think that I could help another in my condition if they had not placed
their intelligence in matter. This I have not done, and yet I am slowly

failing. Won't you write me if you will undertake for me if I can get to you? (*McClure's Magazine*, 1907)

All of this is puzzling. Looking back across the years, after she had become established in her new faith and was recognized as its leader, did she read more into the episode than was rightly there? The convergence of her own testimony, written close to the event, and that of the doctor, the latter speaking not simply in personal interview but carefully from notes taken at the time and under oath in the form of an affidavit, would seem to force the objective student to some such conclusion. Doubts about the accuracy of her reminiscences from childhood and youth are certainly justified by other evidence, such as the conflict between her declaration that she joined the Congregational church at the age of twelve and the witness of the church records giving a date for that event which would make her seventeen years old at the time.

Whatever may have been the literal facts about the fall on the ice and the subsequent recovery, there can be little doubt that this was a crucial moment in her life's experience. She was undoubtedly confirmed by it in a purpose which may have been slowly forming in her mind in relation to the healing ministry of religion. Not that she at once saw the way clear before her, for her own ideas had not yet matured. Certainly it was of paramount importance to her that Quimby's work should be perpetuated, as can be seen in her letter urging Mr. Dresser to take up where Dr. Quimby had left off. Undoubtedly the experience of the fall on the ice had a great influence upon her; and this, together with Mr. Dresser's refusal to assume responsibility for Quimby's cause, had much to do with her own resolution to restore the healing emphasis to the Christian faith.

According to her recollections, this was really her third healing experience: one had come through prayer in association with an aged minister, then another in the Quimby healing, and now she herself had been healed through reading the New Testament account of Jesus' healing of the man with the palsy. In the two earlier experiences, the healing had proved temporary. Would it be so

with this one also? That it was not a once-for-all matter is clear
from her letter to Mr. Dresser. All through the years afterward
there were recurrent attacks of illness with which she had to
struggle. But from this crucial event onward she was primarily and
increasingly concerned with the power of religion to heal. Slowly
but surely she worked her way through to the philosophy of healing
which is now Christian Science. She did not by any means enjoy
immediate success. Followers for the strange new teaching were
not quickly found or easily held, and she was still to know a good
many years of pain, of loneliness, of hostility, and even of
persecution.

Casting her mind back across the decades, she once fixed upon
1853 as the time when she really began to experiment on the
premise that "mind has a science which, if understood, would heal
all diseases." (*Boston Post,* March 7, 1883) On another occasion
she went back to 1844 as the time when she was "convinced that
mortal mind produced all disease." (*Christian Science Journal,*
V, 116)

Meanwhile the Patterson fortunes steadily declined. Life with
the vagrant dentist grew more and more difficult until, in 1866,
Mary and Daniel separated permanently. For a while Mary received
small sums from her husband, but these dwindled. It was seven
years before she filed for and secured a divorce on the grounds of
desertion. Afterward Daniel Patterson drifted into abject poverty,
ultimately dying in the poorhouse in 1896. Ironically, Mary was
then enjoying fame and undreamed-of prosperity.

After the final separation Mary Baker Patterson lived for several
years in rented rooms, never very long at a place, and apparently
never very happily. Contradictory stories are told about her life
during these years. The important thing is that she began definitely
to practice healing successfully and, while her impressive claims to
curing others were sometimes challenged by the patients—as in the
case of John Clark of Lynn—there were quite a number of attested
recoveries of people under her care. Within an hour of her ministrations her niece recovered, according to reputable witnesses, from
a severe case of enteritis following typhoid fever, although the

attending physician had pronounced her condition hopeless. (Clifford P. Smith, *Biographical Papers*, p. 65) In view of similarly authenticated recoveries in Mary's practice later on, it is not difficult to believe that during this pioneer phase of her work the felon on one patient's finger disappeared overnight; that another patient, delirious from fever, was restored almost at once; or that a cripple, after sixteen years of confinement, left her wheel chair and walked. It seems quite unlikely that a movement pinned to physical healing could gain the momentum that it so soon achieved without exhibiting some such phenomena—whatever their true cause—as confirmation of its efficacy.

Mrs. Patterson—who had by this time resumed the name of Glover—was not only in the healing practice; she was also engaged in trying to set down the philosophy underlying her works and to perfect her techniques. In her experiments and conclusions at this time she was unmistakably influenced by the Quimby theory and example, as she frankly admitted throughout all these formative years.

Those in whose homes she lived testified that Mary Glover spent long hours every day and night writing—writing down her thoughts about healing, her interpretation of Scripture, instruction in the curative art. Often she would let fellow-boarders or roomers read her manuscript and discuss it with her. One of these was a shoe-worker, Hiram Crafts, who became her first serious pupil. On invitation from Mr. and Mrs. Crafts, Mrs. Glover went to live with them, apparently receiving board and lodging in return for her teaching. After five months they moved to Taunton, Massachusetts, where Hiram advertised himself as a doctor, guaranteeing to cure his patients or refund their money. He was moderately successful, the first Christian Science practitioner—though not so called—of a long and numerous line.

With her pupil launched professionally, Mrs. Glover went on a visit to her sister Martha's home in Sanbornton Bridge, only to encounter renewed antagonism to her unorthodox ideas, practices, and associates. The opposition was led by Abigail, but it was also shared by Martha. An even more distressing experience awaited

Mary, for on her return to Taunton she found that Mr. and Mrs. Crafts had decided to terminate their arrangement with her. Once more she was without a home.

The story of the next few years is not a cheerful one. She went from one home to another, well received at first only to be forced to move again before very long. Unpleasant stories of her are told, stories which her devoted followers assert have been the result of bigotry, narrowness, or envy, the lot of one who comes with a new and at first unpopular doctrine. Her enemies—and it may be said, also, objective students of the time—cannot see it in quite such simple terms, believing that where there was so very much smoke there must have been some fire. No final decision can be made on the evidence available. There is little profit in repeating the charges and countercharges, for her opponents see nothing good in her past, while her more extreme followers find nothing at all that is in any way less than perfect. Probably neither side is completely justified in its view.

Every indication points to a very human woman with an insistent idea which she was bound to get to the world somehow. She was known to be outspoken and not always tactful as a child and young woman—for instance, while in her sister's home she offended guests who believed in slavery, arguing heatedly against that institution; and it is not too difficult to suppose that her insistence upon what her detractors thought were crackpot ideas would irritate and even infuriate them. Certainly the diaries of those who later lived in intimate association with her in her home testify that she had a quick temper and a sharp tongue which she did not always restrain. It is not surprising that the effect upon persons who were not more than mildly friendly to her ideas should prove irritating in the extreme and lead to open hostility.

As early as 1868 Mrs. Glover had tried running an advertisement in a Spiritualist magazine. In it she declared that anyone who wanted to heal the sick with a certainty "far beyond any of the present modes," such as "medicine, electricity, physiology or hygiene," could learn to do so from her instructions. She guaranteed "unparalleled success in the most difficult cases," adding that "no pay is required unless this skill is obtained." (*Banner of Light*, July 4, 1868)

A Mrs. Wentworth, whom she had met through Hiram Crafts, was already sufficiently impressed with the possibilities of her healing system to pay three hundred dollars for a course of lessons, this amount to be taken out in board and lodging over a period of time. There is no question that at this point Mary Baker Glover was freely ascribing the mind-healing method she was teaching to Quimby. She brought with her to Mrs. Wentworth's house a manuscript entitled "Extracts from Doctor P. P. Quimby's Writings," which she allowed Sally Wentworth to copy. During her stay here she completed a manuscript which she called "The Science of Man or the principle which controls all phenomena." Embodying the Quimby teaching, the original, still preserved, shows interlineations in Mary Baker Glover's authenticated handwriting. Inevitably some of her own developing thought crept into this work, but certainly not enough to invalidate its Quimby origin.

Before long, trouble developed with the Wentworths. This time she was able to return to the home of a previous host, Sarah Bagley. With Miss Bagley she found peace and quiet, where she could work without the distractions which had been hampering her all along. Here Richard Kennedy, a bright twenty-one-year-old relative of Sarah's, took an interest in the new teaching and came often to discuss it all with Mrs. Glover and Miss Bagley. After a while it was decided that Mary and Kennedy would take a house in Lynn, where he would practice and she would teach her system of healing while continuing to write. Richard, who had paid nothing for his instruction, was to give her a percentage of the fees received from his practice.

In 1870 Richard Kennedy hung out his sign as Doctor. Soon patients were passing through his office in a steady stream, and so many of these people were persuaded to take up the healing art that Mrs. Glover was no longer confined to teaching one pupil at a time. A class was announced, with a stiff fee of three hundred dollars each as the tuition. This put a practical limit on the number of those who would seek instruction and assured at least a seriousness of purpose which she had not always found among those to whom she had given instruction without charge. If three hundred dollars for a dozen lessons seems high, when the average worker was receiving less than a thousand dollars a year, it should not be forgotten that by this modest expenditure one could set himself up as a Doctor and charge fees comparable to those of the orthodox medical practitioners of the day.

This step established Mary Baker Glover at forty-nine as a professional and gave her a source of income which she sorely needed. She was now definitely launched on a new career. It would still be five years before the first edition of *Science and Health* would appear, and quite a while before Mary would see in her teaching an original discovery of her very own, to be called "Christian Science." For the time being, she called her teaching "Moral Science" and assigned its origin to "one individual who healed me, Dr. Quimby of Portland, Me., an old gentleman who made it a research for twenty-five years, starting from the standpoint of magnetism thence going forward and leaving that behind." In writing out this answer to a student's query, she said that since her introduction of it, for "eight years I have been founding and demonstrating the science." (Studdert-Kennedy, *Mrs. Eddy*, pp. 170-71)

Mrs. Glover prepared a catechism for her pupils to study in advance of the class sessions, supplementing this with other manuscripts. Perhaps the most striking feature of the course, as recorded by an admittedly loyal member of the group, Samuel Putnam Bancroft, was the physical manipulation which preceded the actual instruction periods. "Before studying we were treated by Dr. Kennedy in order to render us receptive," writes Bancroft, and he describes the treatment as a manipulation of the head and solar plexus. "The theory, as we understood it, was that these were considered the most sensitive portions of the body. Mrs. Eddy [Glover] taught us, however, that there was no sensation in matter. To some this seemed a paradox." Although she gave over her instruction in the main to dispelling sickness and other discord as illusions of material sense, from which the patient must be awakened, in her catechism she did say this: "Rubbing has no virtue only as we believe and others believe we get nearer to them by contact, and now you would rub out a belief, and this belief is located in the brain. Therefore, as an M.D. lays a poultice where the pain is, so you lay your hands where the belief is, to rub it out forever." (Bancroft's *Mrs. Eddy as I Knew Her in 1870,* sponsored by Mary Beecher Longyear in 1923 and later certified as correct by Clifford P. Smith)

Mary Baker Glover's later repudiation of physical manipulation as being incompatible with her basic premise illustrates well the development of her own thought. All during these and later years she was feeling her way, gradually clarifying the theory in her own mind. Time and again she discarded ideas and practices which she eventually came to regard as mistakes. She wrote and rewrote the material of instruction which she was giving to her students. Copies of some of these papers are still extant, showing whole sentences stricken out or revised drastically.

As might be expected, it was easier for her to change her own mind than those of some of her students. Richard Kennedy, for example, would not go along with her when she abandoned massage. While continuing in the healing practice for many years, Kennedy never relinquished the physical manipulation shown him at the start—even after his teacher publicly denounced the practice in her first edition of *Science and Health* (p. 193): "Sooner suffer a doctor infected with smallpox to be about you, than come under the treatment of one that manipulates his patients' heads, and is a traitor to science." As a witness in a lawsuit in 1879, Kennedy testified that he frankly could not grasp the idea of healing by purely mental means. A woman who came to him for treatment and had to take down her hair while he ceremoniously dipped his hands in water, then felt his soothing touch upon her head, was aware that something concrete was happening. This doubtless had a psychological effect on patients that a strictly mental treatment might not afford.

It is often denied that physical manipulation was ever a part of Mrs. Eddy's theory and practice, but we have her sworn state-

ment on this subject. When, in the above-mentioned suit—brought
by Mrs. Eddy against a student for unpaid tuition—Mrs. Eddy was
called to the stand, she testified under oath that she had taught
"the application of hands and water," adding that "that was not
my principle, it was my method." While she did not now teach
that as her method, she admitted that "before 1872 I taught manipulation and the use of water." Just why she had taught "the laying
on of the hands" she could not say, but supposed "it was because
I saw a hand helped me." After all, she concluded, "the principle is
mind operating on the body." Again, in her manuscript for the
unpublished "Repaid Pages," written in 1896, Mrs. Eddy states:
"When I taught my first student, I said, 'You may dip your hands
in water and manipulate the head,' and this was after I had discovered, in 1866, the proof that God, the divine Principle of man's
being, does all the healing." Plate I, opposite page 48, reproduces a
page from her manuscript on which this statement appears, showing
interlineations in her own handwriting.

Others also refused to follow their teacher, preferring to cling
to some of the ideas and techniques which she pronounced outmoded. For such students there was no place for development in
the system. It hardened down at the point at which they received it,
while she moved on. This has been a constant feature of the movement. It is the firm belief of a considerable number of persons,
who dissent from the official view, that Mrs. Eddy never ceased
to advance in her theory and practice, and that, in the true spirit
of the Founder, Christian Science must always continue to evolve.
To them the present hierarchical insistence on maintaining Christian Science at the precise level at which Mrs. Eddy left it represents a fundamental betrayal of the very spirit of the woman they
think to honor.

Some of her students became quite successful practitioners.
One of them, to whom she had given a great deal of special instruction, set up a practice in Tennessee and flourished for a time. Then
he lost his power, so he said. Concluding that he had been taught
mesmerism under the guise of "Moral Science," he demanded that
Mrs. Glover reimburse him for the tuition paid and the loss sus-

tained in his Tennessee venture. When she rejected his claim, he attacked her in a letter to the press. She came back in the same paper with a vigorous defense of herself and her teaching—something she was to do many times in the years that followed. Finally he challenged her to a public demonstration of her science, defying her to raise the dead, to walk on the water, to live without air, to restore sight to one whose optic nerve had been destroyed, to set and heal a broken bone without physical aid. Mrs. Glover chose not to answer this challenge, perhaps because the general reader could be counted on to consider the demands entirely unreasonable. But there were to be many other attacks which were less easy to meet.

The dissolution of her partnership with Richard Kennedy had a decided effect upon Mrs. Glover. It had been a profitable venture economically, giving her a larger income than she had previously known. Gradually she came to think of Kennedy as an implacable enemy, indeed as a powerful opponent who could through "malicious animal magnetism" work her harm. Up until this time she had apparently not theorized seriously on the potentialities of thought to work evil as well as good, but the idea was later to become of cardinal importance to her.

Soon after her break with Kennedy, Mrs. Glover gave up the comfortable quarters where she had taught and he had practiced, and for the next three years she lived in rented rooms or in the homes of some of her students, writing and rewriting in an effort to set down in intelligible fashion the ideas that were crystallizing. Thus did *Science and Health* begin to take form. While evidence of Quimby's thought may be found in all editions up to the last of her textbook, many think, she was definitely moving away from the basic Quimby concept and creating a basically different system of her own.

What were the influences that were shaping her thought? Here there are various theories. The simple explanation, and the one accepted by the orthodox followers of Mary Baker Eddy today, is that her writing was the result of "inspiration." God revealed it all to her. There are many references in her writings, at least in her later ones, clearly indicating that she herself looked back upon her written works as inspired.

But how does inspiration come? Is everything inspired wholly original, or does the inspired writer take into his mind ideas and impressions which come to him out of his environment and work them over, reject some, modify others, or put them together in new ways not previously done, adding some fresh insight which may be the result of no known external influence? When one appears with an idea or a system that seems unique, or at least is quite unknown to his contemporaries, it may well seem to them original and the result of inspiration. Even then, critical minds may seek to determine if there may not be some earlier known or unpublicized source from which it was drawn. But when a system is launched which does have marked similarities to other known systems, the question of possible dependence inevitably arises. Here of course it must be recognized that two persons may bring forward the same idea quite independently. It will be recalled that Alfred Lord Wallace and Charles Darwin arrived at the theory of evolution at about the same time without any dependence of one upon the other. To mention but one more outstanding example, the Russian chemist Mendelejeff formulated the epoch-making Periodic Law of Elements simultaneously with its formulation by Meyer in Germany.

In the case of Christian Science there is a very close similarity to certain other systems of thought, all of which were to some degree current in New England during the years when Mrs. Eddy's views were maturing. One of these is Hinduism in its Vedanta form; and Mrs. Eddy's writings also abound in ideas undeniably present in the prior writings of Berkeley, Hegel, Fichte, and others. Was she acquainted with any of these? She does state that in her youth her "favorite studies were natural philosophy, logic, and moral science," and she cites with implied familiarity the works of Socrates, Plato, Descartes, Locke, Leibnitz, Spinoza, Berkeley, Hume, Kant, Fichte, Hegel, Huxley, and Spencer. But at no point that I have been able to discover does she give evidence of having read the Upanishads, the basis of Vedanta. Certainly she does not quote from the Upanishads or mention them.

We do know that the contemporary "Concord group," some of whom she knew personally—including Ralph Waldo Emerson and Bronson Alcott—were well acquainted with Indian metaphysical thought. In fact, it was somewhat the vogue among thoughtful people of that community and period. She could easily have become acquainted with the major concept, that of the unreality of the phenomenal world and the consequent idea of matter as illusion, without ever having read a book on the subject or being aware of Hindu origin. If she did thus take over a basically Hindu philosophical idea, certain it is that she worked it over, related it to Christian teaching, and drew from it corollaries of a practical sort which Hinduism itself never did. To be sure, the practice of Yoga has been employed as a therapeutic method—chiefly the Hatha Yoga (or bodily Yoga)—but the healing effects of this are seen to be rather in the discipline of the physical body than in the way Christian Science purportedly heals.

The same could be said of the other systems. Even if it were proven that Mrs. Eddy got her fundamental conviction of Mind as the exclusive reality from one or the other of them, it was she, not they, who drew from this premise the practical conclusions which form the working basis of Christian Science.

The most serious attempt to fix upon Hegel as the real source of her metaphysics is to be found in the book *Mrs. Eddy Purloins from Hegel* (A. A. Beauchamp, Boston, 1936), written by the Rev. Walter M. Haushalter, at this writing the rector of an important Episcopal church in Philadelphia. Here it is charged that Mrs. Eddy made direct use of a manuscript by one Francis Lieber, an exposition of "the metaphysical religion of Hegel," which was turned over to Hiram Crafts, along with a letter dated April 1, 1866, for delivery before a Boston Kantian group of which Crafts was secretary. It is alleged not merely that Mrs. Eddy was influenced by what Lieber wrote, but that she actually plagiarized substantial portions of the manuscript, including the heart of her famous "scientific statement of being." The book offers as evidence parallel pages from the writings of Mrs. Eddy and those of Lieber. The degree of verbal identity between the two writings is such that to regard this identity as the result of sheer accident would be entirely unreasonable.

Naturally this work has been disputed by the Christian Scientists, who call into question the genuineness of the source document itself. The official repudiation of the document in the *Christian Science Sentinel* (XXXIX, 611-12) rested upon the findings of handwriting experts engaged by the Mother Church authorities. But when I personally undertook to compare the handwriting of the Lieber document with manuscripts known definitely to have been written by Lieber, I found so many of their statements unsupported by the facts that I was quite unconvinced they were right in asserting, at least on the basis of the handwriting alone, that the document had to be spurious.

When I called this to the attention of a church representative at headquarters, I was told that there was other evidence besides this, and that anyway it was unthinkable that a woman of Mrs. Eddy's character should be guilty of literary piracy. Aware of the repeated charges that she had used material from other sources without acknowledging her indebtedness, I asked about such things as "The Man of Integrity," an article of about 250 words taken from Lindley Murray's *Reader* and used practically unchanged by Mrs. Eddy without a suggestion that she had borrowed it. I could, I said, understand how she might have taken certain brief quotations from *Philosophic Nuggets*, which are admittedly in her published works, and repeated them in her writings without realizing that they were not her own; but to account for verbal identity of recall to the extent of whole paragraphs on the basis of unconscious memory seemed to me unreasonable. Nor was I convinced by the lengthy correspondence which followed.

In the end I was told that the Board of Directors of the Mother Church had in its files unmistakable evidence—letters reputedly written by the owner of the Lieber document—proving that fraud had been practiced in an attempt to sell that property to the church. A difficulty arose here, since I had become acquainted with the well-known and reputable citizen involved and had been told by him that he had written no letter save one to make an appointment with a representative of the Board. Here was a clear contradiction, in terms not of interpretation, but of fact. Where lay the truth? The spokesman for the Board, in the office of the Committee on Publication, said in a letter that I probably wondered why the church did not settle the Hegel-Lieber controversy by either taking it into the courts or else inviting in "a scholar such as yourself to satisfy himself of the facts and publish his findings." But this they had decided against, saying they preferred that some disinterested scholar outside the church undertake to argue the manuscript's fraudulence on the basis of its own internal evidence. Indeed, the writer said it had been brought to their attention that just such a book was soon to be published.

This book, *Ordeal by Concordance*, by Conrad Moehlman, was brought out in 1956. It purported to prove the spuriousness of the disputed document, chiefly from internal evidence; but it proved unconvincing. Nothing short of external evidence, such as the Board claims to possess, can finally determine the issue.

When a devout church member, much disturbed by the Haushalter book, asked the Board for material with which to refute the charges, he was told it ought to be plain that Mrs. Eddy could not have been influenced by Hegel's ideas since his works had not in her day been translated from the German. Moreover, said they, Hiram Crafts could hardly be considered likely to deliver such a paper before the Kantian Society in Boston, being only a shoe-worker and thus unfamiliar with such matters. But the perturbed member reminded the Board that the official *Life*, by Sibyl Wilbur, described Crafts as a Kantian transcendentalist.

Actually, New England was a hotbed of philosophical discussion during Mrs. Eddy's time. It is difficult to imagine her escaping exposure to it. And *The Secret of Hegel*, by Stirling Hutchison, published in 1866—the very year Mrs. Eddy gives as marking the inception of Christian Science and nine years before *Science and Health* came out—contains many statements which one who is very familiar with the subject finds implicit, if not explicit, in the Christian Science textbook. It would not, therefore, be surprising if by this time papers on Hegel had been prepared and read in such groups as the Kantian Society. That careful checking by myself and others has so far failed to turn up any record of that society can hardly be taken as proof positive that such a group never existed, but only that it may have been small and quite informal, one which sought no publicity and published no programs. I myself belong to such a group, the existence of which I am sure that no one would be able to prove a hundred years from today.

As a matter of fact, I am not myself convinced of the genuineness of the Lieber document. But I am certainly not as yet convinced that it cannot be genuine. In my own mind it must for the present stand as a possible, though by no means certain, source from which Mrs. Eddy may have drawn some of her ideas.

When, in 1883, Mrs. Eddy was accused of plagiarizing from Phineas Quimby, she took the position that Quimby had been more of an impediment than an aid to her in her search for Truth. Characterizing him as an illiterate mesmerist, she explained her former endorsements of him as due to a tendency on her part to overestimate people. She declared that what she was now expounding was an original discovery which came to her, after his death, as an instant and ultimate revelation. "I must write down Christian Science Mind-healing as the antipode of Mr. Quimby's theory (if he had one!), and of his treatment of disease." (*Christian Science Journal,* V, 109-18)

For our purposes in this book it does not seem necessary to establish the particular source of Mrs. Eddy's thought, whether it was completely original or dependent upon others. Eventually she did work out a system which, while it has many points of similarity to Quimby and other sources, is substantially different from all of them, and certainly goes far beyond what any of them dreamed of. My own personal opinion, formed over years of study of Christian Science and the many books written about it and about Mrs. Eddy, is that her system had its origin in a variety of ideas, converging from sources not always recognized by herself, to form as they passed through her mind something different from all the rest. In their practical outreach, they combined to achieve a vigorous, dynamic movement teaching a gospel of healing for mankind, such

as had been the early concern of Christianity. This seems, to one who
stands outside the movement, enough to say. For one woman, past
middle life, to gather together these ideas, rethink them, and give
them to the world in so solid an institution as the Christian Science
church is a prodigious accomplishment sufficient to rank her among
the outstanding religious leaders of the nineteenth century.

It was not until March, 1875, that Mary Baker Glover bought a
house of her own in Lynn, Massachusetts, and finally had a fixed
residence again. Here she surrounded herself with loyal followers,
and never again was she to resume the lonely wandering of the
years since the death of George Glover. She was to live in several
different places thereafter, but always in her own home, to which
she admitted those she wished to have near her.

Hiram Crafts had left her; Richard Kennedy also. But others
had been drawn to her side who were later to play leading roles in
the developing movement. Three of these—George Barry, Elizabeth
Newhall, and Daniel Spofford—enabled Mrs. Glover to get her
Science and Health manuscript into print when no commercial firm
could be found willing to undertake its publication. But even these
ardent disciples were to become estranged in due course. For every
one who fell by the wayside several others were to spring up as the
movement gathered momentum, and so the ranks of the little army
increased despite the recurring defections. It was out of these
inauspicious beginnings that the Christian Science organization
was to take form.

Among her followers at Lynn none was more devoted than Asa
Gilbert Eddy, a young sewing-machine agent who was introduced
to her by Daniel Spofford and quickly rose to favor. He was, by
the way, the first student to assume the title of "Christian Science
Practitioner." After a brief courtship Mrs. Glover consented to
marry "Dr." Eddy, and the ceremony took place on New Year's
Day, 1877. Thus she acquired the name by which she is now
universally known.

Mary Baker Eddy was rapidly making friends, but also making
enemies. When she was attacked she struck back vigorously. Even
so she gradually won somewhat grudging recognition even from

those who were not at all convinced by her teachings. She sometimes
went into the courts to defend her interests. Increasing numbers of
followers were found at every turn, some of them only to be quickly
alienated. She was a person apparently to inspire either almost
fanatical devotion or bitter antagonism. People were seldom neutral
in their attitudes toward her.

Mrs. Eddy early ceased to do much healing work. She concentrated her attention on the task of constantly revising her textbook
and extending her gospel by preaching, then teaching, as well as
through publication of pamphlets, magazines, and books. She was
engrossed in problems of organization and administration, then in
building the Mother Church. But she was now a woman well past
the average age of active participation in and leadership of a lusty
new movement.

Under the stress of all these responsibilities, it is not strange
that ill health once more overtook her. She attributed her physical
difficulties now to the influence of her enemies, chief of whom she
nominated Richard Kennedy. To ward off the attacks which she
believed to be behind her pain and weakness she surrounded herself
with persons who, at her call day or night, were supposed to defend
her mentally from such outside assaults. In this task they were
apparently not always successful. Her teeth required attention, and
finally she had to have artificial dentures. Her eyes needed correction; she felt obliged to resort to glasses. She also suffered inter-
mittently from kidney stones. There were times when the pain
would not yield to the purely metaphysical methods, and a physician
had to be called to administer morphine.

On occasion Mrs. Eddy sought in the public press to justify her
recourse to material aid. When speakers at an Episcopal congress
brought out that Mrs. Eddy, in the face of her claims that there was
no sensation in matter and that she could restore carious bones, had
herself surrendered to dental extractions and employed anesthetics
in connection therewith, she answered in the *Boston Herald.* From
the very first edition of her textbook, she pointed out, she had advocated surgery "until the advancing age admits the efficacy and
supremacy of Mind." As for the anesthetic, she explained that

refusal to co-operate fully with the dentist would turn his mental protest against her, so that "his mental force weighs against a painless operation, whereas it should be put into the same scale as mine, thus producing a painless operation as a logical result." (*Christian Science Sentinel*, III, 216-18) When challenged at a public meeting for wearing glasses, Mrs. Eddy retorted that she "wore glasses because of the sins of the world"—an oblique reference, perhaps, to the general "mental malpractice" to which she often said she was subjected.

Because her recourse to dentists, oculists, and physicians was seized upon by her opponents as representing the failure of her teaching, efforts were made—and still are made—to keep her sufferings and her reliance upon material aid from public knowledge. But the diaries of her intimate associates, when they were finally published—particularly that of Calvin Frye, her long-time faithful secretary—made it all too clear that their beloved Founder had many bad moments in which she sought relief through other means and methods than straight metaphysical treatment. Confronted with the Frye disclosures long after Mrs. Eddy's death, the Mother Church Directors admitted that she had taken anesthetics on occasion for relief from extreme pain. But her teaching permitted this. According to *Science and Health* (p. 464), if a Scientist finds himself in too much pain to treat himself mentally and is unrelieved by fellow-Scientists, he can summon a doctor for "a hypodermic injection," so that "when the belief of pain was lulled, he could handle his own case mentally." The Directors asserted that "the Master himself momentarily felt a sense of separation from his divine source, for he cried out, 'My God, my God, why hast thou forsaken me?' but he never abandoned his fidelity to divine Principle." To this they added: "Neither did Mrs. Eddy." (*Christian Science Journal*, XLVI, 669)

The loss of her devoted husband on June 3, 1882, was a harsh blow. Although Gilbert Eddy died from organic heart disease, according to medical diagnosis, his widow announced through the newspapers that he had been murdered with arsenic mentally administered by "certain parties here in Boston who had sworn to injure" the Eddys. In another interview she said she could have saved her husband had he not assured her that he had the situation well in hand. "I have cured worse cases before but I took hold of them in time," she declared. Once again she had become a widow and, according to letters she wrote at the time, she was a very lonely woman even though surrounded by faithful followers.

As her power and influence grew, from time to time Mrs. Eddy handed down bylaws for the direction of her followers. One of these made it incumbent upon any Christian Scientist whom she summoned to leave his or her home and occupation and come to Mrs. Eddy's home, there to serve her for three years at a nominal salary and in any capacity Mrs. Eddy desired. To disobey the summons was to risk excommunication from the church. And if the student left before the expiration of this term, "such student shall pay to Mrs. Eddy whatsoever she may charge for what she has taught him or her during the time of such service." (*Manual*, pp. 67-69) But it was considered a great honor to be so chosen, and those who lived thus close to the adored Leader are greatly honored today by the church, however menial their duties may have been in her home.

As Mrs. Eddy's economic condition improved and she became a person of wealth, she adjusted her living accordingly. She gradually withdrew from detailed direction of the organization, though in her isolation she still held the reins of power and determined quite fully the course the church should take. Her public appearances were gradually reduced to a daily drive. Even those who waited on the roadside to catch a glimpse of her as she passed were notified through the press to refrain from doing so. Gradually she had become something of a legend, long before her death.

Attempts were made to force her out of her obscurity. As so often happens where any secrecy is thrown about a person, ugly rumors arose. It was alleged that she had died, or was dying, and that it was not she, but a substitute who issued forth each day for the carriage ride she had come habitually to take. To dispel these suspicions when the newspapers became clamorous, she agreed to meet representatives of the press, and did so. What different reports emanated from this meeting! It is almost impossible to believe that the accounts in the *New York World* and the *New York Journal* could be referring to the same event. The *World* described Mrs. Eddy as a pathetic, crack-voiced crone, painted, bewigged, and artificially sustained for the interview by stimulants, giving an agonizing performance calculated to deceive the public. The distinguished Arthur Brisbane, on the other hand, found Mrs. Eddy's face free from wrinkles, her handclasp firm, her voice deep and resonant, her eyesight exceptionally good for a woman of eighty-six, her wit quick, and her mind keen—the whole picture one to convince even the hardest skeptic that here stood a great but modest woman, quite at the height of her powers and a match for many half her age.

Out of the ensuing controversy between rival newspapers was born the "Next Friends Suit," a legal action by her relatives who sought to take her affairs out of her own hands, on the charge that she was physically and mentally incompetent. But after a dramatic hearing in her home, to which the court adjourned, the suit collapsed in what has been properly regarded as a triumph for the venerable Leader. Obviously Mrs. Eddy was still in control.

Her later years were troubled by disaffection on the part of some of her most ardent disciples. Augusta E. Stetson, head of the New York church and probably the most powerful figure in the whole movement next to Mrs. Eddy, was castigated and banished from the church she had built. Josephine Woodbury, claiming that a child born to her was immaculately conceived, greatly embarrassed Mrs. Eddy and was driven out of the organization. Dr. Julia Field-King fell from grace and was shipped off to England. But one by one these cases were disposed of without noticeably impeding the growth of the movement as a whole.

Mrs. Eddy was now a very old lady. Many believed that she would never die. Others believed that if she died she would be resurrected as Jesus had been. Of all this speculation she apparently took no notice, but simply went on about her business of revising the textbook, supplying occasional bylaws, issuing infrequent messages to her church.

Then, one day, the frail old lady lay down wearily with pneumonia. The year was 1910 and she was eighty-nine. It was Sunday,

December 4, when the First Reader of the Mother Church paused before the regular benediction and said to a stunned congregation: "Mrs. Eddy passed from our sight last night at 10:45 o'clock, at her home in Chestnut Hill." Thus the world was quietly apprised that Mary Baker Eddy had passed off the human scene. Henceforth her teaching and her movement must stand or fall without the steadying hand of their Founder. The Christian Science organization would have to make its way in the world without her guidance, save as that guidance was preserved in the textbook, the *Manual,* and her other writings. What would happen now?

3

The Organization

FROM MANY statements of Mrs. Eddy's it seems clear that she did not regard organization as essential to religion. Rather, she expressed distrust of it, and seems to have yielded somewhat reluctantly to the idea that her new faith must have a tangible institution if it was to make its way successfully in the world.

In the first edition of *Science and Health* (p. 166), Mrs. Eddy wrote: "We have no need of creeds and church organizations to sustain or explain a demonstrable platform that defines itself in healing the sick and casting out error," and "the mistake the disciples of Jesus made to found religious organizations and church rites, if indeed they did this, was one the Master did not make." To the end of her days she continued to republish, in *Miscellaneous Writings* (pp. 91-92), her *Journal* statement of 1892 that "it is not indispensable to organize materially Christ's church," that "if this be done, let it be in concession to the period, and not as a perpetual or indispensable" thing. She never retreated from her stand that "after this material form of cohesion and fellowship has accomplished its end, continued organization retards spiritual growth and should be laid off . . ." (*Retrospection and Introspection*, p. 45)

Yet she did set up a religious organization, one as tightly organized as any in existence. Why? Was it, as some prominent followers of Mrs. Eddy say, because the church organization was and is indispensable to getting her book into circulation? Certain it is that the sales of *Science and Health* were negligible before the Scientists were marshaled into a disciplined group. Or was it, on the other hand, as equally prominent followers assert, obviously with official approval, because Mrs. Eddy "saw that she must bring her discovery into the field of established Christian religions" that she launched the Christian Science church? (*Christian Science Sentinel*, XLIX, 1961)

Time and again Mrs. Eddy reiterated her basic precept that every individual is entitled to freedom of thought and action in religion or science. "Let us serve instead of rule . . . and allow to each and every one the same rights and privileges we claim for ourselves." (*Miscellaneous Writings*, p. 303) Yet there is nowhere now any more centrally controlled religious organization than the church she founded. As a matter of fact, it is the rigidity of the organizational structure with its extraordinary controls over its branch churches, its members, and particularly over its teachers, readers, lecturers, practitioners, and other responsible leaders, that has been the occasion for most of the conflict that has been aroused. It has been organization, rather than doctrine, which has been the principal reason for rebellion and dissent for a large number of truly faithful and convinced Christian Scientists.

How has this come about? Who was responsible for this institutional development? Was it Mrs. Eddy herself, or is it something that has grown up with the passing years?

First let it be said that there really was no church organization at all until thirteen years after the date, 1866, given by Mrs. Eddy as marking the inception of Christian Science, and until four years after the publication of her textbook, *Science and Health*, which appeared in 1875.

There had been, it is true, a fluid group of personal followers of Mrs. Eddy who met from time to time. There was no headquarters for the movement, save Mrs. Eddy's own home. On June 8, 1875, eight persons pledged together to pay Mrs. Eddy the weekly sum of five dollars to speak to them Sundays. They even called themselves "the Christian Scientists." But after five weeks these meetings were discontinued. About a year later the Christian Scientist Association was organized to assemble Mrs. Eddy's students, but was in no sense a church. It had no regular meeting place but came together in private homes in Lynn, Roxbury, or Boston. Its purpose was not so much to extend the faith as to bolster and develop those who had already accepted it.

But as the movement went on expanding, through the circulation of her book and through the increasing number of students who had become practitioners, Mrs. Eddy gradually became convinced that some form of organization was unavoidable. Almost all of her followers came to her from the established churches. They were accustomed to working within organizations. It is not unlikely that they brought pressure to bear on her. Now no longer engaged in getting her book in shape, her major preoccupation for several years, but faced with a growing movement and the many problems attendant upon this, she finally took formal steps toward a definite church organization in 1879. Twenty-six charter members of the new church, which called itself "The Church of Christ (Scientist)," secured a charter from the state of Massachusetts. Their declared purpose was "to carry on and transact the business necessary to the worship of God." The headquarters were in Boston. But this initial church did not last a full decade, and its dissolution was followed by a period in which there was no formal church organization.

Meanwhile there was no church building. In Boston, meetings were held in the Baptist Tabernacle on Shawmut Avenue when it was available, otherwise in the home of one or another of the Boston students. Mrs. Eddy continued to live in Lynn, going to Boston to conduct services. Meetings were also held at Lynn, although attendance there was often as low as five and seldom exceeded twenty persons. But in Boston the crowds increased. Many able people, later to carry heavy responsibility in the movement, were attracted through these public meetings.

At first the services were quite informal, becoming more formal as the numbers grew. The main characteristics of present-day Christian Science ritual began to take form as the meetings settled into the habit of beginning with a silent prayer, followed by the audible recitation of Mrs. Eddy's then current interpretation of the Lord's Prayer, after which one student would read from the Bible and another from *Science and Health*. Then Mrs. Eddy would speak.

Sometimes one of the students would speak in Mrs. Eddy's place, and this personal preaching continued to be a feature of the regular services until Mrs. Eddy eventually abolished it in favor of Readers confined to her own writings, read in conjunction with the Bible.

In 1880 Mrs. Eddy rented for her meetings Hawthorne Hall, where many of the great authors and teachers of the time had lectured. Here the elite of Boston were accustomed to come. It was a bold stroke, and it brought to her expanding movement a new prestige. Also, it made her teaching the center of attention and of criticism from the prominent religious and scientific leaders of the day.

The Hawthorne meetings were held at three o'clock in the afternoon. It was long before Mrs. Eddy put her meetings at an hour that would conflict with the regular worship services of the established churches. It seems almost certain that for quite a while she hoped that her new teaching would find a place within the already established churches, and that there would need to be no separate institution to carry it on. But in this she was bitterly disappointed. From the start she fell under heavy attack from the churches. Bit by bit she became convinced, the record indicates, that there was no escape from the necessity of organized effort if her faith was to spread and maintain itself in a hostile world.

Throughout the years since 1866, she had taught students who in due course became practitioners. But there was nothing in the way of official recognition for them. In 1881 she sought and was granted a charter for a teaching institution, to which she gave the name of the Massachusetts Metaphysical College, with the privilege of granting degrees. Chartered under the short-lived Act of 1874, it was the only school of its kind to enjoy that legal status. The act was repealed in 1883. In dissolving her institution in 1889, Mrs. Eddy again gave evidence of her doubts about organization in an article she wrote for the *Boston Traveler*. "From the scant history of Jesus and of his disciples," she said, "we have no Biblical authority for a public institution."

Conducted at first in her home at Lynn, the Massachusetts Metaphysical College was transferred to Boston in 1881, after the open rebellion of a substantial part of the Lynn following convinced Mrs. Eddy that her further work must be conducted in the larger city. In Boston, therefore, in a rented house at 569 Columbus Avenue, she set up her headquarters and announced the courses for her college. Henceforth Boston was to be the center of her expanding movement. Already the faithful few who had remained with her at Lynn had ordained Mrs. Eddy, in an original ceremony consisting of a simple pronouncement by a selected spokesman, as pastor of the Church of Christ (Scientist).

Hawthorne Hall, which seated over two hundred people and had seemed so large when first engaged, was outgrown and the still larger Chickering Hall was rented. Her followers began to talk of a church building of their own. Meanwhile the *Christian Science Journal* was launched in 1883, a modest little periodical consisting of eight pages, first named *Journal of Christian Science* and issued bimonthly. Its purpose, as stated by Mrs. Eddy in the first number, was "to bring to many a household hearth health, happiness and increased power to be good and to do good."

As her students scattered to centers outside Boston, Christian Science groups sprang up all over the United States. By 1884 so much interest had been generated in Chicago by her followers that Mrs. Eddy went there herself to teach her largest class to date. The class, which included six men and fourteen women, ran three weeks.

Mrs. Eddy called attention in the *Journal* of February, 1886, to the need for teachers, and urged her students by letter to establish regular schools, to be called Christian Science Institutes, as soon as each could get as many as half a dozen students together. A number of these enterprises were launched throughout the country—though not always under the suggested name. The California Metaphysical College appeared in San Jose that year. In Chicago the Christian Science University was set up, and even in Boston itself the Academy of Christian Science was headed by Josephine Woodbury.

Mrs. Eddy carried on an extensive correspondence with the heads of these schools, counseling and sometimes commanding them to do this or that. For example, she ordered Sue Bradshaw to remove

her school from San Jose to San Francisco, and Miss Bradshaw did
so. Nevertheless, despite such uncompromising direction, a number
of the school heads developed ideas at variance with those of Mrs.
Eddy. This must have disturbed her greatly and led her to seek
means by which some effective measure of control of those using
the name Christian Science might be enforced. How could this be
done without organization?

Her immediate students had banded together, but this association was localized in the Massachusetts Metaphysical College. In
the January, 1886, *Journal*, Mrs. Eddy advocated the formation of
a National Christian Scientists' Association, and in February the
first meeting of the new Association was held in New York City—
where, at Mrs. Eddy's behest, Augusta Stetson had already developed a flourishing Christian Science church. A year later, the meeting of the Association at Boston's Tremont Temple brought together
Scientists from fourteen states. Two years later the Association met
in Chicago with over eight hundred delegates present, and when
Mrs. Eddy appeared in person at Chicago's Central Music Hall,
over four thousand people gathered to give her a great ovation.
It was a climactic experience in her career, and only once again did
she appear in a large public gathering, when she spoke before a
thousand people at Steinway Hall in New York three years later.
But from the Chicago triumph on she was definitely a national
figure, and it was obvious that Christian Science had become a
national movement.

Meanwhile in Boston trouble had arisen. During Mrs. Eddy's
absence in Chicago, thirty-six members (about a fifth of the Boston
congregation) decided to withdraw from the society. Irked by Mrs.
Eddy's failure to stand by her student, Abby H. Corner, when
Mrs. Corner treated her own daughter in childbirth and was
indicted for murder when both mother and child died, they determined to resign. They were faced, however, with a serious obstacle,
since Mrs. Eddy had ruled that anyone who broke with her Association must be denounced publicly as "immoral," and this could gravely
impair an individual's standing in the community and handicap his
practice. In the absence of the secretary, who had accompanied

Mrs. Eddy to the Chicago convention, they succeeded in getting the society's records from his wife, and with these they sought to ransom themselves. Mrs. Eddy wrote them that she had not come to her elderly student's defense because she knew beforehand that Mrs. Corner would be acquitted; but the recalcitrant members refused to surrender the records until Mrs. Eddy granted them unqualified releases from membership.

In connection with this event, Mrs. Corner was repudiated in the *Boston Herald* as a quack, and charged with presuming to handle a type of case for which she had taken no specific preparatory course at Mrs. Eddy's college. This attack was signed "Committee on Publication." Here is the first appearance, so far as I have been able to discover, of the title and office of *Committee on Publication*, foreshadowing the development of a public relations department wielding extraordinary influence.

The record shows that Mrs. Eddy sought to control her followers ever more closely, even in the matter of such writing as they might do on Christian Science. When in 1884 one of her primary students, Kate Taylor, issued a pamphlet, *Selfhood Lost in God*, Mrs. Eddy announced that Miss Taylor was not entitled to write, pointing out that she had not joined the Christian Scientists' Association. Ursula Gestefeld, one of her leading followers in Chicago, published *A Statement of Christian Science*, which expatiated on *Science and Health*, giving Mrs. Eddy fullest credit. At once the *Journal*, which had run advertisements of Mrs. Gestefeld's public lectures on Christian Science and had featured articles on the subject from her pen, pronounced her not only incompetent but unfit to comment on Mrs. Eddy's textbook.

In 1887 Mrs. Eddy had introduced an amendment to the constitution of the Association declaring that no person could be a member "who does not use for his textbooks The Bible and *Science and Health*, or who uses any other textbooks in this cause." Extending this prohibition, she published a set of rules in the *Journal* (VI, 54) forbidding teachers to use or to allow their students to use any books on mind-healing other than her own. This was but the beginning of a whole series of restrictions imposed by Mrs. Eddy

FOOTSTEPS IN THE DISCOVERY.

Homeopathy is the intermediate step from alopathy and matter to mind. Dr. Quimby's theory and practice was the intermediate step from animal magnetism , spiritualism, and matter to mind. But neither of these theories or practices were Christian Science. Momeopathy agrees that the drug heals the sick while the fact remains that the drug wholly disappears in some of their prescriptions wherewith the sick seem to be healed. Dr. Quimby used to repeat "there is no intelligence in matter." While at the same time he used water and manipulation to heal his patients.

Christian Science starts from neither of these grounds, it is predicated alone of Christ healing through Mind, not matter, and Christ is Truth, and Truth is Life and Love. And Life, Truth and Love--yea Spirit, not matter, heals the sick. To prove this true I instance my own experience for example. When I taught my first student, ~~largely the way the way hypnotic way of Quimby theory practice and taken up.~~ After I had discovered, in 1866, the proof, the divine Principle, *that God of man's being* ~~which~~ does all the healing. My next step was to learn from *rule and method* experiment and experience the ~~scientific application and the~~ *the of for applying it through practice* scientific ~~rule of the divine Principle which heals.~~ *for applying Truth to man's physical* ~~Then I immediately called a halt to all material uses or applications in healing, and to use mental means alone, hence~~ *before the patient understand the Truth here for* *I halted as to the use of material real means or mental means* *for such a result and left the student to learn from experience.*

PLATE I

Page from a manuscript of Mrs. Eddy's concerning physical manipulation, showing interlineations in her own handwriting.

and still maintained by the Board of Directors as the present effective head of the church.

Mrs. Eddy not only repudiated Mrs. Gestefeld, but wrote the Chicago church demanding her expulsion. When George B. Day, the pastor, suggested that Mrs. Gestefeld ought to be allowed to appear and answer the charges against her, Mrs. Eddy replied that there was no need for this, asserting that the Boston church had excommunicated people without giving them the opportunity to defend themselves in person. Ursula Gestefeld was duly expelled.

Through the instrument of public condemnation some measure of control was extended even beyond the borders of the organization. When Emma Hopkins, then the editor of the *Journal*, left with another student on an independent speaking tour, Mrs. Eddy denounced them in the *Journal*, under the caption *Beware False Teachers*, declaring that "their journeying is done for the ducats," that their pupils were victims of a swindle, and that "they never could have been true Christian Scientists." (V, 157) This could not have failed to turn away some of their clientele, and it must have had a sobering influence upon potential deserters lingering at the edge of the organization.

As early as 1886, the young Christian Science organization had decided to build a church of its own instead of continuing to rent public halls for its meetings. With a down payment of $2,000 the Scientists purchased a site, subject to a mortgage of $8,763.50. At the end of two years they had paid off $3,800, only to find themselves without sufficient funds in their treasury to meet the final payment. The mortgage was foreclosed and the land taken from them.

Before this, however, Mrs. Eddy had secretly bought up the mortgage. At the foreclosure proceedings, she retrieved the property through an agent for $5,000, and it was deeded over to her personally. This parcel of land had sold three years before for $10,763. In the *Journal* (X, 133-34), Mrs. Eddy explained: "I had this desirable site transferred in a circuitous, novel way, at the wisdom whereof a few persons have since scrupled," the transaction being of "a type morally and spiritually inalienable, but materially questionable—even after the manner that all spiritual good comes to Christian Scientists to the end of taxing their faith in God."

At this juncture she admonished her church "to drop all material rules whereby to regulate Christ"—in short, to disorganize. If they would obey at once, they need not be without a church building, for she would deed the land "now valued at $15,000" to "those who shall build a church edifice." Acquiescing, the members surrendered all voice in the project while Mrs. Eddy took complete control by delivering the property into the hands of a small group of her closest followers to be administered under her direction.

The increasing cares of her organization—church, association, college—bore heavily upon Mrs. Eddy. She had already sought to relieve herself by having others take over the instruction of classes, but there was an uncompromising demand for her personally to teach. Finally she boldly closed the Massachusetts Metaphysical College and suspended her own teaching entirely. In a resolution adopted by the College Corporation on October 29, 1889, it was declared that the material organization, like the baptism of Jesus, was no more than a "suffer it to be so now," which must be abandoned for "a spiritual formation wholly outside of material regulations, forms and customs"; that this meant the President, Mary Baker G. Eddy, must sacrifice an extensive income from the prosperous college, but that she was ready to do this for the good of the cause. The corporation was declared dissolved.

The *Journal* remarked that "the College disappeared that the spirit of Christ might have freer scope among its students" and that "the bonds of the Church were thrown away so that its members might assemble themselves together to 'provoke one another to good works' in the bond only of love." (VII, 454, 455) After the church, too, was dissolved, Mrs. Eddy observed: "This measure was immediately followed by a great revival of mutual love, prosperity, and spiritual power." Here again we note the Founder's tendency to regard religion and organization as incompatible.

The public meetings went on as before. Only there were no business meetings. Whatever controls existed were in Mrs. Eddy's own hands. Organized rebellion, at any rate, seemed no longer possible. Was it for this reason that she proceeded as she did? She controlled the property and could withhold it or permit its use, despite the fact that the church as a group had paid a substantial amount toward the mortgage. And it is noteworthy that there was no halting of the organization of local churches throughout the field. Indeed, there were apparently no objections whatsoever to their organizing.

A building fund was set up by the trustees, and gifts came from all over the country in response to articles in the *Journal* urging people to contribute. By March, 1892, it was announced that the fund had reached the sum of $23,172.08. Then one of the trustees became skeptical of the legality of the deed under which he held office. Mrs. Eddy was sure it was all right, but the Massachusetts Title Company refused to insure the title under the circumstances. The trustees resigned, after conveying the property to Mrs. Eddy for a consideration of one dollar, and the money in the building fund was returned to the donors.

There was now no Church of Christ (Scientist) in Boston; only an unorganized group continued to carry on the services as usual. There was no college. There was land for a building, owned wholly by Mrs. Eddy. What would be the next step?

In September, 1892, Mrs. Eddy executed a deed of trust transferring the property to four of her most devoted disciples—Ira O. Knapp, William B. Johnson, Joseph S. Eastaman, and Stephen A. Chase—who were required to erect a church building within five years at a cost of not less than fifty thousand dollars. The trustees were constituted a self-perpetuating Board of Directors, empowered to fill any vacancies in their body, to appoint pastor, speaker, or reader, to maintain public worship, and to make the needed rules for accomplishing all this. The deed stipulated that failure of the Board to fulfil the conditions of the deed would cause the property automatically to revert to the donor, Mary Baker G. Eddy.

In the spring of 1892, according to a letter quoted in Bliss Knapp's book, Mrs. Eddy had suggested that if her followers thought best she would not stand in the way of their reorganizing their church. But this, she implied, would entail tribulations. "When we will not learn any other way," she warned, "this is God's order for teaching us." By midsummer she was persuaded to pick out a dozen Scientists to be entrusted with the incorporation. The chosen twelve were: E. J. Foster Eddy, Stephen A. Chase, William B. Johnson, Mr. and Mrs. Joseph S. Eastaman, Mr. and Mrs. Ira O. Knapp, Julia S. Bartlett, Mary W. Munroe, Ellen L. Clarke, Janet T. Coleman, and Eldora O. Gragg.

But again she had a change of mind, deciding against her followers' setting up their own church. When they met in Miss Bartlett's rooms for the purpose agreed upon, Dr. Foster Eddy was there to present instead Mrs. Eddy's plan for founding the church on the trust deed above mentioned. Later Mrs. Eddy was to point out that this was not the Board of Directors' church, or anybody else's church, but definitely "my church." (Stetson, *Sermons*, pp. 218-20) Eventually she stipulated that all such deeds must include the phrase "Mary Baker Eddy's Church." (*Manual*, p. 102) Plainly, it was to be hers, not theirs.

The trust deed having been executed on September 2, 1892, Mrs. Eddy directed that the twelve charter members appoint a chairman and a secretary, then vote in, besides themselves, twenty persons whom she had carefully picked to join them as "First Members of the First Church of Christ, Scientist." They were required to accept three fundamental statements of belief, but this presented no obstacle since the tenets were such that any member of any Protestant church at that time could readily accept them. There was nothing in them that was distinctively Christian Science, save perhaps the phrase relating to "healing the sick, and raising the dead,—resurrecting a dead faith to seize the great possibilities and living energy of the Divine Life."

The tenets, incidentally, have survived with little modification. The chief difference between this early version and that finally settled upon lies in the elimination of a phrase expressing belief in God's present and future punishment of sin. Now the tenet reads that sin, being cast out by spiritual understanding as an unreal belief, is punished only so long as the belief lasts. (*Manual*, p. 15)

According to a letter from Calvin Frye to William B. Johnson, Mrs. Eddy decided to add two more names to the list of twenty; but before this could be acted upon another letter asked that these two names be withdrawn. It seems quite clear from all this that Mrs. Eddy was in complete control of the situation. She had installed her own Directors. She had chosen the twelve charter members. She had picked out the additional First Members. She had drawn up the tenets to which they must subscribe.

On October 5 a general meeting was held at which, at the request of Mrs. Eddy, those present were invited to join the church, and forty-nine did so. Still the membership was left quite without effective voice. The First Members, later called Executive Members, were permitted to elect officers annually and to hold quarterly meetings for the transaction of such business as "might properly come before them," but the real control lay in the hands of the Board of Directors, who apparently did whatever Mrs. Eddy directed them to do. Unmistakably, it was she who held the reins.

Appeals were made in the *Journal* to unite with the Mother Church. At the end of the first year there were just under three thousand members, 95 per cent of whom lived outside the city of Boston, which had become recognized as the headquarters of the whole Christian Science movement. There were local churches, to be sure, but many of their members were also members of the Mother Church and subject to control from Boston. This number almost invariably included all local leaders.

While the church and the college had been closed back in 1889, the National Christian Scientists' Association had been permitted to continue. To its care the *Christian Science Journal* had been entrusted in May of that year. The *Journal* was deeply in debt at the time. Now, three years later, there was a substantial surplus in the periodical's treasury, vigorous editorial and business management having put it back on its feet. At this point it seemed wise to Mrs. Eddy to "disorganize the Association," and then to repossess the *Journal*. Accordingly, at its annual meeting in 1892 the Association voted itself out of existence, to meet but once more, this time as a "voluntary Assembly of Christians" at the Chicago World's Fair of

1893. In a letter, Mrs. Eddy said that God had bade her to ask the Association "to vote giving the *Journal* back to me" and that she could see the wisdom "of again owning this Christian Science waif." Now its owner once more, she appointed a committee of three of her most trusted students to manage it. Thus the *Journal*, too, was completely under her control.

The long deferred church building finally became a reality. Mrs. Eddy appealed by letter to fifty of her followers to contribute $1,000 each, dating their contributions December 25 as a Christmas gift to her personally. Most of them acceded. Other gifts poured in. Soon enough money was in hand, and the cornerstone was laid in the spring of 1894.

Paid for in full, with a substantial surplus remaining over, the church was dedicated on January 6, 1895, its marble inscription proclaiming it "a testimonial to our beloved teacher, the Rev. Mary Baker Eddy." In it was set aside the opulent "Mother's Room," which was described in the *Journal* as lavishly appointed. This room was held sacred to Mrs. Eddy's occupancy and visited with obvious reverence by Scientists for many years. It was to be closed in 1908, following Mark Twain's scathing ridicule of it as a shrine in his popular magazine articles and in his book, *Christian Science.*

Now that her church was solidly established, Mrs. Eddy could live in semiretirement and effectively control it without appearing personally in Boston. Only once did she stay overnight in the Mother's Room, and only twice did she ever visit her church after it was built. Now she dwelt apart in Concord, New Hampshire, but still kept a tight rein on the life of her church through letters and by means of summoning one or another of the Directors or other functionaries whom she had installed. From time to time she sent down bylaws and asked that they be adopted. So far as is known, no suggested bylaw was ever refused.

The first codification of the bylaws was undertaken at her request by a committee in 1895. Known as the *Church Manual*, it was to undergo incessant revision thereafter, either by addition of new bylaws or by modification of some of those previously given. Indeed, it went through eighty-nine editions before the revising was terminated by Mrs. Eddy's death in 1910. One of its provisions is that it can never be amended without Mrs. Eddy's consent, so it stands today as the basic law of the Christian Science church.

A sidelight on the development of the authoritarian trend is provided by Mrs. Eddy's letter of February 27, 1903. To her Directors she wrote that they should never abandon the bylaws. Even if she had not been personally with them, the Word of God and her instructions in the bylaws had led them hitherto and would remain to guide them safely on. (*Christian Science Sentinel,* XVI, 1010) This statement is frequently quoted in support of the Board's claim to perpetual authority under the present-day *Manual.* Another passage from the same letter, however, stresses the importance of the combined sentiment of the church *remaining* loyal in support of its *present* (current) bylaws. The particular bylaws to which that letter demanded obedience were altered in less than three weeks after the letter was written, and they were to undergo drastic revision through the sixty-one differing editions of the *Manual* during the ensuing eight years.

Although the rules were mainly meant to meet situations of a general nature affecting the whole church, now and then a specific bylaw was clearly aimed at a particular person, for some failure or breach of loyalty. An interesting one arose from the refusal of Mrs. Eddy's adopted son, Foster Eddy, to leave Boston and to go to Philadelphia at her command. This bylaw, which could "only be annulled by the unanimous vote of every member of this church," required that any student of Mrs. Eddy's who disobeyed her when told "to leave a place in the field that she knows it is for his or her interest to leave" must be dropped from the membership roll and treated as a disloyal student. In handing down this bylaw for adoption, Mrs. Eddy wrote the Board that she could not be their Leader unless given the authority to direct them and, secondly, that they should pass the rule because she would never be "entering a complaint against a member of this church" except under God-guided impulsion.

In April, 1895, she sent down a bylaw abolishing preaching from the pulpit, requiring that henceforth "the Bible and *Science and*

Health with Key to the Scriptures be the pastor on this planet of all the churches of the Christian Science denomination." This was accepted by the churches everywhere. Even prominent pastors like Mrs. Stetson, of the great New York church, yielded without a murmur.

Mrs. Eddy now controlled every word spoken from the pulpits. In addition, she decreed that her name be announced whenever any of her works were read or quoted publicly. Nothing was said about properly crediting authors of other quotations given in public, and, indeed, seldom is the source given of quotations originated by others than Mrs. Eddy. A bylaw stipulated that Mrs. Eddy alone be called "Leader" (replacing the previous requirement that she be called "Mother"). Emphasis and inflection were to be determined for the Readers throughout the field. The stereotyped delivery noticeable in most Christian Science churches is not entirely due to coincidence. How this comes about will be evident from the following account of a case which is by no means the only one known.

In 1944 a popular First Reader received a letter from his Board instructing him to repair to the local Reading Room and there peruse the article by Professor Hering in the January 6, 1906, volume of the *Sentinel*. This article was found to set forth writer Hering's interpretation of I John 3:1-3, and his contention that if everyone read it the same way, this would bring about greater uniformity in the Christian Science services. In Hering's opinion, readers sometimes placed undue emphasis on the pronoun *we* in the first verse; furthermore, he regarded the words *he* and *him* in the three verses read as pronouns for Deity and contended that the passage must be so read as to bring this out. Also, he said, the word *correlative* was being slighted by some readers in tying in passages from *Science and Health* with the Bible.

Now it so happened that this First Reader, a successful practitioner and a leader in his community, did not concur with Professor Hering in his interpretation. Was the Reader to be allowed no latitude whatever for individual understanding and expression? If he was tempted to defy the implied order to mend his inflections, he must weigh the consequences. Already he was being accused of disloyalty to Mrs. Eddy for his untraditional delivery of her words. How could a reading style be so construed? Well, it seems that the Hering proscription was to be taken as coming from the Leader herself, since it was printed during her lifetime and allowed to go unchallenged by her in the periodicals. To take issue with his fellow-members, who were wedded to the traditional accent, would subject this Reader to the grave charge of violating Article XI, Section 3, of the *Manual*, the penalty for which could be his removal in disgrace from the pulpit.

If it should be thought that this is a rare instance, let it be noted that the Hering article has been repeatedly brought to the field's attention by the Boston Directors, a bulletin having appeared in the church periodicals as recently as January 30, 1954. This episode illustrates the almost incredible thoroughness of the control evolved.

At the beginning, the First Members did have some functions of a more or less trivial nature to perform, leaving the important decisions to the Board of Directors who, as has been seen, were directed by Mrs. Eddy. After one particular vote by the First Members, Mrs. Eddy required each one to state in writing his reasons for so voting. So unsatisfactory did she consider their reasons, reports Knapp, that for this and other considerations she changed the bylaws, removed all business from First Member control, and lodged it in the Board of Directors. This put an end to any semblance of democratic control in church affairs, and was the beginning of the exercise of complete control by the Board of Directors, who apparently did her bidding without question.

Further implementing her leadership, early in 1903 Mrs. Eddy added a fifth Director to her Board, in the person of Archibald McLellan, an able and devoted follower. McLellan was already editor-in-chief of the church periodicals, so that his appointment in effect merged the publishing authority with the church authority, bringing about a total centralization of power at "headquarters."

Although disciplinary cases were left to the Board according to the *Manual*, its author sometimes took a hand in the proceedings. In one instance, after the Directors tried a First Member on charges of immorality, found him guilty on the evidence presented, and excom-

municated him, Mrs. Eddy ordered him reinstated to full membership, restored to his office as a First Member, and re-entered in the
practitioners' registry in the *Journal*. In the next case of the kind, the
Board merely admonished the erring brother and put him on probation, thus keeping him within the church and checking his wayward
course.

This idea of probation, used increasingly in subsequent years,
operated effectively to keep troublesome members in line, if only
by encouraging hope for eventual reinstatement. Excommunication
was resorted to, even by Mrs. Eddy, but only when a member had
gotten quite beyond any hope of control.

When a serious conflict developed between her Board and the
powerful Augusta Stetson, with whom Mrs. Eddy maintained more
than cordial outward relations, Mrs. Eddy took occasion to disclaim
any involvement in the case. In a *Sentinel* notice (XII, 130), she
declared it was not her province "to interfere in cases of discipline."
Asserting that the Directors did not trouble her with their problems
of dealing with individuals in the Mother Church or with members
of the branch churches, she said her sole connection with church
affairs was through her published rules, open for all to read, rules
which the Directors invariably followed.

The pronouncement did not, however, tie her hands when the
situation waxed critical. Secretly pronouncing Mrs. Stetson's behavior "impious," she urged her Directors to act against this student.
Then on October 12, 1909, she wrote Archibald McLellan to find out
quickly whether the church could be prosecuted for suspending or
expelling a student, ordering that, if it could de done safely, Mrs.
Stetson be excommunicated. She concluded her message by pledging
Mr. McLellan to secrecy in the matter. Augusta Stetson, according
to Knapp, was then forever excommunicated from the Mother
Church in accordance with Mrs. Eddy's written instruction.

It was no longer simply The First Church of Christ, Scientist, in
Boston. It had become The Mother Church, a *ruling* church, in
keeping with its Founder's own description. (*Miscellany*, p. 13)

PART II

Development of the Organization Since Mrs. Eddy

4

The Struggle for Power

MRS. EDDY died in 1910. No longer could harassed leaders turn to her for guidance or reinforcement. If differences were to arise, as they would arise among the very human people delegated by her to carry out her purposes, who would decide between them and give the final word? Would trouble and dissension ensue, as in the case of so many movements after the death of the founder, and the movement be split into warring factions?

These were questions that occurred to many both within and without the church. The outside observers, to some extent hostile, probably hoped that such would be the case. But disappointingly, from their point of view, no such thing happened. The "field" generally had become accustomed to the direction exercised, at least outwardly, by the Mother Church Directors as Mrs. Eddy's agents, and so there was little or no sign of revolt when within a week of her passing the Directors proclaimed themselves, in effect, Mrs. Eddy's successors. In a syndicated press release, the Committee on Publication set forth the Board's position:

The adequate written instructions and directions of Mrs. Eddy, under which the Christian Science movement has grown and prospered, including the by-laws which place the direction of the spiritual and business affairs of the Church entirely in the hands of the Christian Science Board of Directors, will continue to guide their actions. (*Chicago Tribune*, December 10, 1910)

Under the emotional spell cast over the workers by the loss of their beloved Leader there was at first the utmost harmony among them. Indeed, the Board asserted through the press that "hundreds of telegrams and letters received from branch churches and societies throughout the world show that it has the unswerving loyalty and support of the entire denomination." Apparently without exception the church members accepted the Board in Mrs. Eddy's seat of authority, and the church continued on its way with no perceptible change. But the seeds of future trouble were there, and it was inevitable that sooner or later they would germinate and come to life.

For Mrs. Eddy had either consciously and purposefully or else unconsciously—this question is still being hotly debated—left the organization in a very serious situation. She had left its members with a *Manual* which they had been accepting as divinely inspired, but this *Manual* contained provisions which Mrs. Eddy's departure made it impossible to fulfil literally. It required that all members adhere strictly to the letter of its bylaws; at the same time it made essential bylaws inoperable without Mrs. Eddy's written (in some instances oral) approval.

Why not amend the *Manual* and go on developing, meeting changing situations as they arose, with new bylaws, just as Mrs. Eddy had done all along and as most growing organizations are accustomed to do? This *Manual* is often referred to as the "constitution" of the church and likened to the Constitution of the United States. The latter of course provides for its own amendment as required by events, but the church *Manual* forbids any amendment whatsoever without the consent in her own handwriting of the Pastor Emeritus, Mary Baker Eddy. And now her hands were stilled in death. Sections 1 and 3 of Article XXXV make it very explicit that no new article of belief or bylaw can be added, or any existing article or bylaw either annulled or modified, without her written consent.

The president is annually elected by the Board of Directors subject to the approval of the Pastor Emeritus. Technically, therefore, if the church continued more than a year after her death, it must do so without a president. Since the office is simply an honorary one, this difficulty could easily be surmounted. But the clerk and treasurer were also subject to her approval, and their terms were for only a year. Readers must be elected by the Board every three years, but the names of candidates must be submitted to the Pastor Emeritus and none could be elected over her objection.

A major consideration was that the Board of Directors, while self-perpetuating, could fill a vacancy in its membership only after the candidate, chosen by a majority vote, was approved by Mrs. Eddy. How then could the Board of Directors of the Mother Church continue to function beyond the remaining life span of a majority of the then living Directors? If the *Manual* must be taken literally, as has always been and still is officially maintained, how could any member of the present-day Board lay claim to his or her post?

Without Mrs. Eddy's approval of the specific action, no trustee-ships or syndicates could be formed for carrying out the purposes of the church; no special meeting of the members of the Mother Church could be called; the librarian could not be appointed; no vacancies in the editorships of the periodicals could be filled; and no Committee on Publication could be assigned. Furthermore, no important move by the Committee on Publication could be made without the sanction of the Board of Directors subject to the approval of the Pastor Emeritus; no one could sit on the business and finance committees without her consent; the annual appointment of lecturers was subject to her approval in each individual case; no person unacceptable to Mrs. Eddy could be employed in connection with the publication of her books or the editing of the church periodicals; and vacancies on the Board of Trustees governing the Christian Science Publishing Society could be filled by the remaining trustees only subject to Mrs. Eddy's approval, in addition to which she reserved the right to fill such vacancies by appointment.

How, in view of all these limitations, none of which could by any possibility be carried out literally, could the Board of Directors, who were obviously in the position of central command, carry on and at the same time be entirely loyal to the Founder who had deliberately written these restrictions into the *Manual?* While she had herself freely and frequently amended her bylaws as occasion required or inspiration prompted, she had forever put it beyond the range of their powers to do the same.

That the Board early felt the reality of the difficulty is evident from a letter written by Frederick Dixon, editor-in-chief of the church publications, to the Board offering his resignation. Dixon reports that one of the Directors, Archibald McLellan, told him that the Board had felt it necessary to consult their attorneys as to the possibility of carrying on the affairs of the Mother Church in view of the fact that they could no longer do so according to the *Manual*. (Quoted by Studdert-Kennedy in *Christian Science and Organized Religion*, p. 138)

Here was a real dilemma. The Christian Science organization was a growing concern, holding extensive properties, conducting a million-dollar-a-year business of publishing and distributing literature, with far-flung branches around the world, all trying loyally to follow their beloved Leader's directions. Various courses of action lay open to them. Those who believed in Mrs. Eddy's personal infallibility—this was then and is now a very large proportion of her following—were confronted with the necessity of explaining away what appeared to be a fatal contradiction.

One faction began to emerge with the argument that Mrs. Eddy had, with prophetic vision, left it so that the human organization would have to disappear when death took away her divinely inspired control, after which her now-adult movement could go forward on the ideas contained in her writings. Widely accepted, this view found its way into print a few years later by way of a pamphlet written by Geoffrey Hamlin. The position is aggressively maintained by the Paul Revere group today.

Another possibility, it seems to the writer, would have been for the Board of Directors simply to recognize that the Mother Church could not operate under the *Manual* as Mrs. Eddy left it, and then to reorganize the church—as Mrs. Eddy had found it necessary to do whenever she reached an impasse—so as to continue along essentially the same lines, using all that was usable in the *Manual*. This would of course have had to be done within the framework of prevailing legal requirements and would, I feel sure, have been sustained by the courts. It could have been argued very cogently that this would be a mode of carrying out Mrs. Eddy's general desires. To be sure, there are passages aplenty in her writings expressing a fundamental distrust of organization per se; but courts are human and most judges, reared in an organization-conscious society, might be likely to assume the necessity of some institutional form for the preservation and propagation of a great idea. Such a simple course would have been so frankly practical as to obviate any need for either sophistry or strained interpretations to justify it.

It is true that such a bold step might have led to some conflict and division in the ranks. Events have proved that the Board was in a position of great power and authority. Certainly there was no one of great consequence to challenge it.

Another course would have been to recognize the fact of an ongoing organization which was measurably well carrying out the Founder's will, and simply ignore the difficulty—proceed as though it did not exist—at least until challenged. This apparently was the course chosen in the early days following Mrs. Eddy's death.

But in the end the Board chose to go on using the *Manual* in so far as possible, deliberately disregarding the portions that made its own functioning impossible, while at the same time asserting undying loyalty to Mrs. Eddy and to the *Manual*. In doing this the Board held teachers, lecturers, officers, and even ordinary members under the rigid discipline prescribed in the *Manual*, literally adhered to, while the Directors themselves refused to follow it literally. But this policy came as a slow growth and found its final adoption only at the end of a long court battle, the Great Litigation, a struggle for power that finally gave that position court sanction.

Under the circumstances it may seem amazing that there was so little trouble in the organization following the death of Mrs. Eddy. But there was almost no opportunity for factions to develop, and there was no one outstanding person who could by any means be regarded as her successor. At one time Mrs. Stetson may have had some possibilities in that direction, but Mrs. Eddy had taken care of that. Though a powerful figure in New York, Augusta Stetson had been publicly repudiated by the Mother Church and even expelled from the branch church which she had built.

The Board of Directors was the trusted group and the logical one to carry on. It was a self-perpetuating body in no way account-able to the membership of the church. Though the *Manual* asserts that each branch church shall be "distinctly democratic in its government," nothing of the sort was asserted for the Mother Church. To be sure, there had been a group called "First Members" who did for a while have some routine matters of business to attend to, but Mrs. Eddy silenced this group in 1901 and abolished it in 1908, after which the Board assumed its functions. This was to be a bone of contention in the legal battle.

The point here is that the Mother Church had never been a democratically conducted organization. Its members had, and have, no voice whatsoever in its government, and its authorities are obliged to give no accounting to the membership. Church members had always been under almost absolute authority, first that of Mrs. Eddy, then that of the Board of Directors who, during her lifetime, did her bidding unquestioningly. Even before Mrs. Eddy loosened in death her tight hold on the instruments of control, the Board of Directors had become, in the terminology of church members everywhere, "headquarters." On various occasions it had been the custom for individuals, congregations, and officers or local church boards to write to Mrs. Eddy affirming their loyalty and devotion to her, until gradually this had become a test of their faithfulness. Perhaps then it was quite natural that after Mrs. Eddy died, these manifestations were offered to the Board of Directors who were recognized as replacing her. To this day the practice is common, especially with students' associations. Often the sentiment is rein-forced with substantial donations.

If on the surface of things there seemed to be the utmost har-mony, down underneath all was not sweetness and light. At least not for long. The relationship between the Board of the Christian Science Publishing Society and the Board of the Mother Church was somewhat ambiguous. The Publishing Society had been set up under an independent trust deed and, despite the Mother Church Board's centralized control of all members as such, some measure of autonomy by the publishing trustees began to emerge.

The idea of a Christian Science publishing house had first made its appearance in early 1875, when George Barry and Elizabeth Newhall, calling themselves the "Christian Science Publishing Company," undertook to bring out Mary Baker Glover's *Science and Health*. Mrs. Glover—she was not yet Mrs. Eddy—had sought in vain to find a publisher willing to take on her manuscript. She was fervently convinced that her book must be gotten to the world at any cost; but she had bought a house in Lynn, which was at once her residence and the headquarters for her burgeoning movement, and had not sufficient capital left to enter into such an undertaking on her own. Between them, her students Barry and Newhall put up fifteen hundred dollars initially, and then they came forward with an additional seven hundred dollars to cover changes in the text which Mrs. Glover believed necessary after the proofs had been approved and the plates cast. Daniel Spofford, another ardent disciple, entered the picture as sales manager, and he contributed five hundred dollars for an advertising fund. These were goodly sums in those days.

Even so, serious difficulties and considerable delay were encountered. The enforced postponement, Mrs. Glover later decided, proved to be an advantage, for it enabled her to write an additional chapter which she pronounced indispensable to the work as a whole. In the added section she attributed the entire trouble to "malicious animal magnetism" which was arrayed against the expression of Truth.

Science and Health was found unexpectedly difficult to market. Not that insufficient labor was expended, for the little band of missionaries even resorted to hawking it from door to door. Advertisements featured glowing testimonials attributing healings to the reading of the book. It was promoted as a holiday gift item. Review copies were sent to newspapers and magazines. But the reviewers scorned the strange new gospel. After two long years of unflagging toil—during which time both George Barry and Elizabeth Newhall had become disaffected—little more than six hundred dollars could be counted to show for all that had gone into the crusade. And when Spofford turned over this negligible amount to backers Barry and Newhall in partial reimbursement for their expenditure, keeping none of it to cover his own losses, Mrs. Glover declared that failure to turn these receipts over to her as the author constituted betrayal by those she trusted.

Thus in bitterness and ignominy ended the first attempt to found an independent publishing facility for the movement. But this was not to be the death of the idea. It was to be resurrected and nurtured during the ensuing years, eventuating in the present-day Christian Science Publishing Society, with its multimillion-dollar publishing house at Boston and its great army of volunteer salesmen constituted by the membership of the church throughout the world.

In 1878, Mary Baker Glover Eddy's *Science and Health* was published in abbreviated form, under the imprint of Asa G. Eddy, Lynn, and it is to be noted that her textbook was always thereafter to be put out under her personal direction by a student (or students) whom she denominated her "Publisher." During her lifetime *Science and Health* ran through 382 editions, from its first in 1875 to its last in 1908; but she kept it separate from all other publishing activities, retaining the control and all proceeds for herself.

In passing, perhaps it should be noted that the "Christian Science Committee on Publication" was never, as might be inferred from the title, a publishing agency. Rather, it was always a public relations office.

In 1883, Mrs. Eddy, assisted by some of her students under the name of the "Christian Scientists' Publishing Company," launched the *Journal of Christian Science.* Herself the editor of the periodical in the beginning, Mrs. Eddy soon shifted the task to one and then another of her students, still keeping tight rein on the selection of material for its pages as well as on editorial policies. Her voluminous correspondence shows that she left little to chance, and there were frequent changes of editors.

In the spring of 1889 Mrs. Eddy transferred the ownership of the *Journal,* which was now somewhat in debt, to her students' association. Around this time "The Christian Science Publishing Society" was a name which had begun to appear, and it was under this banner that the Association now issued the periodical. Then in 1893 Mrs. Eddy decided to repossess the now-prosperous *Journal*, and title was transferred back to her.

The *Christian Science Quarterly*, listing citations from Mrs. Eddy's writings and the Bible to be studied daily and then reviewed in the Sunday services, was first issued in 1890. It contained the "International Series" of Bible lessons used by other denominations, and with these a special committee undertook to correlate passages from *Science and Health*. The *Quarterly* in its present form emerged in July, 1898, an essential component of the church ritual. Its production remained permanently the responsibility of the Publishing Society, which now and then brought out a pamphlet or tract as well.

The weekly *Christian Science Sentinel* did not appear until near the end of 1898. It seems to have been designed to stress specific application, whereas the *Journal* stressed doctrine, although there has never been any clear line of demarcation between the two periodicals in basic character. How closely Mrs. Eddy supervised every department of her movement is indicated by her firm surveillance and direction of the periodicals. When statements or articles displeased her, as they often did, she unhesitatingly rebuked her editors, sometimes in notices which she required them to print in their columns. For example, an editorial by John B. Willis, called "Watching versus Watching Out," was repudiated in the very next issue of the *Sentinel* in an editorial similarly titled and signed by Mary Baker G. Eddy. (VIII, 40-41, 56)

In 1908 a prominent Christian Scientist, who had been on the staff of the *Boston Globe* for many years, wrote Mrs. Eddy urging the desirability of establishing a Christian Science daily newspaper. He ended by saying: "I think that many would like to read a paper that takes less notice of crime, etc., and gives attention especially to the positive side of life, to the activities that work for the good of man, and to the things really worth knowing." (Quoted by Bates and Dittemore, p. 422) With characteristic forthrightness, Mrs. Eddy sent word on August 8, 1908, to the Publishing Society to "start a daily newspaper at once," calling it the *Christian Science Monitor*. They could, she added, consult with the Board of Directors of the Mother Church, whom she had notified of her intention.

So a great and unique newspaper was born. The first issue appeared on November 25, 1908. By the non–Christian Science world the *Monitor* has generally been regarded as the greatest contribution the Scientists have made to modern American life. Subsidized by the church, it has been spared the pressures which advertisers often exert on the public press. The burden of subsidy is lightened by two things: every member of the church "who can afford it" is obliged "to subscribe for the periodicals which are the organs of this Church" (*Manual*, p. 44); and, secondly, the whole membership is mobilized behind a tireless drive for subscribers and paying advertisers. To a man, the membership works religiously at this task. Indeed, it is the opinion in some responsible quarters that the zeal manifested in this connection antagonizes many, thus tending to hold down circulation, and it is a fact that the total circulation of the *Monitor* has not greatly increased during recent decades. It is believed also by some that the *Christian Science Monitor* is handicapped by the sectarian connotations of its title, as was anticipated by certain of Mrs. Eddy's top advisers when she first proposed and then insisted upon naming it so. The paper has not been merely a house organ or a religious propaganda sheet, however, but has proved a genuinely constructive influence, respected and honored by newspapermen as well as by the educated public in general.

These, then, were the products of her Publishing Society at the time of Mrs. Eddy's death in late 1910. Before she left the scene she had taken certain radical steps to stabilize her various institutions, but these very steps were to open the way for a grave upheaval in the movement, the only major schism the church has experienced.

In February, 1898, Mrs. Eddy drew up a deed of trust which established the Christian Science Publishing Society as a separate legal entity on a permanent and solid basis. In preparation for the event the Society had relinquished to her by bill of sale all its assets on January 21, 1898, including equipment, copyrights, stock, fixtures, and even the cash balance on hand. Mrs. Eddy in turn deeded it all to three of her chief lieutenants—Edward P. Bates, James A. Neal, and William P. McKenzie—in consideration of one dollar and their pledge to fulfil faithfully the terms of her trust deed.

The trustees were to manage the business "on a strictly Christian" basis, acting on their own responsibility entirely, without consulting Mrs. Eddy on details and subject to her supervision only should she elect to advise them. Net profits were to be turned over to the treasurer of the Mother Church. The "First Members"—whom she later disbanded—were to have final say about the disposition of such funds within the limits set by the *Church Manual.*

The trustees were to employ needed help and to remove employees at their discretion or in accord with the needs of the business. They were also to employ persons to prepare the Bible-lesson sermons for the *Quarterly* and to publish the *Quarterly,* as well as pamphlets, tracts, and other literature "so as to promote the best interests of the Cause," Mrs. Eddy reserving the right to make such changes as she might think advisable.

The next section is particularly important:

Whenever a vacancy shall occur in said trusteeship for any cause, I reserve the right to fill the same by appointment, if I shall so desire, as long as I may live; but if I do not elect to exercise this right, the remaining trustees shall fill said vacancy. The First Members together with the Directors of said Church shall have the power to declare vacancies in said trusteeship for such reasons as to them may seem expedient.

It was around this section that the Great Litigation largely turned. It is quite clear that Mrs. Eddy retained in her hands effective control of the trustees during her lifetime. Did she intend that after her death—which she clearly anticipated in another clause providing that upon her decease the copyright to the *Journal* should pass into their hands—an equally final control should rest in the hands of the Board of Directors of the church? This was the question which, more than twenty years later, the court was called upon to decide. In the process the church was to suffer incalculable injury. ···

Now so long as Mrs. Eddy lived the centralized control which she maintained over all her projects would tend to preclude any conflict of interest or of divided authority. But after her departure what would the situation be? She had, six years earlier, drawn up a similar deed of trust establishing the Mother Church, in which she turned over the church property to four (and eventually five) trustees, all ardent disciples who could be trusted to carry out her wishes, just as she now turned over the Publishing Society property to three other trustees. By this latter step she had created two separate trusts, each self-perpetuating and irrevocable. Now she had two boards of directors, each board required by law to abide by and fulfil the conditions of a different deed of trust. She stipulated that the trustees under the church deed "shall be known as the Christian Science Board of Directors" (*Manual*, p. 130), and of course the trustees under the Publishing Society deed were to operate as "The Christian Science Publishing Society." The church trustees were thereafter popularly referred to within the organization as "the Directors," while the directors of the Publishing Society were nearly always referred to as "the Trustees." (For the sake of simplicity, this usage will be followed generally here, but it must be kept in mind that each of the two groups was a directing board composed of trustees, the members of each being sworn to carry out the specific terms of their respective deeds of trust.)

So long as Mrs. Eddy was firmly at the helm and both boards were comprised of faithful and obedient followers, this situation presented no difficulty. Her over-all authority obviated any clashes of opinion, dissolved sectional differences, merged all controls. But the Founder's death in 1910 necessarily changed all this.

The effects of the change were not immediately apparent. As far as the rank and file of members were concerned, ingrained within them was the idea of unquestioning obedience, and the mechanics of the organization generally had become matters of routine by now. The membership having no voice in official matters, dissension at this level was virtually precluded. But at the top stood two autonomous bodies. As has been seen, for some reason known only to herself Mrs. Eddy had chosen to put the publishing business into hands different from those to which she entrusted the church affairs proper. She could simply have designated her Directors to set up and run the publishing business, but she did not do this. Instead she created two relatively independent centers of power. Then she compounded the problem by giving them overlapping duties and functions. Thus the boards would be forced to maintain an absolutely harmonious relationship to avoid real calamity. In some quarters this was interpreted as a divinely inspired plan for compelling her followers not to rely upon human expedients for survival and success, but to turn unreservedly to the demonstration of Christian Science over mundane affairs.

On the one hand, in their deed she charged the Trustees "energetically and judiciously to manage the business of the Publishing Society . . . upon their own responsibility," and then pointed out in the *Manual* (pp. 81-82) that the Publishing Society alone "selects, approves, and publishes the books and literature it sends forth." On the other hand, she was to charge the Directors with what seems to be a kind of general oversight of the activities of the Trustees, by inserting the provision in the *Manual* (p. 44) that the Directors shall see to it that the various periodicals "are ably edited and kept abreast of the times." Similarly, after her dissolution of the First or Executive Members group, Mrs. Eddy sought in the *Manual* to grant the Directors power to remove any Trustee "for such reasons as to the Board may seem expedient," without however empowering the Directors to fill the resultant vacancy. The Trustees alone could appoint every successor on their board (p. 79).

The Publishing Society deed stated that Trustees might not serve unless they were "loyal, faithful, and consistent believers and advocates of the principles of Christian Science" as taught by Mary Baker Eddy in her textbook. Who was to determine whether or not a Trustee was loyal? Who, actually, but the Board of Directors? After all, there was no other authority or court of appeal in case one's loyalty was called in question.

If disputes should arise on any score between the two boards, to whom could the Trustees appeal for a decision? Certainly not to the church membership, for each board existed not as the result of the people's choice but by Mrs. Eddy's fiat. Each was a legal corporation, set up by consent of the state and answerable to no one save Mrs. Eddy, who now was gone. The church itself was not and is not today incorporated.

Disruption between the two boards was made impossible at first by a peculiar circumstance: Mrs. Eddy's right-hand man, Archibald McLellan, was editor-in-chief at the Publishing Society while remaining also a director on the Mother Church Board. Thus, whatever the legal status of the two bodies under their respective trusts, they naturally operated as one under this linkage.

What would happen, though, when McLellan should follow Mrs. Eddy off the scene? Was there anyone at hand big enough to fill his shoes? And, if so, would such a one be granted that dual and strategic position of power by colleagues and potential rivals no longer under the Leader's control?

After McLellan's retirement no individual was ever again to be assigned such a key role. Friction between the two wings of the organization was not long in appearing. The trustees on both boards sought increasingly to enlist the support first of certain officials, then of ordinary members out in the "field," and thus the rift widened to such proportions that it could no longer be concealed from the public nor evaded behind the scenes. Ironically, Mrs. Eddy's "safeguards" had turned out to be traps.

In 1912 a precipitating element was injected into the situation, in the person of Herbert W. Eustace. A leading practitioner and teacher in California, Eustace had always enjoyed exceptional freedom, respect, and authority in his own remote domain. Summoned to Boston to fill a vacancy on the Board of the Publishing Society, he came east quite unprepared for the rigid customs and attitudes which had become entrenched at headquarters, where the Board of Directors reigned supreme.

The inviting officials could hardly have anticipated intractability, since Eustace had gone on record, as far back as 1904, as advocating the authoritarian concept of centralized control. This had been the theme of his address to the General Association of Teachers at Chicago. On that occasion he likened the church to a military organization, an army which could not exist without "loyalty to and support of the constituted authorities," which he said meant unbounded, unswerving, unqualified, unconditional, uncritical obedience, as "expressed exactly by the poet Tennyson, in his lines: 'Theirs not to make reply, Theirs not to reason why.' " True, he traced all authority back to Mrs. Eddy as the commanding general, but did not the Directors now occupy, to all practical intents and purposes, her place in her absence? In any event, it became increasingly clear in the immediate years ahead that, sworn to uphold the Deed of Trust constituting the Publishing Society, a legal document formally drawn up by Mrs. Eddy, he could exercise considerable independence by looking to it as his primary authority in the execution of his trusteeship. He was to carry his fellow trustees along with him in this view.

An early cause for dissension arose when William D. Mc-Cracken's editorials in the church periodicals were construed as advocating evolution and progress in Christian Science thought. To this idea some of the older members objected. McCracken seemed to be suggesting that Mrs. Eddy's teaching was not the final revelation of Truth. They took their objections to the Directors, who were moved to instruct the Trustees to see to it that no ideas be permitted in the official publications which had not been settled upon as correct during Mrs. Eddy's lifetime.

There were other incidents. The Directors rebuked the Trustees over certain expenditures, covering such comparatively minor items as stationery, a car for the accommodation of out-of-town visitors to the Publishing Society, and so on. In 1916 the Directors presented a long "memorandum of understanding" to the Trustees, which defined the relationship between the two boards and held that the Trustees were entirely subordinate to the Directors. But this evidently settled nothing, for the situation continued to deteriorate.

In the regular course of their publishing activities the Trustees announced a new pamphlet by Frederick Dixon, *Purification*, but before it could be released the Directors notified them that the Publishing Society could not proceed without specific authorization from the Board. As the pamphlet was a reprint of articles which had already appeared in the *Monitor* with the Directors' approval, the issue was now clearly drawn—namely, that the Trustees were expected to act only under the guidance and permission of the Directors.

On January 3, 1918, the Directors sent a written proposal "that the present members of the Board of Trustees submit their resignations to The Christian Science Board of Directors to take effect when their resignations are accepted by the Board of Directors." As spokesman for the embattled Publishing Society, Eustace declared that surrender to such a demand would be contrary to his "highest understanding of Principle" as well as contrary to civil law. At this juncture the Trustees sought legal counsel—very eminent counsel, consisting of Charles Evans Hughes (afterward Chief Justice of the U.S. Supreme Court), Silas H. Strawn, and Sherman L. Whipple—and in their rejection of the Directors' proposal they quoted the findings of said counsel: "If there be any conflict between the terms of the Deed and the language of the Church Manual, the legal and moral obligation of the Trustees compels them to respond to and obey the mandates of the Deed. Should they do otherwise, they would violate the compact which they made by their acceptance of the Trust."

Unsuccessful in their endeavor to secure the resignation of the Trustees in a body, the Directors sought to remove one Trustee. On March 17 they served Lamont Rowlands with a "Notice of Dismissal," in which he was accused of reckless insubordination and contentiousness, of putting selfish interest above the interests of the Christian Science movement, of "a disposition to invent or adopt interpretations of our Church By-Laws that pervert their meaning and annul their effect," of trying to alter the established relationship between the two boards, of joining "with other persons, including several eminent lawyers wastefully employed," in an effort to "set up said Deed of Trust against the By-Laws and government of The Mother Church," and of threatening the Directors "with litigation if this Board exercise its right and power to remove any of said Trustees."

Why Rowlands, a minor figure in the controversy? Why not

Eustace, as the ringleader? The Trustees were to allege that it was because Rowlands was the least known and therefore the least influential member of their body, the one whose removal would occasion the least disruption.

Their hand forced, the Board of Trustees of the Publishing Society petitioned the Supreme Judicial Court of Massachusetts, under date of March 25, 1918, for an injunction against interference in their affairs by the Board of Directors of the Mother Church. Many of the salient points given above were recited in their Bill of Complaint, the complete text of which is to be found on pages 983 ff. of the *Proceedings in Equity*. Under this title is gathered into one volume of 1,360 pages, followed by a supplement of 204 pages, the verbatim report of the entire case of the Trustees vs. the Directors. It was first published in extenso and without comment in the *Christian Science Monitor* by mutual agreement of the two boards, but the issues of the *Monitor* containing this material have been removed from the Christian Science reading rooms. At the conclusion of the litigation the Publishing Society put it out in book form as a limited, subscription edition, and this volume is still to be found in some of the larger libraries in the United States.

Mrs. Eddy's plan for promoting and extending Christian Science involved, the Trustees pointed out, two great branches of activity: the first was the organization of the church, for the study of her doctrine as set forth in *Science and Health* together with the Bible; the second was the effort to increase the world-wide circulation of publications on Christian Science. These two branches of activity she put into the hands of different sets of trustees, retaining a large measure of control over both boards, each of which was made up of her own personally selected agents. Although the Board of Directors had been formed in 1892, when she set up the Publishing Society six years later she did not grant them any authority over the publications, nor had the Directors any participation in the Publishing Society.

In her Trust Deed of 1892 Mrs. Eddy had conveyed to the trustees known as the "Christian Science Board of Directors" certain property, and given them certain powers and duties relating to the

Mother Church, its organization and discipline, retaining however her general control of them by right of removal and appointment. Then in 1898, through another trust deed, she conveyed the property used by the Christian Science Publishing Society to a different board of trustees, delegating to them the authority connected therewith which she had reserved up until that time to herself alone. She named no member of the Board of Directors of the Mother Church as trustee of the Publishing Society, doubtless in pursuance of her distinct purpose of keeping the affairs of the Publishing Society under different control and management from that of her church.

From that time on the Trustees had held and managed the properties and business conscientiously and in such a way as to make it successful and prosperous, paying over annually large sums to the Mother Church for the promotion of Christian Science. For the period of six months ending October 1, 1918, they had turned over as profits from their conduct of the business the impressive sum of more than $450,000.

But since Mrs. Eddy's passing in 1910 the Directors had gradually tried to assume and exercise powers never assumed or exercised during Mrs. Eddy's lifetime, even requesting the Trustees to abstain from the exercise of powers which they had before exercised. In general the Trustees supplied requested information about their business and sought to conform to the requests, but the Directors had demanded more than this, insisting that the Trustees "make open, specific and public acknowledgement that the Directors were the supreme and final authority with reference to all of the affairs of the Publishing Society and the management of the Trust created by the Trust Deed of January 25, 1898."

In October, 1918, the Directors made formal demand upon the Trustees that they should no longer manage the Trust as they had been doing, but should thereafter act in all matters concerning it in conformity with the direction of said Directors and with certain wishes of Mrs. Eddy allegedly expressed in the *Manual* and otherwise on occasions long after the date of the Deed of Trust, although these alleged expressions and statements were admittedly inconsistent with the terms of the Deed of Trust and in derogation of the powers and duties of the Trustees therein declared and defined. The Directors did not demand that the Trustees do or refrain from doing any particular thing; the demand was that the Trustees accept the Directors' claim of supreme authority, agreeing in writing that they would thereafter discharge their duties in accordance with the Directors' interpretation of the *Manual*, even where such interpretation was inconsistent with and contrary to the provisions of the Deed of Trust. If this were granted the Directors would be arrogating to themselves all the duties and powers of the Trustees of the Publishing Society as well as those of the Directors of the church.

Legal counsel advised the Trustees that the Deed of Trust was complete and in itself irrevocable. The power under the deed to declare vacancies was invested in the Directors *together with* the First Members; hence the Directors could not alone make such a declaration. The source of the powers and duties of the Trustees is the Deed of Trust, so to it they must look. Neither subsequent provisions of the *Manual* nor subsequent declarations by Mrs. Eddy could have any modifying effect upon it. If there exist any conflict between the Deed and the *Manual*, clearly the Trustees are obliged to obey the Deed's mandates.

The Trustees asserted it as their belief that the action against Rowlands and the attempt to secure the resignations of all three was part of a plan to put in their places three men who would be subservient to the Directors, and that the refusal of Eustace and Ogden to elect a successor to Rowlands would be taken as an excuse for declaring their own posts vacant. They vigorously disputed the charges against Rowlands on which his notice of dismissal purportedly rested.

According to the Trustees, the Directors had stated to others, in substance, that it was their purpose to obtain control of the Publishing Society or destroy it; that if the Trustees refused to surrender, the Directors intended, as one of them had said, "to make the Publishing Society an empty shell" by using their authority and influence in the field, persuading Christian Scientists to cease subscribing to the publications of the Society, in favor of new publications which the Directors contemplated issuing. If the

Directors were not restrained it was the belief of the Trustees that
the cause of Christian Science would suffer irreparable damage
through their actions.

An injunction was therefore sought against the Directors, preventing them from "carrying out any purpose or plan, by either
direct or indirect means, to compel the plaintiffs or any of them to
resign their offices as Trustees; to impair, destroy, or in any way
injure the business of the Christian Science Publishing Society as
conducted by the plaintiff Trustees . . ."

On March 25, 1919, the court issued an ad interim injunction
against the Directors, their agents, attorneys, and counsellors in
compliance with the Trustees' petition.

The Directors on April 4, 1919, filed a lengthy reply to the
charges, which was in substance as follows:

The Directors challenge the assertion that they are directors
only of the Mother Church. They say that the Mother Church is the
central organization of which all the other Christian Science organizations are but branches; that it was never Mrs. Eddy's intention to
separate the Publishing Society from the other activities of the
church; that the Trustees are working under the authority of the
Mother Church over which the Directors have final control. This
they declare has been the recognized relationship, unquestioned by
the Trustees until quite recently. They aver that they did, prior to
the 1898 Trust Deed, participate in the work of the Publishing
Society.

The Directors admit Mrs. Eddy provided that vacancies were
to be declared on the trusteeship by the Directors and the First
Members jointly; but they assert—without here substantiating it—
that with the abolishment of the First Members group, its duties,
rights, and powers survived to and are still vested in the Directors.
Mrs. Eddy provided, in Article XI of the *Manual*, that no one
unacceptable to the Founder and to the Directors could be elected
to the responsibility of publishing her books or editing her periodicals. They admit that never during her lifetime did she give any
authority to them over the publications of which she was sole
author, but aver that she did by will bequeath all of said publications

to the Mother Church in trust for the promoting and extending of her teaching.

The Directors deny that the Trustees have energetically and judiciously conducted the affairs of the Society, or properly discharged their duties. John V. Dittemore, who had just been dismissed by his fellow-Directors from their board for incompatibility, entered a separate answer in which he specified in great detail the shortcomings of the Trustees.

In their answer the Directors deny that in disposing of Rowlands they had any such purpose as alleged by the Trustees. They deny that they had any intention to make the Publishing Society "an empty shell," but aver that it has always been their purpose to support and promote the business of the Society as an integral activity of the Mother Church. They deny some of the allegations regarding what was asked of the Trustees, but admit their request that the Trustees sign the following statement: "It is mutually understood by the Trustees and the Board of Directors that the Board has final authority in regard to the editorial policy and final authority in regard to all matters affecting the policy of the Mother Church or the cause of Christian Science." They admit that they required the signing of this agreement as the price of their continuance in office of the Trustees.

The issue was sharply and clearly drawn. A decision must be rendered by the court, for there seemed to be no agreement between the two boards.

On June 3, 1919, the Bill of Complaint came up for a hearing before the court. The first day was marked only by preliminary sparring, and it was not until June 11 that the hearing really got under way. Meanwhile, on June 3 the Trustees brought contempt proceedings against the Directors for violation of the ad interim injunction. After a week of argument before Judge Braley, of the Massachusetts Supreme Judicial Court, the court found the Directors guilty of contempt by violation of the injunction. Each of the Directors (except Edward A. Merritt) was fined fifty dollars, while the eminent Christian Scientist Clifford P. Smith, as counsel for the Directors, was sharply rebuked and fined one hundred dollars.

The announcement of the court's decision came as a shock not only to the officials but to the members of the church throughout the world. It had seemed to them a foregone conclusion that the court would decide in favor of the Board of Directors. Instead, the Directors were branded as guilty of illegal action in violating the injunction, and were required to pay a fine or go to jail. Could it be that the court in the end could possibly find the Trustees right and the Directors wrong? A very substantial majority of the membership was behind the Directors. If the Board's hands were tied legally, was there no other way by which the desired ends could be accomplished without incurring legal penalty? There definitely was.

Meanwhile on the eleventh of June the hearings on the Bill of Complaint were begun, and on thirty-four days of that very hot summer—spreading through June, July, August, and September—the case was argued, and numerous witnesses were examined and cross-examined by as astute a group of lawyers as could be found in the United States.

While there were many involvements in the proceedings, there was really but one fundamental issue, that as to whether the final and absolute control of the church was vested in the Board of Directors, as they insisted, or whether there existed two separate and independent bodies with independent functions, autonomous bodies which might, however, work together harmoniously to achieve the purposes of the founder of the faith. This latter was the claim of the Trustees. They held that the ultimate governing agent in Christian Science must be Principle rather than a group of people, however noble, good, and wise they might be. In a letter written to the Directors six months before filing their Bill of Complaint the Trustees had said: "We can conceive of no government by Principle except by trusting each employee to make his own demonstration of Principle. Each individual [in Christian Science] must be held responsible for his own demonstration." In his testimony before the court Eustace held that the enforced subservience of the Trustees to the Directors would at once stop all development toward the allegiance to Principle alone which was the conceded objective of Christian Science teaching, and that as a result the Directors would eventually extend their absolute control to every phase of the church's life.

Attorney Charles Evans Hughes in his summary argument before the court put his finger squarely on the issue at stake when he said:

No one could dispute the desirability of harmony. But there are two conceptions of harmony. One is the harmony produced by despotic power; the other is the harmony that results from a unity of ideas and common views of a religious truth. It seems to us most unjust to Mrs. Eddy, most contrary to her teachings, to assume for a moment that she relied upon the exercise of the despotic power which these Directors have arrogated to themselves.

Hughes was greatly impressed with and quoted Mrs. Eddy's well-known statement that organization has both value and peril, that it is requisite only in the beginning, and that "after this material form of cohesion and fellowship has accomplished its end, continued organization retards spiritual growth, and should be laid off." (Retrospection and Introspection, p. 45) Of course, he observed, "Mrs. Eddy believed in organization and selected her forms of organization, but her confidence was in Truth as she conceived and taught it. She believed that the Truth would have a harmonizing power, that it would bring all those devoted to the Truth as she taught it together in unity of action, not through forms of organization."

As Hughes saw it, the very fact of her setting up the Board of Trustees when there was already in existence the Board of Directors evidenced her fear that "autocracy might result if the entire power of organization was in one hand." Further evidence of that fear was Article X of the Trust Deed, in which she invested not the Directors alone, but the Directors and the First Members together with the power to declare vacancies in the Board of Trustees:

The unity which these [Directors] wish, the unity of despotic power, the control absolutely of this entire government of Christian Science in the church and in the publications and everywhere else, that is the unity which might well destroy the very faith or the organization for the propagation of the faith to which they profess to be devoted.

In the end, Judge Dodge, the Master before whom the hearings were held, sustained the Trustees in all three of their major contentions:

First, the Trustees had declared the dismissal of Rowlands illegal because it was not decided by a majority vote of the Board of Directors as constituted at the time Mrs. Eddy drew up the 1898 Deed of Trust. In this the Master concurred. Of the five Directors, Dittemore refused to vote either way. Neal was not present, but gave his assent by telephone. This the Master did not regard as a valid vote on a question of such importance. Merritt was not a member legally for the purposes of removing a Trustee, since he was successor to the fifth member added to the Board of Directors by a bylaw in the *Manual* rather than in the original legal establishment of the Board in 1892. Thus only two votes were legally cast against Rowlands, an insufficient number to remove a Trustee.

Second, the Trustees had declared the Directors legally powerless to remove a Trustee without the concurrence of the now-abolished First Members. The Directors maintained that the duties and powers of the First Members had passed to them. The Master decided against the Directors:

My ruling must be that [the incapacity of the First Members] has rendered any exercise of the power to remove a Trustee impossible, either according to the terms in which the Deed of 1898 gives it or according to the intent manifested. Such exercise of the power having thus become impossible, removal of a Trustee would require resort to a court.

Third, the Trustees charged that the Directors had proceeded arbitrarily and without legal right in abolishing the First Members originally and in assuming their powers (including that of declaring a vacancy in the trusteeship). The Master's finding expresses doubt as to the Directors' functioning thus in matters requiring legal sanction, though they might function in other matters so long as the church membership as a whole agreed. There was never any legal sanction for the setting aside of the First Members. It was they who, according to the minutes of the meeting of September 23, 1892, elected the first officers of the church. Though the Board of Directors was then in existence, its members were not designated as among the church officers. It was not until 1895 that a bylaw directed that the officers of the church be elected not by the First Members but by the Board of Directors. But even then no mention is made of the Directors as officers of the church. This does not appear until the year 1908.

In 1901 the First Members adopted a bylaw providing that "the business of the Mother Church hitherto transacted by the First Members shall be done by the Christian Science Board of Directors." As to this the Master observes:

Whether or not the making of by-laws for the Church's government was, properly speaking, "business" whose transaction its voting members could thus transfer to a different body, wholly independent of their control, may well be doubted. Since 1901 no by-laws have been voted on by the First Members, but only by the Board of Directors, to whom Mrs. Eddy seems to have sent all proposed amendments or additions proposed by her. This practice was accepted by the First Members and by the Church generally without question.

But, said the Master, "with regard to them, my ruling is that none of them are by-laws made under the authority of the Massachusetts statutes. Their authority must be regarded as derived solely from the mutual consent of the church members to be bound by them."

This ruling would of course mean that for legal purposes the subsequent revision (February 20, 1901) of the bylaw concerning the right of the First Members and the Directors jointly to remove Trustees to read "the Board of Directors shall have the power to declare vacancies in said trusteeship for such reasons as the Board may deem expedient" would have no binding effect. The Trust Deed, a legal document specifically requiring the consent of the First Members in order to declare a vacancy, could not be set aside by an extralegal modification of the *Manual* of the church. That is, while the church members might consent to be ruled by the Board of Directors, even to complete elimination of the First Members as such—as was done by a vote not of the First Members or the church members but solely by the Board of Directors itself—such consent could not be held to modify the provisions of a trust set up under state law. If for any reason it became impossible to operate under the original terms of the trust, as now was the case since there was no longer a body of First Members, then the only recourse was to the courts. The Directors could petition the court to do what they could not themselves alone do legally, namely, declare a vacancy in the trusteeship. To proceed otherwise, as they had done, was illegal.

There was much more to the Master's findings; e.g., he did not find that Rowlands had failed in the performance of his duties as Trustee, as the Directors had alleged, nor did he regard the employment of counsel by the Trustees as a reason for dismissal. But these are minor points. The important thing was, from the standpoint of the Trustees, that the Master had sustained their major contention: the legal right of the independence of the Trustees of the Publishing Society from the complete control of the Board of Directors of the Mother Church.

In his final summary the Master recognized the necessity of close co-operation between the Directors and the Trustees; but, he continued, that this co-operation

is impossible unless the Publishing Society Trustees are subjected to the supervision and final control of the Directors, does not so plainly appear as to require the conclusion that Mrs. Eddy must have intended such subjection when she established the Trust. Had she intended it there would have been provision in the Deed of 1898, establishing it in express and unmistakable terms; it is hardly supposable that instead of such provision the Deed should have made the Trustees subject only to her supervision, as it does in paragraph 3. Neither in the terms of the Deed nor in the subsequent by-laws do I find anything which makes it unreasonable to suppose that she apprehended no such danger of dissension between two boards, both composed of firm, loyal, and consistent believers in her doctrine, as would require the express subordination of one to the other in order to secure the necessary cooperation between them.

The Master handed down his decision on February 20, 1920. Shortly thereafter the Directors sent out a letter to all the members of the church saying that the findings of the court were unfavorable, but that this decision was subject to review by the Supreme Judicial Court of Massachusetts, first by a single judge and later by a panel

of five judges. Some months would be required before the case
was finally settled.

The decision, although it was not final, had a sobering effect upon
the field. The membership was by no means so certain now that the
Directors would win their case in the end. A strong wave of emotion
swept the majority group who were loyal to the Directors. The
Board's hands were tied by the injunction, so that the Directors could
do nothing (such as declaring a boycott of the publications issued
by the Trustees). But the authority of the Massachusetts court did
not extend beyond the state, so there was nothing to hinder individuals or even groups in other states from seeking to make the
Publishing Society "an empty shell." So groups sprang up in various
sections of the country who openly counseled members to cancel
their subscriptions to the periodicals. As the *Manual* was held up as
sacrosanct, superior even to any legal document or trust, the members were caught in what appeared to be an unresolvable conflict
posed by the *Manual* itself. Importuned to crush the Publishing
Society Trustees by cancelling all subscriptions and paid advertising,
they were yet confronted with the unconditional requirement in the
bylaws that they support the periodicals.

A group calling itself "The Executive Committee of the Christian
Science Delegates of New York State" issued bulletins purporting to
keep the field informed of what was going on in Boston. They
definitely urged the boycott of the official church periodicals, declaring that "whatever is not conducted legitimately or in strict conformity with our Mother Church *Manual* should not be partaken of
even in the slightest degree." This and other such efforts were
augmented by certain of the Christian Science lecturers, who undertook in their travels to spread the word throughout America and
abroad through private conferences with local leaders everywhere.

In one of its bulletins the New York committee boasted of the
effectiveness of the campaign to starve out the Trustees:

In spite of several recently published assertions that the tide of protest
from the field against the actions of the Trustees is turning, the following
statistics indicate a continuously increasing list of branch churches and
practitioners who are openly standing in support of the *Manual*. The

figures indicate the number of churches and societies and of individuals
[practitioners] advertised in the *Christian Science Journal* in January
1920 and in the issues of January, April and July of 1921.

	Jan. 1920	Jan. 1921	Apr. 1921	July 1921
Churches	1,808	687	511	447
Practitioners	6,581	2,801	2,525	2,098

That is, almost 62 per cent of the churches withdrew their
advertisements from the *Journal* within the first year after the
Master's ruling was handed down. Within a year and a half only
24.2 per cent of the churches were continuing to list their notices
in the *Journal*. Advertisements were withdrawn during the first year
by 57.5 per cent of the practitioners, and by July, 1921, only 31.8
per cent remained in the *Journal* registry.

While most members of all Christian Science churches continued
to buy the indispensable *Quarterly* from the Publishing Society, the
subscriptions to the *Journal* and *Sentinel* steadily declined. In the
end 70 per cent of the *Sentinel* and 80 per cent of the *Journal* and
the *Monitor* subscriptions were canceled. (Studdert-Kennedy, *Christian Science and Organized Religion,* p. 186) In the local churches
those who persisted in their refusal to condemn the Trustees were
made to feel the heavy disapproval of the "loyal." And even today,
close to four decades later, it is not unusual, I am told, for boards
of local Christian Science churches to confront applicants for membership with the question of where they stood "during the controversy." Applicants who were not in the organization during the
litigation period are undoubtedly mystified by the question, for the
subject is never mentioned in the periodicals, issues of the *Monitor*
containing accounts of it are not to be found in the reading rooms,
and discussion of it is frowned upon throughout the field. It is a
well-known fact that when a newcomer to the organization asks
about that historic conflict, or about any of its principals, he is simply
reminded that "our Leader enjoins us to avoid voicing error."
Persistent curiosity is viewed with suspicion. Even today, some
branch church questionnaires for applicants contain this query:
"Are you loyal to the Board of Directors of The Mother Church?"

As might have been expected, the Directors took exception to the

Master's report, and various persons sought to intervene in the case, doubtless with the view of defeating the Trustees and giving aid to the Directors. A Mrs. Hulin, a member of the Mother Church, petitioned the court to pronounce the Board of Directors competent to declare a vacancy; in the event that this was not allowed, she further asked that the court itself remove the Trustees and appoint suitable persons in their places. The petition was rejected by the court.

In an unprecedented move the attorney-general of Massachusetts was apparently persuaded to file a petition having somewhat the same effect. This was likewise argued and denied. Moreover, the attorney-general was severely criticized by the court for bringing such a petition in the way he did. Said Mr. Justice Pierce:

The Attorney-General ought to boss the job. He is not an intervener, he is the Commander of the field; he does not ask realtors or anyone else what he should do, but he does it; he does it as representing the sovereignty of the State. I do not like the idea of the Attorney-General dragging himself in here as the fifth wheel.

Furthermore, from the remarks of the justice it appeared that at the moment at least he was accusing the attorney-general of confusing the issue by bringing in matters that were not really involved in the case. The issue, he thought, was very simple; namely, whether in removing Rowlands the Directors were acting legally or illegally.

Some of the petitioners appear not to have been fully aware of their participation in the proceedings. For example, on May 14, 1941, Gilbert C. Carpenter, Jr., wrote in a letter: "I was amazed when I read of the intervention of the Attorney-General to find my father was one of the eight realtors and First Members that he represented. I mention it because my father says he knew *nothing* about it at all!"

Justice Pierce caused great consternation in the field when it was disclosed that he had said:

Supposing the Court should say in this particular case to whoever writes the opinion, "it may be the by-laws and it may be that the *Manual* ought to be considered in doing these things in this decision, but after all it isn't of very much consequence, the primary question here is as to whether the Board of Directors under the constituting instrument has power to remove the Trustees notwithstanding the fact that they had only half the power they had before the happening of certain events, which events they created themselves." That is the fact in this case, the Board of Directors have made themselves, if they have this power of Kings, by by-laws that they passed when they froze out the First Members.

He added: "I am only saying it might happen; I do not say it will because it may not." But this statement, coming from the court, created serious apprehension as to what the final decision might be.

It was not until November 29, 1920, that the final arguments of counsel for both parties were heard by the full Supreme Judicial Court. Here there was no introduction of witnesses or new evidence, but only summaries of the respective sides of the controversy. The distinguished Charles Evans Hughes spoke for the Trustees. Ex-Governor of Massachusetts John L. Bates argued for the Directors. Others represented John V. Dittemore who, having been (as he contended) illegally dismissed from the Board of Directors and replaced by another, had figured all through the litigation; and the Commonwealth on behalf of the attorney-general's petition.

It was almost a year before the final decision of the full court was handed down on November 21, 1921. The decision was written by Justice C. J. Rugg. In substance it sustained almost entirely the findings of the Master on questions of fact. But the decision itself was adverse to the Trustees, in effect sustaining the Directors' claim to ultimate and supreme authority, based largely upon the court's belief that, despite the formal objections which might properly be raised to the verbal statement of the Trust, the intention of the original donor was adequately fulfilled by the action of the Directors.

The court declared it had no right to pass upon the question as to whether the removal of Rowlands was or was not wise. Having satisfied itself that the Directors were acting in good faith—with one reservation—in ousting Rowlands, and that no essential legal right of his had been violated in the process, it clearly affirmed the right of the Directors so to act. That was, to the court, the crux of the whole matter. Did the Board without the concurrence of the First Members, who no longer existed, have that right? It was the decision of the court that it did.

Of course, the court agreed, the terms of a trust deed cannot be changed by subsequent events. But "its words are to be interpreted with reference to the subject matter to which they relate." Thus "the fair interpretation of the words is that those possessing ecclesiastical functions at the time vested in First Members and Directors should be the depositaries of the power of removal, by whatever names they might be called and however their number might fluctuate according to the polity of the Church." To construe the words otherwise would be to stick to the forms and ignore the substance. "So far as concerns the power of removal of a Trustee under the Trust Deed of January 25, 1898, the organization of the Church in accordance with its polity has consolidated these powers, previously shared by the First Members and the Directors in concurrence, and placed them wholly in the Directors." As for "the Board of Directors" and "the First Members," the court concluded that "these terms are ecclesiastical" and must be interpreted as referring to the governing authorities of the church as determined by church polity. Under this interpretation, the dismissal of Rowlands was held to be legal and the Bill of the plaintiff was therefore dismissed.

Thus the Board of Directors had won their battle and were declared in effect to be supreme in all matters relating to the conduct of the Mother Church. After years of struggle they had achieved their aim. From that time until now no one has successfully challenged their supremacy and total control of the organization.

From the practical standpoint it is difficult to see how the court could have decided otherwise. Had it done so, there is no doubt that there would have been an endless succession of charges and countercharges before the court. The *Manual*, on any literal interpretation, is plainly inoperable. Yet here was a substantial organization not only engaged in religious practices, but a holder of property, and carrying on an extensive business of publishing and circulating literature. Should it simply go out of existence, dissolve itself, become a movement only, not an institution? It would be too much to suppose that judges, practical men, believers in institutional religion, would come to such a conclusion.

The court seems really to have proceeded upon the premise that the church is this kind of church because people want it that way. Again and again the decision pointed out that the general membership, while not having voting rights, nevertheless had acquiesced in the changes. The inference clearly seems to be that ultimately the members have accepted the polity of the church by not opposing it. There is, to be sure, no method provided by which they might register their opposition to the changes; but obviously, if they were too deeply dissatisfied they could leave the church. There is no compulsion upon them to remain in it. Large numbers have remained, indicating at least tacit approval. As to whether the organization is good or bad, effective or ineffective, the court did not feel called upon to pronounce an opinion. What the court did decide was that the organization as it had evolved did measurably well carry out the intent of its founder.

Great numbers of Christian Scientists did not agree with the court. How many it is impossible to say. Clearly the majority did agree, and have loyally supported the Board of Directors in its conduct of the church's affairs. Some resigned from the church and became free-lance Christian Scientists, and some allied themselves with kindred movements.

On November 26, 1921, the Trustees published a brief statement in the *Monitor,* saying they had sought faithfully to conform to Mrs. Eddy's wishes in establishing the Trust, and to obey the laws of the land as she had always admonished. They differed from the Directors in their interpretations of Mrs. Eddy's wishes and purposes and had sought a legal interpretation of the legal instrument defining their duties. That interpretation had now been given. It was authoritative and to them final. They would co-operate with the Directors who, as the law had been declared, were entitled to dominate the Trust in the appointment of their successors.

Then the Directors refused to consider the final accounting offered by the Trustees, demanding that the Trustees first resign, after electing their successors (who were to be subject to the approval of the Directors), and remove themselves from the Publishing Society. The Trustees therefore petitioned the court to allow them to submit their accounts while they still had access to the relevant and supporting records, and be discharged from all further responsibility in the matter of the Trust, from which they asked to be permitted to resign, conveying to their successors the Trust properties in due form.

While the full court had reversed the finding of the Master in Chancery, and had in effect upheld the right of the Directors to declare a vacancy on the Board of Trustees, only the Trustees might elect a successor to fill a vacancy. Herbert Eustace and Paul Harvey were still Trustees. The simplest thing, it would seem to an outsider, would have been to let the two resign as they wished to. But they would not resign, understandably, without first getting a legal discharge showing that a complete accounting had been made of their stewardship. And why, one wonders, was this not quietly allowed?

Meanwhile the Directors wrote both Eustace and Harvey, on December 14, 1921, notifying them that the Board had scheduled a hearing to be held December 19, at which time each might be given the opportunity to show cause why he ought not to be removed from his trusteeship. Twelve detailed charges were made in justification of the Board's intention to declare their posts vacant. These were, briefly: that the Trustees had failed to fill the vacancy created by Rowlands' removal; that they had mismanaged the Publishing Society to such an extent that it had lost most of its sales of literature—70 per cent of the *Sentinel,* 80 per cent of the *Journal,* 80 per cent of the *Monitor*—and the former profits of the Society had become a serious deficit; that they had wrongfully used trust funds by paying extra sums to certain individuals; that they had refused to give an accounting to the treasurer of the Mother Church; that they had wastefully paid a large sum to a public accountant; that they had lost the support and confidence of most of the branch churches and members; that they had brought on the Great Litigation; that they were no longer loyal Christian Scientists; and so forth.

I am bound to say that the charges look bad, particularly that of the misuse of trust funds. If this were true were not the Directors right in wanting to get rid of the Trustees? Then I read Eustace's reply, in the *Supplement to the Proceedings* (pp. 7-10). Eustace refused to attend the hearing in the Board Room, charging that it would certainly not be an impartial tribunal. "Since you would be both accusers and judges," he wrote, "what profit could there be in my joining in this idle ceremony?"

Eustace had not refused to appoint a successor to Rowlands. He had only insisted upon a proper accounting as a prerequisite, and this had been refused. He had then asked the court for relief. He finds it difficult to treat seriously the loss of circulation in the periodicals as the fault of the Trustees. "You know in your consciences that these losses have occurred in spite of our best efforts, and in consequence solely of the things you yourselves have done and approved." He went on to say:

You know in your hearts, and every Christian Scientist knows, that the injury to the periodicals was caused by the insidious propaganda which you have wholly inspired and approved. If you will appoint a fair and disinterested tribunal, we will lay before it such proof as will convince the Christian Science world of the insincerity of this charge and the duplicity of your conduct. I challenge you to such a hearing.

Concerning the misuse of trust funds, a very grave charge, the Trustees had only made payments in keeping with standard practices and in conformity with precedents established by the Directors themselves. As for the Directors' questioning the propriety of salary payments to employees who were receiving payments from other sources, did not the Directors themselves receive salaries from more than one source? The detailed letter sounds entirely convincing to an outsider. If Eustace's statements therein are correct—I have not found them questioned save in a very general way by counsel for the Directors, and certainly no specific evidence was offered to refute them—it is easily to be seen why no legal action was ever sustained against the Trustees on this score.

Other charges were also answered one by one, but the one as to expenses for accounting deserves attention. After a certified public accountant had been brought in and put the books in proper shape,

practically our entire accounting department suddenly and without a moment's notice left their appointed tasks, many of them going imme- diately into your employment. Our books were left in a condition posi- tively disgraceful; pages were torn and mutilated; footings were inaccu- rately cast; and in general there had been interposed difficulties to prevent a correct accounting. This occurrence, which from facts within our knowledge had the approval of the Directors if it was not directly inspired by them, caused the remainder of the expenditure of which you complain.

Again, the outsider might find it harder to believe this kind of charge if he had not come upon the same thing so often in other cases in the movement. Over and over again, loyalty to the Board of Directors, or to what may have been regarded as Christian Science, has led people to behave in a way difficult to justify.

The next legal action came when the Directors notified the court of the removal of the Trustees Eustace and Harvey, and petitioned for the appointment of three men of the Directors' choice. This was taken on December 30, 1921, and was countered by a petition on the part of the Trustees for the appointment of receivers for the Publishing Society.

Finally the Trustees did present their resignations. They did not, however, present them to the Board of Directors. Rather, they resigned to the court, thus requiring the court to appoint their successors. (The Directors still had no power of appointment, but only that of removal.) They thus maintained to the last their strict obedience to what they regarded as the legal requirements of their Trust. They did this in the belief, expressed in a letter they had written earlier, that Truth cannot perish from the earth and that their course would ultimately be vindicated, for "Principle will overturn and overturn and overturn until He whose right it is shall reign."

5

The Central Authority and Its Controls

THE BATTLE was won. The Board of Directors had been declared by the Supreme Judicial Court of Massachusetts to be the final authority in the Christian Science church. It had been a long struggle, but it was over now. To be sure, the issue might conceivably have been carried to the Supreme Court of the United States of America, since the organization was engaged in interstate activities. Even yet one hears among the dissenters the suggestion that it still may one day be brought before that highest tribunal in the land. But I doubt whether it ever will be. It would be a long, costly struggle. The official church group has the necessary funds to defend the case if ever it is brought; but no one with the funds, or the will and determination to raise them, has come forward to renew the fight. In general the dissenters seem rather to have reacted against all organization and to be unwilling to make the effort to salvage the kind of institution which might result if they were victorious.

Meanwhile the Board of Directors carries on. Gradually it has gathered all the reins of control into its own hands, and from its position of power determines the direction the organization takes, and to a considerable degree determines also its detailed operation.

For example, as a teacher of religion who tried to bring before his pupils living representatives of the various forms of religion, I once wrote to the local Christian Science organization inviting them to suggest one of their number who could so represent Christian Science and answer the questions my students might ask. I received a reply saying it was not their custom to do such things, and that I must rather ask the Board of Directors in Boston. All the other local religious groups had freely sent their representatives without reference to any superior authority.

Accordingly, I wrote the Mother Church Directors. Their reply was that they would be glad to send one of their lecturers, for a fee of one hundred dollars; but no questions or discussion would be permitted. We did not, under the circumstances, have a Christian Scientist address the class!

To be sure, this occurred some twenty years ago. But have things changed essentially? Late in 1951 I invited a famous Christian Science teacher, who had been for many years certified in the *Journal* registry but who was currently in disfavor with the Board, to address my class. Shortly afterward I had occasion to visit Boston and, in conversation with a present-day member of the Board of Directors, was taken to task for this. "Why did you go outside the 'recognized ranks' of Christian Science to get someone to speak to your class?" he asked. I told him of my unsatisfactory experience of two decades back. He professed to be unable to believe my story. All I had to do was to write him personally, he assured me, and someone would be sent without charge and authorized to answer questions. I have not availed myself of the offer for lack of opportunity, but even here I note I must write one of the Directors. It could not apparently be done locally, unless by the resident Committee on Publication, who is of course under the direct control of the Directors in Boston.

The taboo against free discussion of Christian Science by those within the jurisdiction of the church organization is well known. Article X of the *Manual* is frequently cited, a rule against unauthorized debating. Despite diligent inquiry I have been unable to find any evidence that debate on the subject has *ever* been authorized, the rule apparently being interpreted so broadly as to exclude discussion. On the other hand, I have been able to document cases where practitioners and teachers have been reprimanded, even penalized, for discussing Christian Science among friends.

When a class in the philosophy of religion at Pembroke College in Brown University reached the subject of Christian Science, a follower of Mrs. Eddy protested against "unauthorized" comment. The instructor was agreeable to having an official spokesman from the church to continue the forum through this phase of his course. But open discussion was not to be countenanced. Instead, the Committee on Publication was assigned the task of presenting a written statement. Only after the "Christian Science Board of Directors in Boston, Massachusetts, kindly gave him the necessary permission [to respond to the ten questions accepted for answer], with the proviso that the answers be formulated and submitted for its revision in advance," could he proceed. The carefully prepared and officially edited paper was then read publicly in the college assembly hall.

Even the aftermath was revealing. It has long been the practice to seek publication in the local press of public addresses on Christian Science; but *reprints* are severely frowned upon, presumably because of the inroads they threaten on the established body of church literature. Accordingly, no objection was made to the printing of the Brown University address in full by the *Newport County Sentinel* of February 5, 1931. But when popular demand brought forth a reprint, the Boston authorities expressed disapproval. Thereafter orders for the reprint were returned with a slip reading: "At the request of the author we have withdrawn from sale and circulation the pamphlet." Today this reprint is a highly prized item, widely copied and passed about among Christian Scientists.

How are the powers of the central authority exercised? In a number of ways. In general they rest upon the fact that indirectly, if not directly, almost every person who possesses any considerable influence within the church owes his position to the Board.

There are, to be sure, some elective officers at the local level; but every branch church officer is required to be a member of the Mother Church, and is therefore under the immediate jurisdiction of the Boston Board. He is allowed to function only so long as he is a member in good standing, and his status may be changed at any time for such reasons as the Directors deem expedient. He may be suspended or excommunicated where necessary.

All the business or temporal concerns of the organization are

under the control of the Mother Church Directors. The considerable
properties are held under their direction. The production and circulation of literature is a major function they regulate. They take the
responsibility for preserving the purity of the doctrine through their
authority over Class Instruction, the accrediting of teachers, both
primary and normal, and the appointment of the lecturers as well
as approval of every word spoken by them from the platform.
Increasingly, also, they have felt it their duty to protect the faith of
the membership by the regulation of what all members shall study
or read. And, finally, even the local churches are under the guiding
hand of the Board and may be restrained by threat of excommunication in extreme cases of difference in their ideas from those of the
central authority. Effective control in these and other areas has been
exercised through a number of methods, a primary one being
authority over Class Instruction, perhaps the most basic and dis-
tinctive feature of the ongoing Christian Science organization.

THE ORGANIZATION has a system of congregational worship, to be
sure. It also has its Sunday school for those under twenty years of
age, as well as its public lectures; but it is "Class," as the institution
is known colloquially, that underlies all of these and is the most
indispensable element of all. Although Mrs. Eddy declares that her
textbook "contains the *complete* Science of Mind-healing" (p. 147),
she indicates that Class Instruction provides the student with something the textbook does not (see *Miscellaneous Writings*, p. 35); and
the more notes and transcriptions of the various teachers one peruses,
the more obvious it becomes that "Class" is a unique institution,
quite unlike the presentation *Science and Health*.

Before Mary Baker Eddy had ever thought of starting a church,
even before she had written *Science and Health*, she had opened her
classes, and it was through her pupils that she first began to be
known. It is not difficult to see why her classes should have made an
appeal for, as she advertised, through Class Instruction one could
become a healer. And this could become the source of gain.

Mrs. Eddy's very first students were taught not in classes but
individually. In the beginning she appears to have taken as students

any who applied, inviting and even urging the attendance of some who did not apply. Nor did she limit them to Christian Science converts, certainly not at first, and even at the very end of her teaching career she is known to have taken into her class a news-paperman who was neither then nor later a Christian Scientist. (See documentation on George H. Moses in the *Christian Science Mon-itor*, June 19, 1929) Among many whom she personally solicited was a Unitarian minister, James Henry Wiggin, whom she took on his own terms. (See *Miscellany*, p. 318) Nor did she prohibit anyone from attending more than one class with her.

As time went on Mrs. Eddy developed what came to be called Primary and Normal classes. Enrollees in the Normal classes were supposed to have attended a Primary class first, but this was not uniformly the case. Almost half of her last class—every member of which was granted the title of C.S.B. for his attendance—had not had previous instruction. When others had become teachers, she accepted into her Primary class students from their Primary classes. Also, some of those who had studied with her went back and took instruction from other teachers. This is clear from a bylaw, announced in the *Journal* of July, 1895, which read in part:

> Careful observation has shown Mrs. Eddy that a student who has been taught by her and afterwards takes lessons of a student, is not benefited but darkened and deteriorated thereby. Therefore ... no student of hers can be a member of the Christian Scientist Association, or considered loyal, who from this date, June 5, 1895, shall take lessons with or sit in the class of a student having been taught in a class by the author of our textbook and the Discoverer and Founder of Christian Science.

The trend evidenced here to regard every pupil as the personal ward of his teacher has continued and developed, one of the results being a compartmentation which minimizes controversy between teachers over the control of students, as well as over doctrinal differ-ences which would tend to come out in any normally free inter-change where students consulted each other or each other's teachers.

At first this personal allegiance was enjoyed by Mrs. Eddy alone, as many episodes show. For example, when James J. Rome, a clergy-man who had become attached to Mary E. Dunbar by attending her class, sought to enter the class of Julia Field-King, Mrs. Dunbar in emulation of Mrs. Eddy was reluctant to release him. The matter reached Mrs. Eddy's ears and she, characteristically, took charge of the situation. She wrote Dr. Field-King: "Yes, dear one, teach Mr. Rome." Meanwhile, she wrote Mrs. Dunbar: "Let Mr. Rome go into her class and watch the effect of this on him."

But with the acceptance of the idea as legitimate, its adoption by the teachers generally precipitated increasingly disruptive conflicts. By 1896 Mrs. Eddy found it expedient to rule that a student going through Class fell under the permanent jurisdiction of the teacher thereof, from which there was no escape unless that teacher became officially discredited or the pupil advanced to teacher status himself. In 1896 the *Manual*, then in sixth edition, for the first time forbade a teacher to assume any direction of another teacher's students. Though frequently changed, the rule has survived in essence, so that today it is considered out of order for a student of one teacher to consult with another teacher (so long as the teacher of the class he attended remains alive physically and officially).

In 1881 Mrs. Eddy obtained a state charter for the Massachusetts Metaphysical College. This carried with it the right to grant degrees, a right enjoyed by no other institution of its kind, for this was the only one so chartered under the Act of 1874, which was repealed in 1882. Thus was Mrs. Eddy's own instruction formalized and carried on during the decade of the eighties. She was President as well as Founder, and indeed the sole faculty member.

A typical announcement of the offerings of the college in the December, 1885, *Journal* lists three courses: (1) the collegiate course in Christian Science metaphysical healing, in twelve lessons, tuition $300; (2) a course in metaphysical obstetrics, in six daily lectures, open only to students of the college, tuition $100; and (3) a Normal course, in six daily lessons, open to those who had taken the first course, tuition $200. There was also a course in theology announced, tuition $200, but apparently it was never given.

The evolutionary nature of the "Class" idea is illustrated in what happened with the "obstetrical course." According to fully authenticated records, this course consisted of instruction in certain physical essentials of delivery, coupled with appropriate "arguments" to a successful and painless childbirth. Although Mrs. Eddy at the time declared, "I think I can do more for a student in this than in any other class," and although in the Abbey Corner case during 1888 she pronounced this particular course absolutely indispensable to the fully equipped practitioner, by the year 1901 she was repudiating it entirely. In the twenty-fifth edition of the *Manual* she ruled that obstetrics was not Science, and would not be taught thereafter.

At first there was apparently no limitation on the number of pupils in each class held in the college. Nor were the classes of the other teachers out in the field limited. This was plainly indicated when Mrs. Eddy wrote her pupil Clara Choate, a popular Boston teacher: "I hope that you are not supposing that I feel bad that you take fifty students in one class." It was not long after this that Mrs. Eddy began to curtail the classes of all the teachers. For a while she permitted them to hold three classes annually, each class containing no more than thirty-three pupils, and granted them the privilege of calling their pupils together for an association address every three months. (*Manual*, 1st ed., pp. 15-16, in 1895) This was changed and changed again as the *Manual* went into edition after edition.

In 1889 Mrs. Eddy closed her college and the corporation was dissolved. (*Journal*, VII, 454-55) She had repeatedly called public attention to the legal foundation for granting degrees which her college alone enjoyed; now this legal basis was relinquished, never to be restored. "State honors perish," she wrote at this point, "and their gain is loss to the Christian Scientist." (*Journal*, VII, 433)

Meanwhile she wanted "it understood that I do not require Christian Scientists to stop teaching, or dissolve their organizations." And so instruction continued to be carried on by individual teachers and by other "colleges" and "institutes" scattered over the country— e.g., the California Metaphysical College at San Jose (see July, 1886, *Journal*)—none of which, she reminded the field, were authorized to grant degrees. In 1891 she told her followers that "Christian students should have their own Institutes, and, *unmolested*, be governed alone by divine Love, in teaching and guiding their students." (*Journal*, IX, 182-83)

With the publication of her collected articles, under the title of *Miscellaneous Writings,* in 1897, Mrs. Eddy suspended all teaching throughout the field for one year, violators of the decree being made subject to excommunication. In place of the teaching was to be substituted her newly published book which she declared was "calculated to prepare the minds of all true thinkers to understand the Christian Science textbook more correctly than a student can." This, with *Science and Health,* her other published works, and the Bible, she pronounced the only proper instructors for the hour. At the same time she declared it the duty of every Christian Scientist to circulate and sell as many copies of her new book as possible, warning that failure to obey this injunction fully would render any member of the church liable to excommunication. (*Journal,* XIV, 575)

A year later, in March, 1898, she served notice through the *Journal* (XV, 781) that the ban was lifted. Teaching could now be resumed, but "loyal students" would teach no more than two classes during the ensuing year, each to contain not more than thirty pupils. This rule was soon changed to its present form, which limits every Primary teacher to one class of thirty pupils annually.

Mrs. Eddy held her own last class in 1898, summoning about seventy persons to Concord, New Hampshire, where she was then living. Some of these people were not even Christian Scientists, some were interested in the subject but had not had Class Instruction, some had been class-taught by other teachers, some had already attended one or more classes which she herself had taught. This memorable class consumed about six hours altogether, the first session running two, the second four hours.

The same year, 1898, Mrs. Eddy chose three of her leading students—Edward A. Kimball, Septimus J. Hanna, and Laura Lathrop—to set up a "Board of Education," the avowed purpose of which was to provide the field with teachers. While this was the real beginning of the Normal Class, which is the only path by which one may now become a teacher within the church, clearly this board was not at first proposed as a teaching agency. In notifying her followers of its creation, Mrs. Eddy announced that Scientists who

were loyal, "whether they have become thus by studying my work
on Christian Science or by class instruction," were eligible to appl
for *examination* by this board, and that if they passed the examina
tion, the board would then decide which candidates were "qualifie<
for the high responsibilities of teaching Christian Science." Th<
approved candidates would be granted teaching certificates
Exempted from these requirements were such students as alread<
held certificates from the Massachusetts Metaphysical College
(*Journal*, XV, 518)

It is noteworthy that the candidates for teaching licenses wer<
not then required to be class-taught, Mrs. Eddy ruling simply tha<
students of her textbook and other writings, if successful in healin<
through what they had gained therefrom, might apply for examina
tion as a preliminary to certification as teachers. However, by th<
time a covering bylaw reached the *Manual*, it specified a course o<
instruction lasting from three to seven days, to be taught from th<
chapter "Recapitulation" and from the "Christian Science Platform
in the textbook, and stipulated that nothing be taught contrar<
thereto. (*Manual*, 8th ed., pp. 48-49) Teaching had come to a stand
still, of course, with Mrs. Eddy's ban of March, 1897, and the variou<
"institutes" and "colleges" appear to have faded out. Thus the groun<
was prepared for this innovation.

The *Journal* (XVI, 555) offered application blanks and an<
nounced that the Board of Education was authorized to send ou<
only twenty-one teachers annually. As they were to be allocate<
according to the need in certain localities, applicants were assure<
that failure to receive a certificate need not be regarded as a mar<
of unworthiness. The initial sessions of the Board of Education
held in the Mother Church during the first week of January, 189<
were attended by 167 candidates—from which it would appear tha<
the number of students was not limited, even though twenty-on<
only could be accredited to teach. (*Journal*, XVI, 807-10) By March
1900, a new bylaw limited the number of applicants "that can b<
received for examination" to thirty-three, out of which no more tha<
twenty-one could be authorized to teach. (*Sentinel*, II, 468) Wh<
the limitation? To this I have found no official answer, although <

said that disruptive competition among the teachers in the field ould not otherwise be curbed.

At the outset Kimball was made the teacher in the Normal ork, holding his first class in 1899 and continuing in that capacity ntil he resigned the post in 1904. Kimball's original outline from hich he taught, fortunately preserved together with transcripts of is classes, indicates that the candidates were *instructed* rather than *examined,* and that most of them were veteran students of Mrs. ddy's writings beforehand. In view of this it is curious that the ollowing bylaw was retained from 1899 all the way into 1902: "A tudent of the books of Mary Baker G. Eddy shall not take lessons om another student, but is eligible to examination by the Christian cience Board of Education." (*Manual*, 25th ed., p. 46)

Although a decade earlier the Massachusetts Metaphysical College had been dissolved, its charter surrendered, and the right to onfer degrees on a legal basis ended, one finds frequent references o it subsequently in the church periodicals, as though it had been the Board of Education effectively continued. (See *Journal*, XVII, 03, *passim*) As for the "degrees," even since the dissolution of the ollege those who have had Normal Class Instruction enjoy the privilege of writing C.S.B. (Bachelor of Christian Science) after their ames in the *Journal* registry. Those who have been through Primary class out in the field use the initials C.S. The C.S.D. (Christian cience Divine) was given only by Mrs. Eddy personally, so there re almost none living now who hold that title.

Thus gradually the idea of Class evolved. Restriction as to umber varied from time to time. In 1903 the twenty-fifth edition of the *Manual* (p. 52) stated that only the teacher in the Board of ducation could receive more than thirty pupils and teach more han one class yearly. In 1904 the forty-first edition of the *Manual* p. 85) suspended Normal classes for three years, and thereafter the ormal class of thirty students could be held but once triennially. ll thirty were, however, automatically certified to teach. This meant king the annual output of teachers at an average of ten for the hole world. The tuition fee was and remains a hundred dollars. It as in 1901 that the teaching of "obstetrics" was declared not Science and forbidden. (*Manual,* 24th ed., p. 70) In 1903 Mrs. Eddy ruled that only class-taught students would be eligible to enter the Normal class. (*Manual,* 33rd ed., p. 80) From 1904 on, Christian Scientists were forbidden to teach Roman Catholics—that is, without obtaining written consent from the Catholic church authorities. (*Manual,* 41st ed., p. 77) Could such consent be obtained?

Perhaps the most important step in the evolution of Class was the attempt to fix the content of instruction for all time. With the setting up of the Board of Education in 1898, it will be recalled, Mrs. Eddy ruled that Primary classes be taught from the chapter "Recapitulation," and that the Normal classes be taught from that same chapter along with the "Christian Science Platform" in her textbook. In actual practice there is very little difference, if any, between the Primary and the Normal class teaching, as can be readily discovered by reading transcripts of both Normal and Primary classes given by the leading teachers. An objective study indicates that the Normal class serves chiefly as a refresher course, bringing back into line any who might be harboring unorthodox ideas, and is probably far more valuable as a control mechanism than for educational purposes.

While no teacher could long survive officially who admittedly violated any *Manual* provision, as a matter of fact a study of the vast array of reliable class notes available proves that classes generally are by no means confined to the prescribed material. Out of two or three dozen top-ranking teachers whose instruction I have perused, not one stays specifically within "Recapitulation" (plus the "Platform" in the case of Normal courses). The only official action that is ever taken to standardize the teaching is through disciplinary measures taken against individual teachers who are reported out of line.

Obviously, it is not difficult to sustain a charge of *Manual* violation, since anything other than teaching by rote would involve some departure from the prescribed textbook material. In challenging one of their teachers, on January 12, 1945, the Board of Directors of the Mother Church wrote that they would be glad to have a written undertaking from him that he did not, or would not in future, discuss or permit to be discussed, in his classes and association meetings topics not readily and directly to be deduced from and confirmed by reference to specific passages in Mrs. Eddy's published writings and based definitely on the chapter entitled "Recapitulation" and on the *Manual*. Conformity to this, said the Board, could not in the slightest degree limit this teacher's authority, freedom, and inspiration. (Letter to John Lawrence Sinton) This teacher claimed, and unquestionably believed, that he was complying strictly with the *Manual* requirements, despite the Board's contrary stand. Who decides in such a dispute? The Board, of course. The Board wrote that it stood ready to supply the proper interpretation or opinion in all such matters, and in this man's case the verdict was "guilty" and the penalty suspension.

The subtlety of the arguments that can be brought to bear effectively in sustaining such charges is well illustrated in the penalizing of teachers Doorly and Sinton. Sinton was accused by the Board of failing to adhere literally enough to "Recapitulation," while John Doorly, on the contrary, was accused of fostering a misconception of Christian Science by laying "undue emphasis on the order of the synonyms for God" through insistence upon retaining their order as given in that very chapter.

Naturally, given the extreme limitation put upon the numbers accepted into the Normal class and therefore upon the number who may teach Primary classes, certification is a privilege greatly coveted. Selection of candidates is made by the Board of Education. The Board of Education is appointed by the Board of Directors of the Mother Church. It is not difficult to see where the controls lie. One is not likely to be admitted to teachership if he is for any reason suspected of being at variance with the Board in his ideas of doctrine or if his loyalty to the organization, represented by the Board, is at all in question. Since it is natural that the major leadership of the church shall come from the teacher group, it is clear that here is an unusually strategic point for the exercise of control. When it is recognized that the Board has an indirect control of the admission to the Normal class and a direct control of the continuance of the individual franchise to teach, it is readily to be seen that both candidates for entrance and already licensed teachers need to be very much on their guard that there be no occasion to question their loyalty.

Much is to be learned about the settled concept of Class from the application form which must be filled out by every candidate for the Normal class. The applicant is required to have successfully practiced Christian Science healing for three years, to be of good moral character, and a "thorough English scholar." He is queried about his age, marital status, thrift, financial solvency, his personal prospects for recruiting full classes, his parental background and race.

(With regard to race: until recently there were no Negro teachers. Although this provision is not mentioned in the *Manual*, Christian Scientists of this race are now required to place the designation *colored* in parentheses after their names in the practitioner registry of the *Journal*. Negro patients are not admitted to the Christian Science sanatoria at Chestnut Hill and San Francisco. In 1955 the Board stated in a letter that this was because of the "generally prevailing sentiment," and that Negroes might be embarrassed in case their presence at the sanatoria occasioned unfriendly comment.)

The candidate's general health is inquired into and he is asked specifically if he has any noticeable physical disorder or defect; whether he has, or ever has had, any Roman Catholic connections; how he conceives of Mrs. Eddy's place in prophecy; and what his view of the *Manual* is. The candidate's church record, as to length and harmonious relations with others, looms large in the forty queries. He must secure the recommendation of five Mother Church members, preferably from his own community, and it may be assumed that the caliber of these endorsers would carry some weight.

He is expected to use "authorized literature" exclusively, and he must agree to consult the Board of Directors before publishing any books or articles on any subject, or before taking part in any civic, political, or charitable activity. And he is asked point-blank if he is in accord with the Board of Directors of the Mother Church.

One of the chief requirements is that of *loyalty*, and it is stated that only loyal Christian Scientists' pupils are eligible for acceptance

This means that the candidate is disqualified if the teacher with whom he went through Primary class, however long ago, is not *currently* in favor with the Board. Here is something that goes quite beyond the loyalty of the person himself who is applying. The outsider may find it difficult to understand the logic and justice of this, but Christian Science officialdom is satisfied to explain it this way (*Sentinel*, XLVII, 1924): "So close is the relationship of teacher and pupil that the faithful teacher imparts, knowingly or unknowingly, to his pupils the benefit of his own spiritual status." The authorized teacher, says the article, who fails to maintain a vigilant watch and entertains the suggestion that the official requirements are not important, is bound to weaken his pupils and strip himself of the authority to teach. The implication that this stripping of authority is automatic is, of course, hardly accurate, since it is the Board which strips the offending teacher. There are, however, those who believe that a teacher's removal is the direct result of his defection, his removal being accepted as proof of defection on his part.

The statement goes on to say that the pupils of such a teacher may be deprived of their status and compelled to seek admission into some other teacher's class to regain their standing, once again having to submit proof that they are worthy of authorized instruction. Only by being "retaught" by a teacher in favor with the Board at the moment, again paying a hundred-dollar fee, can the pupil return to the bought and worked-for privileged position of which he finds himself deprived through no fault of his own.

Surely this is one of the most remarkable aspects of the Class idea. The instant a teacher falls from official grace, his pupils are cast down with him, regardless of the fact that they entrusted themselves to this teacher on the Board's own published endorsement in the *Journal*, going through his class perhaps many years before his repudiation by the same Board and at a time when he was demonstrably innocent of any offense. Every teacher, then, not only has his own position and welfare to consider, but must move with supreme caution lest his pupils be penalized for his own actual or supposed defection.

Now what does being disloyal mean? Disloyalty to the teaching of Mrs. Eddy, according to the church authorities. But Mrs. Eddy lived a long time, she wrote much, she revised often. She kept *Science and Health* in a constant state of alteration, continuing to revise it even after having declared in the book itself that it was the complete statement of Christian Science. Of course there came a time when this was terminated by her death, the current revision being then proclaimed the only proper basis for teaching. But even so, there are in *Science and Health,* as in the Bible, passages which are directly contradictory. Who shall decide in such a case which is the proper teaching? The answer is, the Board of Directors. They constitute the ultimate court of resort in such matters, as they themselves have declared. Every opinion, every interpretation, must yield to their decision, and the Board is a self-perpetuating body of five people, completely beyond any democratic control from the membership of the Mother Church itself. If there are differences of understanding, the majority group on the Board is in a position to perpetuate its views and to root out any in conflict.

If a teacher's view should differ from that of the dominating faction, he must, if he wants to get anywhere, bend—or seem to bend—to the will of that faction. There are various ways in which he may do this. One is simply to accept the dominant or orthodox view, or at least to act as though he does. Another is to make enough concessions to it to get by publicly, and go on, rather precariously, teaching privately what may not be uttered from the housetop. Another way seems to be to conceal one's thought in a mass of verbiage capable of either interpretation if called in question. Since matters in dispute are of a rather subtle nature, this is not so difficult as might be supposed. And there is always the possibility that the individual who does this is not definitely aware of the fact that he is doing so. It may be that he himself is honestly unable to detect any serious differences between the positions. At least practically, he thinks, they yield about the same results.

The inevitable result of this almost watertight compartmentation is the fostering of many conflicting versions of Christian Science. This has become inescapably evident time and again when the various teachings have been brought into the light by controversy with the Board, as well as when they have occasionally drifted out into the field through relaxation of vigilance on the part of their proponents.

It is a well-known fact that most teachers of Primary classes forbid the taking of notes; and where notes are permitted, the pupils are usually forbidden to show them to anyone else or to circulate them freely. Why should this be? Outside Christian Science, in most ordinary classes teachers encourage note-taking, believing that the student will thus get more adequately what the teacher is trying to say and will be able better to recall and reflect upon the teaching than if he trusted wholly to his memory. To be sure, there is no provision in the *Manual* which regulates such matters, but the taboo against notes has grown up and become as the laws of the Medes and the Persians. Published notices from the Board to the field have fostered the "no notes" tradition. One of the grievances the church has against Arthur Corey is that he has assembled the notes which have been taken in the classes of leading teachers, releasing such of the material as he deemed appropriate through his book, *Christian Science Class Instruction*.

Why this pall of secrecy thrown about Class Instruction? Various persons have suggested to me the following reasons. Secrecy, they say, serves several purposes:

1. It keeps Class something of a mystery. It therefore becomes of interest to know what is contained in it. If Class Instruction were published freely, who would pay the hundred-dollar fee for membership? This may or may not be true. Many think that it is so. Certainly one result of the secretiveness is the atmosphere of esotericism which today envelops the whole institution of Class. The characteristic aura of mystery is hardly discouraged by such typical articles as "Becoming a Student" by Lucy Hayes Reynolds (*Sentinel*, XXXIV, 203-4). Some prominent teachers are known to have circulated this particular article among their prospective pupils more than a decade after its publication. How is the rank-and-file persuaded to regard Class? "Once in the classroom," says this official piece,

what may the receptive student expect to experience? Surely it is an occasion fraught with portentous spiritual possibilities; one where student and teacher lay personal selfhood and material thinking on the altar of divine Science, to be taught of God, one where the informing and instructive nature of the Pentecostal spirit baptizes with divine intelligence.

Official confirmation of this position is to be found in the Board's notice to the field in March, 1954 (*Journal*, LXXII, 149-50).

2. It avoids divisions within the church. How? When the fiction is preserved that all teachers are teaching the same thing, there is less ground for the development of cliques within the church, the following of one teacher rather than another. The restriction against any teacher's taking into his class the pupil of another teacher in good standing (except of course in the Normal class), aids at this point, for Christian Scientists obedient to the no-notes rule would have no way of knowing of the differing versions in the field.

3. It protects the teacher, in several ways. Students are notorious for reporting wrongly what a teacher has said. I have had the experience over and over again of being misunderstood, misinterpreted, and misquoted. This represents something of a hazard in today's world. Suppose the student mistakenly reports that I spoke favorably of communism. I could get into very serious trouble. Shall I therefore forbid the taking of notes? Of course I do not. The loss, I decide, is greater for the student than is the risk for myself. But Christian Science teachers generally have apparently decided otherwise in the case of Class Instruction.

Presumably all are teaching faithfully the doctrine of Mrs. Eddy. At least if no reports of what goes on in the class are allowed to be circulated, it cannot be known if the case is otherwise. If an oral report is given of something taught which is contrary to orthodox belief and practice, the teacher can always assert that he was mistakenly reported. Thus a measure of freedom is given to the teacher. This means that there can actually develop a certain amount of variation within the church without the teacher's coming into conflict with the central authorities, and the church is spared heresy trials. George Shaw Cook, a leading teacher, always forbade any note-taking whatsoever, and when a fairly thorough transcription of his 1940 class was discovered to be in circulation, he wrote every member of that class to ask that anyone be reported who had been seen taking notes. While the more liberal Bicknell Young had his pupils bring notebook and pencil to class, he sometimes cautioned against promiscuous circulation of his statements, saying in at least one association meeting, "You wouldn't want to get your teacher into trouble, would you?"

While Young's question implied that his own primary concern was his personal jeopardy, the Board declares notes objectionable only because the inevitable inaccuracies lead to adulteration and eventual loss of Truth. However, I am told—on authority I have good reason to trust—that most of the teachers tell their pupils simply that Class is a sacred event which must be protected from the depredations of mortal mind, citing the fate of Hezekiah, who showed all his treasures only to have them carried off to the land of the heathen. It is not infrequently argued that Science is subject to dangerous misuse, and this passage from page 459 of *Science and Health* is quoted: "Committing the bare process of mental healing to frail mortals, untaught and unrestrained by Christian Science, is like putting a sharp knife into the hands of a blind man or a raging maniac, and turning him loose in the crowded streets of a city."

The Corey book was denounced in the classes and association addresses of William D. Kilpatrick, the late Manager of Committees on Publication. The pupils of Paul Stark Seeley were directed to paste a sticker on their notes, warning "whomsoever it may concern" that the accompanying material was the personal and private property exclusively of the transcriber, to be copied by no one, and to be turned over to the secretary of the Seeley Association in case of the owner's death. The William P. McKenzie pupils were asked to turn back all association papers without delay to the secretary, in whose office one copy only of each was to be kept on file, all others destroyed. Those who might have lost their copies could "send an affidavit" to clear their names at headquarters. The Board of Directors of the Mother Church wrote the McKenzie pupils on May 27, 1948, that they thought it best to guard the copies of association addresses so well that they would never be passed about among Christian Scientists as some other unpublished statements had unfortunately been circulated, and asked that they employ such safeguards as they felt were adequate to insure this protection. And the papers in question here were *printed* papers, from which the hazards of misreporting and miscopying had been precluded. Even so, it will be observed that *among Christian Scientists,* not just outsiders, free circulation was not to be tolerated.

Those who disregarded this taboo, either in or out of the church, were to be denounced as "traitors." For example, the 1947 Annual Report of the McKenzie Association, commenting on Arthur Corey's declaration of independence from ecclesiastical control, said that Corey was a student of Bicknell Young but that he had betrayed both his teacher and his teaching. About this Corey wrote in a letter (December 20, 1953):

I paid for and received my Class instruction unconditionally. Neither was I asked for nor would I have given any pledge of secrecy. Certainly I could not have been expected to know, from my side of the fence, that secrecy had become traditional and was to be taken for granted. I gave the Christian Science Church my heart and my hand because it claimed to be democratic, to honor private conscience, to unshackle thinking, and I stayed with it conscientiously until I had been in it long enough to learn firsthand that it actually practices an unparalleled system of thought control over its communicants. Apparently these people assume that anyone who accepts their organization at its face value, by the same token embraces the unwritten rules, customs and traditions they have tacitly adopted, even though such hidden patterns are incompatible with the Church's public declarations of policy.

The practice of condemning dissenters is not exactly new in the movement. Back in the seventies Mrs. Eddy's own Association of Students had the following provisions in its constitution: "Resolved, that anyone who wishes to withdraw without reason shall be considered to have broken his oath" and "that breaking the Christian Scientists' oath is immorality." How Mrs. Eddy expected her followers to apply this rule is indicated by what she wrote in the *Newburyport Herald* in January, 1878. Denouncing one of her leading pupils by name, she explained that the constitution required that a member's "immorality" be made public. "The motive for this article in the Constitution," she wrote,

was to prevent a member going astray, or in case this could not be prevented, to forewarn the community, so ignorant of the evil that can be done by this student, of the secret agent for mischief that a mental malpractitioner becomes. May the direct line of duty from which I never swerve, be taken by those of our worthy students as we know it will be finally, and Truth will triumph over error.

How this trend has survived the years is shown by a number of communications sent to Corey. A typical one was postmarked from Boston in August, 1952. Signed by a *Journal*-registered practitioner stationed at Columbus, Ohio, it read: "Moral idiocy is a pitiable thing—even when it appears to be deserved, for surely it cannot be escaped that you will at some time have to be healed and awakened from this fraudulent, criminal nightmare you are in." Enclosed with the note was a check drawn on the Shawmut Bank of Boston, filled out: "PAY TO Arthur Corey $ The shock necessary to awaken him DOLLARS."

Meanwhile the Manager of Committees on Publication, official spokesman for the church, publicly denies "that certain teachings of Christian Science are concealed from public gaze and transmitted only through class teaching." His statement insists that "Christian Science classes no more conceal from the public gaze the teaching of Christian Science than a college class in algebra conceals the facts of higher algebra from the public." (*Christian Century*, May 14, 1952)

It is difficult to overstate the importance of getting into the Normal class. Observe first that it has a very decided economic advantage. While it is perfectly possible to become a practitioner without achieving this distinction, indeed without even having had Primary class instruction, a practitioner who can write C.S.B. after his name in the *Journal* registry has a tremendous initial advantage over other practitioners. There can be no question that he is sought out more frequently than the others, especially by persons who are accustomed to commanding the services of the best. Of course the C.S.B. who does not produce results is unlikely to retain all of his clientele, but he does have the initial advantage professionally. It is a little like a doctor who belongs to the College of Surgeons, for example. But there is a second economic advantage. The C.S.B. is privileged to teach once a year, and if he can fill his class he has an additional income of $3,000 for a series of talks lasting not more than twelve days at the outside. As for his expenses in this connection, they are negligible, since he can usually teach in his own place of residence.

Even more important considerations must be taken into account. First of all, there is the prestige attached to his position. There cannot be, under the restrictions of the *Manual*, a very large number of church-sponsored teachers, so that the teacher is indeed one set apart and often regarded with awe. As the effective guide and counselor of all his pupils, who look upon him as their mentor, he exercises over them a remarkable measure of control. They can attend no other class than his in all their lives—providing he does not arouse the disapproval of the Board—save the Normal class. They are forever known as his students. He meets them once a year to deliver his association address, and even if he dies no other teacher can address them, only speakers of less than teacher status being permitted to address associations whose teachers have gone. No aspirant to becoming a teacher himself would be likely to be considered without the recommendation of his teacher. Prestige and power are strong motives.

But to this must be added also the fact that this is the road to preferment in the church. With few exceptions, only those who can display C.S.B. after their names are elevated to membership on the Board of Directors of the Mother Church. The same applies to the Board of Education, the Publishing Society Trustees, the editorial boards, and the office of the Manager of Committees on Publication.

All this may aid in the understanding of the almost sacrosanct view which is held concerning the matter of Class itself, an attitude of reverence which certainly extends to the teacher. I was once talking with a Christian Scientist concerning the organization of other churches in comparison with that of Christian Science. I happen to be a Methodist. I was telling him the difficulty John Wesley had in getting properly episcopally ordained clergymen to administer the sacraments to his converts, converts made by outdoor preaching after the doors of the churches had been shut against him. He, only a presbyter, after studying for himself in the New Testament the beginnings of the Christian church, ordained men to administer the sacraments to his people, thus breaking the *apostolic succession*. "Why, we have the very same thing in the Christian Science church," this Scientist said, pointing out that Mrs. Eddy had declared herself the exclusive revelator of Truth to this age and had assumed the prerogative of handing down the power to teach to her immediate disciples, who then would pass it down in an unbroken line from generation to generation. He called my attention to George Channing's "Authorized Teaching" (*Sentinel,* XLVII, 1921-25), as an up-to-date and authoritative proclamation bearing this out.

The Channing statement, wholeheartedly endorsed by the Board in letters to the field, declares that Christian Science teaching is spurious except when done in classes conducted by teachers selected by their similarly ordained predecessors; that no other way exists by which authority to give class teaching may be obtained; that only those students who are chosen by a teacher so ordained have a right to be taught; that it is unthinkable that one lacking the teacher's status (conferred by church authorities in the direct line of ecclesiastical descent) could usurp it by a short cut, and set himself up as capable of teaching; that the use of the actual words of some authorized teacher's correct instruction by such a "pretender" could convey no understanding of Christian Science; that the pupils imbibe spirituality from a teacher when his status is unimpaired, but, by the same token, are contaminated by any elements of disobedience in him; and finally that wisdom, as reflected by Mrs. Eddy, demands single allegiance to and support of "*authorized* Christian Science teaching."

The above article was brought out upon the publication of Arthur Corey's *Christian Science Class Instruction* in 1945. The publication of such a book under such a title was doubtless considered a threat to the very institution of Class as an exclusive prerogative of the church, and so the organization's claim had to be vigorously upheld. The *Manual* stipulates that a member of the Mother Church may not teach pupils Christian Science unless he has a certificate, but Corey had resigned from the church and was therefore no longer under the jurisdiction of its bylaws. Much was then made of the fact that he had not personally attended a Normal class in Boston. It was maintained that even if he had studied correct transcripts of Normal classes, he could not actually teach Christian Science without this prescribed step.

As to the contention that one is fitted to teach only by the Normal class, I confess that, writing as an outsider, I find it difficult to see how one series of lessons, traditionally limited to half a dozen brief sessions, can be regarded as preparation for the teaching of as difficult a subject as Christian Science. Of course, the enrollee is supposed to have prepared himself by a rigorous study of *Science and Health* over a considerable period, but not under the guidance of a teacher; and there was a time when even this was not required for Normal class entrance. In contrast to the prolonged periods of study in colleges and theological schools which have come to be almost a requisite for any degree of leadership in the churches generally, the maximum requirements of the Christian Science group seem meager indeed.

Conceivably, of course, the ability to "elucidate the Principle and rule of Christian Science, through the higher meaning of the Scriptures," as demanded by the *Manual,* might exist even though one had not had the privilege of Normal class, if he were a diligent student of Mrs. Eddy's writings. As a matter of fact, Mrs. Eddy herself says that "it is not absolutely requisite for some people to be taught in a class, for they can learn by spiritual growth and by the study of what is written" (*Miscellaneous Writings,* p. 317), and also that a student who had had only Primary class instruction, but is imbued with the spirit of Christ, is a better healer and teacher than a Normal class student who partakes less of God's love (*Retrospection and Introspection,* p. 47).

It is hard to see how the extra few sessions at the Normal class level could greatly add to one's competence to teach. There is considerable testimony to the effect that, indeed, the Normal class instruction is not greatly different from that given in the Primary classes. Certainly the rather full notes of teaching given in Normal classes which I have examined have not impressed me as adding anything significant to what is given at the Primary level. It would seem to an educator, however, that the system might well serve as a selective device by which to assure the top leadership of the church that only persons holding the right ideas and having the proper attitudes toward the central authorities of the church would be in a position to influence those who do the actual teaching or the rank and file of practitioners and local church leaders.

All this seems to lead inevitably to the type of ecclesiastical monopoly which Mrs. Eddy deplored in *Science and Health* (p. 141). The Board has, not surprisingly, declared the organization "the watchful and tender guardian of human consciousness in its ascent Godward" (*Sentinel*, XLIX, 1114), and in their letter of August 12, 1946, to John Lawrence Sinton, they assert that any attempt to teach or lecture upon Christian Science in any manner other than as provided for in the *Manual* of the Mother Church by Mrs. Eddy constitutes an attack upon the sufficiency and finality of the revelation embodied in *Science and Health,* its author's establishment of the church organization, and her divinely inspired provisions for its growth and progress. Already the field had been warned through the *Sentinel* (XLI, 311) that any preference for "the irregular and unauthorized" is distinctly a manifestation of mortal mind, and reminded that if there were need of additional literature on the subject of Christian Science it would naturally be recognized and satisfied by the Board of Directors. What are the implications of such a statement? Does it, as some have thought, imply infallibility?

IN THE FORMATIVE STAGES of her church Mrs. Eddy was accustomed to preach in the regular services—as were her followers. The sermons were an integral feature of the worship procedure. There was a testimony meeting also, held in the beginning on Friday evenings but moved up to Wednesdays later on, in which members told in public of their experiences of healing as well as of religious and moral victories. Thus was the faith propagated by preaching and testimony.

There were a number of very effective preachers in the larger churches, such as the Rev. George B. Day in Chicago and the Rev. Lanson P. Norcross in Boston. Augusta E. Stetson, who occasionally substituted for Mrs. Eddy in the pulpit, was sent to New York to found First Church, where she became famous for her sermons. Mrs. Stetson's preaching drew such crowds that the overflow became a problem. Then in April, 1895, it seemed good to Mrs. Eddy to abolish such personal ministry. She decreed that henceforth the reading of her textbook, in conjunction with Biblical passages, should constitute the sermon. The Readers were required to open with the announcement that what they were about to read was "authorized by Christ." Each Sunday all the churches read the same lesson, which was—and still is—made up of citations from *Science and Health* and the Bible as published in the *Quarterly.*

This drastic edict was accepted without any apparent opposition and remains the rule of the church. The preaching had been a very definite attraction, the loss of which might deprive the movement of a real asset. In any case it was compensated for, at least to some degree, by the creation in 1898 of a Board of Lectureship. This, like the other major developments in Christian Science history, was no sudden or unforeseeable step, but was the outgrowth of a solidifying trend. Mrs. Eddy herself had lectured as far back as 1864, when she talked at Warren, Maine, on "Quimby's Spiritual Science"; and she was to confide to Irving Tomlinson that among the various means and methods she found necessary for promulgating her doctrine, from pioneer days onward, were "writing and preaching, teaching and lecturing." She had commissioned certain of her students on occasion, as when she sent George Choate to Portland, Maine, in 1880, not merely to heal and teach but to lecture. Others of her following took the initiative, with tacit approval, as when Ursula Gestefeld advertised her lecture, "The Popular Craze: Christian Science or the Mind Cure," in the February, 1887, issue of the *Christian Science Journal.*

Apart from its obvious purpose of promoting the movement, the Board of Lectureship is enjoined in the *Manual* to reply "justly" to public condemnation of the cause, and to "bear testimony to the facts pertaining to the life of the Pastor Emeritus," Mary Baker Eddy.

The lecturers are elected annually and, while the *Manual* does not stipulate how or by whom they are chosen, it is certain that they are subject to the approval of the Directors, who have assumed Mrs.

Eddy's prerogatives in all such matters. Each lecturer is required by the bylaws to mail a copy of his lecture to the clerk of the Mother Church before delivering it from the platform. Presumably if anything objectionable is found in the lecture it must be revised before delivery, or at least the lecturer is subject to discipline if he delivers it in its unapproved form. Thus the content of the lectures is kept true to the officially accepted interpretation of the faith.

A natural question arises. Do lecturers always read their lectures, or recite them in the exact form in which they have been officially approved? The answer is that they do not. I have heard lecturers who obviously spoke extemporaneously, making reference to some event of the day or hour which could not have been in any written or approved version of their talk. Shorthand records of a series of public addresses by a certain prominent lecturer, for example, exhibit considerable extemporizing on his part, prior to his withdrawal from the public platform a few years ago.

What guarantee is there that the lecturer is faithful to his original? The publication in full of his talk by some local papers would provide no check, for such papers seldom if ever work from a verbatim shorthand transcription, printing instead from the regular advance copy supplied editors by the lecturer or his sponsors.

The corrective at this point is the fact that seasoned members of the church are likely to report anything that seems to be out of line with the well-known and accepted interpretation which "headquarters" maintains. Historically this has happened again and again. There are documented cases in which lecturers have been challenged and admonished by the Directors for deviating from their script. And there have been dismissals of lecturers by the Directors for just such causes. After his expulsion from the *Journal* registry, the renowned Peter V. Ross wrote his students, under date of May 23, 1947, that "a Boston letter suggested that I stop lecturing because I did not stick to the literal text of my discourse, recommended its wide circulation, and produced the Digest of the Bible."

When it is recalled that election takes place annually, so that every lecturer's record is subject to review by the Directors once a year, it can easily be seen that the control is quite effective.

The post of lecturer is one of the most remunerative within the church. During the years of or immediately following the Great Litigation, a list of the lecturers and their annual incomes over a period of years was published. As long ago as the twenties most of them were earning over $10,000 per year, and some as high as $25,000 and over. This income is in most cases augmented considerably by their healing practice and teaching of classes, as the advantage they enjoy through appearing on the public platform brings them their full quota of patients and pupils. While some of the lecturers are men and women of independent means apart from lecturing, theirs is a position of great honor in the movement, not to be lightly cast aside. To a number of them, lecturing represents their main financial resource, and they would hardly be likely to jeopardize so comfortable an income. One would have to have very strong convictions indeed to risk such a loss.

A bylaw specifies that the lecturer must not meddle with or disrupt local church organizations whose guest he is. Receptions and other festivities following a lecture are discouraged. While exceptions are provided for, this rule is almost never violated. Although free discussion is not specifically forbidden by the *Manual*, Article X, which is against public debate on Christian Science, is interpreted by the authorities and almost universally in the field to prohibit free discussion. An offense charged against John Doorly, one of the most eminent of the lecturers for four decades, was that he met informally with individuals and groups for discussion after the formal lectures were delivered.

Each branch church, as well as the Mother Church, is required to call on the Board of Lectureship for at least one lecture a year. In addition, the Directors may provide lectures at such places and times as seem to them desirable, the lecturers being obliged to accept such assignments.

Thus it is apparent that where and when the lecturers shall speak and what they shall say are well within the control of the Board of Directors. It is not likely that one who differs from the orthodox, or Boston, view of Christian Science, of the church, or of its Founder, will be employed as one of the chief means through which the movement is presented to the general public. A perusal of the biographical sketches given in the *Sentinel* of the different lecturers at the time of their appointment shows that the selection of speakers is anything but casual. In the background of each appointee is to be found a long history of devotion to the church organization. Some appear to have reached the lecture platform through their work as Committees on Publication. Others are veteran teachers who have demonstrated their value to the organization through the fulness of their classes and the undeviating loyalty of their pupils to the church. Not infrequently others have been assigned to the platform following some signal service rendered the authorities. For example, Virgil O. Strickler came to the favorable attention of Boston when he testified against his teacher, Mrs. Stetson, during her controversy with the Board of Directors. Another furnished testimony supporting the Board's charges against his teacher in Kentucky. One in New York, who campaigned for the Directors in their litigation with the Publishing Trustees, was elevated afterward to the status of lecturer.

The lectures are well publicized. The public is cordially invited to attend by the Readers at church services, paid advertisements are run in the daily press, poster cards are placed in store windows, and publicity material is released to the newspapers. Church members are encouraged to get non-Scientists to come. The lecture is a major point of contact with the public; hence it is of first importance that those who interpret Christian Science on such occasions conform to standardized views. Here is a good place for the authorities to exercise control. It is a fact that they do so.

"Loyal" Christian Scientists accept rigid controls as thoroughly proper, which is of course their right. No one under the jurisdiction of the church speaks without authorization, and on formal occasions what is said must be approved in advance by the authorities. Recently on my university campus the interfaith group arranged for a meeting at which one young representative of each faith stated what he *personally* believed. The Christian Science representative *read* a carefully prepared statement taken from an official source and so announced. Even the Roman Catholic student had prepared his own statement of belief. But not the Christian Scientist. This has

come to be the normally accepted practice among even Christian
Science youth.

FEW RELIGIOUS MOVEMENTS make greater use of the printed page
than does Christian Science. What people of other faiths, unless it
be Jehovah's Witnesses, are more active in the exhibition of their
literature in public places? One finds their reading matter in railway
stations, bus terminals, airports, hotels. Wherever people are likely
to be waiting around and need something to help them occupy their
time, one is likely to find copies of the *Christian Science Monitor* and
Journal and *Sentinel*.

And Christian Scientists do read their literature and the Bible.
Few other denominations can boast so large a percentage who daily
follow a reading and study plan designed to build them up in
their faith.

It is important, however, the church authorities think, that the
right books and the right periodicals be read, those that interpret
aright the subject of Christian Science. How shall this be effected?
By exercising control over the production and distribution of literature and being sure that no mistaken interpretations creep in. But
what are mistaken interpretations? Who decides what interpretations
are right and which are wrong? The central authority, which is of
course the Board of five Directors in Boston, to whom, as they
believe, has been committed the right and responsibility for
maintaining the purity of Mrs. Eddy's doctrine.

Accordingly there has come to be a body of "authorized Christian
Science literature," which it is recommended that everyone interested in the subject read, and the reading of anything else on the
subject is, if not openly condemned, at least discouraged. Certainly
among the church members the distribution of non-approved literature is taboo, and practitioners and teachers accused of circulating
or recommending it are brought under censure and even severe
discipline by the authorities.

Actually there is no mention in all Mrs. Eddy's writings of
"authorized" or "unauthorized" literature. There is a section in the
Manual headed "No Incorrect Literature," which forbids any mem-

ber of the church to buy, sell, or circulate literature which is not correct in its statement. This of course goes back to Mrs. Eddy's time. She does not spell out in detail what is to be regarded as correct and incorrect. The present leadership does. That is, it lists those books and periodicals which are correct or approved. By implication it may be taken that it is quite safe to read the approved books, but not the unapproved. Indeed it goes farther, openly denouncing specific publications through notices printed in the church periodicals, identifying such works unmistakably by description if not by name, and securing their condemnation outside church ranks by official press releases and letters in the daily newspapers.

Frequent articles in the *Journal* and *Sentinel* stress the exclusive use of approved books, and only approved books are on call at the Reading Rooms which are maintained in most places where there is a Christian Science church. In recent years, as the copyrights have neared expiration, all of Mrs. Eddy's books have been conspicuously stamped "Authorized Edition"; and the idea that nothing on the subject of Christian Science, the church, or its Leader can properly be released except through Boston headquarters is generally accepted within the organization. All else is definitely suspect. As a matter of fact, the word *authorized* has been and is now so used as to become, with the average Christian Scientist, synonymous with *authentic*.

How incisively the lines are drawn may be readily illustrated. To a member who asked what constitutes "authorized literature," the Board of Directors replied on January 4, 1929, that such would be Mrs. Eddy's writings—only those currently approved for study and circulation, it must be added, for the delving into her earlier editions has been declared anathema—and such material as is put out by the Christian Science Publishing Society. The Bible may be looked upon as "part of our authorized literature" since "it is sold by the Christian Science Publishing Society." Current newspapers containing authorized Christian Science lectures may be considered "semi-authorized literature." But the reprinting or circulation of such papers later is frowned upon. Such things as Bible aids and commentaries, ordinarily found useful by other religionists, are not encouraged, and Readers are dissuaded from employing "so-called helps in their work," such as might be compiled by other Readers out of their experience in the pulpit. (*Sentinel*, XLIII, 331)

The imprint of the Christian Science Publishing Society itself, ordinarily accepted as sufficient guarantee, suffers certain exceptions. In answer to a branch church query about the legitimacy of such periodicals as were put out by the Publishing Society during the Great Litigation, the Directors wrote, under date of August 21, 1934, that while some Reading Rooms keep these numbers for historical reference, they were not to be regarded as "authorized Christian Science literature."

It is true, as a church spokesman affirmed in an exchange of correspondence in the *Christian Century* (LXIX, Nos. 10 and 20), that the Board of Directors publishes no such list of forbidden books as the Roman Catholic *Index*. But it is also true that one of the charges made against certain of the teachers who have been disciplined was the circulation of unauthorized literature, the correctness of which was not at issue.

Every effort is made by Christian Scientists to guarantee inquirers, as well as their own church members, as to the safety of books they might find in the public libraries. Local representatives call on the librarians of the public institutions, requesting the privilege of pasting a printed slip in all books on the subject, giving the listing of approved books and periodicals drawn up in Boston. I have found several Methodist and other seminary libraries which have permitted this to be done, and I have visited public libraries which have refused to have their books so marked. Where it is permitted, this list is pasted in both the approved and the unapproved books. In some libraries the approved books are segregated in the card indexes and so marked.

Not only is the attempt made to designate the safe books, but the Christian Scientists also seek to prevent the publication and circulation of books which they regard as in any way inimical to their cause. Pressures are brought to bear upon publishers to refrain from publishing books deemed adverse, or to recall them once they are published. *The Quimby Manuscripts*, by H. W. Dresser, is a case in point. When in 1921 Dresser published in his book Mrs. Eddy's revealing correspondence with Phineas Quimby, which proved clearly at variance with certain official claims about her relationship with Quimby, the book was promptly suppressed. The much discussed mystery of how this was achieved is explained by Dresser in a letter dated May 21, 1922:

No action was brought concerning the Eddy letters. The Eddy Trustees here in Boston wrote to the publishers, T. Y. Crowell Company, referring to an action that got through the Supreme Court of Massachusetts regarding property rights in the ideas contained in personal letters, whoever might own the letters, and requesting the publishers to take the letters out of the book. The counsel for the publishers looked the matter up and, intimating that a suit might follow if the publishers did not take the letters out, advised the Crowell Company to write that this would be done and the sale stopped. Accordingly, I was asked to prepare a substitute chapter. I did so reluctantly, merely summarizing and not quoting from the letters. Then my publishers took out the important parts of the chapter, the summary of the letters, and put in the emasculated remainder.

If the publisher of an offending book cannot be persuaded to withhold publication or recall all copies released, then a nation-wide effort is made to interfere with their distribution. Bookstores are requested not to sell them and threatened with boycott if they do so. This is justified by Section 13 of Article VIII of the *Manual*, which declares that no member of the Christian Science church shall patronize a publishing house or bookstore that sells "obnoxious books." Again, Mrs. Eddy does not define obnoxious books. The Board of Directors seems to assume that any book which falls under its adverse judgment is an obnoxious book, which publishing houses should not issue nor stores circulate, under penalty of boycott.

These are general rules or statements which need to be looked into in some detail. Are they actually enforced? For an answer to this question one might look to the case of one who, a Christian Scientist himself—though withdrawn from church membership—sought the co-operation of the Board of Directors in his publication of a life of Mrs. Eddy.

6

The Studdert-Kennedy and Dickey Cases

BEFORE HE LEFT England for America in 1915, Hugh Anketell Studdert-Kennedy, for many years foreign editor of the *Christian Science Monitor,* had conceived of one day writing a full-length biography of Mary Baker Eddy. Even after his resignation from the Christian Science church, in protest against the growing autocracy in Boston, he never gave up the idea. Indeed, after withdrawing from the organization he had written a book called *Mrs. Eddy As I Knew Her,* designed to answer the chief attacks on her, and this book had been used in very large numbers by the Christian Science Committees on Publication in their public relations work for the church.

Studdert-Kennedy had found neither Dakin's *Mrs. Eddy* nor Bates and Dittemore's *Mary Baker Eddy* acceptable. Nor did Lyman Powell's biography seem to him to be the answer; it cut too close to the official line to convince the general public that it was not another propaganda book. He went to the trouble and expense of subscribing to a clipping service after the Powell book appeared and found, his correspondence indicates, that the major media discussed it as a "procured" book.

An eminent publishing house offered him a contract to write a word-for-word refutation of the Dakin book. But that was not what he wanted to do, so he refused. The Bates-Dittemore book he found full of new source material of the greatest possible value to the historian, but in his opinion the use made of the previously unpublished documents was not fair in many instances, and left a wrong impression of Mrs. Eddy and her work. More and more he felt the compulsion to write a book of a different kind, one that would be neither an attack on nor a defense of Mrs. Eddy, but as true a story as could be written of her, allowing the reader to make up his own mind about her.

By the spring of 1938 his purpose had crystallized to the point of his discussing it with Constant Huntington, head of Putnam & Company, Ltd., in England. Huntington was an admirer of his who had discovered him through his book *The Visitor* in a London bookstall, and had afterward published some of his books. Indeed, it was in connection with the Putnam edition of one of these, *And I Will Give Him the Morning Star,* that Studdert-Kennedy was brought to London and given opportunity to mention his heart's desire. The publisher was interested to the extent of asking that a rough synopsis be drawn up of what he intended writing, and in August, 1938, he extended to Hugh A. Studdert-Kennedy a contract for the projected book's publication.

At this point it seemed to the prospective biographer that he should seek access to the files of the Mother Church, which contained ten thousand or more of Mrs. Eddy's letters and a mass of other firsthand material. To get this it was necessary to enlist the aid of the Board of Directors, so he sought an opportunity to present the matter to them.

Although Studdert-Kennedy had withdrawn from the church more than a decade before this and had published his book *Christian Science and Organized Religion,* a critical study which the officialdom of the church regarded as offensive, he was received cordially by the Board and allowed to present his subject. The warm reception is not surprising when it is considered that he was proposing something which should benefit the movement substantially, and that, furthermore, overtures had been made by Christian Scientists high up in official circles to bring him back into the organization.

He recited to the Board his ambition to write a life of Mrs. Eddy which would not be in the nature of a defense of her, for none was needed, but would be "an appreciation from start to finish" which took her greatness for granted. He read from a letter Huntington had written him confirming the agreement to publish, "that the day has come that it should be possible to present a life of this great spiritual genius which will state the facts quite simply, as in the case of any important character," since this expressed his own belief. The book would deal with "Mrs. Eddy's ideas, background, and surroundings, rather than a refutation of the allegations, etc., which largely through ignorance and malice have been brought up against her."

Naturally the Board asked to what extent he desired their involvement. Studdert-Kennedy, according to the Board's own transcript of the conference, replied that he thought "it would be a most dangerous thing for the success of the book if you had anything to do with it. I think this has been the charge against all the books [the officially approved biographies of Mrs. Eddy]. They have been procured books for a purpose. I think the less you have to do with it the better." There was certainly no lack of directness in this reply.

But what would he expect from Christian Scientists? Nothing, was his answer. "I don't want it to be a book for Christian Scientists to buy to convince a friend. I want to write a book to be read by the man in the street. . . . I have spent twenty years in my small way defending Mrs. Eddy, and I am just simply through with it."

The chairman of the Board then inquired what would be said in the Preface to bring out his, Studdert-Kennedy's, own relation to Christian Science. To this Studdert-Kennedy replied that an inconspicuous note expressing his own deep gratitude to and appreciation of all he owed to the writings and teachings of Mrs. Eddy would be about as far as he could go, and he would let the rest speak for itself. To which the Board chairman replied that what he had told them was very interesting, certainly a novel proposition, and that they would mull it over.

In a letter to Constant Huntington eleven days later, Studdert-Kennedy reported on his interview with the Board who, he thought, "took it very well." After three or four days William R. Rathvon, the Board chairman, telephoned to him that the Board had considered the matter and "felt quite justified in the view that I should go ahead with my plans, and that they would do anything they could to help me." Rathvon had gone on to suggest that Studdert-Kennedy call

Judge Clifford P. Smith, editor of the Bureau of History and Records of the Mother Church, and even made a specific appointment for him to see Judge Smith.

At their first conference Judge Smith had been "ominously courteous," but soon became very much interested in the project and assured him of the fullest co-operation. Before leaving, the Judge loaned him a copy of one of the rarest of Christian Science books, "the suppressed biography of Mrs. Eddy, *Mrs. Eddy as I Knew Her in 1870* by Samuel Putnam Bancroft," allowing him to take it along with him to California. (Letter of October 21, 1938)

In a letter dated November 10, 1938, to Huntington, Studdert-Kennedy reported that his old friend William P. McKenzie, a member of the Board who had been absent at the time of his interview, had written him a cordial letter in which he said that he felt, too, that he had an understanding of what the biographer was seeking to do, and agreed that a book about Mrs. Eddy ought to come out in true literary form, uncontaminated by propaganda or any sense that their Leader could not stand on her actual life and demonstration without requiring defense.

Studdert-Kennedy thought this cordial letter indicated that the more the Board considered the matter of his biography, the more they liked it. He thought this revealed an almost revolutionary change of thought, and was very happy about it. Subsequent events disclosed that he had been overoptimistic in his interpretation of the Board's attitude, but McKenzie did prove a most valuable friend.

With the publisher's contract and the Board's support, Studdert-Kennedy plunged eagerly into research and writing. He was greatly impressed by the documents in the Bates-Dittemore book, he wrote Judge Smith on November 25, 1938. "The book itself," he observed, "is of course vitiated and disqualified as legitimate biography by reason of its obvious bias. But the documentary material of which such poor use has been made is excellent—so excellent, indeed, that I am wondering now again, as I have wondered before, to what extent it is really authentic."

Over and over in the voluminous correspondence, Studdert-Kennedy expressed his distaste for giving the Bates-Dittemore book any publicity, a sentiment he could be sure the Board heartily shared. Yet how could he use the indispensable source material it contained "in such a way as to place the book where it belongs"? Of course if the same material could be discovered in the church archives the Bates-Dittemore book could be by-passed. So again and again he asked specific questions of Judge Smith who, from time to time, sent him not a little material—but without saying anything directly about the book's authenticity.

Finally Studdert-Kennedy's uncompromising pursuit of this matter was rewarded. In a letter dated December 1, 1938, Judge Smith faced the issue and admitted frankly that most of the documents quoted by Bates and Dittemore were actually to be found in the Mother Church archives, explaining that the bulk of the copying mentioned by Dittemore in his preface had been done by him while he was a Director of the Mother Church and from documents to which he secured access in his official capacity. Smith wrote that in his view "most of the detailed information" in the Bates-Dittemore book was authentic, that while accurate data and genuine documents could be so presented as to give a false and unfair impression, he nevertheless could say that the different degrees of bias of the two authors had not prevented them from publishing "a good deal of actual information."

Here was a stunning disclosure, carrying far-reaching implications. That a book which had for six years borne the blanket condemnation of the church authorities should now be privately certified by the chief of their Bureau of History and Records as historically authentic came as somewhat of a shock. It was especially surprising that Judge Smith, who was known from Mrs. Eddy's day on down as perhaps the most taciturn of the top-ranking officials, should make such a sweeping admission in writing. It was something unprecedented.

Huntington, in a letter dated February 2, 1939, declared himself happy over the progress of the book and the support given to it by the Boston authorities. He thought it splendid of the church people to be so helpful, but he added that it was the only wise thing for them, "for such a book as you are writing will do more for

Christian Science than anything else that has been published since *Science and Health*." This may have been the prejudiced view of the book's publisher-to-be, but it indicates the attitude of a man who, if not a Christian Scientist, was a warm sympathizer.

Studdert-Kennedy was deeply immersed in books and documents, slowly digging out the facts he was to set forth in his book. His use of materials, particularly of the Bates-Dittemore book, was indicated in a letter to McKenzie dated September 27, 1939. Everything had worked out well. His intention had been not so much to present new material as to "render available to the world in general and Christian Scientists in particular the great mass of material Mr. Dittemore accumulated for the Church and used in his book, but which he distorted so shamefully by misinterpretation."

The first draft completed, copies were sent to Huntington, McKenzie, and Judge Smith. To Huntington, Studdert-Kennedy wrote, "Hope you will like what I have done." It would need some working over; but as it stood it represented, he thought, about 95 per cent of what he wanted. On January 22, 1940, he said to McKenzie, in sending him a copy for the Board, "While I very earnestly wish . . . not to involve the Board in any way, I need hardly say how glad I will be to have any expression of opinion or any criticism the Board may have to offer, and what earnest consideration I will give to both."

Whether Studdert-Kennedy realized its import at the time or not, one reading the correspondence from the vantage point of close to two decades later can hardly fail to see in McKenzie's letter of March 4, 1940, the signs of impending trouble. Though he writes, "Your present appraisal of Mrs. Eddy's victories stirs the reader to enthusiasm," he says in the next sentence, "One person recently placed in my hands your book about organization, as if it were important for me to know of it. I soon returned it with the comment that it was a 'dead book,' because dealing with things that no longer exist." Again, in a letter of March 30, there is a suggestion that all may not be well. Studdert-Kennedy wrote: "I hope it may be possible for a conference to happen again, whereby differences of viewpoint, if they should come up, may be reconciled."

It was not until April 11 that a letter came from the Board of Directors. It went straight to the point.

The members of this Board had read his typescript. One impression that they had gotten from this reading was that he had presented Mrs. Eddy's experience in such a way as to give the thought that it was one of troubles rather than of triumphs. It is interesting to contrast this with the statement of McKenzie quoted above. Evidently the Board was not unanimous in its judgment.

The second impression the Board got was that the new work made a distinction, in the same way Studdert-Kennedy's earlier book *Christian Science and Organized Religion* had done, between the "discovery" Mrs. Eddy had made of Christian Science and "her founding thereof." This they regarded as clearly contrary to what she herself intended in her frequent reference to herself as "Discoverer and Founder of Christian Science." To her thought, the Board asserted, it was one indivisible whole. This, they said, was proved by statements made in the preface of *Science and Health* (xi:22-24) and *Miscellany* (251:26-2).

Studdert-Kennedy had spoken of advertising this book in the *Christian Science Monitor,* just as he had others of his books in that paper, but now the Board would withhold that privilege so long as he differed with them on the proper view of organization. They felt impelled, their letter said, to ask whether he was now able to express an attitude toward the Christian Science organization other than that expressed in his former book, and whether he would be willing to state plainly this retraction or change of thought in his new biography of Mary Baker Eddy.

Studdert-Kennedy was stunned by this ultimatum. Was a public recantation by him to be the price of the Board's approval, even though no more than tacit, of Mrs. Eddy's biography? On April 16 he wrote the Directors that he gathered from their letter that they regarded this question as fundamental. As for where he stood, the record would show what he thought.

I can only say that my attitude toward organization in general has never changed and is epitomized ... where Mrs. Eddy says, "Growth is restricted by forcing humanity out of proper channels for development, or by holding it in fetters." I only claim my own freedom, as I think I made clear in talking with you in the October of 1938, and for all else I have nothing but hope and benediction. My attitude toward the Christian Science organization is again what it has always been: one of unfeigned rejoicing at every sign of progress and every record of achievement. My fundamental demand upon myself is a recognition of the fact that material organization has no permanent place in the outlook of ascending man. I feel deeply that this is what Mrs. Eddy meant us to understand.

He wondered if it were not possible to leave him out of the argument and consider the book simply on its own merits as a biography.

In a letter to Constant Huntington on April 17, 1940, Studdert-Kennedy wrote that it was all "very silly and beside the point," but that it might be sufficient to prevent anything in the form of an endorsement from the Boston authorities. Still this was not too much of a disappointment, except as it revealed that the broader outlook he had hoped and believed was developing in the Board had not come about. He had reason to believe that the Board was divided, for at least McKenzie was on his side. Indeed, the more he thought about it, the more he felt relieved that the book would go out without any strings attached to it. There was a large and increasing number of people all over the world who were interested in Christian Science but not in the least interested in the church, to whom he would far rather appeal than to the church organization.

Huntington wrote Studdert-Kennedy on May 3, 1940, that his book enshrined a gracious and vivid personality; that it consistently brought out the unimportance of worldly standards, bringing home the lesson that truth flourishes equally, if not better, in humble surroundings; that the spiritual aura surrounding Mrs. Eddy had not been urged upon the reader, but had been allowed to enter into the reader's conception to such an extent that one could not but follow the biographer in placing her among the prophets. Huntington then cautioned Studdert-Kennedy against the temptation to claim some spiritual quality in every incident of a life such as Mrs. Eddy's, suggesting that he try to avoid idealizing and defending his attention to petty matters.

Although sympathetic, McKenzie had to act with discretion as a member of the Board. As he said in one letter, he had to work along with his fellow-Directors. He therefore was careful throughout his voluminous correspondence with Studdert-Kennedy to write only from his home, and with pen and ink, leaving no duplicates. He was not in a position to advise Studdert-Kennedy, he said, but he thought it a good plan to send the manuscript to Lord Lothian, then British Ambassador to the United States, one of the most influential laymen in the Christian Science church. This, it is worth remembering, was *after* the Board had read and commented upon the completed book, and it is further noteworthy that McKenzie did not suggest that Studdert-Kennedy alter his manuscript in any way before forwarding it to Lord Lothian.

Despite the cares and responsibilities of his post, with Britain at war and seeking desperately to get help from America, the Ambassador read the entire manuscript and wrote Studdert-Kennedy on June 14, 1940: "I think I have read all the hostile lives of Mrs. Eddy and I have always thought, as you have done, that they ought to be answered—or, at any rate, that a biographer should take into account what they have alleged and deal with it indirectly if not directly." These hostile books, he thought, would continue to be a veritable mine from which later opponents of Mrs. Eddy could dig out material for yet other attacks for years to come, and it was therefore essential that there should be some satisfactory answer to them. "That, I suppose," he continues, "is why I enjoyed reading your book so much. It is by far the best account that I have yet read of what one might call the human aspect of Mrs. Eddy's life. The spiritual interpretation, of course, is done once and for all in *Retrospection and Introspection.*" His *only* suggestion, he wrote, was that Studdert-Kennedy might quote a little more from Mrs. Eddy as to the nature of her spiritual discovery, such as the passage in *Science and Health* beginning at line 19 on page 108.

Here was high praise for the book from a top-ranking Christian Scientist. Evidently there could not be too much that was obviously bad about it.

Meanwhile Judge Smith had read the biography and had written a rather lengthy and detailed criticism for the Board of Directors, a copy of which he sent to Studdert-Kennedy.

The Directors wrote Studdert-Kennedy on June 28, 1940, that they had not been satisfied with his April 16 reply to their letter of April 11, and that they had been expecting something more satisfactory from him ever since. Now, as they had heard nothing more, they stated explicitly that the Board did not and would not approve the publication of his typescript as submitted. Furthermore, the Directors were making Judge Smith's "comments and corrections" their own. An objection not before raised had for Studdert-Kennedy an ominous ring: the typescript when they saw it, they said, included a large number of quotations from letters and other writings of Mrs. Eddy which should not be published without the express permission of the Trustees under her will, the legal holders of her literary rights. In other words, it was within their power to block the book through legal action if he attempted to publish it despite their disapproval. Was this to be taken as a threat?

Finally, the Directors said they regarded the typescript as "very different from the oral prospectus" given them by Studdert-Kennedy during their conference with him on October 10, 1938.

To this Studdert-Kennedy replied on July 5, 1940. The book, so far as he could see, conformed very closely with what he had originally proposed to them, and he felt keenly the implication which had been repeated several times that this was not so. "I have been living with this book for the last twenty years," he wrote to the Directors,

and I had known for the last five or ten years almost exactly what I was going to do with it. It seems to me almost impossible that I should have given you an impression which diverged to any great extent from what I actually planned. I certainly had no reason for doing so. However, I feel that in the circumstances, the only satisfactory way of settling this question is to ask you to send me a copy of the rescript of our discussion . . . I think if you will read it again you will find that your recollection of the discussion is not always in conformity with the fact.

In this letter he stated that if the Board considered his attitude toward organization a fundamental obstacle to their approval of his book, then nothing more remained to be said. If this were not the case, however, he would spare no effort to explore with them for a common ground. Indeed, much had already been accomplished in this direction, as he and his publisher had agreed with Judge Smith on many of the proposed changes—although for reasons different from those advanced by the Judge. (For example, they too felt it best to delete the quotations from Dickey's memoirs, but only because what Dickey had to say therein was both unimportant and lacking in literary merit, and not because, as Judge Smith contended, the Dickey book was "objectionable"—this being quite inadmissible from a literary point of view.)

Replying to the criticism that his book gave the impression of Mrs. Eddy's life as one of troubles rather than triumphs, Studdert-Kennedy said he was sure he had made it clear that one of his chief purposes was to "dissipate the false impressions of unclouded serenity that had been built up about Mrs. Eddy." He continued: "Serenity she had, to a degree that none of us can even contemplate, but it was the serenity of understanding, which counted troubles as nothing." Then he quoted her as saying: "I rejoice with those who rejoice, and am too apt to weep with those who weep, but over and above it all are eternal sunshine and joy unspeakable." "That," he wrote, "was the real Mrs. Eddy."

As to the use of quotations from Mrs. Eddy's writings, he pointed out that he was including nothing which had not already been published and, much of it, before the public for many years. All this material would be credited to the best available source. His only desire was "to produce a biography of our Leader which shall help to place her before the world in some measure as the world must some day see her."

At this point McKenzie wrote, under date of July 6, 1940, that he was gratified with Lord Lothian's commendation of the book, as this would influence others to approve. (Again, be it noted, McKenzie refers to the unaltered manuscript.) Who were the "others" who seemed to count so much? The Directors? Was McKenzie's strategy that of mobilizing pressure against the Board's opposition?

McKenzie thought it might also be well to have a Mrs. Katherine English, of Vancouver, B.C., read the manuscript. She was an influential teacher on the West Coast and carried some weight with the Board. He sent Mr. and Mrs. Studdert-Kennedy a personal letter of introduction, and on July 17 Mrs. English wrote them that she was looking forward to reading the manuscript. McKenzie was to write her of Studdert-Kennedy: "There is worth in that boy far beyond what his severe critics believe. The situation here is a curious one, mixed up with deep feelings and arguments of the past. There is a lot of ignorance and prejudice in the situation." Would this pave the way for favorable support?

In reporting on September 6 to Huntington on Mrs. English's reaction, Studdert-Kennedy wrote: "The most interesting aspect of her review was the fact that it was particularly the points criticized by Judge Smith that she most commended," especially the treatment of the Woodbury incident, which Smith insisted should be deleted entirely. She had not gotten at all the impression which the Judge seemed to be laboring under, that the book showed the Christian Science movement "in a repellent light." As a matter of fact, when she was asked specifically about it, she said that no such thought had even occurred to her in reading the manuscript.

In October, 1940, the Board wrote again to Studdert-Kennedy, raising once more their objections to his attitude toward organization per se. They had meanwhile sent him the requested transcript of the much-disputed 1938 conference at Boston, the contents of which provided nothing to support their contention that Studdert-Kennedy's book had turned out to be "very different from the oral prospectus" given them on that occasion.

Answering that he regretted their return to this personal question, he said there seemed little he could add to what he had already written them. First of all they must dismiss the idea of including in the Preface or anywhere "an expression of my own attitude as to organization or anything else connected with Christian Science." The reader could not be properly interested in a biographer's personal views, and any injection of them could well strike the reader as an impertinence. Propriety would require a biographer to keep himself as much as possible in the background, letting his subject occupy the entire stage.

But more than that, he had no different attitude to express than that which he had been entertaining for twenty years or more without change. It was true that the Directors had quoted passages from Mrs. Eddy's writings which seemed to run counter to his position, but they had overlooked other passages which definitely supported his own conclusions.

He trusted his letter did not sound ungracious, for it was not so intended. He would appreciate the Board's help and approval, their advice and recommendations, but he did not seek their formal endorsement, since he must safeguard his book from the suggestion that it had been written to order or was in any sense at any point "procured." He said he thought the Board must be contemplating a much fuller endorsement than he had ever had in mind, since all he was asking the Directors for was permission to credit the archives of the Mother Church rather than the anathematized Bates-Dittemore book.

On December 2, 1940, the Board wrote that it would naturally be most undesirable if the biography upon which he was working should advertise the book by Bates and Dittemore. For this reason, their letter said, they were offering a specific agreement to verify quotations from Mrs. Eddy's letters which Studdert-Kennedy had quoted from the Bates-Dittemore book, providing he placed in the Preface a statement that the quotations had been verified by the Bureau of History and Records without any implied approval of the volume as a whole.

To this Studdert-Kennedy replied promptly, accepting their offer without reservations. His December 10, 1940, letter of acceptance made this a definite contract between them. Everything seemed to have worked out well, and with his contract in his pocket he felt safe in cabling Huntington in London to proceed with the composition of the book, a costly undertaking hardly to be entered upon lightly.

The year closed on a happy note when Mrs. McKenzie gave her blessing in these words: "We both greatly appreciate the work you are doing to make better known the wonderful life and labors of our beloved Leader, Mary Baker Eddy." (Letter of December 30, 1940)

The new year opened auspiciously with a handsome token of appreciation from McKenzie. On January 12, 1941, he wrote Studdert-Kennedy: "I have felt that you would like a picture of her [Mrs. Eddy] by Jean J. Pfister, similar to paintings exhibited at S.F. and N.Y. fairs." He had already paid the artist, instructing him to send along the painting and with it a bill of sale and receipt. He explained that as an officer of the church he could not give personal directions, but that as a fellow-Scientist he gave his love and best wishes for success in the project. When he wrote, "It may be so that you can use your picture as you deem wise," Studdert-Kennedy took this to mean that McKenzie was really sending the picture along for the book. "I am very hopeful that we may be able to use it ultimately in the book," he wrote back on January 20. In the continued exchange of letters, the subject was frequently mentioned, and to dispel any uncertainty Studdert-Kennedy specifically proposed such use. McKenzie's response was that he had instructed the artist to send the receipted bill so that "your ownership will be unquestioned," adding, "Shall be glad to see colored reproduction *which will make a perfect frontispiece.*" (Letter of June 6, 1941)

On January 29, 1941, Studdert-Kennedy wrote Huntington that he had been going through the manuscript once more, but had made very few changes. He felt confirmed in his judgment concerning it when he received back the typescript which he had sent up to Mrs. English to read and saw "in how very few cases she had suggested even minor changes." He concluded that as it stood, with changes indicated in his letter of April 22, 1940, and in further communications during the summer, "it is about as good as I could make it." He was delighted that publication was set for the autumn. The private diary of Mrs. Studdert-Kennedy contained this entry for January 29, 1941: "Best news. Constant Huntington will publish the book this autumn."

But when Studdert-Kennedy wrote his letter of January 29, 1941, he did not know that a letter of the most serious import, written by the Board of Directors on January 28, was already on its way to him. Mrs. Studdert-Kennedy's diary record for February 4 carried this word: "Hugh had letter from Board of Directors reversing their

decision to okay documents in book and challenging statement in
Christian Science and Organized Religion."

It will be recalled that it was on the basis of the Board's letter of
agreement to allow his crediting of certain materials to the files of
the Mother Church, really the only thing which Studdert-Kennedy
was interested in having at the hands of the Board, that he had
cabled Huntington to proceed with the composition of the book.
Someone would have to bear the not inconsiderable expense which
the composition of the book entailed, but the Board apparently felt
no responsibility in the matter. Their letter of January 28 simply
stated that "after mature consideration" they had decided that they
would furnish no credentials or material for his book since he had
refused to repudiate the stand he had taken in *Christian Science and
Organized Religion.* It had been a decade since that book was published, but the Board asserted that Studdert-Kennedy was still in a
position of having denounced one of Mrs. Eddy's demonstrations—
i.e., the Christian Science organization—"as essentially evil."

The Board's letter not only stated their refusal to honor the
agreement into which they had entered with Studdert-Kennedy
nearly two months before; it went on to say that the Trustees under
the will of Mrs. Eddy, the holders of the copyrights, concurred with
them and asked them to inform him that the courts had ruled that
publication of letters without the consent of the writer or his legal
representative was prohibited by American law and, presumably,
by English law also. They did not explicitly declare that if he published Mrs. Eddy's letters without their consent legal action would
be taken, but this was clearly implied. They had previously, in the
Christian Science Sentinel (XL, 291), advertised their successful
prosecution of at least one violator of the publishing rights held
by them.

In this whole matter, so the Board letter to Studdert-Kennedy
stated, the Directors had decided *unanimously.* Later it came out
that the decision was taken at a time when his friend at court,
McKenzie, was absent.

Here was a serious setback, but Studdert-Kennedy did not seem
to be too badly discouraged. On March 28, 1941, he wrote to

Huntington that he still believed everything would work out satisfactorily. Powerful influences in Boston were working in his favor,
and McKenzie was devoting himself unofficially to straightening
out the difficulties. He did not feel that it was at all necessary to
have the co-operation of the Board. Still, he felt he should leave no
stone unturned to secure it if possible.

Huntington's reply of April 2 is revealing. He wrote that
Studdert-Kennedy had his sympathy in all he was enduring at the
hands of the Board. "What a light it throws on organization behind
the scenes!" he could not but remark. Nevertheless, he continued,
there was some satisfaction in the fact that the Directors had been
stirred up to the point where they were bound to make good publicity agents for the book when it appeared, even if their advertising
did prove inadvertent. He thought Studdert-Kennedy's method of
patient and respectful consultation was the right one. He was, he
confessed, completely indifferent to their final decision, since they
would probably change it the next day anyway. Again, on April 17
he wrote that he was no longer concerned about the attitude of
"our Boston friends." He was sure Studdert-Kennedy would handle
the situation in the most effective way. He preferred that they not
put the book on the Index, if it could be avoided by punctilious
effort not to be led into an apparent infringement of their injunctions.

On February 12, 1941, Studdert-Kennedy drafted a letter to the
Board expressing his profound regret, not merely because of the
inconvenience and expense involved, and the possibility of legal
proceedings, but because he had cherished the hope that his book
could go out without any taint of controversy among Mrs. Eddy's
own followers. "As to the question of legal proceedings," he
told them,

I cannot but feel that if it were possible to stop a book like mine on any
count of material used, then it would have been much more possible to
have stopped for the same reason such books as the Dakin book, the
Springer book, the Bates-Dittemore book, to mention only three of several. I cannot believe for a moment that, devoted as you are to your
great trust, you would have allowed such an opportunity to pass by to
stop these slanders. Moreover, it would be as you know a very easy matter
for me to make such changes in the book as would render it unassailable

on this account. All such questions are, however, merely side issues as far as I am concerned.

This letter was not sent, but it might as well have been, for on April 30, 1941, the Board renewed its efforts to get a retraction of his former writings. Admitting that the offending book, *Christian Science and Organized Religion,* had been issued as long ago as 1930, they said that presumably it lingered on in individual memories and on library shelves. The trouble was, they said, that he and they did not find the same meaning in his book.

The eagerness of the Board of Directors to secure a public repudiation by Studdert-Kennedy of his ideas concerning the organized church is, under the circumstances, quite understandable. Still, one wonders why Lyman Powell, who had earlier written one of the most vitriolic attacks upon Mrs. Eddy and her church, was granted access to the files of the Mother Church without being likewise required to recant, in his approved book on Mrs. Eddy, his former stand. Possibly the fact that he was an outsider would explain this. Nothing an outsider could say would be as damaging, they evidently thought, as that which one who had been a member in good standing might say. They had given the widest publicity to Dittemore's last-minute repentance before his passing off the scene in 1937. If Studdert-Kennedy could likewise be brought to recant the effect would be tremendous.

There was little Studdert-Kennedy could do but reply, as he did on May 18, 1941, that it only remained to decide what course should be taken if they agreed to disagree with reference to organization per se, since he would yield no further. There were three courses open. The first would be for them to honor their agreement of December 2, 1940, permitting him to fulfil his end of that contract; the second would be for him to write a new Preface which would cite, in a friendly tone, Judge Smith's certification of the Bates-Dittemore book, by way of authenticating his own source material properly; the third would be to tell frankly in his Preface the whole story of his negotiations with the Board and let the reader draw his own conclusions. This last course he found most distasteful, especially since he had striven so long to the end that this book should—not alone in his own opinion but in that of others whom both he and the Board respected—"go out with the good will of all concerned and without any trace of that bitterness and controversy which has characterized all too much of the stately unfoldment of the Christian Science cause."

In a journal entry for February 11, Mrs. Studdert-Kennedy wrote: "Had a puzzling letter from McKenzie, ignoring the Board of Directors' letter, in which they virtually threatened Hugh with suit and reversed their decision."

A letter from McKenzie, dated June 6, 1941, told that he had become Chairman of the Board of Directors. In it he commended Studdert-Kennedy's strategy in keeping to the case in point by discussing only the Preface.

Studdert-Kennedy had of course kept his publisher informed fully as to his relations with the Board. On June 10 Huntington wrote expressing some disgust with the behavior of the Directors on several counts. He concluded that, although they had certainly threatened legal action if everything did not go their way, he felt the threat was an empty one and might well be ignored.

Mrs. Studdert-Kennedy's diary entry for June 25, 1941, reads: "The first batch of proofs. Hurrah! They look very good."

The Board wrote on August 14, 1941, acknowledging receipt of part of the galley proof. On examining it they had found more objectionable matter than they had discovered in the transcript (although this had, before composition, been corrected in accord with the criticism of Mrs. English and to some extent that of Judge Smith). They were, they said, in the process of preparing a résumé of the points they found objectionable.

On September 8, the Board wrote that the book was the opposite of what they had expected. They did not find it, as Studdert-Kennedy had promised in the 1938 conference, exclusively an appreciation of Mrs. Eddy's greatness. He was not to have put anything into his book, they asserted, which the Directors could "legitimately object to"—the question of who would judge the legitimacy of their objections was not mentioned, but evidently it was to be taken for granted that they would be their own final court of appeal—nor was he to lay emphasis on any point in Mrs. Eddy's life which might indicate "difference of opinion," nor include a single "element of controversy."

These objections, it is worth noting, were to a manuscript which had been put into their hands many months before, which they had once agreed might be published with their permission to credit certain materials found in the Bates-Dittemore book to the Mother Church archives. In addition to this, Studdert-Kennedy had since incorporated into it numerous changes proposed by their Mrs. English and Judge Smith, as well as by Huntington.

When the Board finally got all their objections together, it required seven typewritten pages, single spaced, to state them. Why this had not been done sooner they did not explain. McKenzie had found the manuscript acceptable. So had Lord Lothian. So had Mrs. English. And not even Judge Smith had raised most of the objections the Board now offered, "after further consideration and deliberation."

The Board charged that Studdert-Kennedy was "obliterating the significance" of Mrs. Eddy's "final revelation" in 1866 by relating such historical facts as her appeal to a Quimby practitioner for help two weeks after her instantaneous healing which marked the inception of Christian Science, as well as by bringing up quotations from her correspondence showing that she only gradually emerged from Quimbyism.

Entirely too much of the book was devoted to the Quimby question, in the Directors' opinion, and thus it "revived one of the most controversial incidents" in all Christian Science history. It will be recalled that Studdert-Kennedy's original proposition was to "state the facts quite simply, as in the case of any important character." And the Board had now known for a year and five months, from his answer to Judge Smith's critique on April 9, 1940, that Studdert-Kennedy had "always felt that the Quimby controversy needed to be brought out into the open and thoroughly examined without the smallest suggestion of suppression."

The Board was particularly concerned over the disclosure of behind-the-scenes history which "conveys that membership in this church is likely to involve trouble." Again, they did not want the "unlovely picture of petty jealousy" drawn in connection with Asa G. Eddy's elevation to Mrs. Eddy's inner circle, and they felt the lawsuits, disagreements, etc., of that period must remain "long since buried events." There must be no account of the misdeeds of Mrs. Eddy's adopted son, E. J. Foster-Eddy, even though it did come out of the official records of the Mother Church, because these data had once been published by a disaffected official of the church without their permission, and this was enough to make their "republication objectionable." There must be no documented revival of the famous "Next Friends Suit" from the book of her devoted follower, Michael Meehan, because Mrs. Eddy had once asked the suppression of that book on the ground that it might keep alive "a memory of bitterness and discord." Any information drawn from the Adam H. Dickey book was anathema and "the fact that we deemed it necessary to recall it [the Dickey book] furnishes our reason for legitimately objecting to its further use."

Finally, it was claimed that the quotations attributed to Mrs. Eddy were inaccurate. About this Studdert-Kennedy wrote his publisher:

There is a tremendous feeling in the Christian Science movement about having Mrs. Eddy's writings quoted with exactitude. A misplaced comma is enough to precipitate an explosion in almost any direction. But in this connection I want to make one thing clear: most of Mrs. Eddy's lesser writings were published first in the *Journal* and sometimes I have quoted directly from the *Journal;* where I do this there may be certain minor discrepancies between the *Journal* version and that subsequently republished.

Why did they not simply correct his quotations? "This is of course what the Board specifically promised to do, and they have so far failed to honor their promise." If, then, actual errors were perpetrated, he concluded the Board would be entirely to blame.

It now seemed to Studdert-Kennedy that nothing but a face-to-face talk with the Board would avail anything. Accordingly, he telegraphed them that he was coming to Boston on October 10, 1941, and asked an audience.

But it was not so easy a matter. Although the Studdert-Kennedys had many friends among Christian Science leaders in Boston, no one would see them except McKenzie, who continued cordial; he telephoned several times and even visited them at their hotel. The Board made no response to Studdert-Kennedy's request for an audience. After a week of waiting, he and his wife left their hotel and took a house in Newton Center.

By October 27 the proofs were ready to return to London, and Studdert-Kennedy wrote Huntington that he felt they were under no further obligation to delay publication. It seemed clear, he wrote, that McKenzie was doing everything possible to put the thing through; but whether he succeeded or not, there was already enough support in the movement to give the book a good start; it would win its own way.

Studdert-Kennedy finally secured an appointment with George Channing, First Reader of the Mother Church, a man who years before had urged him to do the Eddy story. It was thought prudent for Studdert-Kennedy to leave his car, with its California license, around the corner from Channing's Boston residence, where the two men met, to avoid the possibility that a passing Scientist might inform the Board of the visit. Channing, Mrs. Studdert-Kennedy wrote in her diary on November 7, 1941, told Studdert-Kennedy that "he had been *warned* by a member of the Board of Directors *not* to see Hugh, and if they knew he was talking to him freely as he did, that he would be unfrocked and kicked out."

Studdert-Kennedy reported his conversation with Channing to Huntington in a long letter on November 10, saying that the talk had led him to believe there was a trend in the Christian Science movement—a trend growing, from the Board's point of view, at an alarming rate—toward liberalism and that complete individual freedom which he himself had sought in breaking with Boston twenty years earlier. The result of the Great Litigation of 1919-21 had been to place the Board in a completely dictatorial position, a position they had endeavored ever since to maintain. They were no longer hopeful of reconverting him, and they feared that the reading of his life of Mrs. Eddy would encourage people to read his other books.

But, he continued, the situation was now no different than when the Board had given him its blessing three years earlier, and then for more than twelve months had accorded him every help and encouragement. He had gathered from his conversation with Channing that the instigator of the Board's about-face had been Stuart Boothe, elected to succeed William R. Rathvon after the latter's death; it was Boothe's disapproval which had brought about the Board's breach of the contract with Studdert-Kennedy, and Boothe had continued to stand in the way of any settlement ever since. He thought the Board was no longer seeking modification, but was bent upon preventing publication at any cost. He felt his publisher should delay no longer in going ahead with the book.

A letter from Huntington dated November 26, 1941, opened a new chapter in this long story. He had just been visited in London by an emissary of the Board of Directors at Boston, one Robert Ellis Key. Lieutenant Colonel Key, who was to win the editorship of the *Journal* and *Sentinel,* was then a Committee on Publication. Huntington wrote that Colonel Key had begun his call in the truculent role of a policeman. But Huntington quickly turned the tables on him by saying he judged from Key's attitude that the Directors were really out to suppress facts, in which case it was pointless to prolong the interview. Any attempt to conceal the truth about Mrs. Eddy was an impertinence with which he would have nothing to do. When told this, Key changed his tone entirely, becoming most respectful toward the publisher, the book, and its author.

Key had secured a set of proofs, and had asked if he might keep them a while. Huntington thought this was no more than a ruse to gain time while Key got new instructions from Boston, and resolved simply to disregard him and go ahead with publication if there was any undue delay.

Huntington went on to thank Studdert-Kennedy for not objecting to some minor changes he had made; he wanted it understood, he wrote, that all such changes were to be canceled if Studdert-Kennedy did not approve them.

On November 25, one of the Directors, Charles E. Heitman, called Studdert-Kennedy and the next day they met in his office.

Heitman asked if something could not be put in the Preface or the body of the book to the effect that its author was not opposed to people's going to church. There had been a case that very week, he said, of a woman who had read *Christian Science and Organized Religion* and then had resigned from the church. Nor was this the only one.

Two days later Studdert-Kennedy sent the Board by letter a couple of changes he had suggested to Heitman. He was to have seen the Board that afternoon, but the appointment was canceled by them. After his letter reached them next morning, however, he was granted another appointment at once—and Mrs. Studdert-Kennedy's diary entry for November 28 reads: "Hugh saw the Board at eleven. A love feast! . . . The green light!"

Studdert-Kennedy wrote the Board the next day, thanking them for the meeting; it was, he said, a source of comfort and uplift to him. He was so grateful that their seeming differences should be so happily composed, and he assured them he would do everything to safeguard and emphasize their Leader's life story upon which they found themselves so fully agreed.

In his appraisal of the situation for Herbert Eustace on the same day, Studdert-Kennedy remarked that Judge Smith's certification in writing of the Bates-Dittemore documents had left the Board in a real dilemma. In the necessary documenting of his book, he would have had to quote Judge Smith's embarrassing authentication of that source, the only alternative to this being for him to cite, with the Directors' permission, the Mother Church archives. They were reluctant to show their hand by having such permission publicized, and even more reluctant to see the Bates-Dittemore book advertised. Amazingly, he wrote, the Board had just extricated itself by simply buying outright the plates, the copyright, and all other rights to the Bates-Dittemore book from its publisher, Alfred A. Knopf & Company, and then waiving, so far as his own book was concerned, all restrictions on the material. He was now, he concluded, protected from any action against either himself or Putnams for "unfair" use of the copyrighted material.

For a while it appeared that the story was about to come to a happy ending. Friends of the Studdert-Kennedys among the Christian Science leaders in Boston, who had been avoiding social contact with them since their arrival in the city, began to issue invitations. On December 2 the Studdert-Kennedys dined with the McKenzies. On December 3 they lunched with Irving and Edna Howe. Mrs. Howe, a long-time friend who had been a guest in their California home, had not been able before to find time to see them. On December 20 they had dinner with the Howes. Feeling that their work in Boston was over for the present, they made plans to return to the West Coast.

On December 19 Studdert-Kennedy dispatched to Huntington his final changes—the last he would agree to. Replying on December 21, Huntington summed up his feelings about the struggle. He supposed one should not blame the Board as a body for weaknesses that were really inseparable from organization, but it was to him a shock to find in the Board's point of view so little spiritual character. He thought the final settlement, while satisfactory from a commercial angle, had much in common with a political deal, such as would have saddened as well as amused Mrs. Eddy. Studdert-Kennedy had properly met them on their own level. Once again the way seemed cleared for publication. But now there were wartime difficulties to cope with, such as the paper shortage.

In a letter to Mrs. Studdert-Kennedy on March 9, 1942, Huntington spoke again of the curtailment of printing caused by the war. He mentioned that Colonel Key was interesting himself in the book and that together they were going over it in a spirit of co-operation impossible in the atmosphere of official Boston. This seemed a little strange to Mrs. Studdert-Kennedy, since her husband had already made the last changes that would be acceptable to him. Thus matters stood for some time.

At this juncture Studdert-Kennedy was to lose his champion on the Board. William P. McKenzie died suddenly on September 8, 1942. His widow wrote Studdert-Kennedy, assuring him that he still had her husband's love and "his cordial support in your work for our Cause through your lovely record of the life of our Leader." To Mrs. Studdert-Kennedy too she wrote a letter of reassurance about the book, stating that she and her late husband had read the manuscript together and had "rejoiced together in its advent." Mr. McKenzie would be sorry, as indeed she was, that publication was now being delayed by wartime conditions. With God at the helm, however, they could not doubt that the book would come out at exactly the right time.

More than four years had now passed since the first conferences between Studdert-Kennedy and Huntington had taken place, and still the book was not published. After a brief illness in the summer of 1943, Hugh A. Studdert-Kennedy passed on, leaving the problem in the capable hands of his wife.

August 10, 1943, finds Mrs. Studdert-Kennedy asking Huntington about the work's status. His September 27 reply said he hoped to have the book ready for press "next year." On January 12, 1944, he wrote that work was being resumed on her husband's "great biography." He appreciated her confidence in his ability to prepare the book for press. He knew what her husband would wish in the way of very slight revisions here and there, after their entirely sympathetic work together. On May 9 he wrote promising to take up with her any "slight revisions" of the book, as well as the matter of the format, which must be rich and dignified.

Writing again on July 17, Huntington spoke of the responsibility he shared with Mrs. Studdert-Kennedy for insuring the book's accuracy as to facts and implications about Mrs. Eddy's life. As for Mrs. Eddy's point of view, he found Studdert-Kennedy's interpretation entirely justified. The exigencies of war precluded the book's publication in 1944, but he would consult her about any slight revisions which might seem advisable.

Mrs. Studdert-Kennedy, in a letter to Huntington on January 29, 1945, alluded to the several-times-mentioned "slight revisions" he might have in mind, asking to see the revised proofs as far as he had gone. Five months later she cabled him to send them on to her. In the same cablegram she asked for the publication date so that it might be announced on the jacket of a forthcoming book which the Farallon Press, the firm she and her husband had founded, was about to publish.

This brought a lengthy reply from Huntington, dated June 7, 1945. He wrote that on the recommendation of Colonel Key he had relinquished the proofs for editing to a Mrs. Flower, secretary to the late Lord Lothian. Mrs. Flower had been slowly working through them, while consulting frequently with Christian Science church officials. In the copy just returned to his office the changes seemed slight, but they were quite numerous. His main task, he said, had been that of combating "a tendency to turn your husband's straightforward narrative into Christian Science propaganda." Of course, he would tolerate no changes which introduced ideas not Studdert-Kennedy's. And he had encountered an attempt to delete well-known facts about Mrs. Eddy's life, something he could not permit. Certain passages had been reduced and others expanded, he said, but he could assure Mrs. Studdert-Kennedy that nothing would be done which went beyond what her husband would have approved.

Mrs. Studdert-Kennedy was naturally troubled by all this. What was really happening to the book? On July 26 she dispatched a cablegram asking that Huntington indicate the changes he himself considered important: "Do not wish biography to come out as a book edited by someone else." In a confirming letter, she said that she awaited eagerly the proofs with the suggested changes, as she felt any delay was unfortunate. She had from the beginning felt that "the Church would either stop the publication of the book or render it innocuous." She herself had withdrawn from the church in 1922, following the Great Litigation. Having been consultant to certain of the Boston officials and a contributor to the periodicals, she had had not a little experience with the church apart from this that she had shared with Studdert-Kennedy, whom she had married after her withdrawal. She was neither as trustful of the hierarchy as her husband had been nor as optimistic about the outcome of their dealings with the church authorities.

Again on September 25 she wrote Huntington, saying she had forwarded to him a gift copy of the latest publication of the Farallon Press, Arthur Corey's *Christian Science Class Instruction.* In this book Corey had mentioned her husband's forthcoming work on

Mrs. Eddy, and the jacket had carried an announcement of it. Already some orders had come in for the biography.

On November 19, 1945, she once more asked Huntington to let her have the proposed changes, informing him that the following autumn—the autumn of 1946—would be the very latest time she would want to see the book released. Orders for it, as the result of the mention in the Corey book, continued to come in.

This stirred Huntington to reply on November 30 that he would get the changes to her by Christmas. She would find *many* suggested omissions, but he hoped they did not affect the author's intention. There had been additions, too. But *the bulk* of the work, he assured her, remained unchanged.

Then, with seeming irrelevancy, Huntington remarked that neither her husband nor he would have countenanced the support of a secessionist group. What was the meaning of this? The more she thought about it the more she was inclined to believe that the key lay in an assertion of Huntington's about the changes — that if she thought anything had been sacrificed, she must remember that much was gained in the process in the tacit approval of the church authorities. She felt sure of this when, on January 23, 1946, after he had received the Corey book, Huntington wrote that he hoped Farallon was not becoming associated with any activity unacceptable to the Mother Church Board of Directors.

This sudden concern for the Board which for nearly six years had put every obstacle in the way of the Studdert-Kennedy book was very disquieting. The Farallon Press had never pandered to the Board. Indeed, Farallon had published *Christian Science and Organized Religion,* the book the Board had so long sought to force her husband to repudiate publicly. Had Boston officialdom finally convinced Putnams that it could muster organizational strength sufficient to make or break the new book? Even if that were so, she could not bring herself to believe that Huntington would sell out, after all they had endured together in defense of a principle. Could it be possible that he had gone over to the Board's point of view?

An examination of the changes he approved in the manuscript

may cast some light on this question. Of the deletions and alterations made, only one embodied a correction for historical accuracy,
a minor matter of date. Four had to do with Mrs. Eddy's ancestry,
three with her childhood and youth, four with her health, and two
with the development of her thought. Some twenty-six concerned
her personal characteristics, habits, or activities. Three referred to
Science and Health, one to the *Manual,* and one to the *Journal.*
Eight had to do with Quimby and two to organization; nine referred
to Mrs. Eddy's getting help from persons later discredited, such as
Arens, Kennedy, and Spofford. Several were concerned with statements or episodes which might reflect adversely on Mrs. Eddy.
Numerious other deletions or alterations of a miscellaneous nature
were scattered throughout the proof. Sometimes only a word was
deleted or replaced by another; sometimes whole paragraphs were
struck out or added. At one point thirty-six typewritten lines of
eulogy, wholly out of keeping with the rest of the book as Studdert-
Kennedy had written it, were inserted. Plate II, opposite page 176,
reproduces a typical galley sheet which will indicate the character
of the changes.

Frequently the effect was to give quite a different meaning from
that obviously intended by the author. Some of the revisions, it is
true, were relatively unimportant. But in general the deletions,
changes, and additions represented an attempt to eliminate or
modify everything the author had written which in any way tended
to detract from the view of Mrs. Eddy which has become official
in Christian Science. This view is the end result of a gradual process
which, if it does not reach the point of deification—a charge that
would be indignantly disputed by present leadership—does, nevertheless, seem definitely to look in that direction. At any rate, there
is a distinct indication that Mrs. Eddy must be carefully guarded
against appearing to have manifested any of those very human
weaknesses and failings to which most of us are subject. She must
be shown to have been utterly original in her thought, never to have
been indebted to other humans for the ideas which her system
included. There must be, even in her childhood or youth, nothing
not fitting in with what she was later to become in official eyes.

Mrs. Studdert-Kennedy's answer, when she had studied the alterations in her husband's book, was forthright and emphatic. She had made a thorough and detailed examination of the marked-up proofs, and she found the whole thing unacceptable. In a letter dated March 1, 1946, she set forth her objections precisely and in great detail.

She had been surprised, in view of Huntington's repeated assertions that the revisions were slight, to discover the wholesale editing to which the book had been abandoned. She had urged her husband shortly before his last illness to reread the book to see if any further changes were desirable or possible, and his reply—his last statement concerning the book—was that there was no point in rereading it, as he was unwilling to make any further changes in it. He had said the same thing to his secretary. She felt that he had fulfilled his end of the contract by producing a noncontroversial book, of which Huntington himself had written that he had enjoyed his reading of the work all the way through, and after finishing it found that Studdert-Kennedy had achieved what they both had set out to do.

She could never accede to any revision of her late husband's work which did not carry out what she knew to be his intention and wish, and she had worked with him on it so constantly that she did not hesitate to accept the legal responsibility and moral obligation to protect and promote his major work as he would want it.

She would gladly accept, as he had done, corrections as to matters of historical accuracy—and exceedingly few had these proved to be. But the deletion of sections which her husband had considered basic to his theme, such as the one on the Woodbury affair, she could not allow. Studdert-Kennedy had written concerning Judge Smith's objections to the Quimby case, the Arens case, and the Woodbury episode: "It is just these points that have been exploited *ad nauseam* by Mrs. Eddy's detractors, and I want once and for all to bring them right out into the open, with nothing at all withheld, and show exactly what they amounted to."

Any modification of the original affecting the color or atmosphere would be quite out of the question, and she regretted to observe that the revision had this very effect.

While her husband had been willing to co-operate with the Board of Directors, he had not sought either their direct or their tacit endorsement. Aside from the fact that the Board's endorsement of a book carried the implication, for most people, that it was no more than official propaganda, the history of the organization showed that "the Board's approval has never been and never will be secured except where the book is wholly innocuous and ineffective, and so of little interest or sales value."

She pointed out that the public generally was interested in freshly written books, so that every month of delay in publication of the Eddy life operated to its detriment. Also, there was the chance that almost any time someone else might come out with a book on the subject which would detract from her husband's work. Besides this, there was a definite possibility that the writing might be plagiarized, the manuscript having passed through so many hands. Indeed, she had reason to believe that such a movement was already afoot. It seemed necessary, therefore, that the book be released at the earliest possible moment. It was, she said, her fond hope that Huntington would write her within the month that he would publish the book promptly and in the form her husband had clearly intended it to have—the only form which she could possibly permit.

The correspondence ends with a courteous letter from Huntington releasing Mrs. Studdert-Kennedy from any obligation to Putnams under the original contract; apparently he was unwilling to proceed with publication under the terms of her letter.

Of course, *Mrs. Eddy: Her Life, Her Work, Her Place in History*, by Hugh A. Studdert-Kennedy, was published. His widow saw to that. The Farallon Press issued the book in 1947 in exactly the form its author had originally proposed, corrected, and approved prior to his death in 1943. Then what happened?

There are scattered but unmistakable evidences that the membership of the church was warned against the work. Letters from the Board itself are at hand stating that this book is objectionable.

The Publication Committees, who work under Board directives, have released similar statements. A woman who sent an advertisement of the book to the Northern California Committee on Publication received a reply from that official that the book was "not authorized literature," that its author had passed on some years before, that he was not a member of the Mother Church, and that, as stated in the Preface, the book as published had been edited by Arthur Corey, a man who was, he charged, "a disloyal student of Christian Science."

Now, someone had to edit the book. The church authorities themselves had made this imperative by altering the character of the work as a whole and then by declining to stand by their agreement on the source material around which the writing was built. The mutilation of the manuscript by officially inspired excisions and revisions had to be remedied; but this was perhaps not the most urgent need resulting from the Board's actions. At the eleventh hour, the legal department of the Mother Church had raised a formidable barrier to the volume's publication. On December 4, 1946, the General Counsel for the Boston organization issued a stern warning to Mrs. Studdert-Kennedy on behalf of the Board of Directors, the Publishing Society, and the Trustees under Mrs. Eddy's will, notifying her that she would not be permitted to publish any photographs of Mary Baker Eddy on which they might hold copyrights, or any letters or even parts of letters which Mrs. Eddy had written or which had been written for her by her secretaries, and directing her to send written assurance that she would do as she was being told. This letter was supplemented by a telephone call from the Committee on Publication, who made it clear that the prohibition included the Pfister portrait which McKenzie had had made for the frontispiece, since it had been painted from a copyrighted photograph in their possession.

Thus Arthur Corey, as a qualified editor, was obliged to replace the Board-controlled documents with material already in the public domain, hidden away in yellowing newspaper and magazine files, and to authenticate the book from these sources. There were some quotations for which equivalents could not be found, and these he had to throw into indirect discourse so as to convey the information embodied in them without infringing upon the copyrighted form of expression (which, it should be said, is the only thing that can be copyrighted). In a very few cases he modified a phrase in a manner which Mrs. Studdert-Kennedy agreed her husband would gladly have accepted had he known of certain historical data which Corey's research work had uncovered. To carry out Studdert-Kennedy's declared objectives, Corey made three brief additions. These in no way altered the character of the book, but were designed to fortify it and its heroine against undue criticism. One of these was a properly authenticated account of Mrs. Eddy's famous last class; another was a passing commentary on the story of Mary's having heard "voices" as a child; the third was a footnote justifying Mrs. Eddy's well-known recourse to human expedients. The book as published was unquestionably what Studdert-Kennedy would have published, and what Huntington would have published had he not yielded to the Directors of the Christian Science church.

A look at some of the book reviews is illuminating. The *Chicago Tribune* headlined a long and enthusiastic notice "An Objective Appraisal of Mary B. Eddy." The review concluded, "This may not be the last biography of Mrs. Eddy, but it will always remain the definitive one." The contrast between this opinion and that of an advocate of the Board's point of view is striking. W. D. Chandler, writing in the *San Francisco Chronicle*, admitted that the book was eminently fair and wholly sympathetic in its treatment of Mrs. Eddy, but went on to say that it was "unauthorized," and that its author had "deserted" the church and was therefore no longer a "true Christian Scientist," though still "professing" to be one. When indignant readers wrote in to say that the Chandler article was not really a book review but an attack on the late author, Chandler took refuge in the assertion that he did not consider it a criticism to report that a man has "quit a faith he no longer finds satisfying." But is that what Studdert-Kennedy had done? The record seems to prove that he remained a devout follower of Mary Baker Eddy, and certainly he continued his work as a public practitioner of Christian Science to the end of his days. Confronted with this, Chandler insisted his remarks were justified by the fact that Studdert-Kennedy "some twenty-five years ago withdrew from the Church." Aside from the question of whether Chandler's position on that score was tenable, it was asked, how could he have authoritative information on Studdert-Kennedy's resignation from the church unless he was aided in the preparation of his article by Boston officialdom? The fact of the resignation had never been published, nor had the Studdert-Kennedys given it out. Chandler denied the charge of collusion.

The net effect of the *Chronicle* article on the general public was, no doubt, to damn the book with faint praise, while making it anathema in the eyes of church members by the opening statement that "true Christian Scientists will not be interested . . . in this biography." To a correspondent who challenged this Chandler wrote: "Under the rules, as you know, a Church member is not permitted to read any literature pertaining to Science that is 'unauthorized.'" Accused by another correspondent of being an agent of the Boston hierarchy, Chandler wrote that he was not a member of the church—but that he had been studying Christian Science for many years.

Perhaps typical of the book's reception inside the church is what happened at the annual meeting of the McKenzie pupils' Association in 1947. A Mrs. Norcott, who conducted the afternoon session, said that she had been asked to evaluate this biography. She had talked with Mrs. McKenzie at length about it, and she read a statement prepared by Mrs. McKenzie which asserted that her late husband had known and liked Studdert-Kennedy when he was on the *Monitor* and had tried to help him understand Christian Science more clearly. He had corresponded only occasionally with Studdert-Kennedy after the latter went to California. When requested to read the Eddy manuscript and comment upon it, he had agreed to do so. "I also read parts of it," Daisette McKenzie went on, and said she and her husband felt the book would do good providing certain objectionable parts were removed. To such expurgation, the statement continued, Studdert-Kennedy readily assented, after which the book was submitted to Lord Lothian with the assurance that these objectionable passages would be deleted. Therefore the favorable comments by McKenzie and Lord Lothian, now being cited by the publishers, referred only to an expurgated version and not to the book as first drafted or as finally printed. She had been informed on highest authority, Mrs. McKenzie stated, that Arthur Corey had restored the objectionable material and had also inserted passages not in the original. She had recently learned, she confided, that Corey had married Studdert-Kennedy's widow. (Mrs. McKenzie's source for this bit of gossip could very well have been the form letter containing it which was by this time being sent out into the field by the Board of Directors at Boston.) Corey, she understood, was carrying on ostensibly as an independent Christian Scientist, having resigned from the Mother Church.

Following the delivery of this statement, Mrs. Norcott, speaking under the legal immunity usually assumed for "privileged communications," made some entirely personal allegations reflecting upon Corey's character, after which she said: "You can judge by this whether the book should be purchased by any Christian Scientist or read by any."

One wonders whether Mrs. McKenzie remembered either her husband's voluminous and enthusiastic correspondence with Studdert-Kennedy concerning the book from its first draft on; his suggestion that Lord Lothian read it without any mention of modifying it; or her own letters—particularly the one she wrote after Studdert-Kennedy's passing in 1943, reaffirming her esteem for the volume and suggesting that now its author would be enjoying the supreme honor of being personally introduced to Mrs. Eddy by McKenzie on the other side.

In the spring of 1949 negotiations were under way in Hollywood for the filming of Studdert-Kennedy's *Mrs. Eddy.* The correspondence indicates that Olivia de Havilland had once suggested to Studdert-Kennedy that Mrs. Eddy's story would make a dramatic and inspiring picture, and that Jesse L. Lasky, dean of the motion picture industry—who was, with Mrs. Lasky, to go through one of Corey's classes—was seriously considering Corey's script of the book for a major Technicolor production, with Dorothy Arzner

favored as director. Among the stars, certain Christian Scientists
expressed enthusiasm for the leading role, not alone because of the
opportunities it offered for histrionics, but also because a movie
might popularize their Leader everywhere, thus creating a
widespread interest in her teachings.

In her column for the Hearst press, Louella Parsons wrote: "Mary
[Pickford] has wanted to make a picture for a long time. At the
moment is reading 'The Life of Mary Baker Eddy,' and may do it
independently." Several other stars were mentioned as candidates
for the role. Joan Crawford wrote that she was enthusiastic, but
then backed away from playing Mrs. Eddy because she feared it
would bring down a storm of "malicious mental malpractice."

Then came the typical reaction. Danton Walker, in a syndicated
report, said that "the Christian Science Church is perturbed over
the rumor that a movie company wants to film Hugh A. Studdert-
Kennedy's biography of Mrs. Eddy, which is not on the approved
list." In his national column, Erskine Johnson said that Christian
Scientists "assure me the whole idea is without official approval"
and that the project "will have plenty of objections from the
Christian Science Church."

After lengthy consideration of the script, Mary Pickford issued
a public statement to the effect that she had decided not to do the
picture herself, and suggesting that a screen biography of Mrs.
Eddy ought not to be attempted without the blessing of the church.
(*Hollywood Reporter*, April 20, 1949) As Miss Pickford's statements
make front-page news, this could scarcely have displeased Boston
officialdom. But then Miss Pickford went on to lend powerful
impetus to the idea of a cinematic biography of Mrs. Eddy by
declaring: "I feel that such a film would find an excellent reception
on the screens of the world." Official reaction was quickly registered.

In a formal proclamation on June 2, 1949, spokesman James
Vincent said for the Christian Science organization: "While we
agree that mankind would be benefitted by an appreciative understanding of Mrs. Eddy's life, we realize that it would not be possible
rightly to portray her character either in a picture or on the stage."
Furthermore, the statement read, "her Church would not look with

favor on any such undertaking." Notice was thus served on the motion picture industry.

From this account of the effort to remake one book into a work that would be acceptable to the official mind, and when this proved impossible, then to destroy the volume's influence, it is easy to deduce the purpose and method of thought control which the Christian Science church, as at present constituted, attempts to exercise.

A SOMEWHAT SIMILAR CASE is that of Adam H. Dickey's *Memoirs of Mary Baker Eddy*. Dickey was Mrs. Eddy's secretary and a member of her household for several years, and so highly did she regard him that in her final communication with the Board of the Mother Church she opened the way for him to be made a Director, to fill the place left vacant by Ira O. Knapp's passing. This she did but a fortnight before her own death.

Dickey relates that two years previously, on August 25, 1908, she called him to her room. She was lying down on her couch, where she customarily rested and not infrequently napped in the afternoons. Asking Laura Sargent and Calvin Frye to leave the room, she took Dickey's hand in hers and bade him promise that in case of her death he would "write a history" of what had happened in his experience with her and "say" that she was "mentally murdered." He agreed to do so. So intent was she on her purpose that she required him to raise his right hand and swear to fulfil her request—in Dickey's own language, to "write a history of what I have seen and heard from your lips, concerning your life." Later, he asserts, Mrs. Sargent brought him a penciled note from Mrs. Eddy reiterating her statements of a few minutes before.

Years passed before he was able to carry out her request, and he died before his account could be published. In 1927, the year after his death, his widow did have it published, believing that she was fulfilling a sacred trust laid upon her husband by the beloved Leader herself.

In the foreword Dickey asserts in effect that everything included in the book, which was of course only a small part of what he had written down, was authentic, drawn from a record he had made during the period of his residence in Mrs. Eddy's home.

The work was published by the Merrymount Press in Boston, and an English edition carried the imprint of Robert G. Carter, 29 Hogarth Road, Earl's Court, London. Copies were circulated chiefly by Mrs. Dickey among her late husband's pupils.

When the Board of Directors of the Mother Church read the book they at once sent out a letter to every member of the Dickey Association, requesting the surrender of all copies then in circulation. The measure of their success may be seen from the fact that not long ago two copies of the Dickey book brought $650 and $1,000 respectively.

Fortunately for the historian, the book was copyrighted in England and America, and therefore copies were deposited as required by law in the Library of Congress at Washington, D.C., and in the British Museum.

But when John V. Dittemore sought to examine one of the Library of Congress copies, none was available. He was told that one copy had been mislaid and that the other had been taken out by a Christian Scientist congressman, who reported that he had mislaid it. The congressman was persuaded to locate and return his copy, and the other missing copy turned up behind some books in another department of the library. (Swihart, *Since Mrs. Eddy*, pp. 307-8)

A *Journal*-registered practitioner informs me that when he sought to refer to a copy which had been donated by Dittemore to the New York Public Library, he was told that it was not open to public examination. Why? I myself did use a photostatic copy of the book in the Rare Book Department of the Boston Public Library.

The letter of the Board to the members of the Dickey Students' Association is quite revealing as to the motives and methods of the central authority in respect to the control of publication and circulation of literature concerning Mrs. Eddy and/or Christian Science in general. Since permission to quote at length from the document is not forthcoming, only the general sense of the communication can be given here.

The long letter opens with high praise for Dickey's character, his teaching, and his loyalty to Mrs. Eddy. It asserts that Mrs. Eddy frequently admonished her associates to shield her private life from the public gaze, and credits Dickey with having so scrupulously adhered to this admonition as to condemn those who failed to do so. Therefore his long-time colleagues on the Board are inexpressibly astonished that he would put into a book so much that would prove harmful if made public. They declare themselves at a loss to understand how the Adam H. Dickey they knew could "do such a thing."

Mrs. Dickey, the letter goes on, greatly erred in publishing her late husband's work without specific instructions to herself personally from Mrs. Eddy to do so. Even Dickey did not pretend that Mrs. Eddy had authorized him to *publish* a history, but claimed only that she had asked him to *write* it. Furthermore, when Mrs. Eddy had ordered the publication of material designed for Christian Scientists in particular, it had to be handled by the Christian Science Publishing Society; yet no one at headquarters had known anything about this book before it was issued.

The Directors felt it very necessary to suppress the book before it could come to the attention of persons who were hostile or too immature to read it without injury. Mrs. Dickey had co-operated with them by writing each known owner of the book asking that all copies be turned back, and the Board had offered to reimburse her for the expense she had contracted in publishing the volume.

Since some had apparently not understood the necessity for the action of the Directors in the circumstances, the letter continued, they were writing to explain. Some of the students seemed to think that their teacher was under obligation to obey Mrs. Eddy's request; but then other persons had been asked to write her history only to be stopped when Mrs. Eddy read what they were writing. What these other people had written contained nothing that was in any way prejudicial to her, and did not invade her privacy or disclose things told in confidence, as Dickey's book did; yet she had stopped them. In evaluating Mrs. Eddy's request of Dickey, the Board points out that she was at the time "contending with an acute physical claim" and that after she had rallied from it she had never again referred to this episode.

Dickey is charged with having transgressed under the *Manual*, specifically Section 10 of Article XI (forbidding unjust publications) and Section 22 of Article VIII (prohibiting violation of a patient's confidences). It is averred that a book does not have to be false to be unjust, and that the Dickey book is unjust in that it emphasizes Mrs. Eddy's human characteristics while touching but lightly upon her spiritual nature.

The book represented Mrs. Eddy as laboring under difficulties, shrinking under attack, whereas, says the Board, she habitually dwelt in the secret place of the Most High, being without fear in carrying out what she discerned to be her life's mission. Also, little was said in Dickey's narrative of her "transcendent wisdom," her unfailing dependence upon God, and her love for mankind, which lay behind everything that she did for the cause.

While some seasoned metaphysicians might feel a certain gratification with the vivid portrayals of error, and some even believe themselves spurred to further conquest over evil by Mrs. Eddy's "battles with physical disorders," all this was more than offset by the injury which unprepared minds would suffer. Meat for babes is not wholesome. Enemies of the cause would gloat, and even the unbiased section of the public was already drawing damaging conclusions from the book.

The letter contended Dickey would have fulfilled Mrs. Eddy's request had he merely written his history and deposited it in the archives of the Mother Church. It is asserted that a "history" is not of necessity a book, and that to "say" does not necessarily imply publication.

The letter closes with Mrs. Eddy's admonition from page 23 of *Retrospection and Introspection,* that "the human history needs to be revised, and the material record expunged."

Questions arise at many points concerning the letter. Did Mrs. Eddy send everything through the Christian Science Publishing Society? The first edition of her *Christ and Christmas* comes to mind as one of several instances where this was not the case. And, of course, Mrs. Eddy's textbook was always published independently of the Society. Was the fact that others had shown what they had written to Mrs. Eddy quite a parallel? When she asked Dickey to write a history, she had asked him to do so in the event of her death, so she could hardly have contemplated reading it before publication. Was this account of life in the Eddy household only one of trivialities, as the letter also charged? Rather, in comparison with some of the diaries of her companions, Dickey's account seems to be an idealized version of her home life. And, judging from the many testimonies of those close to her, was she always calm, poised, unperturbed, "habitually dwelling in the secret place of the Most High"? The letter itself seems contradictory on this point when it sets forth, earlier, the startling suggestion that Mrs. Eddy's exacting a solemn vow from Dickey to write the history might be regarded as an irresponsible act, since she was under such physical suffering that she did not until some time later regain her "mental poise."

In reimbursing Mrs. Dickey for the costs of publication, the Board of course acquired the copyright and so moved into a position of control over the book and all its material.

It is clear that the attitude of the Board was one of protecting a particular view concerning Mrs. Eddy, the one which they had come to affirm, and which the Dickey disclosures and those of other diarists did not support. Such a view would be hard to maintain in the face of a book like this. Therefore the book had to be withdrawn from circulation, even though Mrs. Eddy herself had apparently wanted Dickey to write of his experiences with her, stating what he had heard from her lips, and though she apparently had no expectation of reading the work herself.

7

Arthur Corey and Others

ARTHUR COREY was an enthusiastic believer in Christian Science. After a youthful career in the theater, he left the stage and entered the world of business as secretary to a high official of the New York Central Railroad. As a Christian Science layman he was a devoted member of Twelfth Church of Christ, Scientist, Chicago. He taught in the Sunday school. He became a member of the church's Board of Directors and was chosen as Chairman of the Board. He filled out an unexpired term as First Reader and was then re-elected to a full three-year term in that post, being proffered the opportunity to serve much longer than the maximum period traditionally permitted Readers, an unusual occurrence in itself. He entered the class of the eminent teacher Bicknell Young, for whom he had the very highest admiration and respect. He had begun to practice healing, at first only as a part-time occupation; but finally he became a full-time practitioner recognized in the *Journal,* and was more than ordinarily successful, soon being in such demand that he could not take all the patients who sought his aid.

Meanwhile Corey was a consistent and faithful student of Christian Science. He met often with other practitioners and discussed their common problems. A small group in Chicago occasionally gathered at luncheon, but this did not last long. The little group broke up when Corey discovered that any free discussion in Christian Science was frowned upon. That this was no mistaken notion on his part has since been evidenced by the Board's condemnation of the Gilbert C. Carpenters for discussing Christian Science in their home with friends and members of their household;

by the challenging of John Doorly's right to talk on the subject at informal gatherings of friends and acquaintances; by a letter from the Boston authorities to a practitioner calling "adverse" the report of an unnamed informer "that meetings or visits are held in your home" and "that you speak to those in the group all evening on class teaching"; and so on.

Corey associated with a number of teachers of Christian Science. Some of them sought him out as practitioner and consultant, and he had letters from such outstanding leaders as Edna Kimball Wait— daughter of the man who was probably the most distinguished teacher in the history of the movement—to the effect that the material he had given aided them in their Class teaching and Association addresses. This industrious trafficking in material, carried on surreptitiously throughout the practitioner and teacher ranks, led him to believe that a great deal in Christian Science was being withheld from the people. How much it would mean if some of the magnificent expressions of the great teachers of the subject could be given to the world! Indeed, in a letter to Edna Kimball Wait Corey said it was in reviewing her correspondence with him about the pricelessness of the material shared that the conviction was born that he should attempt such a book if none of the older, more prominent Christian Scientists—like Mrs. Wait herself—would undertake the task. He felt they were duty-bound to break the conspiracy of silence.

Corey had from the first collected everything he could in his field of study. In his library was all the official literature ever printed, including not only the bound volumes of the *Journals* and *Sentinels*, but Mrs. Eddy's complete works in all their countless revisions, from first editions on down. But in addition there was in existence a considerable mass of material such as Class notes, Association addresses, and unpublished writings of teachers and practitioners, the circulation of which, while not forbidden in the *Manual*, was driven underground by a spreading taboo in the church. Corey knew that in fact a great deal of such material was in circulation among the veterans of the organization, and he made it his business to secure and authenticate as much of this as possible.

This he has continued until at the present time he has literally
thousands upon thousands of typewritten pages of such notes,
lectures, Association addresses, and so on, to say nothing of correspondence, diaries, and reminiscences of the great and near-great
who have played stellar roles in the development of Christian
Science. This he not only collected, but studied, until he had a
remarkable acquaintance with what Christian Science leaders had
thought and were thinking. Out of this rich background he began
to fashion his book.

What form should it take? What more effective form than that of
the traditional Class Instruction? This vital feature of the movement
forms the major channel through which Christian Science is passed
along. It is the door through which nearly all the practitioners go,
and through which those who reach the upper range of official
positions inevitably pass. But according to the *Manual*, Class Instruction within the church organization can only be given by one who
has been through the Normal class. While this is the official course
to be followed, it is no certain guarantee that the one who does
follow it is a more profound student of Christian Science than
another who may never have had that opportunity, for the so-called
Normal instruction differs little if at all from the Primary class
teaching, except in being half as long. The *Manual* limits it to one
week, and it has sometimes been much less. Mrs. Eddy's last class,
which conferred the C.S.B. title on each participant, consumed no
more than six hours altogether. It should be clear, therefore, that this
instruction confers an official right rather than, necessarily, superior
competence to set forth Christian Science.

Clearly, if Corey published his Class Instruction while within the
church, bitter factional disputes would immediately be unleashed
which might very well eclipse the teaching he desired to release to
the world. He of course knew that if he were expelled from the
church in the ensuing controversy, his teaching could then be
discredited as coming from a branded outcast. Its circulation among
Christian Scientists themselves would then be greatly curtailed,
while its impact on the general public, which he also desired to
reach, would be severely lessened, for he would then stand in the

character of an "unfrocked" minister of his church, an unenviable position and one which definitely would not lend force to his teaching.

There was nothing in the *Manual* forbidding a student of Christian Science to write or publish his findings. On the other hand, many statements of Mrs. Eddy's could be cited which definitely seemed to encourage that right. She had deplored anything in the way of an "ecclesiastical monopoly" of Truth (*Science and Health,* p. 141), said that some books based upon her textbook could be useful (*Science and Health,* p. x) and that "a student can write voluminous works on Science without trespassing" (*Retrospection and Introspection,* p. 76), and admonished her followers to "allow each and every one the same rights and privileges that we claim for ourselves" while urging that "Christian students should have their own institutions and, *unmolested,* be governed by divine Love alone in teaching and guiding their students" (*Miscellaneous Writings,* p. 303). Had she not iterated and reiterated that true followers of Christ must "preach the gospel to every living creature"?

This seemed to Corey a charter, releasing him from any teaching restrictions. He therefore resolved to write his book, setting forth what, as an accredited practitioner of the church, he had been teaching for six years. Stepping out of the organization with its publication, he would remove himself from the jurisdiction of a hierarchy which he had come to believe was exercising despotic control over the life and thought of its people and hampering its teachers, endangering thus the very truth that the organization had been created to promote in the world.

The more he wrote, the more convinced he became that the organizational machinery of the church was stifling the free spirit of true Christian Science as Mrs. Eddy had declared it. If it were really a science, he reasoned, it would be universal and not subject to control as someone's private revelation. Truth scientifically arrived at must be accessible to anybody in any age, regardless of sectarian affiliations or organizational membership.

One evening he was talking about the science of Christian Science with a prominent citizen of Chicago, John O'Connell. "That's

logical," said O'Connell, "that's convincing. Why don't you put it
into a book? If you do, I can put you in touch with the man who I
think would be glad to publish it." So it came about that O'Connell,
vice-president of the A. C. McClurg Company, enlisted the interest
of his friend Melville Minton, president of G. P. Putnam's Sons, the
venerable New York publishing house.

Putnams took on the Corey project late in 1943, promising to
keep the matter strictly confidential until the very moment of
publication in order to forestall organized opposition from the
church authorities before the book could be securely launched. In
the end, however, Minton submitted the Corey manuscript to a
member of the Mother Church, who was a trusted employee of the
firm, for judgment. The verdict was of course adverse. While an
unfavorable reaction was expected, Putnams wrote, they could not
ignore the fact that "probably a large majority of Scientists will
accept for themselves the official attitude of the heads of the Mother
Church." This, they recognized, would mean a concerted campaign
against booksellers everywhere who dared handle the book, stirring
up ill-will against Putnams throughout the trade. Thus, after a
full year of delay Corey found himself in search of another publisher.

All this is important in view of the claims made later that the
book was not written while its author was a member in good standing and an accredited practitioner in the church. The Putnam
correspondence bears the dates of November 27, 1943, to November 16, 1944. Corey resigned from the church publicly on
February 28, 1945.

With the Putnam door closed, Corey recalled that a book
entitled *Christian Science and Organized Religion* had been put
out by a California firm, the Farallon Press. All he knew about
Farallon was that here was a publisher who was not even indirectly
controlled by the Christian Science organization. He resolved to
make a quick trip to San Francisco. There, on February 17, 1945,
he learned that the Farallon Press was a nonprofit enterprise which
had been established in 1930 by the Studdert-Kennedys as an outlet
for independent Christian Science literature. Buying into the firm,
he joined with Mrs. Studdert-Kennedy in an agreement to publish

his manuscript, he to pay the costs of publication out of his own pocket, with all returns from the sale of the book to be retained by Farallon in support of its public service activities.

Corey returned immediately to Chicago by plane. Eleven days later, at the conclusion of the Wednesday evening meeting, which he as Reader conducted, he read his resignation to a surprised congregation, a prudent move to preclude any misunderstanding or misrepresentation of his position. He was a Christian Scientist still, but now able to speak and write independently without legitimate interference from what he called "the Boston dictatorship."

Christian Science Class Instruction was published in September, 1945. But even before it was off the press, church opposition was marshaled against it. The first attack was based on a statement Corey made in his Preface naming the sources upon which—in addition, of course, to the official literature—his book depended. The names were ones to conjure with in Christian Science, most of them honored teachers and practitioners who either were or had been in perfectly good standing in the church. Indeed, only two out of the long list, Herbert W. Eustace and John W. Doorly, had been expelled from the church. What shocked Christian Science officialdom was Corey's announcement that he had "transcriptions of the private teachings" of these people in the form of full Class notes, Association papers, and so forth. He even went so far as to specify, for example, the notes of Bicknell Young in his Normal classes of 1910 and 1937, as well as in his Primary classes from 1914 to 1936, together with twenty-eight of his Association addresses, 1910-1937; Primary and Normal classes of Edward Kimball; and even those of Mrs. Eddy herself. This meant, of course, that he had not been limited by tradition to the outlook of just one teacher but had enjoyed the approaches of many, with the advantage of being able to study them at his leisure; moreover, it meant that he had had the benefit of the Normal class work, and that from more than one of the foremost teachers. Also listed were memoirs and diary records of more than a score of persons who had lived in Mrs. Eddy's household, as well as numerous letters of Mrs. Eddy and her unpublished books and articles.

174 CHRISTIAN SCIENCE TODAY

At once—before the book was published—those people named who were still under the jurisdiction of the church began to write in, warning Corey of dire consequences if he dared to publish any of this material. The arrival of these letters before the publication of the book, in fact even before the book had been announced, raises the interesting question of how these people knew their names were in the Preface. The sure answer may never be known, but it cannot be overlooked that Putnams, in admitted violation of their pledge, had shown the manuscript to a Christian Science church member before they returned it to its author. It is significant that people all over this country and in Europe began at the same moment to write in about it.

As early as May 24, 1945, lawyers of the heirs of Bicknell Young notified Corey that they were informed he was about to publish a book containing material by Bicknell Young, and in a later letter to him declared that if "his writings are used in any manner you will be held accountable."

In a long telegram Blanche Hersey Hogue said, "I protest that this is wholly unauthorized." In a subsequent letter she declared, "Whether or not anything which may have been presented to you claims to be an accurate transcript of my teaching, I would repudiate it." She added that she would not consider publishing anything "except through the regular publications of our Church organization." Mrs. Hogue immediately afterward wrote an article in defense of this position for the *Sentinel* (XLVII, 1961-63).

Another teacher, Margaret Laird, wrote: "I am herewith respectfully notifying you not to proceed with any such unauthorized publication." In evaluating these objections, to determine whether they were independent or done at the instigation of Boston, collateral evidence must be considered. In Mrs. Laird's case, one of her associates wrote to Mr. Corey, in a letter typical of several from other Laird patients and pupils, that Mrs. Laird was eager to know about the response to the book, since if it was selling well it would be encouraging to thinkers like herself, even if she were not at the moment prepared to take the same step. She had had many inquiries from her students as to what she thought of the Corey book, and her invariable response was that "there isn't anything in it that is not absolute Science." When one student characterized the book as rubbish, Mrs. Laird had told him: "If you call that rubbish, then all that Bicknell Young or Edward Kimball or I wrote is rubbish." (Irma Betts, letter of November 24, 1945) Margaret Laird later wrote Arthur Corey concerning the prospects of publishing her own writings.

Still another, Mrs. Albert Field Gilmore, wrote to protest the use of her late husband's name. Her objection, so she said, was based upon the unauthorized use of Dr. Gilmore's name in company with persons who were no longer identified with the Mother Church. Margaret Murney Glenn Matters wrote that her teaching of Christian Science was her "exclusive personal and private property" and that she forbade not only any and all quotation, but any implication therefrom, and reference thereto. Hendrick J. De Lange wrote tersely that he strongly protested, and that he would "reserve all rights for legal action if this might be necessary."

The very same day that Lucia Coulson sent her protest from England, Kate Buck wrote from Boston that the book had been reported to her. Had Miss Coulson been cabled? It seems likely that Mrs. Buck was telephoned, for certain errors in her letter were the kind that might arise out of a poor connection—as when she addressed her letter to "Martha Corey" instead of Arthur Corey, and in care of "The Maryland Press" instead of the Farallon Press.

Simultaneously, Mrs. George Shaw Cook protested "against the implication that notes of his [her husband's] class teaching in Christian Science constitute any part of the basis or of the substance matter of the book." Corey wondered how Mr. Cook's widow could judge this matter when the book was not yet off the press. In answer he said to her that "people who have written on Christian Science without giving full credit to those from whose teachings they have benefitted have invariably been accused of plagiarism and ingratitude."

When his old friend Edna Kimball Wait felt called upon to put herself on record that she did not consent to the publication of her father's or her own teaching, Corey wrote her that he was glad to

see that her son Budd, who lived with her, had ordered a copy of
the book. He felt sure she would find it interesting and really
worth while, in view of their previous exchanges, but he hardly
expected her to put her approval in writing since that would be
"jeopardizing your standing in the organization." He added that his
manuscript had been checked by the finest legal talent so that no
question could arise later "to mar the joy of the work."

As all these letters and telegrams referred to an unannounced
book, as they had so much in common, and as they all came at the
same time, Corey was convinced that they were not written
spontaneously, but under orders from Boston.

Back in March, when Corey had written Gilbert C. Carpenter,
Jr., that the book was in preparation, Carpenter had said: "I believe
the time has come when the withholding of things is to be over,"
and "I look forward to the day when the mere act of printing or
publishing a book will not be regarded as a crime." Later Carpenter
was to write that when the Board called him on the carpet in
Boston, he had been accused by the Directors of collaborating on
the as-yet-unpublished book. When he denied this, they told him
Corey's work improperly quoted him at length, and directed him
to "investigate." When finally one of the first copies off the press
was dispatched to him and he had an opportunity to examine the
text in full, he wrote the author: "Well, the Board's statement was
not true, was it?"

As early as March 24, 1945, Arthur Perrow, Illinois Committee
on Publication, had extended a luncheon invitation to Corey and
it had been declined, as Corey wanted all commitments on both
sides to be in writing. About this invitation Perrow wrote Corey
on July 3 that "my original purpose was to reason together as two
Christian Scientists who love our Cause," but that now he simply
wanted to serve notice that the Mother Church possessed exclusive
literary rights not only in the published material, but in the letters,
statements, etc., of Mrs. Eddy and her secretaries as well. Corey
was to understand, furthermore, that all publishing rights on the
letters and lectures by teachers of Christian Science were the
property of those persons or their heirs.

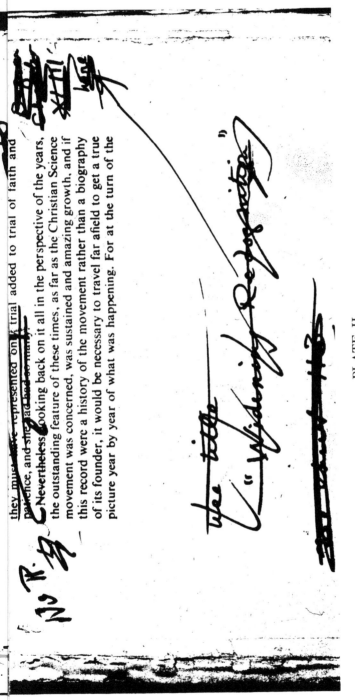

PLATE II

Typical galley sheet of Studdert-Kennedy's *Mrs. Eddy* showing the changes made by Mrs. Flower.

In his answer Corey told of discovering that his financial status had been recently investigated "to determine, no doubt, whether I would be in a position to fight a law suit," and that he had received a thinly veiled threat from a law firm, later admittedly representing the Mother Church.

The Northern California Committee on Publication, James Vincent, came to the San Francisco office of the Farallon Press on August 23 in search of Corey. He telephoned again on August 27 and also on the 28th, but ceased calling when he was told he would have to write a letter stipulating the purpose of his requested conference. No letter came.

On October 4, 1945, a professional process server called at the Farallon office to serve what he called an "injunction" on Corey. When the office secretary declined to furnish Corey's home address she was threatened with legal action. A paper had been served on Mrs. Studdert-Kennedy on October 1, when the process server told her, facetiously perhaps, that she would be sued for a million dollars. Even the printer was threatened.

The so-called injunction read in part:

Please take notice that the letter annexed hereto is intended as and is a prohibition of the publication of any actual or purported class teaching and/or addresses of the complainant, either by quotation, paraphrase, incorporation by reference, implication or otherwise, and also a prohibition of the use of the complainant's name in connection with the publication of any book relative to Christian Science class instruction . . .

It is difficult to escape the conclusion that this paper, couched in the language of the court rather than that merely of a private attorney, and served by a regular process server, was meant to intimidate the recipients. Needless to say, it had no such effect.

The book was published in September, 1945, and at once it had a warm reception everywhere—except in Christian Science official circles. It was enthusiastically read and not infrequently recommended by such eminent Christian Scientists as Peter V. Ross and John W. Doorly, as well as by certain leading members of the Mother Church whose names must be withheld here because they are still active in high church circles. Gilbert C. Carpenter, Jr., wrote on October 16: "It is splendidly written and would convince anyone that you are a thorough scholar . . . I know that your prayer is that it do good, not harm, [and] shall be pleased to hear of its fruits." The sustained popularity of the book among Scientists is reflected in a letter from William Lyman Johnson, dated January 17, 1947, reporting that Colonel Johnson (promotion manager of the *Christian Science Monitor*) "told me last evening that the Corey book is having a large sale." By 1957 the book had reached its nineteenth edition, with increasing circulation on every continent of the globe.

To be sure, there were difficulties in getting even the normal amount of publicity for the volume. Editors who reviewed it were assailed through organized letter-writing campaigns. Advertisements in the newspapers were promptly offset by denunciatory letters, signed imposingly "Christian Science Committee on Publication," which were printed without charge in the same papers following the paid announcement of the publishers. *Time* thought it would make a good item and, according to a letter from one of *Time's* executives, a story was set up ready to run—but it was killed at the last moment because of pressures that can only be guessed at. In deference to emissaries from the church, some newspapers insisted upon emasculating revisions in the advertising copy. When a San Francisco daily held up the initial announcement of the book, the agency handling the Farallon account reported that never had such pressure been brought to bear against an advertisement in this particular paper. Certain prominent merchants had threatened the withdrawal of valuable advertising. When it was suggested that there was a connection between the Farallon Press and the great Hale Department Stores, also heavy advertisers (Mrs. Studdert-Kennedy's father was the founder of that chain), the ad was scheduled and run.

Curiously enough, the *Christian Herald*, which might have been thought of as free from external influence, especially from a church organization, refused to advertise the book, remarking that it would bring a storm of criticism. They had been running a series of advertisements, they wrote, for the *Christian Science Monitor*.

Solicited by Radio Station KFRC, the Farallon Press agreed to buy time for spot announcements—only to be confronted with an eleventh-hour cancellation. The station management had been warned that the Corey book was "controversial." And anyway, they now said, they had a rule against religious books. KFRC, they added, was regularly broadcasting a program for the Christian Science people, whose contract stipulated that no broadcast of material relating in any way to their interests could precede or follow their prográm on the air.

When Farallon complained to Howard Mayer, its public relations counsel, that an organized conspiracy was afoot which ought to be exposed in the public press, Mayer wrote on October 18, 1945, that he had talked with some of the editors in Chicago and that they did not feel they wanted to incur the pressures which they knew would be exerted against them if they should notice the book. "The *Chicago Tribune*," he wrote, "has standing orders to print nothing about Christian Science, simply to escape the nuisance of which they were the victim every time they did so in the past." The essential issue being that of freedom of speech, he thought the religions ought to lead a fight for freedom of expression, since freedom of worship is irretrievably tied in with freedom of speech; but instead religion was here an obstacle. "Regrettably there are those who have so successfully exploited their faiths that there is little hope of accomplishing anything in this direction." When the newspapers and churches had so much at stake, why could not Farallon find enough sympathy and support to spearhead the crusade itself? "I doubt that you are ready to carry the load for such a fight," observed Mayer. Mobilized letter-writers all over the country could create the illusion of vast numerical power, and editors naturally shy away from anything which threatens to stir up religious controversy.

The book did get some publicity. Excellent reviews appeared in a number of newspapers and magazines. A great many Christian Science practitioners and teachers bought copies, and cautious recommendations spread downward through the church ranks. The organized opposition did slow down the sales, but it by no means stopped them.

Naturally inquiries came to the church authorities. One member, for example, wrote the Board of Directors at Boston to ask, specifically and solely, whether the Corey book was correct or incorrect in its doctrine. The Board's answer stated that the book in question was not authorized, nor did it have the sanction and approval of the Directors; that its author was no longer a member of the Mother Church or of a branch church, having withdrawn his membership in both; and that "neither is he advertised or approved as a Christian Science practitioner."

The recipient of the letter sent it to Corey with the statement that it was no answer to her question, and that, since she made her inquiry in all good faith, the Board's evasiveness only served to disillusion her with the church.

To an outsider the Board's letter does not seem inflammatory, but thought throughout the field was apparently prepared to ignite at the official touch. A typical episode: one Rae Wentworth, having received an identical letter from the Board, dispatched a warning against Corey to the proprietor of an inn at Saratoga, California—who, incidentally, was not a member of the church. Under date of October 4, 1945, Mrs. Wentworth wrote she had heard that the inn had had as one of its guests a few weeks previously a man by the name of Arthur Corey, who no doubt *posed* as a Christian Scientist. Because they were apt to be preyed upon if they were not alert, she said, she was quoting from a letter received from the Board of Directors in Boston, so that the proprietor would not be fooled by this man.

On November 9, 1945, the Board itself wrote to Corey, having the letter delivered by an attorney. In this letter the Directors raised no specific objection to the content of the teaching in the book, beyond making the oft-used charge that Mrs. Eddy is quoted inaccurately and claiming that this results in a misrepresentation. They did not, however, offer to supply correct quotations.

Their main objection seems to have been the publisher's blurb on the book jacket. (This had been prepared by Farallon's advertising agency and, since previous books on Christian Science had been effectually discredited by attacks on their authors as uninformed outsiders on the one hand, or as outcasts on the other, the agency felt it important to make Corey's background clear.) The book had been described as the first publication of its kind "authorized by a duly accredited practitioner while in good standing with the Church." The blurb told how Corey had been certified in the *Journal* registry for five (actually six) years, and explained that he had written the book while First Reader in a major metropolitan church. While this was entirely true, the Directors expressed the fear that it would lead to the impression that Arthur Corey was *still* a practitioner enjoying the certification of the Boston authorities. The Preface, admittedly, pointed out that Corey had severed his connections with the church organization and withdrawn his advertisement from the *Journal*, but the Board felt that "in a spirit of fairness and truthfulness" the offending jackets should all be destroyed.

In view of the many letters that came in from various places which were apparently inspired by a common source, and in view of the efforts being made to hamper the circulation of the book and to discredit its author, it is not surprising that Corey regarded the Board, whether rightly or wrongly, as the instigator of most of the opposition and was moved to a vigorous reply.

Declaring their letter a valuable document in the history of ecclesiasticism, Corey upbraided the Directors for attempting to interfere with the freedom of speech, press, religion, and trade guaranteed by the United States Constitution. "So long as you do exercise autocratic powers," he wrote, "the place for independent thinkers is obviously outside your organization, as proven by your disciplining of Peter V. Ross, Margaret Laird, the Gilbert Carpenters, John Doorly, et al., and by my withdrawal ahead of the witch-hunt which might have been directed against the possessor of frankness and initiative." Corey suggested that the Board of Directors should, "in a spirit of fairness and truthfulness," begin housecleaning at home by correcting the form letter about him that they were sending out into the field—a letter which, he charged, was deliberately misleading.

The Committees on Publication throughout the country swung

into action. Gilbert Carpenter, Jr., observed: "If you wanted to stir
things, believe me, feller, you have! Committees on Publication all
over the land are on a hot griddle over it. And I'll bet that makes
you smile as it does me. Our Committee on Publication announced
in public meeting that The Mother Church was going to sue the
Farallon Press. I have my doubts!"

William D. Kilpatrick, then Manager of Committees on Publication in Boston (under whom all state and local committees serve),
went out to Chicago and addressed a city-wide meeting of Christian
Scientists which filled Orchestra Hall to overflowing. It was made
up wholly of church Scientists, for admission was by card only. The
speech was called "Church Unity," but the first half was devoted
largely to the Corey book, containing three announcements of
the title and mentioning the Farallon Press several times. One
admirer of Corey telegraphed him after the meeting: "Your book
received great recognition and you got a million dollars worth of
free advertising here tonight." Another observed that probably
nine-tenths of the people present had never heard of Arthur Corey
or his book until then. Now they knew about both.

A letter from the manager of a downtown Chicago bookstore—
he was not a Christian Scientist at the time but from the reading
of Corey's book he has since become one—affords an interesting light
upon the outcome of Kilpatrick's attempt to stop the book. A woman
had written in to say that she had received a card from the bookshop
advertising *Christian Science Class Instruction,* but that Christian
Scientists would not be interested in "that book" because—and she
recited what has already been quoted as having been sent out by
the Board of Directors. To this the bookseller replied from his home
address in the capacity of a private individual, not as a businessman.
He thanked the woman for her letter, adding that the fact she had
signed her name to it placed her above the average run of Christian
Scientists, for they usually hid behind anonymity. He said that all
their letters contained the same stereotyped phrases, but her letter
was refreshing because at least it gave him a chance to present some
facts. As to her statement that Christian Scientists would not be
interested in the book, he wrote that if she cared to stop in at the

store he would be happy to show her a list of Christian Scientists who had not been ashamed to sign their names to orders for the book, and most of them were practitioners whose names were in the *Journal*.

He went on to say that the Kilpatrick meeting had been open only to Christian Science church members and the doors had been guarded, so that none but the faithful had been at the meeting; yet the next day every bookseller in the Loop had been swamped with requests for the book. Before Kilpatrick's address, only one other store besides his own had carried the book; now almost all the large bookstores were planning to stock it. And all this was the result of telling a large group that the book was anathema.

As for the remainder of her objections, he pointed out that they were doctrinal and did not concern him as a bookseller, but just in the interest of free discussion he would like to record his own opinion. The book might not be approved by the Board of Directors, but didn't she think it was high time that a group of people using the designation *Science* in their official name should measure things for themselves, using the infallible yardstick of Principle, rather than abdicating their right in favor of a human Board of Directors? He then cited Mrs. Eddy's statement that books based upon her book are useful, pointing out that, regardless of what the Board might say about it, Corey's book was indisputably based on Mrs. Eddy's textbook and would enrich anyone who read it. Mrs. Eddy, he said, did not prohibit writing on Christian Science, but, on the contrary, specifically suggested it.

As to her next objection, that Corey was not a Christian Scientist, he could only wonder how one who had been a practitioner, recognized officially in the *Journal* for so long, and Reader in his local church while the book was being written, could be called anything other than a Christian Scientist—even though he had, as he pointed out in the Preface, resigned from the church organization. And as for her objection that "the publication of Class Instruction is a sacred privilege not to be trespassed," perhaps Corey only took seriously the injunction of the Wayshower, "Go forth and preach the gospel to every living creature."

He would be willing to guarantee that if she would read the

book it would make her a more ardent and practical Scientist. Also he would be glad to have her show his letter to anyone she saw fit, including representatives of the Boston hierarchy. (Letter of Richard Booker to Mrs. Marie D. Hidding, October 22, 1945)

The same bookseller wrote direct to Corey relating some interesting episodes having to do with the book. In a letter dated November 15, 1945, he commented:

C.A. came marching in last week and said, "Give me a copy of the Corey book." I said to myself, "Oh-oh!" She looked rather forceful and I thought she would give me a good song and dance. She said: "I understand there is some controversy over the book." I said, "That is so." She said: "I have been a Scientist for twenty-five years, and no Board of Directors is going to tell me what to read. My name is C.A. in case anyone asks you." And she walked out.

Mr. C.D. bought a copy for himself and also one for Mrs. L.W. Mr. D. is a man who thinks for himself and would be part of the backbone of the movement for intellectual independence in the Church.

Staff Sergeant D.R.D. got two copies and said he would have to read his copy under the bed, like he used to read *Diamond Dick* in his youth, because his mother is "an old Churcher from away back."

Some imposing looking duchess dropped in to take a look and was much intrigued with the book, and said she would pick up a copy in San Francisco, her destination on her present trip, so if she comes in you will know her. She will probably fall down a manhole on the way!

In an earlier letter, dated October 15, 1945, this Chicago dealer had written:

A few minutes ago we had a knock-down drag-out fight, almost. A gentleman (I say it advisedly) came into the store and asked how the book was selling. I said, "Very well, thank you." He said: "Well, you won't sell any more. We are getting an injunction against Corey. Everything in the book was stolen." I told him I was well aware of the difficulties of the Church. He informed me: "You had better stop selling the book if you know what is good for you." I asked him for his card. He refused to give it to me. I asked for his name, which he also refused. I told him that we could not recognize anonymous complaints. "Good day, Sir." He was so mad that he shook all over.

We have received a number of anonymous calls, mostly from ladies with cracked voices, beginning: "I am an accredited practitioner of Christian Science," and threatening dire results if we don't stop advertising the book. Practically all the complaints tack on the threat that Christian Scientists will all stop trading with our store.

On the other side of the picture, several practitioners have openly praised the book. They said it would help them a great deal.

We find that two classes of people are buying the book: the general public (not members of the Church) and practitioners. The average member won't touch it without gloves. They are terribly curious, and come in and ask questions, but they don't buy. I have learned to tell the practitioners. They will not call the book by its title.

I put a display of your book in the window flanked on one side by *It's a Free Country* by Ben Ames Williams and on the other side by *The World the Flesh and Father Smith.*

A typical boycott threat, emanating from a *Journal*-registered practitioner, contained this: "It is our opinion that you are rendering yourself a real disservice in promoting the book. I hardly think the general run of Christian Scientists—and you no doubt have some among your clientele—would patronize *for other items* a bookstore handling this particular book."

It must have been evident to the authorities that Kilpatrick's speech in Orchestra Hall had backfired, serving rather to accelerate than to stop the sale of the book. Although the Chicago date was but the beginning of an extended speaking tour, Kilpatrick thereafter deleted the title and author's name from his talks, attacking the book by implication instead.

From various parts of the country came reports of difficulty in getting the book sold in bookstores. An order for a copy, with check enclosed, came from a man in Long Island City, with this note: "I could not get Macy's even to order the book. How about it?"

A letter came to Corey from a stranger in Portland, Oregon, saying that she had gone into the book section of the leading department store there, Meyer & Frank, found on the shelf a copy of *Christian Science Class Instruction,* and alongside it a copy of Studdert-Kennedy's life of Mrs. Eddy, which she purchased. Not having sufficient cash in her purse at the moment, she did not buy *Class Instruction* but returned to the store for it a little later. A clerk told her she thought the books had been removed to a back room and called the department head. He hastened to explain that "unfortu-

nately and quite by mistake" the Corey and Studdert-Kennedy books
had been put on display, but that they were "unauthorized" and as
quickly as this had been called to their attention the books had been
removed. She asked if she might have a copy, but the clerk replied
that it was very doubtful if she could, and recommended instead
Edward Kimball's *Articles and Lectures*, the volume published by
Kimball's daughter and "recognized as correct." The customer
replied that she already had Kimball's work, and so would try
another store for Corey. But, she wrote, "she [the clerk] exultantly
told me that I wouldn't find one anywhere in the city, and I didn't,
though I went from store to store. No one apparently knew anything
about the book. I felt stunned, as I couldn't believe fine books could
be banned in this autocratic way." She concluded: "My purpose in
writing is to let you know how difficult it is to reach the people of
this section, although I am sure many would be as grateful as I am
to have your very fine book."

If there were no more examples than these, one might think the
banning was only a local affair; but reports of like cases have come
from every part of the country and continue unabated to the present
day. A personal friend of the writer happened to be in an Evanston,
Illinois bookstore when a man came in and demanded that the
bookseller remove Corey's work from his shelves. This was in 1950,
five years after the book was first published.

But there is still another angle to the story. Reports show that
some have been dissuaded from buying the book by the widely
repeated charge that it represents nothing more than a money-
making scheme, which would disqualify it under the *Manual*
requirement that "the spirit in which the writer has written his
literature shall be definitely considered." It is a generally known
fact that the Farallon facility has always been a philanthropic
activity, carried on at great personal expense to its sponsors ever
since its inception in 1930. Now the Farallon Foundation, it operates
as a religious-educational public service under the stringent nonprofit corporation law of California. An affidavit from Gottenberg &
McDowell, San Jose's leading firm of certified public accountants,
shows that Corey has never been paid a cent from the returns on the

world-wide sale of his *Christian Science Class Instruction,* all monies being retained by Farallon for the support and extension of its work.

Corey turned his book over to Farallon without remuneration, as his desire was to get it read. Gift copies were sent to a large number of public libraries throughout the country and abroad. Here too resistance has been experienced. Most of the libraries accepted the gift with thanks, placing it on their open shelves. But that was not the end of it. Local Committees swung into action to see to it that if possible the book was removed. Where they could not bring about its removal, they sought to have it relegated to closed shelves, or at least stigmatized as "unauthorized."

Occasionally copies of the book have disappeared out of the libraries. In 1955 I learned that the copy in the Northwestern University Library had been surreptitiously removed, and that even the index card had been taken out of the file drawers, a feat which required the withdrawal of the locking rod through the cards. In other instances, copies are mutilated. For example, the page listing the names of the authoritative Christian Scientists whose teachings Corey studied in preparation for his writing was torn out of the circulation copy at the main library in Los Angeles. A member of the Christian Science Society at San Jose State College reported in a letter to Corey that one of their number had recently proposed setting up a committee to keep his book out of circulation by the college library by borrowing it in relays.

Do Scientists act spontaneously in these things, or do they take their lead from Boston? Corey cites numerous articles and bulletins found in the church periodicals which afford some insight into the situation. For example, in the *Christian Science Sentinel* (XXXII, 89) it is stated that, at the instance of a Christian Scientist, an objectionable book concerning Christian Science was removed from the shelves near Mrs. Eddy's writings in the Los Angeles Public Library; also, through the alertness of the Assistant Committee on Publication, an objectionable biography of Mrs. Eddy was removed from the open shelves of the public library in this Assistant's city. Again (*Sentinel,* XXVII, 329), it is reported that an unauthorized work on Christian Science was removed from circulation at the Chicago

Public Library, and that a plan designed to secure the removal of objectionable books from all public libraries is receiving the attention of Assistant Committees on Publication.

A member of the staff of the Boston Public Library wrote the Farallon office that the Corey book had been placed in their Rare Book Department, which means that it was unavailable except under special circumstances. They advised that the matter not be pursued further, since they simply would not place on the shelves a book disapproved by the Mother Church. Letters to the librarian about the situation remain unanswered. This despite the fact that this same institution had on its shelves at the time fifty gift copies from Farallon of Studdert-Kennedy's *Mrs. Eddy*, thirty of which had been donated at the library's own request.

The Kansas City Library has received more than one gift copy, yet the book is not to be found there. Many people have written that they have asked for it, only to be turned away with the cryptic statement that it is not available. Letters to the librarian elicit no response.

The librarian of the Boise Public Library wrote for seven cents postage to return her gift copy to Farallon, stating that she had submitted it to a local Christian Science practitioner who disapproved of it. This is particularly interesting in the light of other correspondence showing that another *Journal*-listed practitioner in Boise was enthusiastically endorsing the Corey volume.

The Jacksonville Library, while accepting the book for its Circulation Department, wrote expressing anxiety over the aggressive activities of the Christian Science Committee on Publication, and asking how the book should be classified to avoid trouble.

Perhaps the Des Moines case is the most outstanding of all. This city's library accepted the gift copy of *Christian Science Class Instruction* from its author's own hand, then wrote at the top of the title-page: "This book is not an authorized Christian Science publication." And in the back cover of the book they glued a statement headed "Explaining a Controversy About This Book." Plate III, opposite page 208, reproduces a photostatic copy of both the title-page and the statement. In the words of the indignant donor of the book, the library was "using a gift copy from the author to circulate among its readers a highly libelous letter from William D. Kilpatrick, chief publicity agent of the Mother Church."

A letter written not by Corey but by the secretary of Farallon to the librarian at Kansas City, on receipt of information that the book had been withdrawn, sets forth clearly the issue involved. After recalling that most libraries had gladly accepted the book, the letter went on to say that naturally its publishers were very much concerned

about the concerted campaign of a small but highly organized minority which is seeking to limit free discussion of religion by suppressing this book from coast to coast. Librarians and booksellers have written us from all over that attempts at intimidation have followed unsuccessful efforts at persuasion. That a religious group right here in the United States of America should attempt to exercise censorship over tax-supported public institutions through extra-legal methods in the wake of a war we have just fought to preserve such institutions inviolate should rouse every public-spirited citizen as well as every publisher to a militant defense of our American principles. We cannot but feel that any effort to control, through edict, harassment or intimidation, the reading matter in a public institution is striking at the very roots of the public library system. A grave responsibility rests upon us all in these critical days of world upheaval, what with our constitutional guarantee of free speech, free press and freedom of religion under attack. (Letter, Farallon Press to librarian of Kansas City Library, December 19, 1945)

It is quite understandable that the Board of Directors were very much perturbed by the release of the Corey book. It removed the veil of secrecy which hung about the whole institution of Class teaching. And it represented a forthright challenge to the hierarchical control which had been built up across the years. The records prove that the book was read by many loyal Christian Scientists who, for the first time, had their eyes opened to what had been going on in the church; and it rendered many of them highly critical of centralized authority. Not a few believed that there was simply no possibility of reform from within, so they withdrew. How many did so there is no way of knowing.

One practitioner in England wrote, under date of March 29, 1947,

thanking Corey for his "splendid book *Christian Science Class
Instruction*." He had been thinking along very much the same lines
for a number of years, and was pleased to have these ideas analyzed
and clarified so intelligently. He was grateful that Corey had had
the moral courage to take his stand and publish his book. He and
his wife had been instrumental in the sale of between twenty and
thirty copies through their recommendation. He had himself just
followed Corey's example and had taken his name out of the
Journal, in which it had been listed for ten years, convinced as he
was that a better sense of freedom could be found. (Letter of
Walter Shaw, Nottingham, England) Another correspondent from
the British Isles told Corey that the Board had ceased its custom
of sending out an individually dictated letter in acknowledging
withdrawal from membership, and was using a form letter.

When, due to importunities from the field, Arthur Corey really
taught a class, and not one but several *Journal*-registered practitioners attended, and when he admitted into one class not just
thirty but a very large number of students, the opposition was
stepped up. Unfortunately for the advocates of centralized authority,
there was no legal means of controlling his activities. He was quite
beyond the jurisdiction of the church, so that there was nothing the
Board could do to him in the way of discipline. There seemed to be
no lack of students desirous of entering his classes. They came from
every state in the Union, from England, Switzerland, even from
Egypt. There was nothing to be done, unless Corey could be
discredited. It would be pleasant to believe that there was no
official sanction for the repeated attempts to bring his name into
disrepute, and that they represented nothing more than the mis-
guided zeal of fanatical members of the church who thought that
their cause was endangered and so lashed out at the offender.

Just before his largest class was to convene in San Francisco,
rumors were spread in the Chicago churches that Corey was dead.
A Miss Adams wrote from Chicago that at least one point of origin
for the rumor was the provocative question being asked of many by
one of the Publication Committee's staff, "Have you heard that
Corey has passed on?" Some friends became very anxious and sent

telegrams and made phone calls to the West Coast to see if it were true. It is difficult to see what end could be served by such rumormongering, unless it would be to discourage enrolments.

An intimate family friend in Chicago, who had known the book was in preparation a year before its publication and had lauded the project after reading the manuscript of the Foreword and the book's outline, was sent an inscribed copy by Corey. This she returned at once unread—after tearing out the inscription. She was not again heard from.

Another friend, who had received an announcement of the Coreys' marriage, sent her benediction. But in the same letter she said she was returning unread the copies of Studdert-Kennedy's *Mrs. Eddy* and Corey's *Class,* which the Coreys had given her some time back while she was at the Farallon office assisting them in their work. She explained that she had just attended her Association meeting in Vancouver, B.C., and was now convinced that the revelation of Truth had to come to each one direct through the Bible and Mrs. Eddy's writings only. She added a postscript saying that she did not mean to seem cold, for she loved them and always would.

Following Corey's first class, the Board of Directors in Boston was apparently furnished the names and addresses of all who attended the course, for those participants who were members of the Mother Church were soon the recipients of letters from the Board. The practitioners among them were reminded that they were in the *Journal* by sufferance of the Directors, and were called upon to explain their behavior. Whether these letters were the regular preliminary to disciplinary action may never be known, for the recipients promptly withdrew from the Board's jurisdiction. In their letters of resignation from Mother Church membership, they repudiated the authoritarian setup of the church as incompatible with science, and declared there was nothing in Mrs. Eddy's writings which precluded their studying with whomever they pleased and as often as they chose. They had found it possible to identify the Board's informant, a member of the class, since one of the students had changed her address and the Board's letter bore the new address known only to one of her classmates. He, of course, did not resign from the church.

Extralegal devices had to be employed to reach those beyond the jurisdiction of the Boston authorities. One case in point is that of a prominent Harrisburg, Pennsylvania practitioner. This veteran Christian Scientist had filled, at one time or another, about every office in the church. She enjoyed perhaps the largest healing practice in her city. But she was among those who resigned after being reported to the Board for attending a class taught by Corey. Under date of January 26, 1948, she reports:

In November I had a call from the telephone company office saying that they had received a letter from the clerk of the local church, asking them to remove my name from the list of Christian Science practitioners in the classified section of the directory. I said I had not authorized them to do that and wished it to remain as it is. I reminded the caller that I had not belonged to the Church when my name was first accepted, and that the telephone company had not required that I be a church member in order to have my name in the list. I told her that if she would consult the legal department of the company I was sure she would learn that there is no law requiring church membership in order to be listed. (Letter of Mrs. Esther Harris Booda)

Perhaps the most significant thing in this whole controversy is that Corey's *teaching* is seldom if ever attacked, but only his *right to teach*, a right to be conferred only by the centralized authorities. The official position is set forth comprehensively in George Channing's article, "Authorized Teaching," which was brought out in the *Sentinel* (XLVII, 1921-25) immediately following the publication of *Christian Science Class Instruction* and was thereafter featured in pamphlet form at all Christian Science reading rooms. Time and again inquirers have been told by reading room librarians that the Channing article is directed at the Corey book, and Channing's published attack upon a reviewer who gave the Corey book favorable notice seems to bear this out. When a letter to the Board challenged the Channing article, the Directors answered that they considered it excellent and believed that it would be very helpful to the field. (Letter to Edward Kramer, St. Louis, January 15, 1946)

"Authorized Teaching," then, is an authoritative pronouncement deserving our attention. In it Channing asserts that no book or paper purporting to give Class Instruction to just anyone who buys or reads it can possibly give Class Instruction that is valid or desirable. Why? If a teacher unauthorized by the church, he explains, even uses the actual words of a church-sponsored teacher's instruction, that would not enable him to teach. Nor does Channing leave it there, as being merely ineffectual. It is a positive menace. He says that any attempt to benefit from instruction by an unauthorized teacher is not only futile but harmful, for the poison of disobedience and disrespect infects the nonconforming seeker and even contaminates the curious who might give it their attention and interest.

This position is reaffirmed from time to time in the church periodicals. In an editorial in the December 10, 1955, *Sentinel*, for example, Helen Wood Bauman declares that writings "purporting to provide class instruction . . . are not worth one moment of our attention [and] if we adopt them as of value, we are departing from 'the order prescribed by supernal grace.'" *Science and Health*, it is asserted, presents an exact science, employing such terminology as is precise and best adapted to the purpose. "When we accept that terminology as it was revealed to Mrs. Eddy and do not attempt to introduce strange terms in our statement of Science, we are guarding our heritage." A cardinal point of Corey's book had been that inability to state the truths of being in other than stereotyped terminology and phraseology showed a lack of understanding of the underlying ideas and their practical application by the individual.

The effect of all this on the field is reflected in letters from people who have received the regular printed announcement of the Corey book. Of the derogatory responses—which, by the way, constitute less than a tenth of one per cent of those received—without exception the condemnations represent emotional explosions rather than reasoned criticisms or calm rejections. Most of the writers assert that they have not even seen the offending book. A San Francisco practitioner wrote: "What a stinkin' mess you are. Shame. You have no power and you know it." A *Journal* listee in the Panama Canal Zone wrote: "Are you selling any? Ha, ha!" Another wrote from Houston,

Texas: "Don't send any more of this vomit into my home." A more conservative writer called it "garbage." A prominent Christian Science teacher in San Francisco simply slashed the printed announcement across its face and mailed it back to the Farallon office.

Impending retribution was suggested by more than a few. An Albuquerque practitioner wrote, "May God help all who have been disobedient to the Manual," and referred Corey to Mrs. Eddy's statement that the disciples who failed their Master were all punished, each one coming to *a violent death*. Another wrote, this one from Los Angeles: "I received a card from you in which you are wishing to make some money off of a book. Dittemore tried to injure our C.S. Church—*He is dead*. God is at the helm of our Church, and in time error is weeded out and vanishes."

Mrs. Edna Howe, sitting on the Lesson Committee in Boston, wrote a Farallon executive (October 1, 1945): "I am really concerned about a book written by a man named Corey ... The money-changing urge, or perhaps more often the temptation to wish to see one's name on book wrappers instead of written in heaven as Jesus recommended, appears to be always with us."

At all levels the same basic attitude can be discerned, and the common weapon employed is that of vilification.

A Florida editor who had never met Corey wrote him:

Can it be possible that you are the skunk and scoundrel and evil egotist you are said to be by a local Christian Science practitioner? "It is an evil book," said she. "Have you read it?" I asked. "No," she answered. "How then can you judge it?" I queried. "I was told all about it in Boston last summer," said she. She added that everybody from Truman and Stalin down to the cop on the corner had sued you or were about to sue you for stealing material. I told her that I was in no position to know what you had swiped, but that it seemed to me you had gone out of your way to give full credit for every line from the outside. "But he had no permission to use that material!" she wailed, "and his motive is wholly wrong!" "How do you know what the man's motive is and was?" I asked, "have you talked with him?" No, she didn't know you, but she had been told, etc., etc.

The editor then ran an essay, "Condemned Without Reading," in one of his magazines. He did not identify the woman, not even as a Christian Scientist, but at once her husband, who is a prominent *Journal*-registered teacher, wrote him a quite libelous letter about Corey. The libels are not worth repeating, but his justification for them is:

It is not the substance of the book to which my wife took exception, for that substance may be excellent. But it is because of the unquestioned dishonesty of the individual who has published the book. To the inspired thought a beautiful musical composition can sound hideous if rendered by a musician whose character is impure. Therefore my wife was perfectly well justified in questioning the purity of his motives. The underlying motive of the book is base.

An interesting aftermath was that fellow-members of the local church, who were unaware of the above exchange, wrote Corey that this teacher showed he was studying the Corey book by incorporating statements from it in his testimonies given at the Wednesday evening services.

A less impassioned expression of the same position comes from an instructor in a state university who is the author of a church-approved book on Christian Science and philosophy. In answer to an inquiry from the writer, he said: "In general Mr. Corey's text is not incorrect, but we object to his attitude." Granting that there might be room for improvement in the Christian Science movement, he said that "a heroism which defies confidential material and legal rights (copyrights) is not the way." (Lest this stand as a libel, it must be noted that Corey violated no copyrights and that he was under no pledges of secrecy.) This Christian Scientist's letter made it plain that the scientific correctness of the Corey book was not an issue, but implied that the book was invalidated by an immorality in its conception. "Any lasting contribution to Christian Science," he wrote pointedly, "must be on a morally sound basis."

This line of vilification reached its zenith in a scurrilous attack on Corey in the public press—an attack which, incidentally, brought about the downfall of its perpetrator. On October 18, 1948, a Berkeley practitioner telephoned two Corey students in Sausalito to say that a disgruntled follower of their teacher was working with the Christian Science Committee on Publication to launch a newspaper

"smear" series against him. Next day she made the same report to
Mr. and Mrs. Corey, who were inclined to disbelief. On December 8,
1948, the gossip columnist "Freddie Francisco" made Corey his
headlined target for the day in his syndicated column.

But the whole thing backfired. Another gossip columnist broke
what *Fortnight* said was a story known to every San Francisco news-
paperman for three years—"that the *Examiner's* 'Freddie Francisco'
in real life had a lengthy criminal record and a most unsavory
reputation around town for his ruthless tactics." *Time* confirmed the
story, adding that Francisco, a man of eight aliases (Preston,
Lawson, Patterson, etc.), had, following the exposé, been dismissed
from the newspapers on the personal order of William Randolph
Hearst. Some wondered if there was any connection between Francisco's attack on Corey and the fact, brought out by Ann H. Lord,
prominent practitioner, that Francisco had attended the Christian
Science Sunday school and that his closest relative was still active
in the church.

In February, 1952, *Christian Science Class Instruction* having
gone through fourteen editions and never having been reviewed
in the *Christian Century,* I dropped a note to the editor inquiring
if he would be interested in a review. He replied that he would.
So I reviewed it objectively as I review many books, saying something about the author, his point of view, and the general nature of
the work, myself taking no position one way or another with respect
to whether the book was a true statement of Christian Science, or
whether Christian Science itself was true.

Most people, I think, would say it was a fair review of the book.
But the Boston authorities were not satisfied with it. Not long afterward I received a letter from the editor saying that he had had a
letter from the Manager of Committees on Publication of the
Mother Church vigorously criticizing the review. If I wished to see
it and write a reply, he would publish both the criticism and the
reply. (I had been told by veteran Christian Scientists that the
strategy of the church was to attack not the author of an offending
book, but the reviewer who gave it publicity; my experience seemed
to bear this out, both on this occasion and on a previous one, when

in 1949 a chapter on Christian Science in my book *These Also Believe* received a favorable newspaper mention, only to have the Committee on Publication charge, in a published letter, that the reviewer gave "incorrect impressions of both Christian Science and its discoverer and founder, Mary Baker Eddy.")

The letter is important in that, being prepared by the highest public relations figure in the Christian Science organization, their official spokesman, it shows the attitude of the church. So I read it and penned what I thought was a suitable reply, and the two letters were published in the issue of May 14, 1952. Incidentally, the response was so spirited that what is called by many "the Braden-Channing Exchange" was reprinted and circulated to the number of ten thousand copies. Letters came from persons all over the world who wanted to express their acceptance of my point of view.

Channing's letter began by taking the time-honored position that a reviewer who had not himself accepted Christian Science could not possibly understand it sufficiently to write about it properly, and I was accused of "egregious mistakes." To this I answered that I did not believe I had been unfair "to the Christian Scientist movement or to Mrs. Eddy, for whom personally I have publicly, on more than one occasion, expressed genuine respect and admiration, while dissenting wholly from her views." As for not knowing what I was talking about, I had made a serious study of the subject, having read transcriptions taken in the church classes of leading teachers, and had "found no deep esoteric teaching there which an ordinarily intelligent person might not comprehend."

"Christian Science classes no more conceal from public gaze the teaching of Christian Science than a college class in higher algebra conceals the facts of higher algebra from the public," wrote Channing. To this I had to point out that Class Instruction "is undeniably secret, whatever the motive for secrecy may be." The claim that nothing is taught in the classes which cannot be found in *Science and Health* was not quite true, although I had found nothing in the class teaching greatly at variance with the teaching contained in this textbook. But until the veil of secrecy is lifted, some suspicion must remain.

Some of Channing's conclusions were based upon false premises, as he put certain of Corey's words into my mouth, although in my review I had stated I was quoting Corey. Again, he declared that "the Christian Science church imposes no 'official ban' on any book. It does not compile or publish any 'index' of 'forbidden books.'" I had made no such charge, I pointed out; but I asked,

will Mr. Channing deny that there has been a widespread attempt to interfere with the circulation of the book in bookstores and in libraries? I could cite numerous cases of where such an attempt was made. Were these simply the result of individual initiative by overenthusiastic Christian Scientists, or were they under the impression that in so doing they were acting in accordance with official policy followed in the well known case of the Dakin book over twenty years ago? If, as I was told by an important spokesman for the church recently in Boston, the policy of repression has been changed, has the field heard about it? I would be glad for evidence to that effect. Can Mr. Channing supply it?

Disputing Corey's contention that the Board practices regimentation, Channing declared that they "recognize the right of every Christian Scientist to act in the light of the teachings of the Bible and Christian Science according to his understanding." I observed that Corey

had been a faithful member of the church for years. How could he have got the idea? Others who have been longtime members held the same belief. As a matter of fact, I have been permitted to see the entire correspondence between the board and some persons who have ventured to differ from the board's members in their interpretation of Christian Science teaching at some points. I would say that I got the definite impression of attempted regimentation by the board. This could be documented if there were space enough to do so.

The church could not be denied the right to organize itself, I said, on a hierarchical, authoritarian basis if it so wishes and its people agree. But

that the board does exercise complete control over what shall be published and what may be said, at least by its officials, local or general, concerning Christian Science, surely no one can deny; and that the board is constantly disciplining persons who refuse to conform to their rules would seem to me not open to doubt, on the basis of what has been told me by one-time Christian Scientists and of certain cases which I have followed in detail through the correspondence between the persons involved and the board. Some of this is available for publication if desired.

Channing asserted that instruction in the subject by anyone outside the jurisdiction and control of the Mother Church authorities "quite understandably is regarded as improper, unethical and unrepresentative of genuine Christian Science." He explained that "the term 'authorized Christian Science literature' is a descriptive phrase used to identify material published in consonance with the Manual of the Mother Church . . . and thus of an authentic nature." It is generally said that the Christian Scientists equate *authorized* with *authentic,* thus by implication branding everything as spurious and fraudulent which does not issue from officialdom. I did not argue the point.

My letter finished with the observation that many Americans felt the democratic principle should operate in the field of religion as elsewhere, as certain of Mrs. Eddy's writings advocated, and such democratically inclined people would likely sympathize with Corey in his declaration of independence.

But I was not to be allowed to have the last word. Channing came back with a letter in the July 30, 1952, issue of the *Christian Century,* charging me with bias, partisanship, and lack of objectivity. One of his statements should have been challenged, but I was away on a world tour at the time. He said: "We regret that the reviewer, *as he himself has acknowledged,* has relied so heavily on prejudiced and hostile sources for his information regarding the Christian Science movement." [Italics mine.] For the record I must say that this simply is not true. In the first place, I made no such "acknowledgment." Secondly, I had traveled all the way to Boston before publishing my review, conferring with the top officials of the Mother Church, *including Channing,* giving them full opportunity to present their side of the story.

AN ILLUSTRATION of the way in which the Christian Science church goes about the suppression of the writings of outsiders is to be seen in the case of Edwin Franden Dakin's *Mrs. Eddy: The Biography of a Virginal Mind.* Dakin was not a Christian Scientist at all, and his book was brought out by Charles Scribner's Sons, New York, one of America's most honored publishing houses. The publisher's statement of the case, entitled *The Blight That Failed,* and Henry Raymond Mussey's monograph *The Christian Science Censor,* done by the *Nation* in 1930, are the chief documentary sources, but these two pamphlets are not easily to be found today.

Dakin wrote his book and sent it to Scribners; the editors read it, liked it, and accepted it for publication. In due course, public announcement was made that it would appear in the autumn of 1929. Shortly after this, the Christian Science Committee on Publication for New York, Orwell Bradley Towne, arranged for an interview with Scribners executives, and at the meeting drew from his pocket a confidential memorandum prepared by Scribners for their staff. In it the sales personnel were informed that the book might prove unacceptable to Christian Scientists, but that it was in no sense an exposé. It was "not written to show up Mrs. Eddy; it aims to be an honest 'life'.... Mrs. Eddy emerges from this book a woman vastly different from the 'Mother Mary' of the Christian Scientists of the 90's, but a personality more compelling than that incredible figure ever could be."

Towne asserted that the memorandum showed the book to be "false" and "unworthy," adding that "it is a very serious matter to offend several million people." (Mussey points out that at the time the total membership of all 1,913 Christian Science churches was reported by the U.S. Census Bureau to be but 202,098.)

Towne then suggested that the manuscript be submitted to his office "so that the reliability of its sources and the accuracy of its data be checked." There was no corresponding offer to allow Dakin to check his facts in the church archives. This was regarded by Scribners as a proposal that they submit to Christian Science censorship, and of course it was not accepted. They were, they told Towne, quite familiar with what happened to the Georgine Milmine biography of Mrs. Eddy, which had been fought bitterly until the plates were acquired and retired by the Christian Scientists; also, they

knew that the memoirs of Adam H. Dickey had been withdrawn
by his widow, under pressure from the Board of Directors, and that
all distributed copies of the book had been subsequently recalled
from circulation.

After the conference, strong pressures were brought to bear upon
Scribners, through letters and otherwise, to prevent the publication
of the Dakin book. For example, Albert E. Lombard, Christian
Science Committee on Publication for Southern California, wrote a
Scribner editor, Henry H. Saylor, suggesting he intervene. Lombard
reminded Saylor of their old school ties—they had gone to college
together—and said he was sure Saylor wanted to see justice done,
Scribners' high standard preserved, and offense spared "a large
number of respected citizens." He remarked that "some years ago
McClure's Magazine suffered serious loss of prestige" for running
"misleading" statements concerning Mrs. Eddy. "If you are in a
position to discuss this subject with the proper person so that it will
receive judicious consideration," he concluded, "the best interests
of both of us may be served."

But in August, 1929, Dakin's *Mrs. Eddy* appeared and was
enthusiastically acclaimed, with few exceptions, by the reviewers.
One disparaging review was that of Studdert-Kennedy in the
San Jose Mercury-Herald, four thousand copies of which were
distributed among active church workers.

No sooner had the book appeared than a concerted attempt was
made to obstruct it. Bookstores and libraries everywhere were visited
by Christian Scientists who protested its circulation. Libraries were
urged not to buy the book, or if they had already done so, to relegate
it to closed shelves. Bookstores were threatened with boycott if they
ventured to exhibit it for sale. Letters abusive in character came to
Scribners from people all over the country.

In answer to editorial criticism of this campaign of intimidation,
Towne declared: "Protests of individual Christian Scientists may not
be properly interpreted as a boycott or as suppression, and reitera-
tion of assertions to the contrary cannot alter that situation. The
protests made in this case have been by individuals." This simply
was not true. Not only did many of the protests come from Christian

Science churches officially, but they were often so timed together and stereotyped in their content and phraseology as to indicate a common source. At one point alone, nine churches under the jurisdiction of the Missouri Committee on Publication threatened Scribners directly and officially. Typically, a Kansas City church notified Scribners that the Church Manual, which "governs every branch throughout the world," enjoined every member against patronizing a publishing house or bookstore that has for sale "obnoxious books." The Dakin work, they said, fell into this category. Their letter added: "We are calling your attention to this, feeling that if you understood the circumstances you would not want to be instrumental in putting out a publication which was not true and might be detrimental to you."

Many booksellers were frightened and asked the privilege of returning the copies they had ordered. So effective was the Christian Scientists' campaign of intimidation that at one time, according to the publishers, 70 per cent of the bookstores had either stopped selling the title at all, or kept it hidden from the public gaze.

But the decision of Scribners to fight back through national advertising eventually bore fruit. One in their series of advertisements, after stating that many booksellers had been intimidated by Christian Scientists to the point where they were afraid any longer to handle the book, continued:

The result is a situation almost incredible in a free country. You may find that your bookseller either will regret his inability to sell you this biography, universally endorsed by the press of the country, or he may produce a copy hidden away under the counter. Some booksellers actually have the courage to display the book. We hope your bookseller is one of these. Throughout some eighty-five years of publishing, we have been able to say of our books "on sale at all booksellers." We regret that in this one instance we must qualify that statement.

The *Saturday Review of Literature*, one of the many periodicals which carried editorials on the subject, said in its December 21, 1929 issue:

If an honest life of Mrs. Eddy is boycotted because a Christian Science committee does not approve of its interpretations, we have a clear case of extra-legal means to bring about a suppression which no principle of criticism can justify. . . . There is an obvious solution to the disagreeable episode which is the cause of this editorial . . . order a copy.

Ultimately mounting public indignation against the Christian Scientists led the Board of Directors in Boston to try to dissociate the church officially from the campaign of intimidation and repression. In their *Sentinel* disavowal they remarked that Christian Scientists had a right to protest against "objectionable books." But they had been misunderstood by outsiders. "Restraint of untempered zeal" would then be a matter of wisdom. Meanwhile, the *Sentinel* was calling attention, without any hint of disapproval, to the successes of their Committees in such endeavors as getting the book removed from public library shelves.

The total effect of the whole effort of the Christian Scientists, whether acting officially or only as individuals, was to make a best seller of a book which might otherwise have been limited by its relatively high price to a modest circulation. It soon became a one-dollar book, published in the "Blue Ribbon Series," and was thus assured a very much larger reading public. On the jacket of this edition appears a yellow streamer on which is printed in bold letters, "The book that could not be suppressed."

AS A SUPPLEMENT to what I have written of other authors' experiences with the Christian Science organization, some account of my own may be useful. I have already mentioned my failure to obtain access to unpublished source materials held by the Mother Church Directors in Boston. While it is true that one member of the Board kindly offered to furnish answers from the archives to such questions as I might address to him in person, any research worker will perceive at once how limited such help must be.

Research is often a process of discovering material about which one does not know enough to inquire. Indeed, additional questions are always arising out of materials the researcher uses, leading him on to further investigation. Also, a research worker supplied answers to submitted questions would not know whether an answer was given him on the basis of *all* the sources, or only selected ones. With the best will in the world, the archivist designated to answer the questions might not have a sufficient knowledge of a question's context to lead him to more than a partial search for the answer. Though the researcher might himself have the utmost confidence in the Christian Science organization, and believe its officials would do everything possible to supply the material relevant to his research, others reading the results might very well wonder whether or not the research worker's confidence was justified.

Thus, while helpful to a certain extent, such co-operation in no way satisfies the careful inquirer after the truth in the area of study. Even so, this limited co-operation was much more satisfactory than the first offer made by an important official of the church—that if I submitted anything I might write concerning Christian Science, they would consult the archives and tell me whether or not it was true. Obviously this was no help at all.

As a writer who has now and then ventured to print something concerning Christian Science, I have been approached again and again either through correspondence or in person by a Committee on Publication, asking me either to retract something I had said about the subject or to modify it in a subsequent edition of the book in question. This approach has always, I must say, been a courteous one—although I cannot say as much for certain letters from such Committees to editors regarding my published comments on Christian Science—and invariably the official involved has offered to supply what he considered source material which would lead me to a change of mind concerning the offending item. Almost always this proffered material has proved to be only the familiar church-approved books already known to all who write on Christian Science. Consequently, it has had no effect upon my thinking. In one case, with the passage of time and additional research I changed my mind about one thing I had written, and have since in a revised edition of the book modified the statement which had been called in question. I have always been willing to lend an ear to all such suggestions and to discuss the matter in person or in writing with the proper officials.

My experience in securing permission to quote copyrighted material owned by the church people has not been a happy one generally. In my recent book, *The Scriptures of Mankind*, I wrote a brief section on *Science and Health* as one of the newer scriptures to appear in modern times. I said nothing about the book that Christian Scientists themselves had not been saying over and over again for a decade. Yet when I sought permission to quote oft-quoted passages from *Science and Health* and publications of the Christian Science Publishing Society, I ran into difficulty.

First I was asked to give quite specifically the context in which I was quoting the various passages. While no other copyright owners had ever made such request, I acquiesced readily enough and furnished the context in each case. In reply I got a letter—after long delay—stating that the authorities could give final permission only when they had seen the page proofs of the book.

Now anyone who is familiar with publishing knows that any changes made in page proofs are very expensive, for if anything is left out or added it may affect a dozen or more pages of composition which precede or follow it. It is therefore unreasonable in the extreme to wait until such a time before being assured of permission.

I remonstrated somewhat to this effect, but without any apparent result. Finally I wrote to the Board of Directors and said to them that I thought their request was unreasonable, that it reflected a distrust first of myself as a scholar, and second of the integrity of a well-known publishing house. I added that unless I had assurance within a specific time that permission would be given, I would simply throw into indirect discourse the material I desired to use and state in a footnote that, for some reason known to themselves, the Christian Science authorities had refused to grant permission to make a direct quotation from their copyrighted material at this point. Within the specified time I received permission to quote.

In connection with this same manuscript there occurred what seemed to me an unwarranted intrusion by the Christian Science church authorities upon my rights as an author, when representatives of the church appeared at my publisher's office and asked that they might have the privilege of reading the portion of my book which related to the desired quotations. This was done without any request to me for permission. That the publishers permitted it I considered a definitely unwarranted procedure and so told them in no uncertain terms. Here was an intrusion of what I regarded as the control of the official Christian Science organization into the office of a private publishing company which was publishing a book by a non–Christian Scientist.

It is understandable that commercial houses which are obliged at least to make a profit on their total output must be careful not to issue books which might bring them too much trouble, ill will, and possible financial loss. Can it be that such publishers are overestimating the power of this particular minority? Certainly the successful sale of a number of books published without the approval of the Christian Science authorities, and indeed bitterly opposed by them, such as Kratzer's edition of the Kimball teachings over a period of forty years, and of Arthur Corey's *Christian Science Class Instruction,* would seem to reinforce this conviction.

But whether understandable or not, the fact is that a surprising measure of control of what is to be published about Christian Science even by the commercial press does seem to be exercised by the church authorities.

8

Controls over Teachers and Branch Churches

CLASS INSTRUCTION is, of course, basically important in the maintenance of the purity of the Christian Science doctrine. To this end restrictions are thrown around classes; teachers are limited to one class per year of not more than thirty students; there is a general refusal to allow note-taking; each student is limited to one teacher only; and controls are exercised over the teachers' Associations of their students. But the most effective control lies in seeing to it that only the right people are chosen to teach, and that those so chosen continue to think in a straight line, conforming to the established rules of procedure laid down for them in the *Manual* as understood and interpreted by the Board of Directors—and, it may also be added, to any additional rules or standardized ways of doing things that come to be accepted by the Board as necessary.

In the Board's dealings with teachers who have in one way or another fallen under its unfavorable judgment, there seems to be a fairly definite pattern of procedure. First comes a report from the field adverse to the teacher. This brings forth a letter of inquiry from the Board to the teacher, with perhaps a warning. Further reports from the field call forth additional correspondence, which may lead to an invitation to the individual involved to appear at a Board meeting in Boston and answer the allegations. It seems that the accused never knows whence the accusation comes and is never allowed to face the accuser. The Board's judgment usually results in a period of probation for the accused, from which he is rarely restored. At the expiration of the probationary period excommunication follows.

One example of the procedure in such cases may be found in the treatment accorded Gilbert C. Carpenter and his son, the late Gilbert C. Carpenter, Jr. More convinced followers of Mrs. Eddy, Christian Scientists more devoted to her person and her cause, would be hard to find. Among all the writings about Mrs. Eddy that have issued from the pens of followers and onetime followers, those of the Carpenters are outstanding for their touchingly appreciative quality. The elder Carpenter was for a year a member of her household in the capacity of secretary. 'He has been a practitioner for nearly sixty years; and the younger Carpenter was long a teacher, a practititioner, Reader in his church, and finally State Committee on Publication for Rhode Island. Yet both the elder Carpenter and the younger Carpenter were disciplined by the church through its Board of Directors.

For the younger Carpenter, being placed upon probation meant of course that he was stigmatized before the entire field by expulsion from the *Journal* registry and forbidden to give Class Instruction unless and until he was reinstated. He had not been reinstated at the time of his early death in the spring of 1952. It also meant that his Association of students was disbanded, and that all those who had gone through Class with him were deprived of their status and privileges as class-taught students, until and unless they were "retaught" by some teacher currently in favor with the Board. The elder Carpenter is at this writing still on probation, neither father nor son having been willing to resign from the church they both loved so much.

Indeed, so loyal were they that they were loath to be mentioned by name in connection with their difficulties, and gave the author no help in his efforts to unravel their story beyond allowing him to visit their home and see their extraordinary collection of books, pamphlets, and other material related to the movement. The younger Carpenter had organized a foundation for the gathering and preservation of materials of historic interest in this field. He had bought a high-ceilinged, sixteen-room Victorian brick house with a spacious garden, and this he was furnishing as far as possible with articles Mrs. Eddy herself had owned. At the time of the author's visit he

had there her dining-room table, a desk, and other objects, together with many exact duplicates of her own furnishings, bric-a-brac, etc. On the top floor he had a collection of books probably unsurpassed by any other collection aside from that of Arthur Corey or that of the Mother Church itself.

There is ample evidence that the Board regarded the Carpenters with grave disapproval before a complaint from the field provided occasion for formal action against them. A teacher in Washington, D.C., brought the charge against the younger Carpenter that he had violated the *Manual* prohibitions against soliciting pupils, and also accused him of going outside his own territory. She charged that he had encroached upon her field by enrolling as pupils in his class certain people whom he had met at a reception given by his sister in the nation's capital. (Actually, all the leading teachers boast enrolment from various parts of the country other than their own— a fact well known in the field.)

Denial of the teacher's specific charges proved of little advantage, since they no more than opened the way for Carpenter's trial on several other charges, some involving his father. The Carpenters had collected, printed, and circulated material relating to Christian Science without authorization from the Board. This, as we have seen, is strictly taboo, and has gotten not a few Christian Scientists into trouble. It was also regarded as a serious offense that the elder Carpenter, aided and abetted by his son, was every day of the year giving a morning talk in his home, to members of his own household and such friends as might join them at times, on various phases of Christian Science. The general plan was for the younger Carpenter or one of the guests to ask the elder Carpenter some question arising from a newly acquired letter or quotation of Mrs. Eddy, before unknown to him, or to take up some passage from the Bible or from Mrs. Eddy's standard works for exploration. Carpenter would comment at length. Every word was taken down by a mechanical system of abbreviations, then transcribed in manuscript form for filing. These comments have run to as many as a million words annually. The practice has been going on for over twenty years. The younger Carpenter believed, as does his father also, that the comments were divinely inspired. But suppose Carpenter's interpretation, given by inspiration, were to differ from that of the Board?

As a matter of fact, the Carpenters did not differ from the Board on many things. Where the Board ever exalts Mrs. Eddy, the Carpenters take second place to none in their exaltation of her. But even this led to an offense, for they carried their exaltation to the point where nothing Mrs. Eddy said or did was seen as without noble purpose. Even the most petty items found in the diaries of some of the members of her household—items that reveal her as a very human, sometimes impatient, exasperated, weary, querulous, fear-ridden person—the elder Carpenter interpreted as charged with high meaning. In *Mary Baker Eddy: Her Spiritual Footsteps*, a large book of some 450 pages, sumptuously printed and bound, the Carpenters take these items up one by one to show the real purpose Mrs. Eddy had in mind in each situation. While admitting that the facts might be harmful if known to mere babes in the faith, they declare that as strong meat they should be known to stalwart, tried Christian Scientists to whom they would be strengthening.

A glance at some of the chapter headings will indicate something of the range of the incidents they seek to explain:

Mr. Stevenson's Haircut as a Text for Spiritual Unfoldment
Explanation of Mrs. Eddy's Changing Her Mind
Mrs. Eddy's Footsteps as above Human Criticism
Mrs. Eddy's Flicking the Whip on Her Students' Efforts
Mrs. Eddy's Rebuke of Student Who Took a Vacation
Explanation of Mrs. Eddy's Statement Concerning Mental Murder
Handling the Weather under Mrs. Eddy's Direction
Mrs. Eddy and Plagiarism
Mrs. Eddy's Wealth
Mrs. Eddy as High Priest and King
Morphine
"My History Is a Holy One"

These are only a few of the 127 chapters, some dealing with several incidents. For example, the chapter "Explanation of Mr. Dickey's Statement Regarding the Furniture" also includes the explanation of the famous "in-case" meals. It seems that the cook often prepared two complete meals at the same time, calling the second one *the in-case meal* because it was to be ready in case Mrs. Eddy didn't like the first and sent it back—as apparently she did often enough to give rise to the custom of preparing a second. Critics learning of this—as they did through some of the members of her household—might think of it as proving that Mrs. Eddy was overparticular about her food, thought Carpenter, and so he sought a "spiritual" explanation of it. She seemed to notice not at all what she was eating at times, he asserted. But she was spiritually very sensitive. While not concerned about the food she was eating, she did require, says Carpenter, "that it be flavored with scientific thinking, cooked with spiritual understanding, and served with a loving consciousness of man's oneness with God," this being only consistent with "the entire purpose of Christian Science, and teaching the students what they had come to her home to learn." (p. 20) Mrs. Eddy wanted only the demonstration of Christian Science in those who served her. Even if the second meal were not a perfect demonstration, its preparation indicated a loving heart desiring to please her and Mrs. Eddy accepted that. If the cook had had more confidence in demonstration in the first place, it would not have been needful for her to prepare a second meal.

In the chapter dealing with the charges of plagiarism which have been so frequently made against Mrs. Eddy, Carpenter does not make any attempt to show that there was no plagiarism. He assumes for a moment that the charges are provable; but this, he reasons, shows no moral lack. And instead of detracting from the greatness of Christian Science and its "Founder and Discoverer," they rather add to it. His argument is this: Mind knows all things. As two persons turn to divine Mind, they are bound to produce utterances that are similar if not identical. These statements and ideas, being revelation, are not the revelator's but God's, and the one who reveals them is entitled to them so long as he gives the credit to God. Otherwise he is guilty of plagiarism from God. Now whatever came to Mary Baker Eddy from God as revelation, she always attributed to God. It was her intention that whatever she signed "Mary Baker Eddy" and published should be attributed to God, her signature meaning "this came from God." In her reading, she came upon many ideas which she recognized as coming from God that were not so credited by the writers. "Could we not think of her," writes Mr. Carpenter, "as appropriating some of those ideas and restoring them to their rightful place, as revelation, or as having God as their Author?" Even if the world would accuse her of plagiarism, actually the offense would lie at the door of the author who published them as his own instead of crediting them to God. (p. 257)

Mrs. Eddy had no need to plagiarize, he insists. She needed no help from anyone else when all she had to do was to open her thought to God as the infinite source of all ideas. "We know," he writes, "that whatever she took from others must have contained flashes of inspiration which had been held to be the invention of man, and she restored such to its rightful place, as belonging wholly to God." (pp. 258-59)

Not many copies of *Mary Baker Eddy: Her Spiritual Footsteps* are in circulation. Besides the two copies in the Library of Congress at Washington, D.C., which had to be deposited there for copyright purposes, several copies have been placed at points strategically separated geographically to insure their survival.

Though both father and son admitted that they no longer felt they themselves needed the organized church, they felt it should always be supported as "Mrs. Eddy's demonstration" for those who have not outgrown the need of it. In their unquestioning loyalty to the institution, they went to great lengths in justifying the actions of the Board, even when such actions reflected upon them. For example, when the Board publicly denounced certain Eddy notes as "apocryphal if not downright forgeries" after the Carpenters had in print declared the notes authentic, the younger Carpenter wrote:

The Christian Science Board of Directors, who have direct charge of the babes, are functioning properly when they take steps to protect the babes, even to the point of asserting that the "milk of the word" is all there is to Christian Science, since, if the babes begin to discover that there is something beyond the milk before they have taken full advantage of it, they may be tempted to neglect the milk in an effort to obtain the meat prematurely. (Foreword, p. v, of *The Divinity Course*, a compilation printed privately by the Carpenters.)

The inner conflict entailed by their determined loyalty to an authoritarianism which was crushing them is revealed in their voluminous correspondence with Arthur Corey. "I have surely been struggling against brokenheartedness," wrote the younger Carpenter in 1943, and in 1944 he remarked in another letter, "My quarrel is not with the Board, although at times I feel a temptation to wish revenge." Resolutely he would return to the theme that "the Directors are in great danger and we need to do all we can to help them, for Mrs. Eddy's sake." When the Board imposed the probationary period, it had been limited to three years; and when at its expiration he was not reinstated as he had been led to expect, he wrote: "I am in a dilemma which you seem to have solved for yourself very definitely, and I have not solved it for myself." This dilemma had still not been solved at the time of his death in 1952.

When the author visited the Carpenters at Providence in 1951, they seemed free of any resentment toward the Directors. They declared their belief that those who have withdrawn from the church, such as Arthur Corey and Margaret Laird, made a mistake. "They should have remained within the Church and made their demonstration." Yet on June 13, 1952, the elder Carpenter was to write Arthur Corey at length about the failings of the church, concluding: "An understanding Christian Scientist who knows and practices the demonstrating way ... must provide the remedy— why not *you?*"

Nothing, the elder Carpenter assured the author, could separate him from the church, even if he were excommunicated. It takes two to make a bargain, he argued. When he was put out of the local church, he sent it a larger check than usual. Others may say that the Board of Directors are aiming at complete domination of the organization, but with this he could not agree. He felt certain that the Directors were conscientious in doing what they believe Mrs. Eddy would have them do, striving to gain the same results through their leadership that Mrs. Eddy did through hers. On the whole the Board ought to be supported. After all, the Carpenters, father and son, had for many years taught that the Board is simply "the thermometer for the field." If the Directors are failing in their spiritual objectives, it is because they are not sustained spiritually by the field.

A SECOND EXAMPLE is that of Margaret Ledward Laird, who was a student of Bicknell Young. She went through Primary class under him and, years later, was a member of a Normal class which he taught. Young, it will be recalled, was a student of Edward Kimball —in fact, Kimball's best-known exponent—and was not without his own troubles in the church. The rumors afloat after his 1937 Normal class, some circulated by Christian Science lecturers of anti-Kimball persuasion, that the class had been incorrectly taught and would have to be retaught were so persistent and disruptive that the Board found it necessary, in a letter dated August 17, 1939, to assert that the Directors individually and collectively regarded the class as satisfactory. Was this necessarily an admission that the Board regarded Young's teaching as correct? Or was it a bowing to the fact that to discredit Young, and so a Normal class, might have adverse effects on the movement so far-reaching as to be quite out of proportion to the harm such recognition could do? At worst, mistaught teachers could be disfranchised one at a time unobtrusively if that should prove necessary, whereas the repudiation of a Normal class was unprecedented, and in this instance would involve also the reputation and following of the most popular lecturer in the entire movement.

Mrs. Laird was a prominent member of the fashionable First Church of Christ, Scientist, Evanston, Illinois, and she enjoyed a large practice. She served her church as Reader and held other posts of responsibility in the organization. She became a teacher in 1937. In August, 1938, she received a letter from the Board of Directors in Boston citing reports which had come to them concerning things she had said and done.

The Board's letter recited quite a number of allegations which had reached headquarters from unnamed sources, and gave her opportunity to explain. This she did in a long letter. She pointed out that sayings taken quite out of their context accounted for some of the charges. For others she could offer no explanation, but she denied categorically that she held the view or attitude implied by them. Of course, she was to some extent groping in the dark. She did not know who her accusers were, or the incidental circumstances out of which such reports could have arisen. In her many difficulties with the Board during the ensuing years, the sources were in no case disclosed to her, even on the occasion of her personal appearance before the Board in Boston.

In a letter of September 13, 1938, the Board indicated that her explanations were accepted at headquarters, but she was admonished to be very careful about her future statements in order to avoid any misunderstanding.

A letter of July 12, 1939, informed Mrs. Laird that she was once again in trouble. From several persons whose integrity the Board could not question had come disquieting reports. Among other things, she was charged with confusing matter and Spirit in her teaching. She had on occasion recommended unauthorized literature, even giving out typed manuscripts—one of which had fallen into the Board's possession. She was accused of being aggressive in putting out her ideas and in soliciting pupils, of inviting other practitioners to her home to the end of enlisting their services in spreading her teaching. She had, so the Board was informed, told patients it was quite all right to employ medicine at the same time Christian Science treatment was being given; specifically, had she not told a mother to continue giving a child insulin? (In this connection, it is noteworthy that around this time a prominent practitioner had ordered "no medication" for a young diabetic under his treatment, and that the child quickly lapsed into a coma and died, precipitating a front-page scandal in the Chicago papers.) Young people were reported as liking to go to Margaret Laird because she did not condemn their smoking and drinking. She had disparaged other workers and criticized the Board of Directors, so it was said, did not attend church regularly, said much in *Science and Health* was obsolete, and proposed the publication of Bicknell Young's writings. There were other charges of a trivial nature hardly to be distinguished from gossip.

Mrs. Laird's reply was a long one—too long to detail here. To most of the charges she gave an explanation which to an outsider seems satisfactory. That it would satisfy the people involved in the difficult task of administering an essentially authoritarian church is not likely.

On December 31, 1939, a new charge was leveled against Mrs. Laird, namely, that she had accepted a pupil whose wife had previously been taught by another teacher and that she, knowing this, had permitted the wife to attend the class along with her husband, thus violating Article XXVI of the *Manual*.

This letter brought a sharp rejoinder:

The maliciousness of purpose shown in the distortion of facts and the gossip presented to you was not apparent except to one who knew the facts, but here is something which can be proved a slanderous falsehood. A report of this kind, which could have been investigated so easily without bothering either you or me, can be construed in but one way, and that is as a wilful attempt to discredit and injure.

The woman in question had not attended a single session of the class, as could be proved by the thirty persons present. The Board answered on January 26, 1940, that there had evidently been an erroneous report.

Complaint is registered again in a letter from the Board of December 26, 1940, again in a letter dated June 23, 1941, and still again on November 12, 1942, that Mrs. Laird's papers are being widely circulated and read by others than the members of her own Association of pupils. If extreme care were not exercised in the circulation of private papers, the Board reiterated, it would not be long before a great many unauthorized statements concerning Christian Science would be floating about the field which could, if copied inaccurately, contain errors in doctrine. Association addresses must be sent only to members, only members being allowed to read them; no notes or copies must ever be made of them by the students or others; and the papers must be returned after a reasonable period. Even under these restrictions, it might be better to send copies only to those *necessarily* absent from the sessions.

For more than two years there was no exchange of letters. Then on January 4, 1945, the Board wrote that another unfavorable report had reached them, this one from a patient of hers who had become discouraged, since all this patient had learned about Christian Science seemed to meet with Mrs. Laird's disapproval. Specifically, she was alleged to have spoken disparagingly of the Bible and of the church.

She replied on January 16 that the reports were entirely erroneous, that she could not be so misquoted by anyone who knew her unless the misinterpretation was deliberate. "It seems incredible," she wrote,

that an earnest student of Christian Science for more than forty years, a person of exemplary character, a listed practitioner for twenty-five years with many accredited healings, a teacher of Christian Science who teaches what she has been taught and knows that teaching since she had it twice, a deep student of our Leader's writings as anyone who knows me well can attest, should be constantly put on the defensive because of *unconfirmed* gossip.

Clearly Mrs. Laird's patience was being sorely tried by the charges so persistently brought against her by the Board of Directors. She wrote that she was the victim of a smear campaign, concluding: "It seems particularly unfortunate to me that my motives should be so misunderstood by the Board." The Board simply acknowledged receipt of this letter.

A letter dated June 6, 1945, warned Mrs. Laird that yet other reports of her "erroneous activities" had come to headquarters. If Mrs. Laird had scheduled her class for July, she should inform the enrolled students that the class must be postponed. This would allow time for consideration of charges against her. This was naturally a great shock to Margaret Laird. Thirty people had enrolled for her class to be held July 2, and train and hotel reservations had already been made.

In a letter dated June 7, Mrs. Laird begged the Board to see her at once, so that the atmosphere might be cleared and the class held as planned. Again on June 9 she wrote appealing to them "humbly" to take no direct action against her until she had been permitted a just defense of herself and her work, as provided for by the Mother Church *Manual*, as sudden postponement of the class would surely give the appearance of punishment meted out to her before a hearing had been held.

But on June 8 another letter had already been dispatched by the Board, adding still further charges against her. Most of these were no more than variants of charges previously made, but additionally she was charged with having not only approved but even recommended medical and surgical help. The Directors ended their letter with what must have seemed to Mrs. Laird a veritable bombshell. They declared she had "strayed so as not to be fit for the work of . . . a teacher of Christian Science." She was this time *ordered*, not advised, to cancel her proposed class and to do no further teaching until she had been authorized to do so. She was cited to attend a hearing before the Board in Boston on July 23, bringing any evidence she might wish to submit. As a result the class was postponed, and Mrs. Laird journeyed to Boston where she appeared before the Board.

The next letter, dated August 15, 1945, gave the verdict of the Board. It was asserted that all the charges, which were restated in part, had been reviewed along with her own statements and denials, as well as such written evidence as had been produced. The decision of the Directors, reached unanimously, was that she had so strayed as to be unfit to teach Christian Science. The counts against her were that (1) she had written and circulated papers and notes on Christian Science, this constituting unauthorized literature, to her own and other teachers' pupils, and (2) she had made unwise statements concerning Mrs. Eddy as Revelator, the Bible, and the church services. All this was "unethical, indiscreet and unbecoming" behavior for a Christian Science teacher and practitioner. It was therefore ruled that Mrs. Laird be placed on probation for three years, at the expiration of which period, if she had meanwhile maintained the life of a consecrated Christian Scientist, she would be eligible for reinstatement as a teacher. She could not, of course, teach or meet with her pupils while on probation, her altered status being publicized through change in her *Journal* listing. Her pupils were now free to be retaught by other teachers currently in good standing. She must write to all her students informing them of the Board's action, sending a copy of her letter to the Board for approval before mailing it out to her students.

Margaret Laird acknowledged the Board's decision in a respectful letter of August 22, 1945, indicating her determination to follow their directives conscientiously in order to regain her position as teacher.

Early in October it came to Mrs. Laird's attention that the local church in Evanston had omitted all names of her pupils from a list of class-taught students sent out in connection with the election of local church officers. This brought a ruling from the Mother Church Directors that such students might still retain their title "C.S." for use in the *Journal*, on office doors, and in signing applications for membership in the Mother Church. In all other respects, though, they were to be treated as "untaught."

A group of Mrs. Laird's students were moved to write a vigorous letter to the Board in Boston. They questioned whether Mrs. Laird had merited so severe a condemnation as to be pronounced *unfit* to teach. As for the charge of circulating "unauthorized literature," they asked where in Mrs. Eddy's writings there is any prohibition of the writing or distributing of papers by a Christian Science teacher to his or her students. They had been unable to find that anyone was invested with authority either to approve or disapprove such writings by a teacher. The expression "unauthorized literature" appears nowhere in the concordances. Mrs. Eddy had herself said that Christian Science is not copyrighted and that a student could write voluminously on the subject without trespassing. Nor could the private distribution of a few copies of Mrs. Laird's papers be called "publication." They closed their four-page protest with the declaration that they genuinely desired to support the Board of Directors. This Mrs. Laird had taught them. They loved their cause, and all the phases of organization which keep it functioning efficiently. "But we feel outraged at this egregious infringement of our rights and liberties." Referring to the late World War as one between totalitarianism and democracy, they said that some of them had lost loved ones in the fight against "that form of government which demands subservience without consideration of the rights of the individual." According to Mrs. Eddy the *Manual* rules were not "arbitrary opinions or dictatorial demands such as one person might impose on another." In the light of such unequivocal words from their beloved Leader and in the absence of any authority in the *Manual,* "is it any wonder that we are protesting your action in the matter as a purely authoritarian injunction and seek a clarification of your letter of August 15, 1945, to Mrs. Laird?"

This was the year in which Arthur Corey published his *Christian Science Class Instruction,* which created such a furor within the movement. It probably did not help Mrs. Laird's case when a report reached the Board that she had declared that the Corey book "contains the Christ Truth" and that its reading would be of greater help than the reading of the authorized periodicals of the church. When finally she had remarked that in teaching Corey would undoubtedly have full classes, the Board, on December 11, 1946, felt obliged to warn her that she was still on probation and to request an explanation.

On August 13, 1948, Mrs. Laird wrote reminding the Board that the probationary period had elapsed, and requesting instruction as to what steps she must now take to be reinstated. To this the Board responded, on September 10, that they had had adverse reports concerning her activities. The specific charges were (1) that she countenanced the employment of medical aid by her patients, (2) that she had written, sold, and circulated writings on Christian Science, i.e., unauthorized literature, (3) that she recommended the reading of unauthorized publications containing misstatements concerning Christian Science, and (4) that she had made derogatory remarks concerning the Mother Church and its activities. She was formally cited to appear at a hearing in Boston on October 21, if she so wished, to answer the charges.

Mrs. Laird's reply of September 29, 1948, countered that the charges were general, that specific instances were not given which she could explain; most of it was hearsay and should be irrelevant in view of her long years of consecrated service to the cause; that she had never countenanced medical help "except as a humane measure and fully in accordance with the instructions in the

Christian Science textbook." She had never sold, nor had she widely distributed, anything she had written, though she had written for students and patients. And she had written out things to clarify her own thought. But that could hardly be called unauthorized literature. In *Science and Health,* she observed, Mrs. Eddy says writings based upon that book are useful. She found nothing in all Mrs. Eddy's works prohibiting discriminate reading of other literature. Nor had she on any occasion recommended other literature *instead* of the church-authorized. Any of her students could testify that it was upon *Science and Health* and the Bible that her teaching and practice were based. She denied having spoken disparagingly of the Mother Church. While she would be happy to meet with the Board, she felt that it was pointless to take up their time in reiterating what she had already written.

The meeting of the Board was held and a decision reached. So far from reinstating Mrs. Laird as a teacher, it resulted in their deciding to remove her name entirely from the *Journal,* even disavowing her as a practitioner. Her advertisement would be deleted after the November issue. Thus she was in a worse state than before.

Margaret Laird was still a member of the Mother Church and of the Evanston branch church. Not a few of her friends urged that she withdraw completely from the church, but this she was unwilling to do. Did she still hope to regain her position in the organization? Naturally she continued in her healing practice and in her study of Christian Science. She began definitely to prepare a book for publication. The years passed.

On the appearance of my own book *These Also Believe,* which contained a chapter on Christian Science, Mrs. Laird read it and came one day to talk with me. At my invitation she appeared before one of my classes, that on "Christianity Today," in which representatives of various faiths were asked to state their beliefs, then permit questions to be asked by the class. She did a superb job of presenting the fundamental basis of Christian Science, and answered very ably the many questions that were asked. A day or two later a telephone call came. Had Margaret Ledward Laird appeared before my class and answered questions? "Yes, why?" I replied. "Nothing at all," said the voice, "I just wanted to know, thank you." It was the student president of the local Christian Science group at the university. Why did he want to know? Mrs. Laird knew well enough what it meant. Another report would go in to Boston and be added to her already bulging dossier.

Even so, she continued as a member of the church. But when one of the Directors, Ivimy Gwalter, wrote an article for the *Journal* (LXIX, 493-95), advocating the authoritarian control of Christian Science, this was the last straw. Mrs. Laird read the article, and at once, in a letter dated September 27, 1951, resigned from the Mother Church.

In a revealing letter to Alfred Pittman, another of the Directors, Margaret Laird declared that the Gwalter article grossly misinterpreted the bylaws, and brought out how widely their paths diverged. In connection with Mrs. Eddy's rule "No Incorrect Literature," the Board was promulgating the idea that *unauthorized* literature is synonymous with *incorrect* literature, a rank perversion of Mrs. Eddy's meaning. Miss Gwalter said that Christian Scientists must see the necessity for Mrs. Eddy to keep the church under her own control, for it was her church, and to this Mrs. Laird gave assent. But, she said, it was for this very reason that Mrs. Eddy "had made no provision for it to be run by an ecclesiastical board when she was gone." Indeed their Leader had declared, on page 343 of *Miscellany*, that when the enforcement of the bylaws was left to others, trouble ensued.

In view of all this, Mrs. Laird stated that, much as she regretted having to take the step of resigning, since she was now more than ever a practicing Christian Scientist, she could do nothing else and be loyal to Mrs. Eddy and the unfoldment of Truth going on in her own consciousness.

Having resigned from the church organization, Margaret Laird felt free to call her students and patients together for a day's conference. Some two hundred of them responded, and heard Mrs. Laird read a lengthy statement of Christian Science. The pupils were uniformly warm in their praise of Mrs. Laird's stand, and at the same time all still regarded themselves as loyal Christian Scientists.

STILL ANOTHER outstanding figure who fell under the discipline of the church through its Board of Directors was John W. Doorly, of London. He became interested in Christian Science in 1902, joined the Mother Church in 1904, and was listed as a practitioner in the *Journal* by 1907. Having had Primary class instruction, he was accepted for the 1910 Normal class, taught by Bicknell Young, and thus became an authorized teacher. In 1914 he was appointed lecturer, in which capacity he served until 1929. On the occasion of his retirement from the Lecture Board he received an official letter warmly appreciative of his long service. In 1918 he became the second Englishman to be made President of the Mother Church, a strictly honorary appointment but a much coveted one. When approached by the Directors in 1926 he declined to become First Reader of the Mother Church. He traveled and lectured for the church all over the world. All his lectures had, as was customary, been submitted to and approved by the Board of Directors, although he stressed in them the synonymous terms for *God* and the seven days of creation, in line with certain views which were later to bring him into controversy with Boston.

In 1929 Doorly decided he should devote more time to the study of the Bible and Mrs. Eddy's writings, believing that in this lay the secret of better healing, which alone could prove to mankind the all-importance of Christian Science. He had, he thought, discovered in the course of his travels signs of growing danger to the cause in the increasing tendency to substitute belief and religious sentiment for exact spiritual understanding and demonstration. He was convinced that Truth could never be demonstrated until it was understood intelligently and scientifically. And although he had sided with the Directors in their struggle for unlimited authority during the Great Litigation a decade earlier, now he was beginning to note "a lax sense as to the 'essentially democratic' government of the Mother Church."

He had reached the conviction that Mrs. Eddy, through what she found in the Bible and elucidated in her *Key to the Scriptures,* had taken religion out of mysticism, blind faith, and sentimental emotion, carrying it into the realm of exact science. She had, he said, developed a "divine metaphysical system of symbolizing the ideas of the infinite in perfect harmony, rhythm and order, whereby all men could learn, understand and demonstrate the things of God more effectually, more scientifically and more naturally than one could understand and demonstrate even such human subjects as mathematics, music, etc."

Doorly was overjoyed with his findings, as were many to whom he communicated them. But to their disappointment they soon learned that, although Mrs. Eddy had declared "the time for thinkers has come," no independent thinking would be tolerated within the church. They were faced with relentless persecution, and before long Doorly was placed on probation. The removal of his designation as a teacher from the *Journal* registry, followed by the deletion of even his name, advertised to the world his fall from official grace.

Doorly did not take all this tamely, as so many have, but defended himself publicly through speaking and writing. In 1945 he published in London *A Statement by John W. Doorly*. This pamphlet, which contains the greater part of the correspondence between himself and the Board of Directors in Boston, affords a first-class exhibit of the way in which a strongly centralized governing authority deals with those who assert any independence of thought or action. Here, while still on probation, he forcefully declares his own independence of ecclesiastical control:

I shall practice Christian Science as I have done for forty years. I shall also continue my earnest study and research of the Bible and our Leader's writings, and I shall always preach the gospel of Christian Science to all who desire to hear it from me. Thus I shall maintain my democratic and divine right to be an individual, a Christian Scientist, and a member of the English speaking people.

And he stressed the necessity of a larger measure of freedom of expression within the church. "Nothing could be more disastrous," he writes, "than a blind obedience which would destroy the very foundation of her [Mrs. Eddy's] government, involving constant spiritual watchfulness and awareness on the part of the individual members of the Mother Church."

It was in May, 1942, that the Board first wrote Doorly, asserting that for a long time and with some frequency they had received reports of alleged improprieties on his part as an authorized teacher, although they admitted that many good reports had come as well. It was charged that he and his pupils were divided from other Christian Scientists in some communities, and that they contributed to this divisiveness by maintaining an attitude of superiority toward other teachers and their pupils. He and his pupils were also said to hold meetings for the purpose of interpreting Christian Science and sharing such interpretations with other Scientists.

Several infractions of the bylaws were charged as well, it being asserted that he had violated Section 10 of Article VIII in the *Manual*, by using in his Association address report an undue number of quotations from *Science and Health;* also that in printing and distributing this report he had compounded his offense.

Another bylaw, Article XXVI, Section 6, forbids teachers to put their own personal views into their instruction, and this the Board understood he had been doing. They recognized the difficulty of detecting just when personal views enter; but they stood ready, they said, to give an interpretation in any given instance—a clear claim to final authority in all such matters.

What were these personal views? He was said to attach excessive importance to the order in which Mrs. Eddy gives the synonymous terms for *God* in her definition of Deity on page 465 of *Science and Health.* Doorly maintained that if Mrs. Eddy's arrangement were tampered with, her intended meaning would be altered through a shift of emphasis. The Board quoted from former editions of her textbook to show that Mrs. Eddy herself had varied the order of the synonyms. Nor did she limit them to seven in number.

The Directors ended their letter by hoping that he would take heed of the admonition and so preserve his usefulness in the church. Otherwise he stood to mar permanently his long and mainly favorable record as a Christian Scientist. The implicit threat was unmistakable.

In his reply of July 4, 1942, Doorly expressed himself as pleased
that at last he had heard directly from the Board, for rumors were
afloat that individual members of the Board were in correspondence
with his critics, and that other officials in Boston were conveying
to friends and relatives in England information gained from members of the Board about him. The reports might well be untrue, but
frankly the "wolves of religious persecution were in full bay in
London, and the theory was on every hand that the Directors
individually and collectively had unleashed them."

Even so it hardly seemed to Doorly in keeping with the highest
standards of right procedure simply to write and recount charges
against him and his pupils without giving detailed proof or specific
instances. If the Board would supply exact information then he
could deal rightly and intelligently with the matter or disprove the
allegations. Surely they should know the animus and inaccuracy of
writers who feel that they will not have to prove their charges. He
reports that a past member of the Board had once said to him,
"Brother, they write about everybody!" He complains that there is a
persistent report in certain quarters that members of the Board have
encouraged others to criticize and condemn him and his teaching,
and a great many people seem to be well aware of the fact
that the Board has written him, and also of the purport of these
unsupported charges.

Doorly then proceeds to defend his position with reference to the
synonyms. He finds it strangely incongruous that the Board in
defending its position appeals to earlier editions of Science and
Health while he teaches as he is required to do from the final
edition, the one in which Mrs. Eddy's growing understanding of
Christian Science reached its climax. (See Sentinel, XXXVII,
331-32, passim.)

In their charge against him that he and his students got together
for discussion of the basic principles of Christian Science, he asserts
that the Directors make a frontal attack upon one of the most
precious rights of the British and American people, that of free
assembly. If they mean to interpret the bylaw in Article XXVI,
Section 6, so as to deprive any small group of Christian Scientists

of the right to get together to study the Bible and the textbook, it means that they are deliberately cutting across the fundamental law and constitutions of England and the United States. He does not believe that many of his pupils would tolerate any interference on his part in connection with the right of free assembly. But why be afraid of such group discussions?

As long as Christian Scientists believe in Christian Science only as a religion and not as a science, we will be afraid of its being tampered with; when Christian Scientists understand our Leader's revelation as absolute Science, this needless fear will also disappear, for no one can add one jot or tittle to absolute Science, and no one can take it away.

This for him is the real issue. The scientific aspect of Mrs. Eddy's discovery was the truly Christian aspect and was indispensable. This would march on no matter who might resist it.

To this letter, here recorded very sketchily, there was no reply. Instead, charges were brought against Doorly as a member of London's Ninth Church, through its local Board of Directors. Several specific charges were made of infractions of rules of either the local church or the Mother Church. These he declined to answer on the ground that it was outside the province of any branch church to hear such charges, which must constitutionally be judged by the Board of Directors of the Mother Church under the *Manual* requirements. Disregarding this, Ninth Church proceeded against him, declared him guilty on three counts, and suspended him. Thereupon he resigned from membership in the local church and forwarded the whole correspondence to the Mother Church Directors on March 15, 1943.

The Boston Board made no acknowledgment. But on July 30 the Directors wrote him that they had reviewed the transcript of charges made by London's Ninth Church, together with his letters concerning them. Then they brought four charges of *Manual* violation against him: (1) that he "had so far strayed as not to be fit for the work of a teacher of Christian Science" (Art. XII, Sec. 1); (2) that in his Class Instruction he departed from the prescribed chapter "Recapitulation" (Art. XXVII, Sec. 3); (3) that he taught his own personal views and not merely the Bible and *Science and Health* (Art. XXVI, Sec. 6); and (4) that he had assembled a select number of pupils of his own, and those of other teachers, instructing them (Art. XXVI, Sec. 6-7). A meeting in Boston was scheduled for October 28, 1943, at which time and place the Board would take action on the case. They invited the accused to be present if he wished, offering to postpone the meeting to a more convenient date if necessary. No offer was made to reimburse him for the expense of his transoceanic journey, nor to hold hearings at some place more convenient to him. In any event, he was asked to teach no more classes from October 28 forward, pending final disposition of the matter.

On October 9, 1943, Doorly cabled Boston stating that new charges of which he had not before heard were now being brought up against him, and demanding a full statement of all the particulars in order that he might answer them "comprehensively and specifically." But nothing came. Therefore, on December 30 he wrote a long letter answering the charges, but warning the central authorities of division in the church if the fundamental matter of Mrs. Eddy's revelation were pressed. And, said he, "no church that was adding ninety to ninety-five churches annually twelve years ago, but has since steadily declined so that for the past three years it has lost more branches than it has added, can afford a heresy trial, which might lead to division and loss."

Doorly's letter to the Board states that he has consulted legal opinion. His counsel has advised him that the proposed procedure of the Board gave so little evidence of what is considered in England to be equity and justice that he felt it was impossible to deal with it without further and better particulars of the charges and all the circumstances in which they were made. He warns the Directors sharply at one point that if any charges whatever are made against his personal character—not infrequently damaging aspersions had been cast officially upon such distinguished Christian Scientists as Peter V. Ross—he for his part will "take the whole issue to the appropriate Court of Justice, where it will be thoroughly sifted and justice and honesty will decide what is true. Then the whisperers

will be given a chance to whisper on oath to experienced counsel."
He had actually done this once before, he reminded them, and had
been awarded substantial damages.

Concerning meetings of small groups for discussion, that had
happened often after lectures in the cases of men like Judge Hanna,
Edward Kimball, Bicknell Young, and others. Why should it now
be held to be a crime in his case?

He affirms once more his loyalty to Mrs. Eddy, her textbook, and
her *Manual*. He does, however, believe with Mrs. Eddy that "the
time for thinkers has come" and that "unless our Movement will
recognize this, the advancing thought of mankind in this scientific
and progressive era will more and more leave us behind, whereas we
should be in the forefront of all spiritual development and progress."
He includes lengthy exhibits appropriate to each of the points.

Meanwhile the Board had forwarded to Doorly additional accusations, citing published writings and letters of his in support
thereof, and warning that this in no way changed or limited the
original four charges of July 30. By this time the hearing at Boston
had been fixed upon for February 24, 1944, and Doorly cabled the
Board on February 9: "My comprehensive cable dated October 30,
1943, requesting charges specified, was answered by you two months
later on December 29, 1943, was sent ordinary mail and received by
me February 3, 1944, an interim of three months." He found it
impossible to travel to America in time to meet their schedule,
prepared with his defense. The Board forthwith granted him a stay,
making August 4 the deadline, his teaching to remain suspended
pending final adjudication of the matter.

Doorly's cabled acknowledgment of the postponement brands as
arbitrary the Directors' requirement that he refrain from teaching,
declaring it evidence that judgment has already been pronounced
before the hearing. It is unfortunate, he asserts, "that certain letters
from America and articles which have appeared in the periodicals
should consistently give the impression that members of your Board
are not really impartial judges of these charges, but are determined
beforehand to condemn."

In reply by letter on March 16, 1944, the Directors state that they are simply following established practice and have not prejudged his case. In his reply of June 13, Doorly takes issue with such practice, but says that is not the point.

The crux of the whole situation is the solicited controversy over my teaching of our Leader's revelation as both divine Science and divinely scientific. . . . Nothing would be more pathetic or disastrous than that the Directors of the Mother Church should be found opposing the natural and orderly development of Mrs. Eddy's revelation in its inevitable spiritual and scientific aspect, bringing new life and inspiration to our Movement.

On July 20 Doorly's lawyer informed Boston that owing to war conditions it would be impossible for his client to secure transportation so as to be present in Boston on August 4. After more exchanges, the Board cabled on August 3 that in view of Doorly's statement to one of their informants that his counsel advised him not to attend the hearing, and in view of his unwillingness to forego teaching, they would hold the hearing that day.

On August 4, 1944, the Board cabled Doorly that, after full and careful consideration of all the evidence in his case, they had decided to place him on probation as a teacher for a period of three years, at the end of which time they would consider restoring his teaching franchise. Confirmed by letter, this meant that his pupils were now removed from his jurisdiction. They were at liberty to be taught all over again, by any teacher of their own choice currently in good standing. Until they were retaught, they were precluded from attending any teacher's Association meeting. The Doorly Association was of course automatically dissolved. He must notify his pupils of the Board's decision by a letter first submitted to the Board for approval.

In January, 1945, Doorly, while still a member, though suspended, of the Mother Church, published his *Statement,* including of course all of the Board's own statement of the case. Throughout the field many watched to see what the Board would do next, the consensus being that headquarters could do nothing less than disown him publicly. In March, 1946, the Committee on Publication sought an appointment with him, but Doorly refused to see him unless he would first state fully the purpose of his visit. In May of the same year the Board wrote to admonish him, declaring that the publication of the *Statement* was calculated to injure the church, and furthermore that his attempt to teach and lecture "under the guise of giving talks on the Bible" was in direct disobedience to the *Manual*. While they had removed his teacher designation, the Directors had allowed his practitioner's card to remain in the *Journal*. They hoped it would not be necessary to remove his name entirely.

Doorly replied on June 8, 1946, at some length. He challenged the Board to bring forward evidence that his teaching was not in strictest accord with the Bible and the Christian Science textbook. He charged that

during this period of attack upon me, you have constantly been supplied with gossip and unproved accusations by what may now be regarded as a private gestapo, i.e., people who write you copiously about others, well knowing that they will never be called upon to prove a single statement they have made. Your Board should know that such methods as these are universally condemned by all decent-minded people, and it is only a matter of time until these methods defeat their own ends.

He continued:

The mistaken concept that five human beings can tell the rest of humanity exactly what Christian Science is, what they shall think, what they shall read, to whom they shall speak, when and what they shall write, is entirely out of harmony with the thought of our world today. The Christian Science Church organization is in fetters, the fetters of vested interest, of conservatism, of conventionality, of autocracy, and of lack of vision, and your Board is chiefly responsible for these conditions. The marvel is that with a disastrous record of fifteen years of declining membership and fading warmth, your Board does not see the hopelessness of the present policy.

The Directors once more admonished him, in a letter of July 12, 1946, expressing the hope he would see the error of his ways. His reply of July 30 was hardly calculated to smooth things out. So it was inevitable that the Board should at last set another hearing, this one for August 22. To notice of this he did not reply. On August 29, 1946, the name of John W. Doorly was ordered withdrawn from the *Journal*, and he was excommunicated from the Mother Church.

One final letter from Doorly declared that the Board had conferred a great honor upon him. He was glad to be counted among the many men and women "who have been willing to be ostracized and driven out of religious organizations rather than submit to the control and restraint of their spiritual vision." He was quite happy with the outcome. The new freedom of thought that had come to him in recent years had showed him more than ever that church organization might be a necessary restriction for early growth, but if not abandoned when one's thought attained a measure of maturity, it must inevitably bring disaster to the individual and to the organization, as Mrs. Eddy herself had pointed out in *Retrospection and Introspection*.

The Directors had expressed regret at being required to dismiss him from membership—let their regret rather be for their own mistaken policy which had distorted their Leader's mother government into "one of the most despotic oligarchies our world has ever known." They had not really dismissed him from the church Mrs. Eddy founded. The only church worthy of Mary Baker Eddy was, he said, the Church of Christ, Scientist, which she described as "the structure of Truth and Love, whatever rests upon and proceeds from divine Principle." He would, thank God, and increasingly so, always be in that church.

Doorly did not found a rival organization, but he did continue to teach and practice and to write, until death overtook him in 1950. His books are still being published and circulated by the Foundational Book Company, a concern which he set up with a group of his students in London and which continues since his death under the able direction of Mrs. Peggy Brook. She and others of his followers continue to lecture, practice, teach, write, publish, and circulate their own writings as well as his. To how many they minister there is no way of knowing, but there must be a very considerable number of those who are ardent Christian Scientists but who maintain no connection at all with the Christian Science church.

JOHN LAWRENCE SINTON of London is another who fell under the discipline of the Board of Directors and finally resigned from the church. He began practice in 1932 and was a member of Bicknell Young's Normal class of 1937. He was Reader in Fifth Church of Christ, Scientist, Manchester. His undoing grew out of his association with the famous John Doorly.

As was the case with Doorly, Sinton was charged with promulgating unorthodox theories as to the relationship of the seven synonyms for *God* to the seven days of creation, and so on. Sinton, like Doorly, at the end of the controversy with the Board was put on probation and his name stricken from the *Journal*. Deprived of his teaching privileges and discredited before the field by dismissal from the registry, he resigned from the church and published in full his correspondence with the Board.

The controversy followed the same pattern as in the Doorly case: general charges made; specific charges and the names of those bringing them sought for but refused by the Board; the setting of a hearing with the requirement that the accused cease to teach pending the final disposition of the matter—and of course his refusal to do so on the ground that this was not to assume innocence until proof of guilt were provided but, on the contrary, a clear betrayal of British and American principles of justice; the hearing without the accused's presence; and the same verdict.

In his last letter to the Board, Sinton points out a few conditions which he asserts obtain under their interpretation and administration:

You have adjudicated my case and made findings without offering any proof whatsoever of any violation of the *Church Manual*, or any proof where my teaching is mistaken.

Under this same interpretation and administration you constitute yourselves an ecclesiastical court whose word is final, and against which there is no possibility of appeal, unless you yourselves choose to reconsider a case you have decided. There is no democratic provision to cause you to reconsider any given case. In the possible event of a bad blunder in the conduct of affairs—and doubtless Mrs. Eddy corrected many such blunders in her day—the Movement, as at present constituted and operative, has no power whatever of removal and replacement [of Board members]. In other words, you are your own judges on all matters of policy and administration. Yet our Leader writes of the "essentially democratic" nature of her church government.

A further consequence of this kind of administrative policy is the increasing susceptibility of our Movement to mortal mind's malpractice in the form of rumor-mongering, whispering and secret informing, much of which is slanderous, libelous and often actionable at law. The consequences of this policy will accrue until there is either breakdown and disaster, or an honest facing up to the simple and direct requirements of Mrs. Eddy's textbook and the *Church Manual*.

Because of these and other conditions in the church, Sinton found it no longer possible to continue in the organization and so withdrew in 1946. His wife, also a practitioner, followed him in this in 1951. Sinton has since continued to practice and to teach. He has held classes in America, on the West Coast and at Princeton, New Jersey. At Princeton pressure was brought to bear on those in charge of the school facilities to deny him the right to use them, on the ground that he was no longer an "authorized" teacher of Christian Science. The university authorities, not being concerned with divisions within the church, refused to be moved. Sinton has had a greatly increased practice since his withdrawal, and his classes are well attended. Both he and his wife, when interviewed by the author in London, testified to a sense of freedom they never knew within the organization. He was planning to retire from teaching and practice for a year in order to find time to write and publish his presentation of Christian Science, which he, like Doorly, regards as a completely demonstrable science as well as a religion.

Like all the other Doorly leaders, Sinton has conceived a great distrust of organization and wants no organized movement. The result is a very loose association of leaders, each independent, but with common aims and aspirations, who confer now and again on basic matters and co-operate in some ventures, but who are bound by no specific set of rules. Can their ideas perpetuate themselves thus? Or is at least some organization necessary as a carrier for these ideas from one generation to another? In the end will Boston and its hierarchy be the channel through which whatever is of value and importance to the world in the teaching of Mary Baker Eddy will be handed on, or will these more or less independent exponents function successfully in that capacity?

DOORLY'S INFLUENCE reached well beyond England and America. Before World War II there were those in Switzerland who had read his books and heard his lectures. They corresponded with him while continuing in their branch churches as Readers, practitioners, Sunday school teachers, and members of Christian Science church committees. When Doorly was disciplined by the Board of Directors in 1944, these Swiss students fell under the same condemnation since they had studied with him. If they were to continue in the church and teach or practice, they had to be retaught by a currently approved teacher. They were disfranchised. Indeed, in the ensuing controversy, they were excommunicated.

But of what was he guilty? asked Dr. Max Kappeler, foremost of the Swiss dissenters. He had taught nothing he could not substantiate by Mrs. Eddy's own words in her textbook. How could he be penalized under the *Manual?* But he was. He therefore set himself to investigate the question, unable to believe that Mrs. Eddy could contradict herself, championing liberty while imposing serfdom. He published the results of his inquiry under the title *Christian Government: Its Scientific Evolution* (London: Foundational Book Company, 1946).

Dictators, Dr. Kappeler wrote, give orders instead of reasons, thinking their victims impotent. But in his own case and that of other Swiss colleagues this proved not so. They found themselves out in the open, beyond the restrictions of organization, experiencing a sense of freedom they had not known before. They began to give courses and lectures, hold summer school, publish books, and of course they continued with their healing practice. They felt the church authorities had done them a great service. Under organization "the spirit is soon lost, inspiration ceases and unfoldment stops."

Obviously, their interpretation of Mrs. Eddy's writings conflicted with that of Boston officialdom. Essentially they advocated the views for which Doorly was censured. Mrs. Eddy had stressed the point that her doctrine was a science. Well, what are the constituents of this science? To find out, her definition of *God* was analyzed. Why *seven* terms? Why the order in which these terms were finally placed? Are the terms simply interchangeable, as the church authorities argue? These dissenters contended that each synonym has its own specific characteristics and that these characteristics determine the order. This is the very key to the whole Eddy system, they concluded, and is corroborated in the Bible itself. What does Mrs. Eddy mean by "the numerals of infinity"? Or "the divine, infinite calculus"? They asked in vain for an official answer. Indeed, Christian Science officialdom looks with suspicion on anyone who raises the question. One who finds the answer, according to the Kappeler group, is regarded as a heretic to be purged. They only ask questions of *Science and Health,* seeking in it a coherent answer, and this undivided fidelity to the textbook, they contend, renders them immune to deviation and precludes any adulteration of pure Christian Science.

Accused of "Doorlyism," they deny any such distinction, declaring that John Doorly never put any views of his own into his teaching of Christian Science, never added to or took anything away from Mrs. Eddy's presentation of the subject in *Science and Health,* and always insisted they accept nothing from him which he could not prove from the Eddy textbook. They see no reason why they should be called anything but Christian Scientists.

The Misses Emmy Bütikofer and Betty Schurter, both Zurich veterans from the *Journal* registry, and Max Kappeler spearhead what appears to be a somewhat extensive movement, carrying on lectures, classes, and summer schools, as well as continuing in their regular healing practice, since their expulsion from the church. In turn, students of these persons give courses in numerous cities and towns in Switzerland. Some classes have been held also in Germany, and Dr. Kappeler conducted summer courses in London in 1952 and 1953.

According to Dr. Kappeler, each teacher is absolutely independent and works on his own merit, standing or falling on what he knows and does in the line of Christian Science, the only thing they all have in common being the *science* of Christian Science. They are aware of no appreciable interference with their activities from the church organization.

The Swiss dissenters have published a number of pamphlets and books in German and French, and some of Kappeler's works have come out in English. His book *The Structure of the Christian Science Textbook*, when announced in American newspapers during 1955, invited, by its very title, organized opposition from the Christian Science church people. There have been reports from various points that the usual tactics are being pursued against this clear challenge to ecclesiastical monopoly.

THERE IS only one Mother Church in Christian Science. There are many branch churches. Members of branch churches may be and usually are members of the Mother Church in Boston, but this is not at all obligatory under the *Church Manual*. In late years, church membership has been emphasized by the authorities as essential, the church being declared an inseparable part of Mrs. Eddy's basic revelation. But it was not always so. In an official communiqué to all *Journal*-registered practitioners and nurses in 1938, the Board of Directors of the Mother Church declared that, while many individuals belong to the Mother Church and/or a branch church, there are Christian Scientists who do not belong to either. Obviously, according to this official statement, one does not have to be a member of any church to be a Christian Scientist.

From a very early date Mrs. Eddy encouraged the organization of branch churches, some being formed even while Mrs. Eddy's church in Boston was disorganized. Usually the first step is the organization of a Society, which may be constituted with a membership of eleven persons. A branch church must have a minimum of sixteen members, four of whom must be members of the Mother Church in good standing.

According to the *Manual*, the Mother Church shall assume no general official control of other churches. Each branch is supposed to have its own form of government, providing the form is "in consonance with The Mother Church *Manual*." Though it is ostensibly free to govern itself, certain limitations are fixed by the

Manual within which it must operate. There must be in it at least four members of the Mother Church and one of them must be a practitioner whose card is published in the *Journal*. Its membership may not be composed of pupils of a single teacher. No branch church may itself have branches, nor may it associate in conference with other churches save within its own state and for certain common purposes specified in the *Manual*. The article *The* must not be used in the title of any branch church, being reserved exclusively for the Mother Church, The First Church of Christ, Scientist. A bylaw directs that every branch church shall be "distinctly democratic" and stipulates that no person and no other church shall interfere with its affairs. Such churches may be advertised in the *Journal*, being obliged at the same time to recognize all other churches so listed and to maintain "an attitude of Christian fellowship" toward them. All Readers must be members of the Mother Church, as well as of their branch churches. The duties of the branch church Readers are the same as those of Mother Church Readers. Upon the First Reader rests the responsibility of enforcing the bylaws of his local church, but he is warned that "he shall not be a Leader." Incidentally this disciplinary power is seldom invoked, discipline being left as a rule to the central authorities in Boston, with disciplinary action being taken only occasionally by local branch church boards. The services in the Mother Church and those of each branch are identical, except that the Mother Church no longer observes Communion, whereas each branch does so semiannually. Church edifices must not house offices for practitioners.

Are the branch churches really self-governed? What was Mrs. Eddy's fundamental attitude in setting up her organization? She quoted this passage from Benjamin Wills Newton's *Thoughts on the Apocalypse:* "The church at Jerusalem, like a sun in the center of its system, had other churches, like so many planets, revolving around it. It was strictly a mother and a ruling church." Here she observed that according to Newton's description, the church of Jerusalem prefigured the Mother Church at Boston. (*Miscellany,* p. 13) This came out in the May 30, 1903, *Sentinel.*

Can a branch church ever be excommunicated if it fails to follow regulations as set down in the *Manual* (as interpreted by the Boston authorities)? In a newspaper interview of April 30, 1901, answering the charge that she had set herself up as a pope, Mrs. Eddy said that a position of authority had become necessary, that out of experience and prayer she had made a code of bylaws, but that when she had entrusted others with their enforcement, five churches had been subjected to discipline. In this situation she intervened, reuniting them all, so she said. (*Miscellany,* pp. 343-44) Apparently branch churches are themselves subject to discipline.

ONE OF the most vigorous forms of dissent manifested in Christian Science in America is that reflected in a long series of booklets, pamphlets, and circular letters brought out under the pen name of "Paul Revere." For five years the writers did not disclose their identity, although it seems to have been known by the officials of the Mother Church. A reply from the Mother Church Board by long-distance telephone call to a telegram signed *Paul Revere* and giving only a post office box number in Washington, D.C., came to Walter H. Wilson, one of the two men who collaborated in the writing of the Revere material. The other author was Karl N. Smith of Rochester, New York. How they got this information the officials did not reveal. Wilson alleges, rightly or wrongly, that it was through the post office at Washington, a fact which made it difficult for the church officials to discipline offenders Wilson and Smith, since it might involve the officials as well as those from whom the information had been obtained in an unsavory legal difficulty, or at least in undesirable publicity, since the disclosure of such information by any postal employee is strictly forbidden.

The suggestion here is that the information might have been secured by some member of the Christian Science church organization in the employ of the post office, whose loyalty to the church was beyond his loyalty to his employer. If this seems an unworthy suspicion, it is supported by a good deal of evidence from many quarters concerning "leaks" of information in publishing houses, stores, and other places—as in the Corey, Dakin, and other cases. Farallon discovered that even the sales figures on the Corey book, worked out from confidential data in insurance reports, were being transmitted to interested parties in Boston by the insurance broker's secretary, who happened to be a Christian Scientist. Alice L. Orgain found that sections had been removed from copies of her book *As It Is* during the process of printing and binding, and an ultimatum from the Board of Directors in Boston showed that they had advance knowledge of what she was publishing. Eventually Mrs. Orgain was stricken from the *Journal* registry and then excommunicated. Meanwhile, she found herself having to reimburse purchasers of mutilated copies of her book as the result of an unknown informer's depredations. (A. L. Orgain, letter of July 21, 1944)

The attitude of the Paul Revere authors toward the Mother Church is quite different from that of some other dissenters. Although for several years they urged the study of Studdert-Kennedy's *Christian Science and Organized Religion,* the theme of which is that organization per se is the culprit in the strangling of religion by ecclesiasticism, they showed from the beginning a compulsion to correct organization rather than dispense with it. There is no question that in the end they believe organization to be necessary if the essential teachings of Christian Science are to be perpetuated and spread to all mankind. Their writings clearly hold Mrs. Eddy to be infallible, from which it is implied that any institution which she founded must be supported and sustained by her followers.

In consonance with this view, these crusaders accept centralized control as having been wholly right so long as it was in Mrs. Eddy's hands. What they object to is the exercise of such authority by the Directors as her successors. They therefore could not resign in protest, but must remain in the organization while endeavoring to reform it. So, as they write, they took the calculated risk of being expelled by announcing to the world in 1948 who they were. Should excommunication follow, they would merely "be paying the cost of having been members of that immortal band who, down through the ages, have, in the words of Thomas Jefferson, 'sworn upon the altar of God eternal hostility against every form of tyranny over the mind of man.'"

Action against Wilson and Smith was not long delayed. Within a few weeks the first step was taken, that of sending a representative to warn Wilson that the Board regarded the pamphlets as detrimental to the cause of Christian Science, and to propose that their publication cease. Continuation of their publication would jeopardize his membership in the Mother Church.

A second visit, this time of two persons, one presumably to serve as a witness, occurred some two weeks later. Shortly thereafter a letter came from the Board reporting charges that Wilson had "the name without the life of a Christian Scientist," in that he had published materials designed "to injure or destroy The Mother Church" and its activities, as established by their beloved Leader. He had been admonished according to the *Manual*, but to no avail. He was now summoned to appear before a meeting of the Board in Boston, if he so desired, to present any evidence he might have in defense of himself against the charges.

Wilson replied that if the charge was mainly that of being a Christian Scientist only in name, then his twenty-five years of healing, to which hundreds could attest, should be a sufficient refutation. On the other hand, if the publication of the Paul Revere pamphlets was the chief basis of the charge, he would be glad to appear before the Board and to show that they were not inimical to the cause they all loved. Indeed, if in an open discussion the Directors could convince him that he was wrong, he would gladly retract publicly what he had written and would cease further publication. He only asked that since Karl N. Smith was his collaborator as Paul Revere, he would want of course to bring Smith with him to the hearing.

But the Board, in a letter of December 27, 1948, declined to invite Smith to the hearing, while at the same time they made it clear that the chief basis of the formal charge was the publication of the pamphlets.

Wilson in turn declined to attend the hearing on the ground that it was patently disciplinary in character, and it could serve no useful purpose for him to be present.

The Board's emissary on the occasion of his visit had called upon

him in effect "to repent or be excommunicated." Mrs. Eddy had used
the term *repent*, but "to suppose that an interpretation of her by-laws
is correct that empowers a set of five persons whom our Leader
could not possibly know with the right to demand of other Christian
Scientists that they 'repent or be excommunicated,'" ought surely to
awaken the sleepiest Christian Scientist to the realization that someone had flagrantly misinterpreted Mrs. Eddy's instructions. He found
it inconceivable "that our Leader would be so lacking in intelligence
as to formulate by-laws that would keep alive in the consciousness of
her followers a phase of Roman Catholicism so abhorrent to every
Protestant who knows the history of the Dark Ages and the medieval
Roman Catholic Church, and even its present one."

As for expulsion, Wilson wrote,

no excommunication that you can inflict can separate us from the real and
only Mother Church there is, nor make us leave it, or fight the Cause
Mrs. Eddy gave so much to establish. It is still our Church and no one
can really be put out of it. . . . Your love of the Cause impels you to take
your methods, our love of the same Cause impels us to take our methods.
And who is to be the judge of whether or not it is the excommunicators
who are having "the name without the life of a Christian Scientist" or
those excommunicated? Our readers and an increasing number of earnest,
thinking Christian Scientists are growing more sure every day, as the
excommunications of fearless and conscientious members of the Mother
Church increase, that it applies to those who are so mesmerized as to
think they can steady the ark of Truth by excommunications.

The Board met and voted to remove Wilson's name from the
membership roll of the Mother Church. Expressing regret at the
necessity for so doing, the Directors asserted that for twenty-five
years they had lovingly sought to heal the fundamentally wrong
attitude of his which had led them to remove his practitioner's card
from the *Journal* in 1922. They had been obliged three times to
refuse to restore it, they wrote, and now the pamphlets had made it
necessary to take this final step.

Why had Wilson's card been removed from the *Journal* in 1922?
He had supported the Trustees of the Christian Science Publishing
Society during the Great Litigation. That the Board had "lovingly

and patiently worked" with him in the hope of healing him he brands as pure falsehood. "At no time," he says, "was there any evidence of love, nor even human fairness. It was one continuous effort to have me repent or be purged, the same kind of 'loving' effort that has succeeded in purging from our Movement today some of the most spiritually minded and clear-thinking Scientists of our time." He had watched the growth of this ecclesiastical despotism over a period of a quarter of a century. His collaboration with Karl N. Smith in the Paul Revere pamphlets had been resolved upon as one phase of an effort to do everything possible "to correct this growing abuse of power in our church organization."

What position does the Paul Revere school of thought take precisely with reference to the church and its Board of Directors? Chiefly this, that the Board is operating today in violation of more than a score of specific statements in the *Manual*, called the "estoppel clauses," which cannot literally be followed today because Mrs. Eddy is no longer present in the flesh to give her required consent, and yet the Directors purport to be following the *Manual* in all their decisions.

Recognizing that in the famous lawsuit called the Great Litigation the Board of Directors won legal sanction in establishing themselves as Mrs. Eddy's successors in authority, the Paul Revere dissenters believe that, in doing so, they set aside Mrs. Eddy's clear intention to the great detriment of the cause which she founded. So they build unremitting arguments on the theme that the "estoppel clauses" were meant by Mrs. Eddy to be taken seriously, and that if they were so taken, the centralized authority would be automatically dissolved. Instead of an over-all controlling ecclesiastical body, then, the Christian Science church would go forward on an essentially Congregational basis, each local (branch) church independent of any central control, but all bound together as faithful followers of the teachings of Mary Baker Eddy into a genuine and vital Christian Science movement.

This is, of course, the thesis laid down by Geoffrey Hamlin (Wilkinson) back in the twenties, in the wake of the Great Litigation. Frederick Dixon voiced it in his letter of resignation from the Mother Church, when he said that "obedience to Mrs. Eddy can only be achieved by dissolving the material organization of the Mother Church, the spiritual reality [of which] is, of course, indestructible." Herbert Eustace, who long recommended Studdert-Kennedy's *Christian Science and Organized Religion* to his students, today takes the same stand as the Revere school, and points to Mrs. Eddy's early Congregational background in support of the view that she intended her church to follow along Congregational lines after her hand was withdrawn from the controls.

That such a movement could thrive without Mother Church dependence is, they think, demonstrated by the fact that from 1889 to 1892, when there was no organized church in Boston, as many as 119 local Christian Science churches were formed, not as branches of the Mother Church, but as voluntary associations of Christian Scientists with a common cause. Furthermore, at the present time Christian Science societies are being formed and exist for a considerable period as societies before they are recognized by the Mother Church as branch churches. Yet they carry on exactly as churches, their final acceptance as branches being more or less "pro forma."

This is what the Paul Revere people propose should now be done, since anything else would be in violation of the *Manual* provisions. Under this plan, The First Church of Christ, Scientist, in Boston, would continue to function under its Board of Directors as decreed by Mrs. Eddy, but it would simply be one of the many Christian Science churches, greatly loved and revered because of its intimate association with the Founder but having no control over any other Christian Science church. When it is pointed out that Mrs. Eddy declared the Mother Church a *ruling* church, with the branch churches no more than satellites (*Miscellany*, pp. 343-44), Wilson and Smith admit no basic conflict. It is their contention that any seeming conflict in Mrs. Eddy's works is readily resolved when her words and acts are interpreted spiritually.

Mrs. Wilson goes really to the heart of their problem in her pamphlet *Demonstrating the True Concept of Church*. The trouble is, she says, that most Christian Scientists are under the impression that Mrs. Eddy established a material organization, whereas her real establishment was that of "the structure of Truth and Love; whatever rests upon and proceeds from divine Principle." This spiritual concept of Church "supersedes the concept of membership in a centrally controlled material organization in Boston," and the official preoccupation with obedience to constituted authority rather than to Principle. Since error is but a false concept of a spiritual fact, it is not to be corrected by ecclesiastical brute force, so to speak, but by knowing the truth about it.

To be sure, Mrs. Eddy did employ material organization, but only as a temporary concession to the period, pointing out that it was not indispensable to establishing Christ's church, which church she defined as the inviolable bond of love for one another. The resolution dissolving her church organization in 1889 declared that the church had reached the point where it must free itself of the thraldom of man-made laws in order to rise spiritually; also, that to achieve its goal as an institution, progress in spiritual life and the spread of the gospel, they must operate as a voluntary association of Christian Scientists, knowing no law but the law of Love and no master but Christ in the exercise of such ministrations and activities as they had heretofore performed as a church. And Mrs. Eddy afterward observed that this dissolution was followed at once by "a great revival of mutual love, prosperity, and spiritual power."

Mrs. Wilson argues that the *Manual* (p. 133) made legal provision for dissolution of the Mother Church as such, and that the "estoppel clauses" left the obedient follower of Mary Baker Eddy no choice but to dissolve the centralized authority with Mrs. Eddy's passing. As the Paul Revere school sees it, Mrs. Eddy foresaw and provided for this very contingency, leaving unmistakable instructions in her writings. And had she not written that the material form is a "Suffer it to be so now," to be abandoned when Christ, God's Way-shower, should point the advanced step? (*Miscellany*, p. 140)

Eventually Karl N. Smith was excommunicated also.

THE EXCOMMUNICATION of Wilson and Smith did not end the Paul Revere movement, but set off a train of events unique in the

history of Christian Science, and sufficiently newsworthy to generate
national publicity.

Fourth Church of Christ, Scientist, Rochester, New York, was the
home church of the originators of the Paul Revere movement, and
had clearly been suspect, if not in open disfavor, with the Board of
Directors of the Mother Church since the days of the Great Litigation. Fourth Church was one of the few branches which felt duty
bound, under the *Manual* requirement that all Christian Scientists
support the official periodicals, to continue their paid advertisements
in the *Journal* during the time that publication was under condemnation by the Board.

Now the Boston Directors removed the First Reader of that
church, Mrs. Maude S. Hartung, by putting her on probation for
being involved in the Paul Revere activities. As a result of this
action by the Mother Church authorities, the Rochester church on
April 12, 1950, passed a set of resolutions in which it formally
severed its connection with the Mother Church. The members
declare:

In consequence of the stand taken by this church, for nearly thirty years,
against the encroachment of this ecclesiastical power, on the part of the
Christian Science Board of Directors, the church has suffered unwarranted
persecutions and interference with the free and democratic exercise of its
rights as a Church of Christ, Scientist.

The encroachment, "culminating in this recent arbitrary action by
the Board against our Readers . . . has so decimated our ranks that
the church is now forced either to close its doors or take some step
to free itself from this bond of ecclesiastical control."

One wishes that they had been more specific, but they evidently
felt justified in affirming that

we take this step, not only because of the persecutions of our own church
and the resultant decimation of our own membership, but because, in a
far larger way, these persecutions, the many excommunications from The
Mother Church,—and the falling away of interest in Christian Science so
evident throughout the world—are all the effects of the same false sense
of church government; and that the time has come when we must take

this action in order to help establish the true concept of church founded by our beloved Leader, Mary Baker Eddy.

While Fourth Church would no longer tolerate "the attempted control by an autocratic form of government in Boston which is so at variance with Mrs. Eddy's teachings," in severing its connection with the Mother Church it is, it asserts, "not hostile to nor fighting against anything established by Mrs. Eddy; loyal to Mrs. Eddy's teachings; operating in strict obedience to the divinely inspired by-laws left by her; and adhering, in the conduct of its services and other of its affairs, to her explicit instructions in the *Manual*."

What attitude has been taken by the Boston authorities? For one thing, the Christian Science Publishing Society has refused to accept Fourth Church's checks for publications essential to the conduct of church services, such as the Bible, *Science and Health*, the Lesson Quarterly, and others issued by the church, on the ground that Rochester's Fourth Church, although it is a corporation under the laws of New York State, is not a legitimate Christian Science church. This provokes Paul Revere to remark:

Think of it! The American Bible Society distributes Bibles to millions in every quarter of the globe, in darkest Africa, benighted China, even to the Eskimos in the Arctic regions, but the great Christian Science Publishing Society refuses to sell the Bible, *Science and Health*, etc., so much needed for the healing of mankind, to little Fourth Church—little and few in numbers, but mighty in the right.

THE CASE of Second Church of Christ, Scientist, Watford, England, is somewhat similar to that of Rochester's Fourth Church, though there seems not to have been any excommunication of individual members. The similarity lies in the basic motivation of the two cases—a firm conviction that the estoppel clauses of the *Manual* make the operation of the Christian Science church as carried on by the Boston authorities quite illegitimate, even contrary to the desires of Mrs. Eddy herself. To this is added a certain irritation from requirements laid upon the Watford church by "headquarters."

The Watford people wrote the Directors on November 15, 1949, that they were troubled by the increasing demands of Boston for various kinds of information—some of a very personal and private nature—and for material statistics, coming in the form of exhaustive questionnaires; and also by letters from officers and departments of the Mother Church to individual officers of the Watford church, presenting various policies and asking for compliance with them. In some instances these had amounted to directives.

These were but a few of the items which "served to show the extent to which the policies and government of The Mother Church are encroaching upon and fast absorbing the individuality of the branch church with its 'Local Self-Government.'"

In reply, the Board of Directors of the Mother Church, with seeming great patience and reasonableness, cited passages from Mrs. Eddy's writings to indicate her intention that her church should go on in the way it was being conducted. In this connection they cited Mrs. Eddy's oft-quoted letter of February 27, 1903, in which she had said that the word of God and the *Manual* had guided them in the past and would remain to guide them in the future—without mentioning that the bylaws there referred to had been changed shortly after the letter was written. The Directors' position had been upheld by the courts, they declared, but that this did not mean that there was only a legal basis for the present government of the church. They had carefully studied Mrs. Eddy's plan and were endeavoring to carry it out fully.

This failed to satisfy the Watford dissenters, and the Boston Board interpreted their letter of dissent as an implied request for withdrawal, voting to withdraw their recognition as a branch of the Mother Church. The Watford church, while repudiating this interpretation, accepted the severance. At the same time, the dissenters wrote Boston that

our action, rightly understood, is not a termination of our relationship with The Mother Church; it is but the beginning of the right relationship required by the *Church Manual*, which gives The Mother Church her own unique status and government, and to each branch church its own individual place and the requirement to demonstrate its own "Local Self-Government." Therefore, what we are terminating is only our participation in procedure which annuls the by-laws of The Mother Church *Manual* and obstructs their spiritual purpose; by this action we become more closely united with the divine *source* from which Mrs. Eddy's founding proceded, and in which source alone each branch church must find its roots, authority, and government. Surely this entitles us more than ever before to be known as a "branch Church of Christ, Scientist."

Will other churches follow the lead of these two? Paul Revere thinks they will. The author knows of no other churches that have either voluntarily withdrawn or been excommunicated in the whole history of the movement since Mrs. Eddy. This fact in itself may be quite significant. It is clearly so regarded by the Directors, who speak somewhat deprecatingly of the dissent expressed from time to time by elements within the organization, and refer to the "monolithic" strength of the church as a whole. Whether this monolithic aspect of the church is as much a fact as they allege is sharply questioned by prominent dissenters who are in touch with large numbers of people in the field.

9

Christian Science and Law

CHRISTIAN SCIENCE IS of course more than a healing movement. It has a philosophy, a theology, an organization, a discipline; indeed, it is a way of life. But healing is central in it, and probably most of those who have been drawn into it have come because of some experience of healing, or at least in expectation of healing. That many genuinely ailing persons have recovered their health while under its ministrations there can be no doubt.

It is true that some patients have suffered and died while in the hands of Christian Science practitioners, but it is argued that the same charge could be brought against the practitioners of materia medica. Before the Massachusetts legislature in 1898, William Lloyd Garrison contended:

The death of a patient under "irregular treatment," although it may be demonstrated that the greatest care and intelligence were used, is heralded abroad as something scandalous and dreadful, but if any regular physician were to make public the deaths coming to his knowledge from misapprehension of the disease, or because of mistaken remedies used, the public might well be alarmed. (*Christian Science and Legislation*, p. 33)

The official church literature has from the beginning abounded in testimonies as to illnesses overcome by Christian Scientists without recourse to material aid. Critical observers point out that often the diagnosis of the particular disease or ill from which the Christian Scientist patient recovered was not scientific, inasmuch as almost none of Mrs. Eddy's followers is trained to diagnose physical disorders.

In early numbers of the *Journal* the healing testimonies were preceded by the flat statement that they had been authenticated. This has been modified until today the statement is that the healings related have been carefully verified "to the best of our ability," and that the correspondence relative thereto is on file in the Publishing House at Boston. This is somewhat reassuring, but the objective student would want to inquire just what the editors regard as "verification." Is it likely that this word has for them the same meaning that it would have for a medical diagnostician?

Mrs. Eddy's followers complain that generally, when confronted by the attested healings of Christian Science, members of the medical fraternity deny either the correctness of the diagnosis originally, or the cure. Claims of healings impossible from the medical point of view are naturally unacceptable to a doctor of medicine; however, this is not the chief obstacle to providing corroborative medical testimony. Loyal Eddy followers explain that they are precluded from seeking such unassailable evidence by their Leader's teaching that medical examinations are fraught with peril. "A physical diagnosis of disease—since mortal mind must be the cause of disease—tends to induce disease." (*Science and Health,* p. 370) Materia medica, as they call it, is believed to be a channel for mental malpractice, and in the field the warning is often heard that "the doctor will put a law on the patient."

When a testimony is submitted for publication, the verification required is simply that the healing be attested by a member of the church in good standing, and that the word of this witness be supported by that of another member in good standing with the church. "Verification" here obviously does not mean that the healing has had to be confirmed by a competent physical examination before and afterward.

Despite this, there have been numerous cases in which Christian Science healings of an impressive character have been confirmed by competent physical diagnoses. So, while recognizing the possibility that not all the testimonies given represent genuine healings, one cannot reasonably doubt that many people have been restored to vigorous health under Christian Science treatment.

No fair-minded investigator could fail to be impressed by such healings as that of Mrs. David Oliver, the Chicagoan, which was recognized in the *Journal of the American Medical Association* as "the first instance recorded of recovery from generalized blastomycosis," a condition described therein as hideous and desperate. While this medical paper makes no mention of the fact that the patient had turned to Christian Science after the doctors had failed her, it does admit that she recovered quite without medication of any sort. (B. O. Flower, *Christian Science as a Religious Belief and a Therapeutic Agent,* pp. 105-15)

It is a well-known fact that many attempts at Christian Science healing have failed, for one reason or another; and some of these failures have led to serious difficulties for the movement. Practitioners have been brought into court on the charge that they were the cause of their patients' deaths, and this happened not infrequently during Mrs. Eddy's lifetime.

Abbey H. Corner, of West Medford, Massachusetts, having gone through Primary class in the Massachusetts Metaphysical College, attended her own daughter in childbirth. When both the young mother and her child died, the townspeople were highly incensed and brought charges of murder against the elderly practitioner. At the trial Mrs. Corner was acquitted on the ground that her daughter's death resulted from a hemorrhage which might have occurred and proved fatal even if a physician had been in attendance.

In San Bernardino, California, a practitioner was indicted and tried for manslaughter in 1893, on the death of one of her patients. After a five-day trial, she was acquitted. Physicians testified that, as a post mortem examination showed, a surgical operation would have relieved the patient and saved her life. But it was brought out in the course of the trial that the physician who had attended the patient before the practitioner was engaged had recommended no surgery. Who was guilty of her death, then? the defendant's attorneys asked.

In a more recent example, during the thirties a Detroit widower entrusted his eight-year-old daughter to the care of his sister-in-law in Chicago. The child was a diabetic, but had been doing well under regular insulin injections. Her aunt put the case into the hands of a prominent Christian Science practitioner, whose motto was "no medication." Soon the little girl lapsed into a coma and died. The father brought both his sister-in-law and the practitioner into court on a charge of manslaughter, but the defendants were dismissed on the judge's ruling that the aunt, as the child's guardian, was entitled to choose the kind of treatment employed.

The Christian Scientists have not always fared so happily in the courts. One Lotte Post, of McGregor, Iowa, was arrested in 1887, tried three times, and fined for "practicing medicine without a license." She was one of the first among many to be haled before the bench on this particular charge. It was generally felt that too much was at stake to allow religionists, with no recognized qualifications, to invade the healing profession. Other physicians were required to produce their credentials of proper training, submit to examination as to their abilities, and secure a license for the practice of healing. How else, it was asked, could the public be protected from quacks and irresponsible fanatics? If Christian Scientists were indeed to take the place of physicians, why should they not be required to do the same?

The Christian Scientists replied variously. They countercharged that the prosecutions were instigated by organized medicine, seeking a monopoly which must eventuate in a state healing system and thwart all progress by blocking exploration of other methods of healing. It was argued that in every stage of human progress there was a time when wisdom was with the minority, and that the protection of the minority from the tyranny of the majority is the criterion of good government. (Clifford P. Smith, *Christian Science and Legislation,* p. 16) Declaring medicine to be "merely experimental and not an exact science," they quoted Chief Justice Clark of North Carolina's Supreme Court: "An eminent medical authority in this State has said that out of twenty-four serious cases of disease, three could not be cured by the best remedies, three others might be benefited, and the rest would get well anyway." The medical fraternity might hold up its impressive academic background as a criterion, but it could be argued that Christian healing, as exemplified by Jesus, required no such equipment. Clifford P. Smith explained that all the information on material subjects required for the practice of Christian Science is supplied by an ordinary education, since success in this practice is dependent not upon material knowledge, but on spiritual qualifications won through labors far transcending the effort required to win a college diploma. (*Christian Science: Its Legal Status,* p. 36)

Cures were claimed for Christian Science in many instances where the doctors had failed to effect relief, and voluminous testimony was marshaled to support this claim. A great point was made of the "sacred right" of every citizen to choose his own physician, citing the words of Governor Thomas of Colorado:

He may indeed select a healer of doubtful reputation or conceded incompetence, but that is his affair, just as much as is his choice of a minister or attorney. His action may prove injurious, possibly fatal, to himself or some members of his family, [but] it is better so than to delegate to any tribunal the power to say "thou shalt not employ this man" or "thou shalt employ this one."

It was argued that Christian Science is a religion, with "healing its very foundation stone," so that any restriction on its practices would be "a blow at religious liberty." (*Christian Science Journal,* XVI, 101) Quoted often was an editorial from the legal periodical *Law Notes,* which said: "Even if the doctrine is pronounced a groundless superstition, its believers have a constitutional right to hold and follow what seems to them a system of truth."

Out of all the defensive arguments raised, this question of untrammeled freedom to practice one's religion, guaranteed by the Constitution of the United States, emerged as the most effective. It gradually began to turn the tide, and today remains the decisive legal weapon in the defensive arsenal of the Christian Science church.

In 1911, shortly after Mrs. Eddy's death, a case brought in New York City was decided favorably to Christian Science practice in the state Court of Appeals. (*People* v. *Cole,* 219, N.Y. Rep. 98) Supplementing the written opinion of the Court, one judge added: "I deny the power of the Legislature to make it a crime to treat disease by

333333

prayer." This note was caught up by the Christian Scientists and sounded increasingly. Said Septimus J. Hanna:

In undertaking to restrict Christian Scientists in their practice, or to prohibit them, our legislators are saying in effect to the people: You have no right to employ such help as you please. You have no right to ask your neighbor to pray for your recovery to health . . . to commune with God in your behalf . . . even to invoke the divine grace for yourself. (*Civil and Religious Liberty*, p. 51)

Here was an appeal which few Christians, if any, could withstand; and it has not been unusual since then for the Christian Scientists to draw sympathy and even overt support from other churches, as well as from a large section of the public press, in resisting actions brought against them.

Gradually the Christian Science practitioners' legal right to practice has been won in most states. This acceptance has been hastened by energetic lobbying, organized letter-writing campaigns, and so on. As far back as 1898, according to George H. Kintner, writing in the *Journal* (XVI, 96), when legislation inimical to Christian Science was anticipated, many Christian Scientists and their friends, acting on the advice quietly secured from a Supreme Court justice who was friendly to the cause because of the healing of his wife when doctors had failed, sent letters to their representatives in Albany, thus bringing a substantial influence to bear upon the lawmakers. In 1953 a United States congressman related that when he was a member of the California state legislature, that body had been prevailed upon, by an overwhelming flood of communications, to reverse itself on a bill which the Christian Scientists disapproved. "I myself received around seven hundred letters from the village of Los Gatos alone," he said.

Christians, of course, have always prayed for the sick. But they see no incongruity in taking such human measures as seem desirable and helpful at the same time. The Christian Science church regards this position as self-defeating. The Christian Science theory as to the cause and cure of disease is quite the opposite of "materia medica's" theory, wrote one of the leading spokesmen at the outset. Likewise, reliance on material drugs and faith in God's supremacy are opposed and cannot be combined in the healing of the sick. The failure of the prayers of those who substitute faith in drugs for faith in God to effect healing, he asserted, proves their incompatibility. (*Christian Science and Legislation*, p. 35)

Mrs. Eddy's repudiation of materia medica she stated comprehensively in a New York newspaper article, reproduced in the April, 1901, *Journal* (XIX, 2-7), the material from which is today scattered throughout her published writings. The official position today remains essentially the same, as set forth in a proclamation entitled "Concerning Use of Drugs and Medicine" (*Sentinel*, XLIV, 812-13, *Journal*, LX, 174-75, etc., etc.), the theme of which is that "Material medicine has no place in the life of a Christian Scientist." Can such proclamations be disregarded, or are they orders to the field? In striking the famous Margaret Laird from the practitioners' registry in 1948, the Mother Church Directors wrote her that according to reports she had countenanced the use of medical help by her patients.

This uncompromising opposition to medical aid has naturally led to grave legal difficulties. As the Boston organization has steadily acquired greater prestige, there have however been correspondingly fewer prosecutions and convictions. Even so, the climate of public opinion seems to be changing. The courts of late have been frequently ruling against religionists who seek constitutional immunity from medical requirements. In 1952 a Texas judge issued an injunction restraining the family of an unconscious accident victim from interfering with a blood transfusion. These people were Jehovah's Witnesses, and the tenets of their faith prohibited "tampering with the blood" on that sect's interpretation of scriptural authority. (*People* v. *Olliff*) When in 1953 a little girl was bitten by a mad dog at Memphis, Tennessee, her parents declined medical attention on the ground that she had been instantly healed by the Lord through prayer. They were members of the Church of Jesus Christ, whose minister vouched for them. The judge, while declaring respect for their beliefs, made the child a ward of the court and committed her to a hospital for anti-rabies shots. (*People* v. *Smith*) In 1938 the Supreme Court of the State of Washington declared it a crime directly to advise any patient to abstain from necessary medical or surgical care. (*State* v. *Karsonsky*) A far-reaching decision was handed down in 1951 when the Illinois Supreme Court ruled that citizens are free to "practice their religion as they wish, but such practice is wrong if it affects the life of a third party." (*People* v. *Labrenz*) In April, 1957, a Superior Court judge in Chicago ordered a Christian Scientist mother to allow a physician to give her child polio shots if he felt it to be necessary. The judge said: "It is in the public interest that the spread of such disease be prevented at all costs." (Associated Press, April 23, 1957) On the very same date, the California Supreme Court ruled that, under the Constitution, freedom to *believe* is absolute, but that, by the very nature of things, freedom to *act* remains subject to regulation for the protection of society.

The legal right of practitioners of Christian Science to collect fees for their ministrations has been established, but belatedly. For many years, some of the states maintained laws specifically forbidding charges for such professional services to patients. Only recently have Ohio, West Virginia, and Texas yielded on this score. The church has widely distributed a leaflet called *The Laborer and His Hire,* arguing the propriety and justice of practitioners' charges, and Mrs. Eddy is quoted as advising that such charges should be equivalent to those of medical doctors in the community.

The degree and form of recognition varies greatly throughout the country, as can be seen from the *Table of Legal Provisions Upholding Freedom in Religion, Health, Education,* a pamphlet put out by the Christian Science Publishing Society primarily for the convenience of the Committees on Publication. A Colorado statute states that "nothing in this Act shall be construed to prohibit the practice of Christian Science with or without compensation." The Illinois statute reads that the "Act shall not apply to persons treating human ailments by prayer or spiritual means as an exercise or enjoyment of religious freedom." Many of the states add that such permission to practice is subject to certain other laws relating to communicable diseases and sanitary matters.

In only sixteen of the states is Christian Science specifically mentioned in the statutes, the rest using a general formula under which not only Christian Science but other healing movements may operate. This would of course be in keeping with the spirit of the pioneer Christian Scientists who, when the movement was struggling for a foothold, deplored limitations on anyone, however unorthodox, in the exercise of religious freedom of practice. When their own position was insecure the Scientists had argued that discrimination by law between methods of healing had the effect of depriving the people of the right to choose freely between them, created a monopoly, and in effect established a state healing system. Since the exercise of religion was involved, it practically established a state religion, they held. (*Christian Science and Legislation,* p. 41)

But with the gradual entrenchment of the Christian Science organization as a settled institution, there has been a growing trend toward seeking legislative advantages for Christian Science church practitioners exclusively. For example, the Maryland legislators were persuaded to specify that nothing in the laws of their state "shall prevent any Christian Science practitioner duly registered in the Christian Science Journal of the Christian Science Publishing Society, Boston, Massachusetts, from treating human ills in accordance with the tenets of Christian Science or from making an adequate charge for services performed."

It may well be asked if such a law would not make the Publishing Society, in effect, a licensing bureau. Would it not give the church authorities unlimited power over any who might seek to practice? And some would certainly regard this as an ecclesiastical monopoly such as was denounced by Mrs. Eddy. Could such discriminative legislation survive a Supreme Court test of its constitutionality? Committees on Publication have been known to advise patients against payment of bills for services by Christian Science practitioners unlisted in the *Christian Science Journal.*

In earlier periods, judges and juries denied Christian Scientists compensation in accident and other damage suits, on the premise that the Scientists could not pronounce their injuries unreal and then claim damages under the law. The climate has gradually changed, and now practitioners are authorized by statute to sign

certificates for sick leave and for disability claims in seven states—
Colorado, Illinois, Massachusetts, New Jersey, Oregon, Pennsylvania,
and Wisconsin—and for federal employees. In health, accident, and
hospitalization policies, some insurance companies today recognize
the services of a Christian Science practitioner in lieu of a physician
or surgeon. One of these is the Bankers National Life Insurance
Company of Montclair, New Jersey.

Christian Science nurses are exempted from registration in
twenty states. They are not always exempted specifically as Christian Scientists; rather, they come under a general exemption
variously stated but usually in terms similar to those of the California law, which "does not prohibit nursing or the care of the sick,
with or without compensation or personal profit, when done by the
adherents of and in connection with the practice of the religious
tenets of any well recognized church or denomination, so long as
they do not otherwise engage in the practice of nursing." (Sec.
2731) Only four states mention Christian Science nurses specifically.

Though the Christian Science church maintains but two sanatoria, one near Boston and one at San Francisco, there are in
various parts of the country and abroad nursing homes which are
run by and for Christian Scientists. Some of them operate on a nonprofit basis, under a board of trustees or a foundation, to which
Christian Scientists contribute very much as members of other
denominations do to their hospitals. There is a Committee of the
Mother Church on Christian Science Nursing Homes, which certifies
those that fulfil requirements set up at Boston headquarters.

John V. Dittemore, sometime Director on the Mother Church
Board, once reported that an inordinate number of fatalities
had occurred at the two sanitoria operated by the church. Since
that time more stringent rules have been promulgated for screening
applicants. An instruction sheet accompanying application blanks
lays down twenty-one stipulations, including the following:

When the applicant is experiencing physical or other difficulties, TWO
letters of reference must be received before final action can be taken on
his application. If he is receiving treatment, one letter should be from his
practitioner, and it should supply full details as to the nature of the

problem and the phases it assumes. [The writers must] supply details as to the nature and present condition of any physical or other difficulty.... These letters should contain frank statements of the writer's opinion, and he should remember that the welfare of the Benevolent Association, as well as that of the applicant, is to be considered.

People who use tobacco or alcohol are excluded, and under legal restrictions the sanatoria do not "receive maternity cases, so-called mental cases, or those of a contagious or infectious nature."

Ordinarily institutions caring for the sick are subject to state inspection and held to certain medical requirements. These Christian Science nursing homes have won exemption from such requirements in sixteen states—or rather legislation of a general nature, covering not only Christian Science but other forms of religion which practice healing, has been written into the statute books of the states. California, for example, in its law dealing with hospitals, nursing homes, etc., declares that the provisions of the law as to licensing, inspection, and regulation of such institutions do not apply to any institution "conducted by and for adherents of any well recognized church or religious denomination for the purpose of providing facilities for the care and treatment of the sick who depend upon prayer or spiritual means for healing in the practice of the religion of such church or denomination." (*Health and Safety Code*, Sec. 1415)

All this, of course, raises basic questions about sanitation and hygiene. Mrs. Eddy taught that "the less we know or think about hygiene, the less we are predisposed to sickness" (*Science and Health*, p. 389), and "when there are fewer prescriptions, and less thought is given to sanitary subjects, there will be better constitutions and less disease" (p. 175). Thus her followers have always taken a militant stand against exposure to instruction in sanitary and hygienic measures, asserting that "a mind impregnated with theories of sickness and filled with mental pictures of disease, will do more to make a diseased mortal than all the germs and bacteria that were ever propagated." (*Sentinel*, XVI, 463) This campaign against what they term "medical indoctrination" has been very much intensified of late.

In 1950 the New York state legislature passed a law providing that "a pupil may be excused from such study of health and hygiene as conflicts with the religion of his parents or guardian." In reporting this, the *Scientific American* of February, 1952, observed:

Under this provision the State Commissioner of Education has ordered the exemption of Christian Science children from instruction in disease prevention and control. Among the excluded topics are the building up of resistance to disease; control of communicable disease; the importance of pure food and water; what bacteria are; first-aid treatment, and so on.

Publication of this item, which was entitled "The Right to Be Ignorant," brought an immediate rejoinder from the church authorities. In a letter to the magazine, spokesman George Channing denied that the Christian Science church was behind the state action. However, "medical indoctrination" in the schools was deplored on the ground that "such teaching tends to undermine the religious teaching given Christian Science children in the home. In so doing it invalidates a right of individual conscience priceless to all free men."

The official position is set forth in the *Christian Science Sentinel* of July 12, 1952, in a policy statement by the Christian Science Board of Directors—a proclamation which, it was there asserted, had been of great value throughout the year to maintain and extend the legal rights of Christian Scientists. According to the accompanying text, their deepest religious convictions were violated by medical indoctrination, examination, and treatment. The Board lauded an increasing volume of protests firmly made by Christian Scientists against medical examination. It also announced special exemption-demand cards which parents were encouraged to use.

The Board of Directors of the Mother Church declares that to force medication or any kind of medical examination upon a Christian Scientist is to violate his clear constitutional rights. (*Sentinel,* LIV, 1225) Despite this uncompromising declaration, it appears that the church authorities do not oppose, nor do they recommend resistance to, the examination and medication (vaccination, inoculation, immunization, etc.) imposed upon Christian Scientist draftees and volunteers when they are inducted into U.S. military service.

In view of the Board's apparently passive attitude toward the compulsory examination and medication of Christian Scientists drafted by the armed forces, some have found it difficult to understand the militant opposition of Christian Science officialdom to fluoridation of water systems for the prevention of tooth decay. While the quantities of fluorine introduced into the city water supplies are so small as to be generally considered harmless, the church officials have objected strenuously, terming fluoridation a species of mass medication which obliges them, as citizens of a given city or state, to violate a religious principle every time they drink a glass of water. They liken this to forcing a Roman Catholic to eat meat on Friday.

This is a particularly vexed question in view of the fact that the Christian Scientists have accepted without protest the introduction of chlorine into their water supplies. Confronted with this seeming inconsistency, they have held that there is a fundamental difference between the two treatments. In the one case, the chlorine is introduced into the water system in order to destroy certain bacteria to make the water fit for drinking purposes. It is the water which is treated, not persons. On the other hand, the introduction of fluorine into the water makes of it a kind of medicine designed to affect the health. That is to say, it is a medical treatment. Therefore, drinking water so treated is quite contrary to the beliefs of the Christian Scientists.

The fluoridation of drinking water to prevent cavities in the teeth is something comparatively new, and many people, including a few doctors, are not yet convinced of its value. But where fluoridation has been proposed, the fight against it has been led by the Christian Scientists, who in some cases have blocked or secured the reversal of legislation in favor of it.

According to the *Table of Legal Provisions* put out by the church, laws in thirteen states—among them New York and Indiana—exempt children from the requirement of taking health instructions in the schools. Twenty-eight states do not require persons who for one reason or another might be expected to do so to undergo medical examination, vaccination, or treatment if they have religious objections thereto. The Michigan law reads that "no person who objects thereto ... shall be compelled to receive medical or physical examination, medical instruction, or medical treatment of any nature," making no mention of religion as a basis for such refusal. The New Jersey law states that "any person who indicates that he subscribes to the art of healing by prayer as practiced by any well recognized religious denomination, the principles of which are opposed to medical treatment, shall not be required to submit to medical treatment without his consent." The Pennsylvania statute declares that

this Act shall not be construed to compel any teacher, school employe, or pupil to submit to any medical or dental treatment under the authority of this Act, when such teacher, employe, or parent, or guardian objects to the same on religious grounds, or to permit any discrimination against such teacher, employe, or pupil on account of the same.

In eleven states specific provision is made for exemption of children from vaccination, inoculation, and immunization. Here religion is seldom given as the reason, and in no cases are Christian Science children specifically exempted.

When in 1952 it was disclosed that questions on such topics as hygiene, the prevention and control of disease, the importance of pure food and water, the germ theory, and so forth had been omitted from high-school examinations throughout the state of New York, a storm broke. *School and Society* carried an extended article on "Health, Welfare and Religious Freedom," asserting that great harm to the public would result from such legislation as the amendment to the Education Law, Section 3204, Chapter 135, which added the following: "Subject to rules and regulations of the Board of Regents, a pupil may be excused from such study of health and hygiene as conflicts with the religion of his parents or guardian." The article earnestly called for a re-examination of the whole problem of health and religious freedom. At once a movement was set on foot to repeal the amendment. Finally a compromise bill, known as the Morgan-Brydges Bill, exempting children of Christian Scientists from the study of disease symptomology and therapy, but not from the study of the public health aspects of the subject, was passed and signed by Governor Dewey. (*New York Times,* April 9, 1952) Later attempts to repeal the original amendment were defeated, and so at this writing the law stands as defined in the Morgan-Brydges Bill.

A point at which the public has been less tolerant of the effect of peculiar religious beliefs on health practices is the question of contagious or infectious diseases. What is the attitude of Christian Scientists toward such illnesses? In theory or principle there is and can be no difference between diseases among them, for none is real, all are only false belief. All are eradicable, they hold, through metaphysical treatment. Christian Science spokesmen assert that it is the accepted rule among practitioners, out of deference to public sentiment, to report, as they are required to do in most states, cases of a contagious nature.

But here a real difficulty is encountered, for this means that the ailment must be diagnosed as a contagious one. Practitioners are not trained in the identification of symptoms; neither are they permitted by law to make a diagnosis. "Only a registered physician may make a diagnosis," observes the Illinois Committee on Publication in its 1938 bulletin. The Committee advises Christian Scientists to report contagious disease "as soon as the reason for the report becomes evident, unless the disorder is immediately destroyed, as it should be by the effectual practice of Christian Science." But is the practitioner qualified to determine when a contagious disease is destroyed, in the absence of expert medical findings?

Time reported, in its issue of May 29, 1954, the case of a schoolteacher, a Christian Scientist, who each year made affidavit that she was free from any infectious disease. She was, however, under treatment at the hands of a practitioner for "living congestion and over-activity." Finally, under pressure from relatives, she was sent to the hospital where, a day later, she died of tuberculosis. For two years, while suffering from this infectious disease, she was in close contact with a substantial group of students. Efforts were at once begun to make sure that every pupil who had any contact with her should undergo a fluoroscopic lung test to see if any had been infected by her. Meanwhile the *Christian Science Sentinel* (LIV, 1225, *passim*) takes a militant stand specifically against X-ray chest examinations.

Nine states prescribe by law that persons who rely on spiritual means of healing shall not be required to enter hospitals or other medical institutions even in the case of communicable diseases, unless there is no other way of isolating them. Most of these states provide for quarantine in the home. Presumably none of the states free Christian Scientists from some kind of control in case of contagious or infectious disease. I am told by Christian Scientists that they do not seek such release—that what they resist is enforced confinement in medical institutions in which they do not believe, and subjection to the treatment given there; they do not want to offend their neighbors and friends who do not share their beliefs.

One section of the *Table* deals with venereal diseases. In a great many states there is compulsory treatment of these diseases, but in at least eight states there is exemption from compulsory treatment even of these diseases in case such treatment is regarded as going counter to the patient's religious beliefs. Usually, however, as in the California law for control of venereal diseases, all cases must be reported and are subject to regulation as to isolation or quarantine and as to types of employment in which the patient may not engage so long as he is suffering from the disease. Again the question arises of how the Christian Science practitioner is to determine whether his patient is free of the disease without blood tests or other physical determination, since the symptoms of syphilis are not always otherwise evident.

A number of states require prenatal examinations of pregnant women, including a blood test for syphilis. But apparently the woman is not required to furnish the necessary blood sample, for it is specifically stated in several state laws that a physician who has been refused a blood sample by the patient is not subject to penalty for his failure to make such an examination.

We have here sampled, rather than reported *in extenso*, the recognition that has been won for Christian Science in the laws respecting health, medicine, etc. It is a constant preoccupation of the Committee on Publication in each region to keep a sharp watch in his territory. Usually he will be acquainted with some member of the legislature; or there may be one or more members of the Christian Science church in the lawmaking body. These can be counted upon to alert him if any matter affecting Christian Science is to come up during the legislative session. If so warned, he must spend as much of his time as necessary either at the state capital interviewing legislators in the matter, or by correspondence or otherwise seeking to get Christian Scientists and others who might share their views at that precise point to write their representatives. In short, Christian Scientists attempt to influence legislation in the direction their faith indicates.

Christian Scientists, like most minority groups, are extremely sensitive at points affecting their faith and its practice, so they are more easily stirred to expression of their sentiments than members of majority groups. As we have seen, there is one person or several people in each local church whose duty it is to co-operate with the State Committee on Publication. The local agent or agents can usually be depended upon to awaken local members to do something about the question at issue—such as writing letters, enlisting others to do the same, calling upon officials and other influential people, and so on. Since few persons take the trouble to write in their views for or against proposed legislation unless there has been a good deal of publicity given the matter, the overwhelming expression of opinion is often that representing the Christian Science or minority viewpoint. Legislators, therefore, unless the issue is sharply drawn, give their consent to or oppose the proposed bill in accord with the expressed wishes of the vocal group.

The writer once asked a Committee on Publication about what proportion of his time was devoted to legislative matters, and his reply was "about half" of his working hours.

This kind of work is carried on not only at the state level, but at the national level as well. A Committee for the District of Columbia, at Washington, is assigned to watch national legislation. One of the church's very strongest and ablest men is usually given this post.

10

Growth and Spread of Christian Science

THE GROWTH and spread of Christian Science in the early years was very slow. There was strong opposition to it both from the churches and from the medical profession. To the former it seemed a radical departure from what most Christians thought about God, Jesus, the Holy Spirit, prayer, and the nature of the world and man. The idea of the unreality of sin and evil, the repudiation of the current ideas of heaven and hell, cut sharply across the beliefs of evangelical Christians of the time. So Christian Science was bitterly opposed in pulpit and press, and held up to ridicule.

The medical profession had a stake in the matter. If people with a few simple lessons from Mrs. Eddy, or, later, some other teacher, could set up as doctors, then the medical practitioners who spent long years in study and apprenticeship were at a clear disadvantage. And where was the careful diagnosis that they were sure must precede treatment? These untrained healers constituted a menace, in their minds, to public as well as individual health. In fairness to the doctors, it must be said that probably the latter consideration was and is uppermost, for most doctors who are well qualified do not lack for patients.

At first the movement was largely in New England, centering around the neighborhood of Boston. But it was not long before there were churches, healers, and even schools for the training of practitioners in distant parts of the country. Unfortunately, reliable statistics of the growth of the organization are not available, since Mrs. Eddy established a rule that such statistics should not be divulged by members of her church.

There is one way by which the growth of the organization can be ascertained. Since near the turn of the century it has been the custom to list in the *Christian Science Journal* the addresses of all the churches and societies, as well as the names and addresses of practitioners; and a church must have a minimum of sixteen members. Presumably a smaller number may form a society. From this it has been possible to determine whether the number of societies or churches or practitioners is increasing or decreasing. And thanks to the fact that the geographical location has been given by states and countries since 1909, it is possible to discover where the losses or gains have been registered after that date. Of course the number of members cannot be determined from this, since one church may have a mere handful while another may have several hundred.

In the first number of the *Journal* which lists churches and practitioners, that of 1906, there were 926 churches and societies. In the July, 1900, issue it had been reported that during the preceding year 3,600 new members had been received into the Mother Church, making a total membership of 18,131. There were 416 branch churches then, of which 38 had been established during the year, with a total membership of 21,040.

The same report asserted that over a million Christian Scientists were living witnesses to the truth of Christian Science. Obviously this is a general statement, probably meant to include the large number who were in some way influenced by the new teaching. Actually, the Religious Census of 1906 gives the total membership of the church, with 638 churches reporting, as only 85,717. Christian Scientists maintain generally that the United States Census figures concerning their churches are not correct.

In 1911, the year following the death of Mrs. Eddy, there were approximately 1,190 churches or societies and 3,280 practitioners in the United States. By this time there were churches in every state of the Union, five in Africa, two in Asia, 15 in Europe, seven in Australia, eight in Great Britain, and 35 in Canada. There were no practitioners listed in Africa, but there was one in Asia, and there were 33 in Europe, 15 in Australia, 108 in Great Britain, and 63 in Canada.

By 1919 the number of churches in the United States had risen to 1,644, an increase of 38 per cent; practitioners had risen to 6,111, slightly more than an 80 per cent increase. There had been an increase in all the other countries also.

Because of the effects of the Great Litigation, statistics both of churches and societies and of practitioners for the year 1921 or even 1922 have little meaning. By 1931, however, the number of churches had risen to 2,090, about a fourth more than in 1922 and almost as many again as in 1911. Between 1931 and 1941 the number rose to 2,294, an increase of slightly less than 10 per cent. By 1958 the number had increased to 2,372, a gain of but 3.41 per cent in seventeen years. Thus in recent decades there has been a definite slowing down of the rate of increase, at least in the number of churches and societies.

The deceleration of the rate of growth in the number of churches and societies does not necessarily reflect a change in the rate of growth of the membership of individual churches. However, something may be inferred about the general state of affairs in the movement from at least one official document. This is a letter from the Board of Directors of one of the Christian Science churches in Chicago to its sister churches, seeking to enlist greater co-operation in such promotional activities as the jointly sponsored lectures and institutional work. The letter states that sales of *Science and Health* in the downtown reading rooms had fallen off by two-thirds from the earlier high-water mark; furthermore, the membership of the Christian Science churches in Chicago had suffered a marked decline, although during this very period Chicago's population had increased by a third of a million. (Letter of May 3, 1944)

Does such a decline exist elsewhere in the great cities of the United States? The writer does not know. Certainly in Chicago the decline is evidenced by observable dwindling of general attendance. One striking example is that of historic First Church, Kimball's home church and a proud landmark in Christian Science annals, where the once-large membership decreased until it was almost negligible before First Church disappeared in a merger with Ninth Church several years ago; then even the Ninth Church building (now called First Church) went on the block, the services being conducted thereafter in a hotel. (*Woodlawn Booster*, September 19, 1956) Whatever the condition elsewhere, the number of practitioners in this country increased from 8,420 in 1931 to 8,680 in 1941, or a little more than 3 per cent. But by 1958 the number listed in the *Journal* was down to 7,996.

Something of the way in which the church grew may be seen from the following table, reporting the growth in certain selected states. The figures for 1906, 1926, and 1936 are taken from the U.S. Religious Census. (There was none reported in 1916.) The 1946 and 1956 figures are from the *Journal*, only the number of churches being given for these years.

States	1906 No. of Churches	1906 No. of Members	1926 No. of Churches	1926 No. of Members	1936 No. of Churches	1936 No. of Members	1946 No. of Churches	1956 No. of Churches
Mass.	34	43,547	72	8,536	79	8,416	82	83
Calif.	35	2,753	235	16,355	268	25,907	276	349
Ill.	54	5,675	123	16,763	132	21,512	133	142
Kan.	31	1,131	63	2,719	65	2,887	57	52
Ohio	34	2,582	90	9,477	96	12,247	105	107
N.Y.	51	5,671	141	11,530	157	15,875	163	165
Ore.	8	591	48	2,893	50	3,752	53	63
Pa.	25	1,551	64	4,776	78	6,534	81	83
Conn.	10	521	26	1,517	25	2,111	27	32
N.H.	7	431	22	3,190	20	736	20	23

From this it appears that there has been a steady, though not rapid, growth in most of the states. Only Kansas shows a decline in the number of churches—a loss of eight churches or societies from 1936 to 1946, and a further decline of five in the years between 1946 and 1956. In terms of percentage, this was between 1936 and 1956 a decrease from 65 to 52, a loss of exactly 20 per cent. It is true that in the decade 1930-40 Kansas lost in population, but over the period 1930-50 there was a 1.3 per cent population gain. Why the loss in churches? I have found no explanation.

West Coast states experienced rapid growth between 1906 and 1926, with the tremendous westward shift of population. California's number of churches rose from 35 to 235, a gain of more than 600 per cent, and Oregon had 48 instead of eight, just six times as many. California's population increased in the decades 1910-30 by about 240 per cent, and Oregon's by 42 per cent, so the growth of the number of churches outran the population growth percentagewise. Since 1926 California has jumped to 349 in 1956, a gain in 30 years of over 48 per cent. From 1946 to 1956 the increase was from 276; this represented a gain of 26.4 per cent. But from 1930 to 1950 California's population growth had been 86 per cent; Oregon's gain during the decade was from 53 to 62, a little more than 17 per cent, while Oregon's population growth in the decade 1940-50 was 39 per cent. It thus appears that in more recent years the growth in the number of churches in these two areas has not kept pace with the advance in population. Whether or not this is true of the growth in membership, there is no way of knowing.

The following table, based upon the *Journal* figures, shows in summary the growth in the number of churches throughout the world by major geographic divisions. (There are a few churches in other parts of the world not included in the table.)

Year	Africa	Asia	Australia	Europe	Great Britain	Canada	United States
1911	5	2	7	15	68	35	1,190
1919	7	3	9	22	94	46	1,684
1922	3	3	10	35	120	47	1,635
1931	22	7	35	94	219	66	2,030
1941	35	13	48	150	313	74	2,284
1958	40	13	70	175*	344	79	2,372

*This total does not include churches in East Germany.

The table below presents the over-all picture of church growth between 1911 and 1958, together with variations in number of practitioners listed in the *Journal*. Figures given represent totals for the whole world.

Date	Number of Churches	Approximate % gain	*Journal*-listed Practitioners	Approximate % Gain or Loss
1911	1,238		4,732	
1923	1,991	60.0	6,368	34.5
1931	2,466	24.0	10,177	59.1
1941	2,891	17.0	11,154	9.6
1958	3,115	7.7	9,567	−14.2 (loss)

Of the total of 2,372 churches and societies in the United States, 1,726, or 72.7 per cent, were churches and 646, or 27.3 per cent, were societies. As might be expected, the percentage of societies is larger outside the United States, where of the 743 total 382, or 51.4 per cent, are churches and 361, or 48.6 per cent, are societies. Of the world total of 3,115 organized Christian Science groups, 2,108, or 67.6 per cent, are churches and 1,007, or 32.4 per cent, are societies.

The total number of Christian Science church members in the world is difficult to ascertain. In World War II, chaplains were allocated to the Army on the basis of church membership. Christian Science authorities, required to open their books to provide the necessary statistics, reported a membership of 268,915 in the United States.

Assuming this figure to be the approximate membership in the 2,284 local churches or societies reported in 1941, the average membership of the local groups would be 118+. Projecting this figure on to the world plane and assuming that the average outside the United States is equal to that within—an assumption probably not warranted, since 48.6 per cent of the groups outside the United States are societies rather than churches—the Church of Christ, Scientist, with its total of 3,115 churches and societies, would have a world membership of 367,570.

When the figure of 268,915 was given wide publicity as the total membership of the Christian Science churches in the United States, the church authorities declared, in an Associated Press release dated May 6, 1950, that "size alone is not considered important by Christian Scientists." It was explained that "in accordance with its by-laws, the church publishes no membership figures." However, the release said, "outsiders working from figures supplied by the Census Bureau in 1936, place the total well in hundreds of thousands." It is noteworthy that previously, in an official declaration, the Mother Church Board announced an increase in the rate of numerical growth, asserting that "continued growth in numbers is important" since it indicates spiritual advancement. (*Sentinel*, XLIV, 1920-21)

Christian Science has always been thought to be chiefly urban in its membership. The table below presents the number of Christian Science churches or societies found (according to *Journal* listings) in eleven states chosen for geographic spread, broken down by number and percentage according to population of the cities or towns in which they are located. In the last column is given the percentage of the total population of each state which is considered rural; that is, the percentage living in communities of less than 2,500 inhabitants.

State	In cities over 50,000		In cities 10-50,000		In cities 5-10,000		In cities 2.5-5,000		In communities -2,500		% rural pop.
	No.	%	No.	%	No.	%	No.	%	No.	%	%
Calif.	132	32.+	82	23.5	36	10.3	40	11.4	79	22.6	19.3
Conn.	8	25	17	53.1	3	9.3+	2	6.25	2	6.2	22.4
Ill.	37	26.+	55	38.7	30	21.3+	15	10.55	5	3.5	22.4
Iowa	6	12.8	18	38.3	13	27.6	6	12.8	4	8.5	52.3
Kan.	5	9.8	21	40.3	8	15.3	13	25	5	9.7	47.9
N.Y.	53	32.1	48	29.1	27	16.7	21	12.9	16	9.6	14.5
Ohio	30	28.03	46	42.0	13	12.15	11	10.37	7	6.54	29.8
Ore.	11	17.40	10	15.8	11	17.46	19	30.16	12	19.04	46.1
Pa.	21	15.30	34	40.96	16	19.29	5	6.02	7	8.43	29.5
Tex.	34	32.7	39	37.5	21	20.19	7	6.74	3	2.88	37.3
Ga.	9	40.90	12	54.54	–	–	–	–	1	4.56	54.7
	326	27.95	382	32.84	178	15.36	139	11.92	141	12.09	34.2

According to the 1950 United States Census, the average percentage of rural inhabitants of these eleven states was 34.2, or almost three times the percentage of rural Christian Science churches, 12.09. In California, with 22.6 per cent of its churches in rural communities, Christian Science proves to be more rural than the general population, which was 19.3 per cent in the census of 1950. But California is the only state which shows any such ratio. Curiously enough, New York is the only other state in which the percentage of the general population living in rural areas is not more than twice the percentage of Christian Science churches which are located in those areas. In Georgia the ratio is over ten to one, in Texas over twelve to one, while in Kansas it is over five to one. In Oregon it is something less than three to one.

It is interesting to note that only in the far western states have churches gone into the smaller towns in any substantial manner.

Here the growth of the church in recent years has been more rapid than elsewhere. An explanation for this may be that the newer societies or churches have sprung up in places to which, for reasons of employment or otherwise, Christian Science families have migrated, and where they have constituted the nucleus for the start of a new church.

One explanation of the larger percentage of rural churches in California is the fact that a number of them—in fact, about one third—are really not rural in the sense of being in isolated small towns, but are in small suburban communities which have not yet grown to the point of having 2,500 or more inhabitants. There are many such communities in the areas of San Francisco, Los Angeles, and San Diego. A few others are in essentially vacation resorts to which city people go for week ends and their longer vacations. While there is no certain way of knowing, it is a fairly safe assumption that were it not for the part-time dwellers who come out from the city, there would probably be no societies in such resorts.

It will be noted that Texas has the lowest percentage of rural churches. In California, especially in Southern California, the villages are closer together and it is possible that one small-town church may serve several near-by communities. In Texas, towns are farther apart.

If the states we have sampled are representative of the situation in the United States as a whole, it is very clear that Christian Science is, as generally thought, predominantly urban in character. If in addition we knew the membership of the churches, as well as their number, it would be shown without doubt that a still larger percentage of the membership is found in urban than in rural churches. Most of the churches in the smaller communities are of course small in membership also, while in the cities the units are sometimes quite large. Almost 28 per cent of the churches are in cities of over 50,000 people. More than 32 per cent are found in cities of from 10,000 to 50,000, making a total of slightly more than 60 per cent in cities of 10,000 or more. Only about 25 per cent are in towns of less than 5,000, and here is where the churches are likely to be the smallest. It is interesting to note that the Roman Catholic church, which has been largely urban in America, is about 20 per cent rural.

Can any definite trend be detected in the growth of the church? A comparison of churches listed in 1941 and in 1956 shows that in the state of California one church disappeared in Los Angeles, two dropped out in cities of between 2,500 and 10,000, while eight societies or churches disappeared from the list in towns of less than 2,500. On the other hand, eleven new churches were added in cities of over 50,000; eight in cities of 10,000-50,000; and seven in cities between 2,500 and 10,000. During the same period thirty-three societies or churches were added in rural communities. The net gain expressed in percentages was 8.8 per cent in cities over 50,000, but 46.3 per cent in communities of 2,500 and less. Clearly in California the tendency to increase at the rural level is very marked.

In New York State the gain in the number of churches at the rural level was 44.4 per cent; at the 2,500-10,000 level it was 2.13 per cent; and in cities of 10,000-50,000 it was 4.52 per cent. There was a net loss of one church in cities over 50,000. In Illinois there was a net gain in churches at the over 50,000 level of 19.3 per cent; in the 10,000-50,000 of 5.76 per cent. At the rural level there was a net loss of 28.5 per cent.

In Georgia there was no gain in the number of churches in cities of less than 10,000; but there was a gain of 71.4 per cent in cities between 10,000 and 50,000; and of 50 per cent in cities above 50,000.

Finally, in Kansas there was a net loss of one church in cities of over 50,000; two in cities of 2,500-5,000; and five in rural areas, or just 50 per cent. No clear pattern of growth emerges on the basis of this small sampling.

For twenty years or more the Christian Science church has made use of radio programs to get its message to the world. In the earlier days the program usually consisted of an interview with a prominent Christian Science leader, a reading from some of the publications, particularly from *Science and Health*, or testimonies of healing. More recently a series, "How Christian Science Heals," has been broadcast regularly. It consists generally of the testimony of healing by one who has been healed, followed by an informal commentary by a speaker, explaining the approach of Christian Science to such

a situation. The program is written and transcribed under the supervision of the office of the Manager of Committees on Publication
of the Mother Church in Boston, by the staff of the radio section of
that office. The records or tape recordings are then sent to the 800
or more stations throughout the world which broadcast them.

The programs are designed to appeal to the non-Scientist by
showing, through the experience of an actual individual who has
been healed, how God's power is available to heal men of "sin,
sickness, sorrow and limitation." The response to the message is
substantial. I was told by a member of the staff which produces the
programs that 30,000 people wrote in during the first year of the
series, when there were only 600 outlets for it. The mail response in
the summer of 1955 was running from 700 to 1,200 to each program.
Each letter is of course answered, and follow-up material is sent.
Sometimes personal visitation by experienced Christian Scientists in
the local community results from the inquiry. Numerous healings
are reported as a consequence.

The radio ministry is supported by voluntary contributions of
individuals to the State or Mother Church radio fund. While some
of the programs are carried free by the stations, most of the time
is paid for, especially on key stations. There are a few "live talent"
programs conducted by local Christian Scientists, who send their
scripts to the radio staff in Boston for checking before going on the
air. In addition Christian Science takes part in such special network
broadcasts as the "Church of the Air" and others of that nature,
and also in television programs.

The publishing activities of the church are carried on in a large
and very beautiful building at 1 Norway Street, just across from
the Mother Church in Boston. When it became evident in the early
thirties that the older publishing facilities were no longer adequate,
plans were set on foot for a new building. Although the country
was in the midst of the depression, a campaign for contributions
was undertaken. Many thought it was ill-advised to initiate such
a costly enterprise under the circumstances. Nevertheless, it was
undertaken, and seven months before the completion of the new
building, the Board of Directors announced that no more funds

would be needed. The final cost was $4,300,000. The cornerstone was laid on October 17, 1932; completion was on January 20, 1934.

Christian Scientists like to point to the international character of the edifice, signalized in the fact that much of the marble is from Italy, the antique woodwork from England, the ceiling mosaics from Germany, the tile from Czechoslovakia, etc.

Here are published the *Journal*, the *Sentinel*, the *Christian Science Quarterly*, and of course the great daily, the *Christian Science Monitor*, besides much pamphlet material. In all, eighteen languages are employed in these various publications.

An interesting development is the type of building the Christian Scientists are now constructing. Since the dedication of Kimball's home church in 1897, the classic motif has been apparent in most Christian Science church edifices. Architect Beeman, a Christian Scientist, said he sought to translate the grandeur and simplicity of the faith into architectural terms, fronting his temple with a portico having tall, fluted pillars, and raising above the main structure a dome lined with Tiffany glass. Throughout the northern states this style, reminiscent of the Roman Pantheon, has become the almost certain earmark of a Christian Science church—though Methodists and Baptists have also followed this vogue generously throughout the South.

But that is changing. Quite recently new churches have swung toward a modernized Georgian style, modified particularly in the shape and proportions of the steeple. They are functional, and not without a certain beauty. Even farther away from the classic are some of the "contemporary" churches which have been erected in recent years, more than one of them distinctly showing the influence of Frank Lloyd Wright.

One radical change has occurred that is worth noting. In the Watford, England, letter complaining of the centralized control of the Mother Church Board, mention was made of the ways in which the Directors were carrying on propaganda, their use of advertising methods, and so on, all of which seemed to the Watford people out of keeping with the spirit of Mrs. Eddy's teaching.

It is true that for many years after Mrs. Eddy's death the church's selling practices were very conservative. Bookstores were not encouraged to stock *Science and Health,* and were even denied the regular trade discounts granted them by all other publishers. Quite a point was always made of the fact that Mrs. Eddy's writings were to be purchased through the church reading rooms. Around 1945 this policy was abruptly reversed, and an aggressive campaign of direct advertising, subsidized in part or in whole by local branch churches, was launched in the newspapers of the nation. In 1946 a trade edition of *Science and Health* was offered the bookstores, with full discounts and special inducements. The stores were promised assistance and support in pushing Mrs. Eddy's book, and soon some of the great dailies were carrying expensive spreads of display advertising.

Whether this revolutionary promotion was undertaken because of a general falling off in the sales of *Science and Health,* as reported by Eighteenth Church in the Chicago area, or whether it was decided that the bookstore outlet was after all a useful avenue for extending the faith, the step did represent a break with tradition. Whether it fulfilled expectations is not known, of course, but an inquiry among booksellers indicates that the special trade edition of *Science and Health* has proved a rather slow-moving item.

How many copies of Mrs. Eddy's textbook have actually been put into circulation since 1875 can only be guessed. Christian Scientists have spoken loosely of "the millions of copies" that have been sold. Information is not, however, available from official sources.

In the files of the New York Public Library an entry on a card indicates that an edition issued by Joseph Armstrong in 1903 was the 271st thousand to be published to that date. The practice of indicating the number of the edition on a flyleaf was discontinued in 1906, but it is known that at the time of Mrs. Eddy's passing 382 printings or editions had appeared. According to William Dana Orcutt's *Mary Baker Eddy and Her Books* (p. 25), "editions of one thousand copies each came off the press"; and it would seem fair to take this as the usual size of each printing, since Mr. Orcutt's work is a Christian Science church publication—which means that its every statement would have been rigorously checked and weighed for content and implications. Thus it would appear that 382,000 copies of *Science and Health* had been issued by the year 1910, an average of nearly 11,000 copies per annum.

Had that level of sale been maintained through 1957, some 517,000 additional copies would have been published, or a total of 899,000. With the growth of the church and the perfecting of its distributing agencies, the number could have been greater—but hardly in the "millions." Actually, the complaint of the Chicago church raises some doubt as to whether sales have been maintained at a high level. Assuredly, many people buy the book who never join the church; but how many no one knows. The policy of the church forbids the giving out of specific data, and what the reading rooms and the Publishing Society sell is undisclosed.

Has *Science and Health* undergone any changes since the death of its author? A four-page folder was issued early in November, 1954, charging that certain alterations had been made by the church authorities. It was clearly based upon a work *(Progressive Revisions)* by Mrs. Alice L. Orgain, an Eddy follower so ardent as to have said, "I have never read anything but Mrs. Eddy's writings and the Bible since I became interested in Christian Science on Easter Sunday, 1898." (Letter of July 14, 1947)

Since *Science and Health* is believed by every loyal Christian Scientist to be Holy Writ, and Mrs. Eddy, as its revelator, to be God's anointed, the folder-writer thinks it may be startling, if not horrifying, to the great majority of them to be informed that these writings have been "tampered with," "added to," and "taken from." When Mrs. Eddy had spent her mature life perfecting her book under divine inspiration, how would any human hand dare alter a single word? Had not Mrs. Eddy herself once written, "What can improve God's work?"

It seems that in the final chapter, "Fruitage," which is chiefly made up of testimonies of persons healed, a testimony captioned "Insanity and Epilepsy Healed" had been removed and in its place another, not chosen by Mrs. Eddy, "Spinal Trouble and Indigestion Healed," substituted for it. The change appears for the first time in 1925. Again, a testimony entitled "A Priceless Boon" has been left out entirely. In the latest printings "A Grateful Testimony," which was the concluding item, has been omitted. These objections are to changes in the text itself, but it is also objected that there have been changes in the marginal headings, and that Mrs. Eddy's picture, which she kept in the front of her book, was removed after her death.

This raises a critical question of great importance. If the book is God-inspired and not of man, how does a human group have a right to alter it? Of course the answer might be that they do not hold to an absolutely infallible verbal inspiration, but only a general one. But if Mrs. Eddy was divinely guided to write and arrange it as she did, are they under a divine guidance which supersedes hers? May they therefore change anything in the book as they wish?

It is not a mere question of interpretation that is involved. The prerogative of the Board to supply the interpretation has long been accepted by the church generally. Here is the assertion of a right not merely to interpret what divine inspiration had led Mrs. Eddy to include, but to modify what she included, or to omit it completely. Even the Roman Catholic hierarchy, which asserts its right and its sole right to interpret Scripture, has not ventured to alter the canonical content of the Bible; it has said that church tradition is also to be observed, but it does not make any changes in the received Old and New Testaments.

I wrote to the Boston authorities and asked for a statement of their belief and practice in this respect. Their answer was to refer me to an article in the *Journal* (LXXIII, 92 ff.), in which the Board of Directors made "An Important Statement." Coming out in February, 1955, this statement was apparently intended as a rebuttal to the 1954 folder.

The Board's article affirmed categorically that since Mrs. Eddy's passing in 1910 no change whatever had been made in anything she had written; that the text of her writings remained exactly as she had left it, and that of course it always would remain unchanged. A few changes in typography, binding, etc., had been made "due to specific instructions from her or policies firmly established by her." She had established during her lifetime a policy of omitting testimonies which subsequent information had convinced her should not be included, and it was this policy the Board had followed in removing one testimony entirely and substituting another in one case. Mrs. Eddy herself had, in removing one testimony, left the choice of the substitute to her publisher, said the article. The Board was therefore not going beyond what their Leader had authorized in selecting a substitute for one of her testimonies.

A recent Paul Revere pamphlet attacks the Directors, refusing to take their official statement as a guarantee of the complete integrity of the inspired textbook and *Manual,* and there the matter stands.

What about the "social outreach" of the Christian Science church? Most churches have numerous boards or auxiliary societies through which they carry on various functions outside the formal religious services—boards of education, boards of hospitals and homes, boards of domestic and foreign missions, boards of evangelism, of lay activities, of social action.

The Christian Science church does, of course, have the "Christian Science Board of Education," which is concerned solely with the one-week Normal class held triennially, and the Christian Science Publishing Society. There are also the two sanatoria which the church maintains, and the various privately operated retreats for Christian Scientists. And there is the Pleasant View rest home for elderly Christian Scientists, which the church has built on the site of Mrs. Eddy's Concord, New Hampshire residence. There are local committees for the distribution of literature, which are quite active. But aside from the system of Class Instruction, a very limited activity, the church has not entered the field of education.

There is one college, the Principia, in southern Illinois, run for the children of Christian Science parents, but it is in no sense official. It is privately owned and operated as a nonprofit institution by a group of Christian Scientists. Principia began in 1897, when a mother set up a kindergarten in which to teach her own children. Other Scientists asked that they might send their children also, so a year later the school opened formally. Gradually it was expanded to take in the lower grades, then the high school, and finally the liberal arts college. Today a child can start in the nursery school and go through to the Bachelor's degree, all within the Principia. The lower schools function in St. Louis, Missouri, the college in Elsah, Illinois, some thirty-five miles north on the Mississippi River, where it has a two-thousand-acre campus and adequate buildings and equipment for education of five hundred students, the number to which enrolment is limited.

Principia does not duplicate in any way the Class Instruction system of the church. Indeed, it does not include the subject of Christian Science anywhere in its curriculum. It does, however, provide an atmosphere congenial to the faith where the young people of Christian Science families can get a higher education. There are no other schools of a similar nature within the movement; apparently the church has preferred rather to follow its students into the colleges of the country, organize them into societies on campuses where there are enough to function, and seek thus to help them maintain and express their faith among other people. Such campus societies are found listed in the *Journal* along with the regular churches and societies which are recognized branches of the Mother Church.

Most of the branch churches, both in this country and in distant lands, got their start through the activities of such small groups; and nearly every one of these groups, at least in the beginning, consisted of the following of some individual practitioner or lay leader, who brought acquaintances together for the worship services and testimony meetings. This type of propagation has resulted in a world-wide spread of the faith.

There is no such thing as a systematic foreign missionary enterprise within the church. On some occasions the Board of Directors, or Mrs. Eddy before them, did send a person or persons to introduce Christian Science into countries where it had not been known, as in the case of Frances Thurber Seal's assignment to Germany. But this has not been done systematically. More often the faith has been carried to such places by Christian Scientists who, because of business or other interests, found themselves in foreign lands and got together to form a small society which could carry on the customary services. Gradually the native peoples, usually those who could understand English, came to know of it and became interested in joining.

In this connection, it is interesting to note that Mrs. Eddy made it plain, especially in her correspondence with Julia Field-King, that she distrusted translations of her writings into other tongues. Her textbook was finally translated into French, German, Spanish, Italian, and Swedish, but translations are required to show both the original English and the foreign text side by side. Services in the foreign lands are usually read successively in English and the local tongue. No one can become a teacher of Christian Science who does not speak English, for only those who are "thorough English scholars" are eligible for the Normal class certification.

Seemingly, the Christian Scientists show little or no interest in the social aspects of religion, in the sense either of cultivating sociability among the membership, of promoting wholesome recreation for young people, or of working for the amelioration of the adverse social conditions under which much of society labors. Their aloofness from the social work engaged in by the people of other churches has been attributed to the Christian Science view that evil is essentially unreal, and that by accepting its challenge they would be descending to its level and "giving it power." Still, they regard sickness as unreal yet feel bound to come to terms with the fact that people do seem to be ailing and must be brought out of their error to a realization of health.

In the early years of the movement, the Methodists, the Baptists, the Presbyterians who were drawn to Mrs. Eddy and her teachings brought with them some of the customs and practices of their respective groups. But these things did not too long survive. At first there were the usual teas and dinner parties at which Christian Science was discussed, notably those of such society leaders as Clara Choate and Josephine Woodbury. Mrs. Eddy herself appeared at some of these affairs, seeking to arouse and spread an interest in her cause. There were picnics. There was the strawberry festival, reported in the *Journal* (IV, 94), where coffee was served after the ices, berries, and cakes.

Then there came a time when Mrs. Eddy began to express disapproval of such things and a certain restraint settled over the field. When in 1888 Mrs. Eddy was given an overhearty reception at the Palmer House in Chicago, following her address at the Central Music Hall, she said, "Christian Science is not forwarded by these methods." (Wilbur, p. 121) During 1900, in eliminating the vacation period for Mother Church services, she declared that "Amusement, or idleness, is weariness," while rest is to be found in Truth and Love. *(Manual,* 18, p. 40) This marked the beginnings of a trend which has clearly grown and solidified through the years. It was in 1900, too, that she said in her "Message to the Church" (p. 2) that a right-thinking person "takes no time for amusement, ease, frivolity," and this idea was finally emphasized by Section 4 of Article XXXI of the *Manual,* which provides that as a rule "there should be no receptions nor festivities after a lecture on Christian Science."

Christian Scientists are known to admonish each other frequently "not to go out into mortal mind company." It is often pointed out by them that their churches are not social centers. Any social activity sponsored by Sunday school teachers is definitely frowned upon. Efforts to establish young people's clubs or societies have been largely confined to "*Monitor* study groups" and the like. In a very few instances, such things as "The Saturday Evening Club" in Chicago, which sponsored carefully chaperoned dances, have sprung up, but these efforts on the whole have been sporadic and short-lived.

Such organizations as Christian Scientists might evolve for social outlets are handicapped, if not foredoomed, by Mrs. Eddy's *Manual* rule entitled "Church Organization Ample." (pp. 44-45) Here she declares that, requiring undivided allegiance, God provides sufficient and dutiful occupation within the channels of the Mother Church for all its members. In a succeeding rule she adds that members must not join any societies outside those specified in the *Manual.*

There are no women's circles, no ladies' aids, no church dinners, no sociables. There are the regular worship service, the Sunday school (which parents are forbidden to visit unless they happen to be duly appointed officers or teachers), the Wednesday evening testimony meeting, the occasional lecture by itinerant approved lecturers; and that is about all. All these things existed in Mrs. Eddy's time and nothing essentially new has appeared since her demise. The organization of the local churches follows the pattern set down in the *Manual,* its rules having remained entirely unchanged since its author's passing in 1910.

The *Manual* cannot, of course, be revised, because for that Mrs. Eddy's express consent must be given, and she has been gone nearly half a century. Whatever innovations are made have to be brought about somehow within the framework of the *Manual's* fixed rules. This is possible only insofar as it can be done through interpretation, and is actually done by the Board of Directors whenever they deem it necessary. And necessities do arise, for life does not stand still. The world is constantly changing, and Christian Science, like all other forms of religion, has to make itself relevant to that changing life or eventually disappear.

11

Christian Science in Wartime

THE COMING of World War I, only four years after the passing of Mrs. Eddy, presented her movement with a whole series of problems. How these problems were handled is set forth in detail by the church in a full-sized volume, *Christian Science War Time Activities*, issued in 1922. A later volume, *The Story of Christian Science War Time Activities 1939-1946*, issued in 1947, recounts the story of what the Scientists did in World War II.

In October, 1914, the Board of Directors sent out a letter to all branch churches and societies in America stating that the Mother Church in Boston would take up a collection at both services on Sunday, October 25, to help relieve the distress which Christian Scientists in Europe had suffered as a result of the war. They offered to serve as a forwarding agency if any branch churches desired to take a similar offering. This was the beginning of their War Relief Fund. A delegate was sent to England, who asked that a Relief Committee be formed to distribute the fund to those among Christian Scientists in the British Isles who had suffered most. Like committees were set up in France, Switzerland, Germany, and finally in Italy and Holland.

An article in the *Sentinel* for April 3, 1915, announced that already over $82,000 had been contributed for the aid of Christian Scientists, but in addition nearly $30,000 had been collected and disbursed for the succor of non–Christian Scientists. So the outreach of the fund was broadened, and this wider giving had now become an established part of the Christian Science wartime activity, for which additional funds were earnestly solicited. With the entrance of the United States into the war in 1917, a Camp Welfare Committee was also appointed to serve the men who were being inducted into the armed forces. Within sixty days the church in the entire country was organized and beginning the work of following its young men into the great centers of training and embarkation for overseas service. Eventually the two committees were merged and the entire work of the church was carried on under the direction of the single committee, but with the aid of numerous local committees and individuals.

By Armistice Day in 1918, there were in the employ of the committee over two hundred full-time workers, and over two thousand others served in a volunteer capacity as committee members or fund raisers or part-time workers. Their work was on the order of some phases of the U.S.O. In many places they maintained rest centers, which provided opportunity for quiet reading, or writing, or recreation. Unlike the U.S.O., however, such centers staged no shows and furnished no coffee or tea. Naturally Christian Science literature was provided. The report of the committee said that of course its most important accomplishment was the distribution of some forty thousand copies of *Science and Health,* in a vest-pocket edition which the soldiers could keep on their persons. The report stated that more than six million copies of the *Monitor* were given away or sold during the period.

When the United States entered the war there was provision for chaplains, but only from the Protestant churches represented in the Federal Council of Churches and the Roman Catholic church, and all applicants were required to be ordained clergymen. Naturally other groups with considerable numbers of men in the services also wanted representation in the chaplaincy. So a bill was passed in 1917 creating chaplains-at-large, and commanders were authorized to ask for chaplains to serve Jewish, Christian Science, Mormon, Eastern Catholic, and Salvation Army members if they thought there were sufficient numbers of any of these groups under their command. Eleven Christian Science chaplains served during World War I, only one of them in the Navy. In this post they of course carried out the prescribed duties of chaplains regardless of denomination, but they were able to maintain the regular worship services and testimony meetings, as well as to counsel many young Christian Scientists and to practice healing along the lines of their own faith. The report of their work includes many stories not only of healing but also of protection as a result of the chaplains' activities.

All told, the church contributed $2,000,000 through the War Relief Committee. Official Christian Science literature was distributed to the value of more than $300,000, or almost a sixth of the total disbursement. The rest went for housing, rest centers, recreation, salaries of workers, transportation (the committee owned many cars and one launch), clothing for refugees, and knitted garments for military personnel. While the committee's work was begun primarily to meet the needs of Christian Scientists, workers found themselves ministering to and even providing relief for many who had no connection with the church. They learned soon, as did representatives of other religious groups, that human need is nonsectarian, so their ministry had to become increasingly nonsectarian—without, of course, losing sight of those who were bound to them more closely by the tie of a common religious faith.

After the liquidation of the War Relief Committee, the church went on very much as before. In the interval between the wars, Christian churches in general moved in the direction of pacifism. Many of them made solemn pronouncements against war, some nearly pacifist. Many prominent religious leaders became outspoken pacifists, resolving never to bless another war. And the Protestant churches themselves, in their most representative gatherings, declared that war was a *sin*, mankind's greatest *collective* sin.

Thousands of young men under the teaching of their churches became pacifists, repudiated war, and declared their intention not to participate in another war. Many churches provided opportunity for their young people who wished to do so to put themselves on record as conscientious objectors. Meanwhile, under pressure from the churches, the government passed legislation providing that conscientious objectors who could prove that they were opposed to war service because of their religious beliefs might be inducted into the services as noncombatants, who were not required to bear

arms, or into alternative services of a nonmilitary character in what
came to be called Civilian Public Service Camps.

Most of the larger denominations supported their young men
who chose this course, some of them wholeheartedly, some without
enthusiasm. But the Christian Science church was not among these.
Indeed, the Boston church authorities took steps to deprive Christian Scientists of the right to claim conscientious objection to participation in armed conflict.

A few Christian Scientists of draft age took the conscientious
objectors' position. Apparently the matter was brought to the attention of the Board, for they published an article on the subject in
the *Sentinel* of January 4, 1941. In it they declared definitely that a
draftee could not claim exemption as a conscientious objector
without misrepresenting Christian Science, citing the fact that the
formal tenets or platform of the church included nothing in reference
to participation in war or undergoing military training. If the
draftees could establish the fact of their opposition to military
service by reason of religious training and belief quite apart from
membership in a church, that was their privilege under the law;
but to affirm that they did this on the basis of the teaching of the
Christian Science church would be a misrepresentation. In support
of this stand, the Board quoted a saying of Mrs. Eddy (*Miscellany,*
p. 277), to the effect that if the nation's rights or honor were seized,
then every citizen would be a soldier, and even woman would be
"armed with power girt for the hour." In a personal communication,
the Boston authorities state that ten members only of the Mother
Church are known to have been in Civilian Public Service Camps
during the last war.

The *Monitor,* which voices only policies approved by the Board
of Directors of the Mother Church, published in June, 1941, an
editorial on World War II, advocating material arms and military
participation in conflict. It is highly significant that this editorial
has been reprinted and distributed widely by the authorities in
Boston. Likening certain individuals and nations to David, it asserts
that "they know their chief reliance must be on God, but they also
know that, with the assurance of the justice of their cause, they

must pray for wisdom, courage, vision, and then deal humanly with the modern Goliath with the weapons they have learned to use." This position is reiterated and elaborated in such feature articles as "Serving in the Armed Forces," by Herbert Rieke (*Sentinel,* October 30, 1954).

Many Christian Scientists disagree with this position, citing Mrs. Eddy's assertion that "killing men is not consistent with the higher law whereby wrong and injustice are righted and exterminated" (*Miscellany,* p. 277), and her excoriation of war in the *Boston Globe* in December, 1904. In the latter article she asserts unequivocally that "war is in itself an evil," that by fighting much is lost and nothing is gained, so that victory therein is actually defeat, that anything unloving in thought or action "is never requisite, never a necessity, and is not sanctioned by the law of God, the law of Love." (*Miscellany,* pp. 278-79)

Out of this dissent came a Christian Scientist pacifist fellowship. Known as "The Peace Association of Christian Scientists," it is "an international association for the promotion and extension of a Christianly scientific peace, the members of which refrain from participation in war." This was always a very small minority group which, according to its head, was definitely opposed by the Board of Directors in Boston. Some Christian Scientists assert that there was a widespread pacifist trend in the church, but that few individuals had the temerity to voice their convictions after the *Monitor* editorial was so pointedly reprinted and circulated by the Boston leadership. That there is some truth in this report is evidenced by the springing up of other dissident groups, such as the Pacifist Principle Fellowship, "an organization devoted to the welfare of students of Christian Science who are conscientious objectors to war, functioning as a private enterprise and not as an agency of the Christian Science Church." One of this group's booklets, printed in Portland, Oregon, during 1945, gives some of the reasons advanced by this minority, which felt that it was "demonstrating what seemed to be the only possible interpretation of Mrs. Eddy's writings"—and which, incidentally, was made up of seasoned Christian Scientists from all over the country.

When World War II came it was fairly easy for the church to reorganize the War Relief Committee. As early as 1935 the restrictive measures of the Nazis with reference to Christian Scientists created serious problems with which the church had to deal. In 1936 the *Sentinel* gave directions to guide contributions to the loyal church members in Germany. In 1937 a "Literature for Germany Fund" was set up. It could readily be seen that a crisis was near. So when the war burst upon the world in 1939, the church was already prepared to launch into vigorous wartime activity along the lines followed in World War I.

This time war called for the expenditure of more than ten million dollars, and tens of thousands participated in the activity in one way or another before peace came once again to the world. In December, 1939, the Board created Wartime Committees of the Mother Church in the United Kingdom, Canada, and France, and warmly supported every effort of these committees to meet the needs in the war-torn lands. In June, 1940, the Mother Church opened its War Relief Fund, and in September headquarters of the War Relief Committee were set up in Boston. Among seventeen agencies of this nature called to conference in Washington, it was reported that Christian Science ranked fourth in the magnitude of funds raised for relief. With America's entrance into the war there was once more the question of ministry to millions of young men in the armed services, many of them Christian Scientists. Again the camp welfare activities familiar from World War I were inaugurated.

A serious problem for young Christian Scientists was what to do when faced with the requirement of vaccination and inoculation, for the armed services allowed no exception to the rules. In civilian life every effort is made by orthodox Christian Scientists to avoid such things. Legislation has been sought, and in many states successfully, to permit exemption of Christian Scientists from such rules. But submission seems to have been accepted as inevitable under military rule. To prepare young soldiers for the experience a pamphlet was issued which explained that they must submit to this requirement. Mrs. Eddy was cited as recommending that where the laws required it the individual obey and then appeal to the gospel that he be saved from evil physical results. To this was added her statement that she believed in obeying the law. (*Miscellany*, pp. 219-20) They were likewise advised to submit to medical or dental treatment when ordered to do so, but cautioned that this should not be construed as preventing them from seeking the aid of a Christian Science wartime minister, or any other practitioner, if they so wished.

In view of the fact that this might open the way for civilians to slip into the mistaken belief that they too might feel free to employ material treatment while under Christian Science treatment, a lengthy statement was published in the *Sentinel* on May 9, 1942, declaring medical aid incompatible with Christian Science, and citing Mrs. Eddy's statement that it is unwise to take a halting position, expecting to work with Spirit and matter at the same time; that only when there is radical reliance on Truth can scientific healing be achieved.

In *The Story of Christian Science War Time Activities 1939-1946* it is stated that in a number of instances medical rules were set aside when it appeared that Christian Science methods were proving adequate to the case. The book also includes numerous testimonies of healing.

In March, 1941, the first Christian Science wartime minister was appointed, and there were sixty-four such ministers by the time of the Pearl Harbor attack. It is to be noted that these were not chaplains, but civilian ministers. In addition, there were thirty-six volunteer wartime workers on duty in the various military and naval installations in the United States. There were 252 wartime ministers before the war ended, and 1,750 volunteer wartime workers. In World War I there had been a hundred welfare centers; in World War II there were 225 such centers, with many additional study rooms at military and naval encampments around the world. The chaplains, which had numbered eleven in World War I, were now twenty-six in number. All told, the Board of Directors appointed some 4,300 Christian Scientists as full-time paid or volunteer war workers during the years 1939-46.

The distribution of Christian Science church literature by all these workers was enormous. At a cost of approximately five dollars each, 50,000 sets of the vest-pocket size Bible with *Science and Health* were given to military personnel who requested them. Almost $1,000,000 worth of new literature and books were purchased from the Publishing Society for distribution by the Camp Welfare Activities Committee. More than 22,000 copies of the *Monitor* were leaving Boston daily for distribution largely to soldiers, sailors, or airmen, along with huge quantities of the *Quarterly*, the *Sentinel*, the *Journal*, etc. Nor did all of this go only to United States soldiers. There was also a constant shipping of the church literature, as well as food and clothing, to overseas distributors to needy civilians, to prisoner-of-war camps, and to refugees. It is estimated in *War Time Activities* that nearly $4,500,000 worth of clothing was shipped overseas. Altogether there was a great outpouring of money and goods, as well as highly valued personal services, by the church during the war years.

The reports of various chaplains contain accounts of the protection which they believed they were able, through Christian Science, to throw about groups which they served. One chaplain reports that he was with an antiaircraft and artillery battalion for more than a year of combat duty, which took them from the Mediterranean through France, over the Rhine and Danube, into many bitterly contested areas. It would have seemed impossible, from any human point of view, that they should not have had numerous casualties. But hourly Christian Science "work" of a preventive nature was done. The chaplain relates that men and officers urged him to claim the protection offered in the first verse of the 91st Psalm: "He that dwelleth in the secret place of the most High shall abide under the shadow of the Almighty," especially emphasizing the word *abide*. Not one of the men in this battalion was killed by enemy action in the whole year, and even the wounded shared in this good fortune to the degree that all of them would apparently recover. This extraordinary result the chaplain naturally attributes to his work. (*War Time Activities*, p. 169)

Nor is this a unique case. Page after page of like testimonies is given in the book. A thrilling story of the invasion-crossing of the

Channel is told, during which it is said that there was not a man lost aboard the particular transport on which the narrating chaplain served, nor did the ship itself come out with even "the smell of fire," although explosions and destruction occurred on every hand. The chaplain had made hourly use of the cardinal points in the Lesson Sermon given in the *Christian Science Quarterly*. The lesson that week was "God the Preserver of Man," and the golden text was "I am with thee, saith the Lord, to save thee." (*War Time Activities*, p. 173)

Gradually, as demobilization took place, the war work was abandoned. But the appointment of Christian Science chaplains had become a fixed policy of both government and church.

PART III

Development of Christian Science
Thought and Practice

12

Developments in Christian Science Thought

IF ONE WISHES to set forth tendencies in the thought of a movement he must first of all have a clear understanding of the original ideas which underlie it. If divergences are to be noted it is necessary to know that from which later thought represents divergence. Is it possible to set forth a clear, consistent set of beliefs which will be everywhere and by everyone recognized as the teachings of Mary Baker Eddy, and from which, as the revelation of new truth, there should supposedly be no departure?

The answer is, of course, no. The reason for that answer is that Mrs. Eddy lived a long time, that she said and wrote many things, that she simply never was primarily a systematic, logical thinker. This has been the case with most of the founders of new religions. Mrs. Eddy was undoubtedly an exceptional character, a woman of deep religious experience, fired with great convictions and moving under a compulsion which was, she thought, of divine origin. But she was also, possibly against her own wishes, an organizer and a promoter. She had to be to get her movement under way, as she did, in the face of tremendous opposition both from without and from within.

The result is that it is perfectly possible to assert as the true teaching of Christian Science ideas that are almost fundamentally opposed one to the other. For example, Mrs. Eddy writes in *Science and Health* (p. 411) that the procuring cause of all disease is fear, ignorance, or sin, but a few pages away (p. 419) she asserts that neither sin nor fear has the power to cause disease. She refers more than three hundred times in this same book to "mortal mind"—a

great many of the references being to something having volition of
its own and even aggressive, e.g., that narcotics quiet mortal mind
(p. 157), that mortal mind produces table-tipping (p. 80), that
mortal mind is the murderer (p. 104). Yet again and again she
affirms that in reality there is no mortal mind (pp. 103, 487, 591
passim).

It is precisely this sort of apparent contradiction which has led
to substantially different interpretations of Christian Science within
the movement itself. Indeed, Mrs. Eddy herself recognizes the possibility, at least, that people may get divergent ideas regarding the
doctrine from her textbook. She refers in one passage to critics of
Christian Science who declare the textbook inconsistent, basing their
criticisms upon apparently contradictory statements contained in it.
But, she declares, in her volume there are no contradictory statements—at least, none that would be apparent to persons who understood the subject well enough to pass judgment on them. (p. 345)

It is nevertheless true that Christian Scientists of long standing,
noted for their devotion to Mrs. Eddy and her cause, and certainly
well acquainted with her literary output, do find themselves in
violent disagreement as to what she meant in her writings, and are
able to cite numerous sayings of their Leader in support of their
apparently contradictory ideas concerning one phase or another of
her teaching. These differences led to the struggle for control which
went on in the years following Mrs. Eddy's death and which still
continues in our time. By now it has been pretty well decided in
favor of the central controlling authority of the church, the Board
of Directors at Boston, which claims to be the final arbiter in all
matters of faith and practice. Armed with absolute power of
excommunication, it is in a position to weed out those who venture
to differ too markedly from what the Directors regard as the correct
interpretation of Mrs. Eddy's exposition.

But if there is any one portion of her writings which more than
any other may be taken to express Mrs. Eddy's fundamental conclusions, it would probably be agreed by Christian Scientists that it is
to be found in her chapter entitled "Recapitulation." Warrant for
this judgment is to be found in the *Church Manual,* which the

organizational segment of the movement today regards as a divinely inspired book just as much as it does *Science and Health*. Class Instruction, whereby the doctrine traditionally is passed down by word of mouth from generation to generation, is perhaps the most basic feature of institutionalized Christian Science. It is most important, therefore, that it be kept undeviatingly in line with the Leader's teaching. Article XXVII of the *Manual* undertakes to fix this for all time by requiring teachers of Primary classes to teach their pupils from "Recapitulation" only, and teachers of the Normal classes are required to teach from the same chapter supplemented by the "Christian Science Platform" in *Science and Health*, introducing nothing in conflict therewith.

Undeniably, in actual practice Class Instruction is a far cry from any strictly literal adherence to the prescribed chapter. But since "Recapitulation" opens with the declaration that its statements are pervaded by absolute Christian Science, one seeking the essence of what Mrs. Eddy sought to teach, at least at the close of her career, would surely be warranted in centering his attention upon these sections which the *Manual* injunction would indicate to be comprehensive. Obviously her other writings should throw additional light upon these particular sections; but they ought not to differ from what she deliberately chose as the basis of future instruction. If anything had been deemed lacking in these chapters, their author would certainly have indicated where it might be found.

From its opening paragraph the reader might infer that "Recapitulation" is recognizably Mrs. Eddy's 1870 "class-book" revised for inclusion in the first edition of *Science and Health* in 1875. Actually there is but slight resemblance, in any literal sense, between these two early works, and it must be remembered that this chapter also underwent considerable revision throughout the 382 editions of the textbook published before the last version was frozen by its author's death in 1910. Indeed, the changes are significant enough to make the church authorities hold students down to the final revision and frown severely upon any study of the earlier editions. Practitioners and teachers have been disciplined for violating these unwritten rules.

"Recapitulation" is made up of questions and answers, and is clearly intended to be of an explanatory nature. The "Christian Science Platform," on the other hand, is a systematic declaration of faith, with comparatively little explanation such as is given in "Recapitulation." In the one Mrs. Eddy is stating forthrightly the content of her faith; in the other she is arguing and defending it. There seems to be no essential difference in content.

If one were to look for a very concise statement of the essential doctrine of Christian Science, he might find it best expressed in what is known as "the scientific statement of being." Probably no single passage of Mrs. Eddy is more universally known or more frequently repeated than this one. It is a declaration that matter possesses neither life, truth, intelligence, nor substance; that Infinite Mind, together with its infinite manifestation, is all, since God is All-in-all; that Spirit is immortal Truth, while matter is mortal error; that Spirit is real and eternal, matter unreal and temporal; that man is the image and likeness of God, Spirit, hence man is not material, but spiritual.

Here is a clear statement of Christian Science teaching about the nature and being of God and of man. These things are spelled out in greater detail in other questions and answers in this chapter and in the "Platform," but here, it may be safely assumed, is a statement of the essentials. God is All, He is Mind, He is infinite, He is Spirit, He is eternal, and man as God's image and likeness is nonmaterial and immortal. Good, as infinite, is used throughout the whole book as a synonym for God; but early in this chapter seven synonyms— there were eight up until 1907—are given to express the nature, essence, and wholeness of Deity: Mind, Spirit, Soul, Principle, Life, Truth, Love. These synonyms are defined in the glossary at the end of the book.

In the "Platform," Mrs. Eddy affirms that God is individual, yet incorporeal; that He is not merely Father, but Mother as well; that He is personal—"in a scientific sense, but not in any anthropomorphic sense." Here, as elsewhere (p. 116), she draws a distinction between *material* personality as a finite, limiting concept, and the spiritual personality of the Infinite. Life, Truth, and Love constitute the triune person called God, a trinity in unity. They are in essence the same, though in office they are multiform: God, the Father-Mother; Christ, the spiritual idea of sonship; and divine Science, the Holy Comforter. (pp. 331-32)

Jesus the corporeal man was human, but he demonstrated the Christ. Christ is described as the divine message from God to men, speaking to human consciousness. It is a cardinal point that Christ is not a synonym for Jesus, but is synonymous with Messiah, alluding to the redeeming spirituality incarnate in Christ Jesus. Christ Jesus manifested the highest type of divinity possible to a fleshly form in that age. (pp. 332-33)

Since God is All, His unlikeness can have no existence. And since God is good, evil, which is contrary to good, could not be created by God and must therefore be unreal. (p. 339) Evil can be made to seem real only by giving reality to the unreal. (p. 470) Indeed, sin, sickness, and death appear in human experience because unrealities seem real to erring belief until God unmasks them. (p. 472) The fact is that all mental and bodily inharmony is illusion, possessing no reality or identity, even though it seems to be real and identical. (p. 473)

As Spirit's image and likeness, man is the compound idea of God, and this compound idea includes all right ideas. As such he possesses no creative power of his own, but reflects spiritually all that belongs to his Maker. (p. 475) God's idea, man, is incapable of sin, sickness, and death. (p. 475) Jesus discerned through science God's perfect likeness, and this correct discernment healed the sick. (pp. 476-77) It will be well to hold this last statement clearly in mind, for around it was destined to be joined one of the major controversies in the Christian Science movement.

But what about body? Man has, or seems to have, organs, nerves, brain. Does brain think? Do nerves feel? No, there is no intelligence or sensation in matter. Indeed, there is no such thing as matter. It is an error of mortal mind to believe that matter is real, or that sin, sickness, or death could be real. But what is this "mortal mind" which entertains such belief? It is difficult at this point for an outsider to follow Mrs. Eddy's argument, for she goes on to say

that actually there is no such thing as mortal mind. Nor does it help
overmuch to turn to the glossary and read the definition of mortal
mind: "nothing claiming to be something" and "error creating other
errors." (pp. 591-92)

Mrs. Eddy herself senses that there is a genuine problem here
when she seeks to resolve the question: Who or what is it that
believes? Her answer is that Mind understands and that this precludes the need of believing; that the body, matter, cannot believe;
that the belief and the believer are one and the same, being mortal.
(p. 487) Does this answer the question satisfactorily? To the uninstructed, at least, it does not seem clear. And it is to be noted that
in this, likewise, there is a difference of opinion among the present-
day followers of Mary Baker Eddy. One of the very crucial points
of divergence among contemporary Christian Science thinkers
emerges precisely over the question here raised. What of the phenomenal world, the world in which one seemingly lives and works
and thinks and finally dies, and which forces insistently upon man
the difficult problems with which he must deal practically from
day to day?

Is it necessary or important to understand the explanations given
with reference to the nature of Soul and body, of truth and error,
etc., in order to heal the sick—a major preoccupation of Christian
Scientists? According to Mrs. Eddy, the answer is yes, since sickness
is a part of the error which can be cast out only by truth. (p. 472)

Christian Science, Mrs. Eddy goes on to explain, heals and can
heal only on the basis of one Mind, God. (p. 482) Sickness is a
belief which must be destroyed by this Mind. Under the influence
of hypnotism, or even in a dream, men experience acute distress
because they mistakenly believe certain things are happening to
them. Awaken them out of sleep or release them from hypnotic
entrancement, and the distress vanishes at once, because it was
based upon a false belief. Change the belief and the sensation is
changed. If the belief is destroyed, so also will be the sensation.
(pp. 490-91)

In another chapter, called "Christian Science Practice," these
things are made quite explicit. Since the foundation of sickness is

fear, ignorance, or sin, these must be removed if the patient is to recover his health. Disease is induced always by a false sense entertained mentally, and, because disease is an image of thought externalized, the removal of the false sense is clearly the way to cure. (p. 411) The power of Truth must be employed to dispel the dream of the material senses. (p. 412)

The way to heal a patient is to make disease unreal *to him,* Mrs. Eddy says. To this end the practitioner should explain to his patient the complete control of Mind over the physical body, and show how mortal mind seems to induce disease through fears and false conclusions, and how therefore divine Mind can cure by opposite thoughts. (p. 417) In the case of fever, the efficient remedy is to destroy *the patient's* false belief by both silently and audibly arguing the true facts of harmonious being, representing man as healthy instead of diseased, thus showing how impossible it is for man to suffer, to feel pain, to be thirsty or sick. Destroy fear and you end the fever. (p. 376)

So clearly is sickness tied up with the mind of the patient that a physical diagnosis tends to provide disease (p. 370), presumably by suggesting it to the mind—mortal mind, of course. The same idea seems to lie behind Mrs. Eddy's assertion that the less we know or think about hygiene the less we are predisposed to sickness. (p. 389) A practitioner should never talk illness to a patient. (p. 396) At the very first appearance of the symptoms of disease, the testimony of the material senses is to be disputed with Science. No claim of sin or of sickness—and in the last analysis she makes no distinction between the two—must be allowed to grow upon the thought; rather it must be dismissed with the conviction that it is illegitimate, since God can no more be the author of sickness than He can of sin. (p. 390) The physical affirmation of disease must always be met with mental denial. If one believes in inflamed and weak nerves he is liable to attack from that quarter. He may call it neuralgia, but Science designates it a belief. (p. 392)

To be sure, in Mrs. Eddy's advising practitioners to argue audibly and silently the points of harmonious being, there is a suggestion of something more to the curing of disease than simply seeking by argument to correct the patient's thought. It seems that a practitioner heals a patient at once if he is able to reach that patient "through divine Love." (p. 365) The spiritually deficient practitioner is hindered "from reaching his patient's thought" to cure him. (p. 366)

But to what avail the silent argument if the difficulty is to be found only in the mind of the patient—unless the principle of telepathy be invoked to explain the effect of silent argument upon the patient's consciousness? Mrs. Eddy elsewhere asserts that space is no obstacle to Mind, for which reason a patient who is absent from the healer can be healed through Science as readily as if he were present. (p. 179) She speaks of Jesus reading another's thought (p. 56), and says that Christian Scientists have the ability to read the thought of the sick and the sinning, an ability important to success in healing. (p. 95) In her *Christian Healing* (p. 6), she says that the individual's mind alone can produce results upon his body. And, describing "treatment" in *Miscellaneous Writings* (p. 220), she writes that the healer speaks to his patient mentally, saying, "You are well and you know it."

Sin and death are, in Mrs. Eddy's thought, bracketed constantly with sickness and are equally unreal, the illusions of mortal mind, the effects of error. (*Science and Health,* p. 473) They are to be dealt with ultimately as sickness is dealt with, though it is recognized that, for the present at any rate, the complete victory over death seems not to have been attained save in the sense that orthodox Christianity believes also—namely, that physical death does not mean final dissolution of the self. Life, she says, is not attainable through death, but is to be found by following the pathway of Truth both before and after what is called death. (p. 487)

It is abundantly clear that whether she got her ideas from Phineas Quimby or discovered them independently, it is possible to detect a remarkable parallelism, both as to theory of disease and method of treatment, between many of Mrs. Eddy's teachings and those of Quimby. That there are other phases of the teaching which differ markedly is also true. In this connection it is interesting that those who regard themselves as liberals in the movement assert that the majority group, the orthodox wing, of Christian Scientists continue to follow essentially that aspect of the Eddy teaching which is most like Quimby's, rather than what these liberals regard as her more original and profound thoughts.

In 1859, three years before Mrs. Eddy first visited Quimby, he had written: "An individual is to himself just what he thinks he is.... If I believe I am sick, I am sick,... all disease is in the mind ... to cure the disease is to correct the error, and as disease is what follows the error, destroy the cause and the effect will cease." (H. W. Dresser, *The Quimby Manuscripts,* p. 186) These very points appear unmistakably as cardinal propositions in Mrs. Eddy's writings. Even the most casual student will recognize them at once.

Quimby says that all effects on the human frame are produced by belief, and this differs not at all from what Mrs. Eddy repeatedly says. One is reminded of Mrs. Eddy's article "Mental Practice" when Quimby declares: "If your mind has been deceived by some invisible enemy into a belief, you have put it into the form of a disease, with or without your knowledge. By my theory or truth, I come in contact with your enemy and restore you to health and happiness." (*The Quimby Manuscripts,* p. 194)

How does Quimby propose to restore the patient to health and happiness? "Partly mentally and partly by talking, till I correct the wrong impressions and establish the Truth, and the Truth is the cure." Time and again Mrs. Eddy avers that Truth is the cure, and to destroy a patient's false belief, she writes, is to silently and audibly argue "the true facts in regard to harmonious being, representing man as healthy instead of diseased." (*Science and Health,* p. 376) In *Miscellaneous Writings* (p. 220) she describes such a treatment in considerable detail. She there instructs the practitioner to address the patient mentally, silently assuring him that he is well and knows it, supplementing this with both silent and audible refutations of the sick man's thoughts, words, and actions. This course is persisted in until the patient's mind turns into channels of Truth and surrenders to a harmonious state of thought, where he too can say, "I am well and I know it."

The use of the term *mentally* with reference to addressing the

patient, by both Quimby and Mrs. Eddy, as well as their advocacy
of "absent treatment," raises a very fundamental issue. The question
is: how, without talking to the patient, can the practitioner affect
the patient's mind?

At this juncture, Quimby had no hesitation. He frankly believed
in something like telepathic communication. He early began to treat
patients silently and at a distance, just as did many of his predecessors in the field of "magnetic" healing. Dresser publishes the
letter of a correspondent who declared that, on a certain day at a
certain hour, her cousin professed to see Quimby present, describing
him correctly although she did not know him, and the correspondent
inquired as to whether Quimby had actually been present in spirit.
A letter written by Quimby, but not mailed, expressed his intention
of making such a mental visit on that day and at about the hour he
was purportedly seen. Further convincing evidence of Quimby's
own views on the subject is found in a letter he wrote five days
later, in which he said: "If that lady is still with you, I will try to
make myself appear to her eyes next Sunday between seven and
eight o'clock." (*The Quimby Manuscripts,* p. 104)

One more Quimby statement must suffice. "What is disease? It is
false reasoning. True scientific wisdom is health and happiness.
False reasoning is sickness and death; and on these two modes of
reasoning hang all of our happiness and misery. . . . Disease is one
of the natural inventions of error . . . for error is the father of
disease." (*The Quimby Manuscripts,* p. 295)

Talking the patient out of his ailments was clearly one of
Quimby's major concerns, and any student can readily find in her
published works that Mrs. Eddy not once but often advocates this
basic method. Although, as we have said, it is possible to find in her
writings another view—and one in character quite unlike that of
Quimby—it was not until the appearance in Christian Science ranks
of perhaps the most powerful and interesting figure of the movement, Edward Kimball, that this emphasis began to be an important
element in the teaching of Christian Science. It was to dominate for
some years and to be the center of an enduring factionalism.

Edward Ancel Kimball was born in Buffalo on August 27, 1845, the youngest of several children. His father died when he was but three years of age, and he was early obliged to go to work selling newspapers in support of the family. He was thus prevented from pursuing his formal education beyond the grammar school grades; but his keen, vigorous mind led him to acquire an education apart from academic training which made him in the end a thinker of real power, a most able analyst, and a remarkably effective teacher and lecturer. He worked his way up in the business world of Chicago to become a partner, in charge of sales, in the firm of Barrett & Kimball, manufacturers of paving and roofing materials. He married Miss Kate Davidson on May 8, 1873, and of the union two children were born, Wallace and Edna. The latter was to become a well-known leader and teacher of Christian Science.

Beginning in the late 1880's, both Mr. and Mrs. Kimball suffered prolonged illness, for which they found no medical relief. Then, in 1887, Christian Science was brought to their attention and Mrs. Kimball quickly recovered. Her husband progressed more slowly, but eventually he did regain his health. Both of them became enthusiastic students of *Science and Health,* and together went through Mrs. Eddy's Primary class of 1888, again attending a Primary class taught by her in 1889. Both of them were also among the seventy who were summoned to the famous Concord class, the last class Mrs. Eddy taught, which instead of the now-traditional six-day Normal course consisted of but two sessions, requiring but six hours all told. Kimball retired from business in 1890 to devote himself to the cause, and he was given the coveted C.S.D. (Doctor of Christian Science), the title which could be conferred by Mrs. Eddy only.

Mrs. Eddy early recognized Kimball as a most able teacher and leader. Going over the heads of all her ranking veterans, she entrusted him with the honor of presenting Christian Science to the World's Parliament of Religions at the World's Fair in 1893. After the Chicago church elected Kimball its Second Reader, Mrs. Eddy requested the church to make him First Reader, and the elected First Reader stepped down for him. When the Board of Lectureship was established in 1898, he was made its chairman and continued in that post until his death. He became the most popular and influential lecturer of his day, delivering some 1,800 lectures in all parts of the world, traveling over 400,000 miles. He was given the task of making private and semiprivate talks to Scientists in the various centers during his lecture tours.

When in 1899 Mrs. Eddy set up her "Board of Education" as successor to the Massachusetts Metaphysical College for certifying Primary class teachers, Edward Kimball was one of its three members, and it was he who conducted the ensuing Normal classes from 1899 to 1902. These were not the only evidences that Mrs. Eddy trusted Kimball beyond all others. During the Woodbury slander trial, in order to avoid possible seizure of her books in case of defeat, she transferred all her copyrights to him for safekeeping. In 1908, along with Mr. and Mrs. William P. McKenzie, he and Mrs. Kimball were constituted a committee to review and report on a final revision of *Science and Health.* On his return from a lecture tour in Europe in 1909, at Mrs. Eddy's request he was invited by the Board of Directors to teach the Normal class of 1910. But before the date set for the class Kimball passed on—his death occurred on August 13, 1909—and the movement had lost one of its most distinguished and able leaders.

Mrs. Eddy, who was now far advanced in years and herself within a few months of the end of her earthly career, at his passing proclaimed her "beloved" Edward Kimball's teaching correct and clear, adding that even now it remained an inspiration to the entire field. (*Christian Science Sentinel,* XII, 10)

Thus the seal of approval was placed upon his teaching by the very founder herself. This passage was to be quoted again and again by the followers of Kimball when, in later years, his essential teaching fell under the condemnation of the church authorities.

Led off by Mrs. Eddy's own eulogy, the church periodicals were filled at the time with tributes to Kimball. Editor McLellan of the *Journal,* in featuring a letter of praise for Kimball written by the prominent lecturer Frank H. Leonard, called it a "tribute to the teaching of one who was taught by Mrs. Eddy, and who faithfully upheld the gospel which he received." This was the same Editor

McLellan who, after Mrs. Eddy's passing, spearheaded the official attack upon the Kimball school of thought.

Leonard's letter discloses that while Kimball was very popular and his students, next to those of Mrs. Eddy, might be the most envied throughout the church, there had been and were those who disagreed with his interpretation of Christian Science. It had been asserted, for instance, that he taught that there were spiritual organs, but nothing the writer of the letter had ever heard in Kimball's class brought any such impression to him. (*Sentinel*, XII, 91)

The year 1910 saw the passing of Mrs. Eddy; and the major control of the church, which had been firmly held by her up until the time of her death, passed into the hands of the Board of Directors of the Mother Church, with a considerable measure of autonomy being exercised by the Board of the Christian Science Publishing Society (a situation which led to the Great Litigation).

Apparently there were powerful forces in the hierarchy which were opposed to what came to be known as Kimballism, and from that time until the present day pressures of one kind or another have been exerted to purge the movement of its champions. And these efforts have been successful to a considerable extent, at least within the organized ranks. Most of the teachers who admittedly embrace the Kimball interpretation have apparently been eliminated from the organization.

The first overt attack on Kimballism in the church press came in editorials published in the *Journal* and *Sentinel* three years after the death of Mrs. Eddy.

In an editorial in the *Journal* of December, 1913, Annie M. Knott, who was later to be elevated to a Directorship, goes straight to the heart of the controversy when she condemns as "utterly false and unspiritual logic" the argument that one's "own hand cannot be painful or diseased because God's hand is not." This was a direct repudiation of an essential principle of Kimball's teaching. He had emphasized such assertions of Mrs. Eddy as that with Christian Science "can be discerned the spiritual fact of whatever the material senses behold"; and the Leonard letter had already put on public record that "he [Kimball] taught that everywhere are to be found

God's ideas, manifesting the infinity of creation, and that where mortal mind said there was a sick organ, in that very place was one of God's ideas." As the Leonard statement had been published unchallenged, indeed with approbation, during Mrs. Eddy's lifetime, it must have come as a shock to the many Kimball followers when the *Journal* and *Sentinel*, still under the same editor, openly attacked this view now that Mrs. Eddy was gone. Although Kimball was not identified by name, the allusions to him were generally considered unmistakable.

In 1885 Mrs. Eddy had declared that every idea of Spirit is counterfeited in some matter belief, so that every material belief can be regarded as the type and representative of a spiritual verity (*Journal*, III, 133). And in *Science and Health* (p. 267) she said that mortals present more than superficially appears, since errors function as pointers to the one Mind. That Kimball clearly adopted this line of thought is shown in the Leonard letter.

Mrs. Knott argued that it is a mistake to trace our likeness to God by taking the physical body or its members even as symbols of divine ideas. She supported her stand with another passage from *Science and Health* (p. 302), to the effect that man's true consciousness is not to be found in any bodily resemblance to Spirit, but strictly in the mental. The absurdity of seeking anything divine in the place of the human, she indicated, "will be readily seen when we attempt to apply it to the digestive system, brain, nerves, etc."

In an editorial called "Perfect Models" (*Sentinel*, XVI, 371), Mrs. Knott inveighs against "the spiritualizing of matter"—which was the charge commonly made against Kimball. Kimball had specifically sought to redeem the organs and functions on Mrs. Eddy's proposition that scientific understanding "translates matter back into its original language, which is Mind, and gives the spiritual instead of the material signification." (*Christian Healing*, p. 7) It was well known that Kimball always warned against denying body, since a successful denial would be its disappearance in death, emphasizing Mrs. Eddy's thought that if you correct material belief by spiritual knowledge, "consciousness constructs a better body." (*Science and Health*, p. 425)

Mrs. Knott counters this with an anecdote. She says Mrs. Eddy chided a pupil for not being, as Paul admonished, "absent from the body," since God is incorporeal and man is His image and likeness. Getting even closer to a direct Kimball quote, Mrs. Knott says that while Mrs. Eddy enjoins us to "hold the perfect model in thought," this does not "authorize us to say that there is only one eye, ear, or foot." Now it was axiomatic with Kimball that the spiritual idea of which material eye, ear, or foot is the human concept, must be one in its infinity, just as there can be but one twice-two-is-four, omnipresent as idea. Mrs. Knott deplores the encroachment of what she brands the "undeveloped or faulty concepts of Truth" on what she evidently considers the correct understanding, and fears that their dissemination will lead others even farther astray.

The battle lines were now sharply drawn. As against the Kimball emphasis on spiritual perfection in the very place where material imperfection appears, the official view emphasized that "*entirely separate* from the belief and dream of material living is the Life divine." (*Science and Health*, p. 14) Kimball taught that anything wrong in human experience would have to be a wrong sense of a right something, so that Christian Science healing was simply the transforming effect of understanding on the human concept. To deny that eye sees would be tantamount to blindness, whereas officialdom, in the person of Mrs. Knott, declares: "While it is true that mortals are at present dependent upon the body for outward expression of their thought and activity, it is none the less true that the eye does not see, nor the ear hear, but that Mind and its idea alone compass seeing and hearing." She directs attention to lines 2 to 4 on page 261 of *Science and Health* as meeting the need of health by turning thought away from the body to Principle.

Archibald McLellan, the editor-in-chief, in a vigorous editorial (*Sentinel*, VI, 450), says he is surprised to learn through letters from the field that people think the two editorials by Annie M. Knott were ever meant to be directed against any teacher, particularly as condemning "the teachings of a well-known and greatly honored and respected teacher of Christian Science." They had no teacher in mind, he asserts, and were not knowingly condemning any teacher or teaching. Only setting forth the truth. Some of the editors had been taught by "this teacher" unnamed, and they declared that he never taught "the manifestly erroneous views of Christian Science which were condemned in these editorials." But when McLellan typifies the widespread misconception they are correcting by referring to a lady who was told her hand is an idea of God and therefore exempt from pain, the repudiation is obviously directed at Kimball's teaching.

The editors were, McLellan claimed, only doing their duty in expounding the true teaching of Mrs. Eddy, when the receipt of similar letters from different parts of the field showed the need for correcting quite a number of students.

Interesting light is thrown on Mrs. Knott's views, which were of course the officially recognized orthodox ones, by an exchange which took place between herself and a visitor to Boston. In a personal letter dated November 27, 1951, a correspondent writes:

> When in 1942 I queried Annie Knott about this editorial dynamite, she stood pat. Asked how she would treat indigestion while abandoning the body, she countered: "Does Mind in its infinity have anything to digest?" Pressed about the function of elimination, she said: "In all of infinite Mind there is nothing to eliminate, and no place outside of infinity to eliminate it, so there is no elimination." If one succeeded in demonstrating that there is no elimination, I hazarded, wouldn't that be constipation? She only smiled patiently and reminded me that I was very young.

While this exchange may seem merely facetious, it does bring out a fundamental difference between the orthodox point of view, which Kimball labeled annihilation, and the viewpoint of transformation. The Kimball position in this case, as this correspondent remarks, would be that "if anything wrong is a wrong sense of a right something, then indigestion would be replaced with digestion as the unrestricted activity of divine Mind, and this principle would apply to any function, including that of elimination."

A prominent Kimball student declares categorically that since this controversy broke out into print at the end of 1913, no writings have appeared in the church periodicals in which Kimball teaching could be identified, save in two periods. The first was during the

Great Litigation, when Herbert Eustace, a leading champion of Kimball, and his group took over the Publishing Society. Kimball's approach this student finds easily discernible in the editorials and articles in Vols. XXXVIII and XXXIX of the *Journal* and Vols. XXII, XXIII, and XXIV of the *Sentinel*—which volumes, by the way, have been withdrawn from most of the Christian Science reading rooms. The second period was during the ascendancy of George Shaw Cook, an organization stalwart who died in 1944. The titles of the leading Cook articles hint something of this. Cook had "managed to make Kimball precepts palatable to Boston official-dom," says this student, "through a style of presentation which was either too subtly ambiguous to rouse the furies of orthodoxy, or actually represented compromise on his part." He adds that this latest resurgence of Kimballism had its last gasp with Cook's retirement in 1942.

With the passing of so notable a figure as Edward Kimball from the scene, it was natural that his followers should desire that his teachings be perpetuated. While it had not been customary for teachers to publish their material, and some of them had fallen into Mrs. Eddy's disfavor and been cut off from church membership when they ventured to do so, there was no absolute prohibition of publication. Indeed, Mrs. Eddy had left the door open by saying that books based upon *Science and Health* could be useful, and that a student could write voluminously on the subject without violating any rules. But it was to be some time before anything by Kimball appeared.

Despite the stern disapproval of officialdom, the secret treasuring of "unauthorized" writings has always flourished among the followers of Mary Baker Eddy, and it is not surprising that, out of the thousands of papers in circulation, not a few are of Kimball origin. It would seem inevitable that some of this highly prized material would eventually reach print. And so it did.

In Chicago the Rev. Glenn A. Kratzer, who had left the Methodist pulpit to become a Christian Science practitioner, fell into disfavor with the church authorities for publishing some of his own writings. But he continued in the practice and teaching of Christian

Science without benefit of church membership, his study aided and
enlivened by the flow of officially unapproved and clandestinely
circulated writings. At last, through the generosity of a prominent
Kimball practitioner, he came into possession of a large collection
of Kimball addresses, letters, and records of class teaching. It is said
that Kratzer insisted upon paying his benefactor $1,000 to reimburse
him for the expenditures he had made in gathering and copying
these papers.

Kratzer's next step, as reliably reported from several sources, was
to offer the whole collection to the Kimball family, free of charge
but on the one condition that it be published. He was sharply
rebuffed. He then took it to the Board of Directors in Boston, where
he was given a cool reception, and finally to the Christian Science
Publishing Society. Here Trustee Eustace expressed intense interest,
but declined to accept the material for publication.

Although he was threatened with dire consequences if he dared
to publish the collection himself, Kratzer went ahead and issued it
in book form in 1917, under the title *Teaching and Addresses of
Edward A. Kimball*. Since then it has been reprinted again and
again, and still enjoys a lively circulation. It is reasonable to assume
that the Board of Directors decided they could not legally prevent
publication, for no court action was ever instituted to interfere with
the book.

But that is not to say the book was ignored by the church
authorities. Clifford P. Smith, Manager of Committees on Publication of the Mother Church, in a dispatch to the *New York World*
dated March 10, 1928, stated that the Kratzer book was objectionable. Part of it was not authentic, he asserted, although he did not
indicate what part. He declared it had been issued without the consent of Kimball's widow or anyone representing her and over the
objections raised by her and her daughter, Edna Kimball Wait. The
Smith statement also alleged that the book was persistently advertised in a deceptive manner.

It is true that the book is not well edited. It exhibits grammatical
and typographical errors. Mrs. Kimball found the arrangement of
the material offensive, according to Elizabeth Berend, who was

house guest at her Indiana estate when Kratzer sent the first copy off the press with his compliments. Mrs. Berend reports that Mrs. Kimball closeted herself with the book all day, only to come out weeping. "They have made a cookbook of my husband's life work!" she complained, referring to the way in which the material is cut up with paragraph and section captions, and indexed so that the reader may readily look up a Kimball statement on any particular topic, "like finding a recipe," without having to study the book as a whole and thus get Kimball's foundational structure. The fear was that the essential Kimball teaching might be misunderstood, the meaning distorted, by a piecemeal approach through passages torn from their context.

At the time of the book's publication, Mrs. Wait wrote the Board of Directors concerning her desire to sue for an injunction to restrain the publisher from distributing it. She had conferred with Bicknell Young and others, including their attorneys. The Board asked, however, that she take no action until she heard from the Committee on Publication. But no letter ever came.

Following Kimball's death in 1909, there had been some disposition in official circles to consider favorably the publication of some of Kimball's papers. A member of the Board of Directors, William V. Rathvon, at one time urged the Kimball family to collect his writings and notes; but apparently when he saw the Kratzer book he realized for the first time what the Kimball teachings really were and backed away from the idea. Mrs. Wait told more than one of her students that, indeed, Rathvon had tried to maneuver her into damaging admissions about her father's teachings. Edward Merritt, another of the Directors, however, continued to favor the idea of publication.

When it was found that Kratzer's book, though anathematized, was being bought and read by considerable numbers everywhere, it seems that the Board came to the conclusion that a Kimball book sponsored by his own family might divert readers from the Kratzer publication. Thus it was that, with the Board's tacit approval, Edna Kimball Wait brought out a collection of her father's addresses and letters in 1921, under the title *Lectures and Articles on Christian*

Science, having in its preparation the editorial assistance of members of the staff of the Christian Science Publishing Society. Still in print today, the book remains unchanged from its first edition, except for the inclusion in 1938 of a short article called "Letter on Reflection," the same article which, under the title "God and Man," had always been a feature of the copyrighted Kratzer book.

It is true that the Wait volume was never formally authorized by the Board, and has never enjoyed the advantage that officially sanctioned publications have in the organization. But this makes it possible to avoid the whole explosive issue of whether the Kimball teaching shall be accepted as authoritative.

In the Wait book the more radical Kimball statements do not appear, and significant modifications have been made in the material itself. One really crucial change has reference to the *modus operandi* of treatment. In the Kratzer book, after describing disease as "a defective depicting of thought," Kimball asks: In whose mind is this false mental picture to be corrected? His answer is: "I will say in the mind, so called, of the practitioner." Elaborating this point, he goes on to say that when the practitioner clears his own mentality, he will have nothing else to do, and indeed he never can do anything else. After all, he explains, the practitioner "has nothing to do with matter, nothing to do with his patient, so far as that is concerned." (pp. 36, 37) This is equivalent to Kimball's well-known stand that the only patient the practitioner has, in the final analysis, is himself. In the Wait book, the corresponding passage (pp. 420-21) follows closely up to the point where the question is raised: In whose mind? Here the answer is given as: "*Amongst others,* in the mind of the healer." This is not the same thing at all. It is a very radical change, involving the very heart of Kimball's teaching, as can well be shown from other sources.

At this juncture a significant departure from the old order emerges. Quimby's idea was for the practitioner to talk the patient out of his trouble; and the idea is echoed in Mrs. Eddy's writings when she says the practitioner must refute the sick man's thoughts, words, and actions by mental and oral arguments, persisting in this course until the patient's mind yields and his mind is controlled fully by the harmonious thought. Kimball's idea was for the practitioner to talk *himself* out of what might appear to be his patient's troubles, since the practitioner must be dealing with false belief where *he* is thinking. This, too, finds echoes in Mrs. Eddy's writings, when she says that "what you see, hear, feel, is a mode of consciousness, and can have no other reality than the sense you entertain of it" (*Unity of Good,* p. 8), and, again, "Jesus beheld in Science the perfect man, who appeared to him where sinning mortal man appears to mortals. In this perfect man the Saviour saw God's own likeness, and this correct view of man healed the sick." (*Science and Health,* pp. 476-77)

In the Smith dispatch condemning the Kratzer book, it was asserted that no one representing the Mother Church had ever acted or spoken against the Wait volume. And Albert Field Gilmore said in a letter to Mrs. Wait that his editorial against "unauthorized books" was not meant to reflect upon her publication, which he personally found meritorious. Meanwhile, according to veteran Christian Scientists, the Wait book never approached the Kratzer book in popularity throughout the field.

What, precisely, are the Kimball teachings, and how do they differ from the orthodox interpretation of Christian Science? The difference would seem to be really at only two significant points: (1) what the philosophers would call his concept of the phenomenal world, and (2) his idea as to the treatment of disease.

The first of these has been the chief center of attack upon Edward Kimball. In popular terms, it expresses itself in the charge that he taught that there were spiritual organs—the point of the editorials in the *Journal* and *Sentinel.* That Kimball was well aware of this is evident from a long letter he wrote to Judge Hanna on November 29, 1907, congratulating the Judge on the fact that he was to teach the Normal class that year. Kimball here alluded to opposition to the Board of Education which had existed from its very inception. This opposition, he declared, was just as unreconciled as ever. He had heard of a Christian Science lecturer, not himself a teacher, who had denounced the continuance of the "College" as an insult to the other teachers, and said it should be abolished. Kimball remarked that he knew this particular critic disliked both him and Hanna, but observed that it was evidence of the continuing movement to discredit and so bring to an end the Normal class work. Everything that had purportedly been mistaught there was finally imputed to himself, he had learned, before they got through with it.

One of the teachers under the Board of Education, Alfred E. Baker, had sought to dispose of error, matter, by simply wiping out everything in a nihilistic kind of philosophy. Mrs. Eddy had taken Dr. Baker to task about this. While Jesus bade the man with the withered arm to stretch forth his hand, she complained, all the doctor could say was that the man didn't have any hand! She condemned the method used by a Concord practitioner, who had disposed of a case by saying there wasn't any case. The patient had died. Mrs. Eddy denounced such negation, saying the patient got nothing curative out of it.

Mrs. Eddy's exact words to Kimball had been: "Declare, I have a perfect liver, and let the spiritual import of this declaration destroy the false concept of liver." Later she had said to Mrs. Kimball, who reported the healing of a troublesome case through using this declaration, "Yes, you may declare, I have a perfect liver, or there is no liver, provided the thought back of these declarations is right."

It is noteworthy from the above exchange that Mrs. Eddy might be taken as authority for either of two absolutely opposing views: (1) you have a perfect liver, (2) you have no liver at all. Obviously, Kimball fixes upon the first view; for he writes that, in a discussion of the question with Mrs. Eddy, she expressed herself as feeling he was exactly right in his interpretation of her utterance. This led him to use her own words in class, amplifying and explaining them, with the result that much practical healing was accomplished. Most of his students had gotten the correct understanding of this phase of the teaching, but by the time it had been passed on second-, third-, or fifth-hand, it appeared he was teaching that each man had a separate spiritual stomach.

His letter said that thousands had in like fashion misinterpreted Mrs. Eddy's words, with the difference that they generally damned him for their own mistake, but didn't dare damn their Leader.

Enemies of the Normal class work had borne tales about him, saying his teaching was defective because it spiritualized body or matter. But Mrs. Eddy had assured him that she never believed this gossip, which reached all the way to her door, because she knew where he stood.

Kimball felt it would be well to set forth what he taught in order to confirm Mrs. Eddy's own instruction, and proceeded to outline briefly his class presentation of Christian Science. This, confirmed and elaborated, to be sure, in his many published articles, lectures, and class notes, is the most concise and straightforward expression of his thought to be found anywhere. Here are the essentials as he gives them:

Being is primarily Mind or noumenon, and secondarily ideas or phenomena. One, because infinite, it is not made up of duplications. Because this Mind is Life, Power, Law, Good, there is only one life, power, law, etc. (This is sheer monism, of course.)

Now Mind is expressed by means of ideas, and this manifestation of Mind, as an infinity of ideas, is body or embodiment, and it is necessarily one in its infinity. There is, therefore, only one body, not many.

Mind and its expression in ideas constitute not plurality, but unity. Such unity is inorganic, including no organs, spiritual or otherwise. (This would be Kimball's answer to the charge that he taught that organs are spiritual.)

While the manifestation or body is one, it does include or show forth all ideas, all things. (By this I suppose Kimball means that while collectively this infinity of ideas is one, it is nevertheless apprehended distributively in human consciousness.) All things of body, all ideas, are perfect, complete, immortal, harmonious, and under the rule of divine law. If there is but one Mind, the manifestation of which in ideas is body, it may be said, for all practical purposes, "that all men have one Mind and one body."

On the other hand, this does not seem to be the report of human experience, which sees, or seems to see, a countless variety of material forms all about, a whole universe of matter. What of all this? The answer is that the apparently material, including man, is not what it seems to be. It is not matter at all, for matter is not real, but is "subjective error, nothing but belief which calls itself matter." It is false belief, a lie. But there must first be a truth to lie about or it would not be a lie. Thus a material tree or a material body must be a lie about the real tree or the real body, the one and only body that exists, namely, the ideas which are the manifestation of the one Mind.

At this point, it will be observed that a definite dualism emerges. This dualistic postulate, that of the truth *and* the lie, the genuine and the counterfeit, was clear-cut in one of Kimball's favorite statements: "Underlying and behind every material object is a divine idea." Such representative Kimball teachers as George Shaw Cook made this a thematic statement in their classes, and the same thought is discernible in the Leonard letter.

Now was this an alien element, introduced originally into Christian Science by Kimball? Or was it derived from and based on Mrs. Eddy's own teachings? The record provides the answer. It was in 1885 that Mrs. Eddy declared every idea of Spirit to have its counterpart in some matter belief, so that every material belief must signify a spiritual verity at hand. Kimball did not take up the study of Christian Science until two years after this statement was published in the *Journal* (III, 133).

But Kimball appears to be the first leader to exploit this particular phase of the teaching. Before his advent, it is said that the emphasis had fallen on such of Mrs. Eddy's statements as that in *Science and Health* (p. 14) where she declares that entirely apart from the material concept is the divine reality or idea; and it is generally understood that in her classes she stressed the separateness and dissimilarity of "the real and the unreal." The material world, she often assured her pupils, was no more than a false creation of "nothingness calling itself something," simply error generating other errors, a wholly misleading illusion unconnected with fact. It is reported that she illustrated her point forcibly by asking the question, "What is the relationship between twice-two-is-four and twice-two-is-five?" and then answering, "There is none, since twice-two is not five."

With the wealth of material before us, it may be safely asserted that Kimball did not approach the visible universe in precisely the same way. In his letter to Judge Hanna he ties in the actual with the so-called illusory, perhaps endeavoring to establish "the indissoluble spiritual link" which Mrs. Eddy says mortal man must find to save himself. (*Science and Health,* p. 491)

Arthur Corey regards this shift of emphasis as one of Kimball's fundamental contributions to the advancement of Christian Science thought. "If there were no relationship between the truth and the lie," he asks, "how could you reach the lie with the truth to correct it?"

This is the line that Kimball apparently took, for he says in his definitive letter that every normal thing in matter is but a lie about a spiritual fact or idea, and that the spiritual thing is all right, perfect. He cites, and equates it with his own view, the phrase of Mrs. Eddy, "perfect in God."

The practical question here arises: What is the method of dealing with the bodily ills and imperfections in human experience? Is it annihilation or transformation? That is, shall the practitioner deny that there is any body, any eye, any hand, any liver, or shall he make a positive affirmation of the truth of which the apparent ill is the lie? Kimball's own choice is the latter—to discover the truth behind the lie and to establish that truth through realization. Does not Mrs. Eddy say, "Evil and all its forms are inverted good" (*Unity of Good,* p. 53), and "To material sense, earth is matter; to spiritual sense, it is a compound idea" (*Science and Health,* p. 585)?

With existence and experience totally mental, would it save or destroy to establish the thought that there is no eye at all? If there were no counter fact to the concept of body as sick, would not death result? Specifically, "If there were no opposite affirmation to the concept 'my liver is imperfect,' then the ultimate would be a belief of disaster instead of transformation" to health. Mrs. Eddy says the counter fact is requisite in bringing about a cure. (*Science and Health,* p. 233)

Thus to the claim, "My liver is imperfect," the immediate offset would be, "I have a perfect liver in God." More accurately stated, but still the practical equivalent, would be something like this: "Body is spiritual, it consists of spiritual ideas, and every idea is perfect. The idea of which liver is a false concept"—a counterfeit, to use Mrs. Eddy's expression—"is perfect."

This Kimball regards as virtually the same as Mrs. Eddy's statement in earlier editions of her textbook which read: "Realize the presence of health and the harmonious action of organs." (He admits that this may not be the exact wording, which throws some light upon the way he used Mrs. Eddy's statements.) He says he called her attention to this, and told her that the same people who failed to grasp the import of "I have a perfect liver in God" also interpreted her own statement wrongly. Indeed, in condemning his teachings his critics were condemning the author of their textbook.

The letter closes with the categorical statement that no student of his was ever taught that the spiritual man has spiritual organs, or that body is organic, or that there are many bodies. Nevertheless, he does teach the students to be careful about saying they have no arm, etc. True, Mrs. Eddy can and does make such a statement on occasion (she did so specifically in a letter to him dated July 26, 1901); "but," he reasons, "it proceeds from the clear sense of the fact that lies back of the belief of arm." As for spiritualizing matter, Kimball says Judge Hanna knows he does not perpetuate any such rot. (Incidentally, the Judge buried this letter in his files and it did not come to light until after his death, when his secretary turned it over to Edna Kimball Wait.)

It is noteworthy that on another occasion Edward Kimball said:

It is safe to declare that the body is not material, that there is no material heart, etc., but it is no more right to say that there is no heart than to say that there is no God. All things *are*. All things are spiritual. All things are perfect. Heart [the spiritual idea] *is*, and is perfect. Now if this is true, why say and reiterate, 'There is no heart'?"

Was Kimball true to the teachings of Mrs. Eddy, or were his attackers following what she taught? The answer is yes in both cases, for she made statements capable of sustaining either point of view, any number of which may be cited on both sides of the ledger. A Kimball student, considering this, is led to write:

Whether Mrs. Eddy oscillated between the path of rationalism (which Kimball took) and the inspirational path (preferred by the Boston faction), it is difficult to say, for her *Science and Health* is a patchwork of statements from every level and period of her evolution. Any logician can see that she did not always follow through on a given premise. At times she was carried along with irrefutable logic, but obviously she hesitated not at all to sail away with any passing inspiration, on the ground that it must be divine in origin if it came to God's anointed messenger. Kratzer used to say, "I never know when Mrs. Eddy's changing cars!" Kimball tended to fasten upon her reasoned propositions, glossing over such accompanying statements as were incompatible, while the Boston "intuitional" school of thought accepts it all uncritically as unadulterated revelation. The Kimball people, too, accept Mrs. Eddy as the Final Revelator, but they feel her writings must be read with scientific "discrimination," to use Bicknell Young's word, since, to quote Mr. Young, "We can't stay back with the relative statements forever, but must dwell more and more upon her absolute statements if we would progress." (Personal communication)

This does not of course accord with the orthodox stand that Mrs. Eddy made a terminal discovery in 1866, from which she could not possibly waver in spirit or letter throughout all her writings and revisions to follow. The official position is that there are no inconsistencies whatsoever in her writings, and that no modification is detectable or even possible in her basic thought as this thought found its expression in the innumerable statements made and published by Mrs. Eddy between 1866 and 1910.

What, then, about the attitude of the field toward Edward Kimball's unorthodox interpretation? The signs of implacable opposition have always been apparent in some quarters, as when the editors of the *Journal* and *Sentinel* repudiated Kimballism, in principle if not in name, after Mrs. Eddy had passed from the scene. Such reports as the following, written by a veteran Christian Scientist in England, are by no means uncommon: "Here in one of the Christian Science churches I was refused membership because I read and passed around Mr. Kimball's writings published by his daughter. This book was burned by practitioners here, and the Publication Committee had meetings warning about it." In a letter to Edna Kimball Wait of July 7, 1945, William Lyman Johnson told of a class-taught student who, at her teacher's request, "put your father's book into the incinerator."

More recently, the Gilbert C. Carpenters, father and son, were to print in a book of essays "a reproduction of Mrs. Eddy's pencilled corrections on portions of a manuscript that was written by her student Edward A. Kimball." The corrections, if they are in Mrs. Eddy's hand, are hard to reconcile with her unqualified public endorsement of Kimball's teaching on the occasion of his death. To an inquirer who raised this point, the senior Carpenter replied: "*Everything* can be a vehicle for God"—from which the inference was drawn that it was not the form but the spirit which Mrs. Eddy validated in her famous eulogy of Kimball and his "clear, correct teaching." "After all," Carpenter explained, "it was not what Kimball *said*, but *the thought behind his words* which counted metaphysically." Thus one might deny body or affirm body with equal propriety, depending entirely upon the thought behind one's statement. "Mother [Mrs. Eddy] once said, 'My words in another's mouth can be a lie,'" Carpenter writes. Even a correct statement would convey untruth if the underlying thought were wrong, and vice versa, according to this.

Other explanations of a less mystical nature have been found. Recently in conversation with a distinguished Christian Science teacher the remark was made that Mrs. Eddy was very adverse to Kimball and his teaching. How, then, account for her letter commending to the world his presentation of Christian Science as clear and correct? "Oh, that," she said, "was written by Mr. Dickey." Adam H. Dickey was a Kimball student and, at the time, was Mrs. Eddy's chief secretary. "But," I said, "she signed it." "You must remember," the teacher replied, "that Mrs. Eddy was very old and that she signed many things."

On the other hand, Herbert Eustace, eminent Kimball student, insists Mrs. Eddy's endorsement of Kimball must be taken at face value. In his classes Eustace always said that Edward Kimball's advent had brought about a change in Mrs. Eddy's published writings. Asked what this change was, Eustace answered:

She had been waiting for years to see if anyone would really be able to dig out the science of Christian Science from what she had written in *Science and Health*. What a joy to have found at last one who had actually been able to catch her real meaning. It was after she was assured of this fact—the fact that she had written the book so that it could be dug out—that she changed her statement in *Christian Healing*, page 14, to its present wording. (Letter of September 15, 1951)

Checking back on this, I find that up through the 1896 edition (p. 13), the passage in question read: "I have never yet had a student who has reached this ability to teach; it includes more than they understand." The passage was revised for the next edition to express Mrs. Eddy's recognition of a teaching level of understanding not before achieved in the field. Eustace points out that it was at "this time that she opened her College work again and started it out on a metaphysical basis with Mr. Kimball in the chair." (Letter to Clarissa Hale Corey)

There is yet another phase of the Kimball teaching which is of interest. In a letter to Theodore R. Hinsdale, February 5, 1905, he had written to sketch briefly his position, though insisting that to do so adequately would require at least seventy thousand words. Three things must be remembered in understanding the basic concept that all is infinite Mind and its infinite manifestation: (1) that all things real are perfect, complete, normal; (2) that there is nothing in the nature of construction, organism, organization, aggregation, etc., about them; that the so-called material universe is not what it seems to be, but is error; that error, equated with mortal mind, is not a creator but a liar, a lie, or what Mrs. Eddy calls counterfeit, the reverse of Truth (but not Truth reversed as Truth cannot be reversed); (3) that mortal mind—and this is the significant added point—has primary and secondary phases. This is the explanation of the difference between the normal and the abnormal in the so-called material world. The *hand* may be taken as an example of the primary phase, while a *wart* on the hand would be secondary, because it is abnormal.

Discussing this in class, as reported in the Kratzer book (p. 145), Kimball used as an illustration the dollar banknote, or U.S. "greenback," with a blot on it. Behind the greenback is a silver dollar in the

U.S. Treasury, but there is nothing behind the blot, per se, to validate it.

In the Hinsdale letter, Kimball goes on to explain that mortal mind as a whole is a lie about Truth, but it is to be perceived that a specific lie implies a specific truth about which it is the lie. Everything materially normal is a counterfeit of that which is real in Spirit.

Mortal mind distorts its own concepts and images. As an example, Kimball uses a tree which, he says *Science and Health* teaches, exists only as a divine idea in reality, while the claim of tree, i.e., the material tree, is a misconception of reality. But suppose a man cuts the tree down and makes of it various objects—a telegraph pole, a whiskey barrel, a coffin. Are these equally counterfeits of specific ideas of divine Mind? His answer is no. Only the tree is. Then what about the others? They are only secondary errors.

The whiskey barrel is part of the primary lie that man is material, with sentient body needing food and drink, and possessing appetites, both normal and abnormal. The truth of which this is the lie is that man is really spiritual, possessing spiritual senses, sustained entirely by and in Mind. A telegraph pole is but part of the claim that intelligence can be transmitted through or because of matter, the belief in a system of mechanical communication having no prototype in Mind. But behind it all is the spiritual fact that, as Mrs. Eddy writes, thought passes from God to man, "and that the whole of man is to know (reflect) infinite Mind." In belief the coffin may represent death, but somewhere in the background is the fact of infinite Life and man's immortality.

To the question of whether the belief of a table is as real as the belief of a child, Kimball answers no. Positing degrees of reality, he says the belief of a corporeal man is nearer to reality than a wart or a crutch or a coffin or a table. To be sure, the material concept *table* is a lie about something, but it is not the counterfeit of a spiritual table. Behind the table would be the false material concept *tree*, and behind that would be the spiritual fact or reality of *tree* in Mind. In other words, table is a derivative belief and, as such, farther removed from the divine idea of which material tree is a false concept. As Bicknell Young was later to explain it, mortal mind involves itself in a network of lies, and a manufactured object is not as real as a natural object, being a lie about a lie.

As time went on, experience led Edward Kimball to exercise more and more caution. He said:

I used to declare in my teaching for a perfect spiritual liver. I did it because Mrs. Eddy told me to do it. But after finding that my students would go out and make this statement omitting my amplification, and so leave an impression that I was teaching the spiritualization of matter, I quit it and changed my presentation.

He had found it wise to forego naming the organs and functions, although this had nothing to do with the fact that what he was trying to explain was simply that there is some perfect idea of Mind which mortal mind has counterfeited in its presentation of liver. The essential that remained was that the perfect body, the body of right ideas, which is the spiritual body, should be declared for daily. Thus the human concept, the visible body, is brought into line with its divine prototype, the correction or transformation being what we call healing, Kimball concludes.

Now Bicknell Young, who was a Kimball student, carries the development of Christian Science still farther—or at least uses language in which he seems to go beyond his teacher (although he himself would not have agreed that he did). Young was, perhaps next to Kimball, one of the most popular teachers and lecturers in Christian Science history. When Kimball, who was to have taught the Normal class of 1910, passed on, it was Bicknell Young who was chosen to teach it.

Arthur Corey, who was a member of Young's 1936 class and took a shorthand record of all that was said on that occasion, reports Young as saying that what is called the material universe is the spiritual creation dimly seen and incorrectly interpreted. He quotes his teacher as declaring: "Remember that it is the mountain you see through the mist, no matter how dimly and distorted, still the mountain." And, in another connection, Young said: "Everything in the realm of matter or mortal mind indicates something in the divine order of infinite being."

Corey was excited by these utterances and, in a personal conversation with Young, expressed his satisfaction that at this point Young had progressed beyond Kimball. Young was startled, Corey declares, and remonstrated that he had contributed nothing new or different in the teaching. Young held that Kimball had never made a single statement the equivalent of which could not be found in *Science and Health*, and that a Christian Scientist should venture no expression on metaphysics which could not be found in that book. "If I have departed from Mr. Kimball's teaching in any way," he said in effect, "I retract it."

Bicknell Young, the most outstanding of Kimball students, enjoyed widespread popularity, but his teaching was evidently suspect. The fact that he was appointed to teach the Normal class in 1937 has been advanced as evidence that he must have been in good standing with the Directors, since by this time nothing official in the movement was beyond the Board's control. Under the circumstances it is not a little surprising that he was chosen for this important task.

Several members of the 1937 Normal class report that there was quite a stir among them when, at the opening session, it was discovered that Young was to be the teacher. One of them told me that two men, seated directly in front of her, voiced great disapproval of the appointment of a teacher bearing the Kimball stigma, and even some horror that Kimball's daughter, Edna, was present as a fellow-student. Others have confirmed this report, and they add that in the field generally there was an adverse reaction. Rumors were circulated that the Normal class would have to be retaught, breaking all precedent. So insistent was the gossip that the Board was obliged to send out a letter to prevent further disruption.

That Young himself sensed the precariousness of his position may be inferred from a remark he is reported to have made in one of his Association meetings: "You don't want to get your teacher into trouble, do you? Then don't pass notes around of what I have said."

Bicknell Young died in good standing with the church. Some thought it was only because he had so large a popular following that he was not challenged. But a number of the Kimball students and their second-generation successors have not fared so well at the hands of the organization. At least two members of Young's 1937 Normal class, John Lawrence Sinton and Margaret Laird, were disciplined by the Board, and it is said by several of her students that Edna Kimball Wait voiced fears of being "next on the list." Mrs. Wait died without these fears having been realized. Sinton resigned under fire, and Mrs. Laird withdrew from the church after being deprived of official recognition, because of her views, as a teacher and practitioner. Europe's leading teacher, John Doorly, who had gone through Normal class with Bicknell Young, was excommunicated following a heresy trial. A German member of the Doorly faction, William H. Breymann, the Hamburg practitioner, was excommunicated. The eminent Frances Thurber Seal, Christian Science ambassador to Germany, had her troubles after going through Kimball's class, although she did manage to stay in the organization. Helen B. Barrett, prominent Kimball teacher, was stripped of her privileges and denied all standing after she had founded Chicago's Tenth Church. Then there was the Rev. Mr. Kratzer, definitely of Kimball persuasion, who fell into serious trouble with the church authorities and was squeezed out.

Herbert Eustace experienced considerable friction with his orthodox associates in Boston before his excommunication; but his expulsion was the immediate outcome of his unsuccessful attempt to prevent the Board of Directors from establishing complete control of the church, and was not primarily due to his Kimball leanings and the conflicts they unquestionably engendered.

Archibald McLellan was one of the few Kimball-taught students to survive the Boston challenge; but his sponsorship of the anti-Kimball editorials in the church periodicals shows that he himself had gone over to the Boston school of thought.

Arthur Corey is one of the very few dissenters from Boston orthodoxy who did not leave the church while under fire. He had for six years been a *Journal*-registered practitioner in good standing, and was a popular First Reader when he as a matter of principle threw off organization, convinced that organization is a hindrance rather than a help in the spread of Christian Science. He continues to promulgate the Kimball-Young line of teaching, though modified substantially.

George Shaw Cook, who had Primary class instruction under Edward Kimball in 1896 and was a member of Bicknell Young's Normal class in 1910, was among the last of the recognized Kimball exponents to occupy a high post in the church. Cook, known for his circumspection, was editor of the church periodicals from 1935 to 1942. Whether he maintained a clear-cut Kimball point of view and/or succeeded by ambiguity in satisfying the demands of orthodoxy, it is difficult to determine. Here and there in his writings the Kimball thought seems to be expressed unmistakably, but again its near opposite is to be found. Those concerned with philosophical subtleties might wish to examine several articles in which Cook handles phases of the subject ordinarily thought of in connection with Kimball. One, "Demonstration," appeared in the *Christian Science Sentinel* (XLIII, 650). Published in the *Christian Science Journal* were "Mind and Body" (LVII, 278 ff.); "Man Consists of Ideas, Not Organs" (LVIII, 564 ff.); "Concerning Counterfeits" (LVII, 566 ff.); and "The Visible Universe" (LVII, 332 ff.).

In his article on "Organs" Cook takes account of the fact that some students are perturbed by the statement that back of every material thing is a spiritual fact, or right idea. This is the timeworn charge against Kimball teaching, which is evidently still hanging fire. Cook points out that Mary Baker Eddy plainly says just this in *Science and Health*, where she affirms that Christianly scientific discernment discloses the spiritual fact of whatever the material senses behold. This does not mean, he explains, that the idea is located in space back of the object, but that in thought or consciousness it underlies it. Indeed, objects of material sense are in no sense like the spiritual ideas of which they are, to use Mrs. Eddy's term, counterfeits. They do not bear any resemblance to them. So when one says that there is a divine fact or spiritual idea back of hand or foot or stomach or any other organ, all he means is that there is underlying these physical organs a spiritual reality. There are no spiritual organs.

Arthur Corey, who had selected Bicknell Young as his teacher because he regarded Young as the natural successor to Kimball and Kimball teaching as the one school certified by Mrs. Eddy herself to be clear and correct, found the Young class a revelation, gaining his first glimpse beyond the frustrating dualism into true monism. He found the conflict between the "real" and the "unreal" resolved, a conflict which the dualistic hypothesis would perpetuate interminably. As we have said, Corey was greatly impressed by Young's statement that the so-called material universe is the divine creation dimly seen and incorrectly interpreted. Did not this imply that the very man who is seen as mortal must be understood to be spiritual man and immortal? If not, how are you and I to be saved? Are we, rather, to be wiped out and replaced by some alien entity called "spiritual man"?

George Shaw Cook took note of the growing trend to carry the Kimball line beyond its settled dualism, of the truth *and* the lie, for he writes: "Christianly scientific facts correct the erroneous belief, sometimes entertained, that what appears to the physical senses as an object existing in space is actually a spiritual idea, of which we have a material view." (*Journal*, LVII, 332) Cook always emphasized the unreality of the visible and the reality of the invisible. At this point it would appear that Bicknell Young, and certainly Arthur Corey, part company with Cook. Young consistently deplored dualism and pleaded for "oneness" as the basis of demonstration. He even spoke out against Moseley's article "The Divine Idea and the Human Concept" because he said that very expression tended to establish dualism.

Cook explains the healing process in this way: Christian Scientists "find, through realizing that health or wholeness is an ever-present quality of divine Mind which spiritual man reflects and enjoys at all times, an improved belief of health is made manifest in their human experience." (*Sentinel*, XLIII, 650) According to this, all metaphysical endeavor would be to the end of making the world of material belief more harmonious until it could be destroyed or wiped out. That which is humanly visible is unreal, being the product of material sense, and at best is but a belief about a divine reality. The rose in the garden is no more

than an externalized human concept, and while it may be considered to symbolize a divine verity, it is not itself in any way that
verity which it counterfeits. Mind's idea of rose, Cook asserts, is
spiritual and *invisible*. (*Journal*, LVII, 333)

How would this square up with Bicknell Young's teaching?
Young would have had to say: remember, it is the rose you are
seeing through the mist, no matter how dimly and distorted, still
the rose. It was this which Corey seized upon and followed through
to the blunt conclusion: *the human concept is the divine idea as
it appears to you*. He writes:

Having struggled so long with the dualistic hypothesis which always
dominated the Christian Science movement, Bicknell Young's statement
that the material world is really the spiritual creation "seen through a
glass darkly" as it were, meant to me a revolutionary turn in the development of the doctrine, for I certainly inferred from it that this was a way
out of the dilemma of dualism, which otherwise seemed unresolvable.

To Corey this was the only logical outcome of Bicknell Young's
statement.

Corey was not the only responsible thinker to move along this
newly developing phase of Christian Science, although no one
before him appears to have acknowledged it as a distinct trend.
Edna Kimball Wait, Margaret Ledward Laird, and other distinguished Christian Scientists were unmistakably leaning in this
direction. Perhaps they were handicapped by organizational inhi-
bitions in openly facing the issue. Mrs. Wait, discussing it privately, remarked that her father often said, "If you're seeing anything different, keep it to yourself!"

Glimpses of the emerging monism can be caught in a paper
written by Martha Wilcox of Kansas City, in which she speaks
of what she gathered while a member of Mrs. Eddy's household.
Recollection is of course a selective process, and, as Mrs. Wilcox
attended Young's 1910 Normal class, the possibility cannot be
entirely discounted that she was influenced by this experience in
later recording the highlights of the Eddy sojourn.

When Mrs. Wilcox went to live at the Chestnut Hill residence, the first thing Mrs. Eddy taught her, she says, was "that 'the objects of sense' when correctly understood are really 'ideas of Soul.'" How was she shown to apply this in everyday experience? The dressmaker was expected to get Mrs. Eddy's clothes right to the fraction of an inch without benefit of fittings, because "Mrs. Eddy knew that Mind's work and Mind always fit," being one and the same thing, and there is not to be found in Mind the sense of anything being too large or too small. Again, her mistress expected her to know where every single thing in the house was to be found, even things she herself hadn't seen in forty years. "She taught me that there was only one consciousness, and that this consciousness was my consciousness and included all ideas as present and at hand, and she expected me to demonstrate it." This one-world idea even included the weather, for "God governs the weather; He governs the elements and there are no destructive winds or lightning," and from this position Mrs. Eddy expected her students to banish all storms and threats of storms.

In his book *Christian Science Class Instruction*, Arthur Corey precipitates the essential monism to be found in particular statements of Young, and before him Kimball, and all the way back to Mrs. Eddy, so that there can be no mistake about the origins of this trend, and about the distinctly new level which has been reached. Corey analyzes the two main lines of diverging thought in the movement, defining the one approach as negative—"There is *no* this, that or the other thing"—and the other as the positive—"There *is* a truth to *every* thing." He observes that this is an over-simplification, but points out that it is nevertheless the point of cleavage. He rejects the nihilist school in favor of Kimball's transformation idea. "There must be," he declares, "a specific truth about any aspect of existence which we apprehend, no matter how imperfectly we apprehend it."

Corey regards as farcical, and sometimes even disastrous in practice, the extraordinary notion so frequently advanced that by simply knowing that there is no organ one demonstrates that nothing can be wrong with it. Any object that is material to one in belief is so because one is believing it to be material, inter-

preting it so, and obviously merely to call it counterfeit or suppositional would not solve the problem.

"The so-called physical is actually spiritual in the last and only
right analysis, regardless of any interpretation with which you are
confronted," he maintains. "Recognizing the negative statement of
Truth as Truth defined in obverse, you arrive at the point of
glorious transfiguration." (pp. 153 ff.) But, he warns, do not regard
the negative as something apart from the thing negated, for "there
are not two creations, but just one, and that one is spiritual." This
accords with Mrs. Wilcox's recollection that Mrs. Eddy taught
her that it was a mistake to regard the things of creation as divided
into two groups, the one group being spiritual and the other group
material, with the group called material something she had to get
rid of; that, indeed, instead of two groups of creation, there is just
one, and that one is spiritual.

Suppose one is suffering from some heart ailment. If there
were no specific counter fact, disaster rather than redemption
would eventuate. But what is the logical affirmation to counteract
the false belief, the erroneous sense, the material lie? It would be
irrelevant and fruitless to say there is no heart. The affirmation
must be "my heart is perfect." Obviously one could not properly
say this while thinking of the heart as a material object in space.
Such an affirmation can only be made properly from the standpoint of Spirit, from which all things are seen as spiritual. If there
is any truth about heart—and there must be, else one could not
even be aware of a lie about heart—heart must be spiritual, and
therefore "indestructible, safe and sound." (p. 147) With this
understanding, the human interpretation or sense of things—heart
in this case—is spontaneously rectified. Thus healing is a process
of reinterpretation, the interpretation improving apace with advancing understanding.

In a personal statement to the writer, Arthur Corey insists that

my own teaching on reality aims at total, literal monism. I maintain that
we can demonstrate perfection in present experience only by recognizing
that *this* is the divine creation, however it may appear to us at the
moment—just as right where two-times-two may appear to be five, right

there it is really four, and this can be demonstrated or proved solely by staying with the simple fact, certainly not by attacking the five. . . . In essence, Quimby taught *mind over matter*. History records that Mrs. Eddy began with that premise. But scientific thought is dynamic, not static, and she evolved far beyond the Quimby view, at her height levelling off with *Mind instead of matter*. That was half a century ago. Today we have reached the place where it is *just Mind*, period. I should add here that I do not hold with the absolutists, who would retreat into an ideal world. It is vital that one's Mindness be tied in with human experience, applied in an entirely practical way to the handling of conditions and situations with which he is confronted from day to day.

Corey finds support for his argument in many of Mrs. Eddy's statements. He points to *Science and Health* (pp. 507 ff.), where she says that *misinterpreted*, it is *the divine idea* itself which seems to fall to the level of a human or material belief called mortal man or physical body; and to *Miscellaneous Writings* (p. 25), where she says that "Science, understood, translates matter into Mind," calling attention to the capital *M*, with which Mrs. Eddy always signified that she was speaking of *divine* Mind.

"The orthodox type, the faith-Scientist as Mrs. Eddy calls him, clings fondly to his suppositional world paralleling the divine creation, despite the obvious fact that he can never attain his dominion that way." Corey points to the absence of all monistic writings in the official literature as an indication that the dualist faction is in control at headquarters, and observes that those who lean away from the double concept are naturally regarded as unsound. The regular *Memorandum to Contributors* issued by the editorial offices in Boston, he notes, emphasizes the requirement that all writings must bring out the separateness of the two worlds, that of mortal mind and that of divine Mind. In any article acceptable for publication, "a clear distinction is always made between mortals and immortals, etc.," it is ruled. (*Sentinel*, July 16, 1955)

As for the old charge of spiritualizing matter, Corey gets around this by explaining that those who follow out from the Kimball premise are simply *dematerializing thought*, something Mrs. Eddy commends and the orthodox accept. (See *Science and Health*, p. 211; *The People's Idea of God*, pp. 2 and 7-8)

13

Evolution of Christian Science Practice

PARADOXICALLY, both wings of the Christian Science movement start out with the premise that Mind is absolutely All-in-all. Nevertheless it appears that there have long been two main trends of thought in Christian Science with respect to the essential nature of reality. The resulting breach has steadily widened as the two types have pursued their divergent paths and consolidated their arguments. Does this bring about any differences in actual practice?

When one examines the methods employed by Christian Scientists in treating disease, basic differences do appear. In general there seem to be three distinct levels of practice. The first, and one very widely used, seems clearly to be a carry-over of the Quimby influence; that is, since sickness is but an erroneous belief of the sufferer, the cure lies in specifically correcting the belief through argument.

In *Science and Health* Mrs. Eddy says that the relative counter fact is requisite in the curing of disease (p. 233), and that in order to heal by argument, the practitioner must ascertain the type of the ailment, even get its name, arraying his mental plea against the physical, and conforming it thereto, in order to destroy the evidence of disease. (p. 412)

Expanding on this, her book takes up various physical problems and handles them by the method known as "affirmation and denial." Many illustrations are given of adjusting the argument to the claim of belief. Symptoms of disease being but evidences of false belief, the remedy is to change the mental state by arguing in favor of man's innate perfection. Because what is called material body is a mental concept, under the control of mortal mind, the patient's disease belief must be destroyed by showing him how impossible it is for matter to suffer, to feel pain or heat, to be thirsty or sick; and the harmonious facts of being must be declared for. (p. 376) Palsy is no more than a belief that matter governs mortals, and this belief is destroyed by arguing that muscles have no power to lose, that Mind is supreme. (p. 375) If a patient is susceptible to colds, he must be informed that matter cannot take cold. If invalids seek a more healthful climate, Christian Science must tell them that they can be healthy in any climate. Since disease always stems from the mental cause that is a mistaken belief, the state of mind must be constantly watched to forestall bad effects. Never, says Mrs. Eddy, has she known a patient who did not recover when the belief of disease had been destroyed in this way. (p. 377) "A sick body is evolved from sick thoughts" (p. 260), but bodily impressions are deceptive and the evidence of the senses must be rejected as mortal mind illusion (p. 365). The basis of such rejection is that "divine Mind produces in man health, harmony, and immortality." (p. 380)

Unmistakably, the *patient's* consciousness is here involved, so that his co-operation is essential to the healing process. "To the Christian Science healer, sickness is a dream from which *the patient* needs to be awakened." (p. 417) Again, note that it is the patient who is to be "instructed out of" *his* "illusion of sickness." (p. 297) He is aided in this by the affirmations and denials of the practitioner, and he receives like benefit from the reading of *Science and Health*. The practitioner argues audibly on the side of health, denying that it is possible for matter to feel anything, thus destroying *the patient's* belief of suffering. (p. 376)

In the earliest phase of Christian Science development, Mrs. Eddy's methods included physical manipulation upon the patients. Quimby had practiced it regularly, first dipping his hands in water, though he himself declared that the manipulation was not an indispensable part of the treatment. It was used, he said, to establish confidence in the patient, and Quimby believed confidence an important factor in the curing of disease. While it was carried by

Mrs. Eddy into her own teaching, she evolved a different theory or explanation to justify its employment.

In his book *Mrs. Eddy As I Knew Her in 1870,* Samuel Putnam Bancroft, who was a member of Mrs. Eddy's first class and whose loyalty has never been questioned, reports that physical manipulation was a feature of the course. He relates that before each session the pupils were treated by her assistant, Richard Kennedy, not only to illustrate the physical methods used, but to induce in the pupils a state of receptivity. Then Mrs. Eddy undertook to teach them the spiritual methods. "Dr. Kennedy's treatment," he writes, "consisted of a manipulation of the head and solar plexus" —a sort of massage, as we learn from other sources.

In a manuscript prepared for her pupils, Mrs. Eddy explained that rubbing the head was the process employed to rub out belief, and that it was like erasing a wrong statement on the blackboard, to make way for the harmonious demonstration that Principle gives in idea and not belief. She added that the rubbing had virtue only as they, as well as others, believed they got nearer by contact. The belief to be rubbed out is located in the brain, she said; "therefore, as an M.D. lays a poultice where the pain is, so you lay your hands where the belief is to rub it out forever."

Christian Scientists in official circles today deny that Mrs. Eddy ever used manipulation, saying that she merely tolerated its use by her students in the beginning. Sibyl Wilbur, in the officially sponsored biography, writes that Mrs. Eddy had taught certain pupils Principle, but had permitted them to make use of the method of laying their hands upon the patients. (*Life of Mary Baker Eddy,* pp. 203 ff.) It is said that this was not meant to imply that she approved of the practice, and certainly not that she employed it herself at any time.

What is the truth of the matter? Fortunately we can let Mrs. Eddy speak for herself, and under oath. During a lawsuit which she brought in 1879 against two of her students for unpaid tuition, Mary Baker Eddy testified from the witness stand that she had for several years advocated the laying on of the hands with water. "It was not my principle," she said, "it was my method." Why had she adopted this method? She could not exactly explain, except that "it was because I saw a hand helped me." She did not claim that it was original with her, but could not recall whether she had known of it before she had met Phineas Quimby. (*Eddy* v. *Tuttle*)

This is indisputable evidence that Mrs. Eddy believed the physical practice in question aided *her* in *her* healing work, that it *was* her method, for one could not ask for more than her own sworn testimony given in the sobering atmosphere of the Essex County courtroom. It is hardly to her discredit that she employed physical manipulation in the development of her healing practice. Experimentation and the adoption of tentative hypotheses have always been a part of scientific progress.

At this trial Mrs. Eddy admitted she had taught manipulation prior to 1872. But by 1875 she was denouncing the method in her first edition of *Science and Health* (p. 193): "Sooner suffer a doctor infected with smallpox to be about you, than come under the treatment of one that manipulates his patient's heads, and is a traitor to science." In an 1896 manuscript she wrote that she had taught her first student that he might dip his hands in water and then manipulate the heads of his patients, even though this was after she had concluded, in 1866, that God, as man's Principle, does all the healing. But as time went on, experiment and experience taught her the scientific rule and application of the divine Principle in healing the sick, and this led her to renounce material manipulation in favor of exclusively mental means. (See Plate I, opposite page 48, in which is reproduced a photostatic copy of the 1896 manuscript, authenticated by Mrs. Eddy's own handwriting.)

According to the final *Science and Health*, resort to physical manipulation must weaken one's power to heal. Those who indulge such practices do so because they are ignorant of the harmful effects of magnetism, or because they are not spiritual enough to depend upon Spirit (p. 181).

Dramatic though it was, Mrs. Eddy's use of manipulation was no more than a side issue, modifying not at all the essential level on which Christian Science moved in its first stage of practice.

Now we come to the second level of the healing practice. At this point the strictly mental argument is introduced. Not only are such outward activities as physical manipulation abandoned, but full reliance is no longer placed upon audible argument. While the system of affirmation and denial is still to the same end—to affect the consciousness of the patient—a new trend begins to emerge as emphasis shifts to the silent argument of pure thought. Now the practitioner is instructed to plead the case on the side of Truth mentally and silently, varying the arguments to fit the symptoms (p. 412).

Bancroft's documented account has shown us the level attained by Mrs. Eddy's Science of Mind in 1870. Where it was about two decades later is made plain by Mrs. Eddy in an article she wrote for the *Journal* (VI, 249 ff.), an article to be given a permanent place in her book *Miscellaneous Writings* (pp. 219 ff.). Here she says that a healthy state is a state of consciousness manifested on the body. The practitioner's work, therefore, is aimed at changing his patient's consciousness of dis-ease and suffering to one of ease and loss of suffering. She describes the practitioner's treatment as opening with a mental salutation, in which the patient is silently told that he is well and that he knows it. The force of this silent argument is augmented by oral arguments in refutation of the thoughts, words, and actions of the sick man, to turn them into Truth's channels. The net result is to change from sickness to health the consciousness of the patient, so that he acknowledges that he is well and knows that he is.

In her *Private Directions for Metaphysical Healing*, copyrighted January 19, 1881, only a short time before the appearance of the *Journal* article, Mrs. Eddy makes this even more clear. Again she stresses the silent argument, and seems to imply that the oral approach might be optional when she says that "after this, *if* you fix the Truth stronger by so doing, talk it audibly." She speaks of "the Truth you bring *mentally* to destroy the error." Disease is an image in mortal mind. "If a cancer, or malformation, or whatever it may be, argue it out of belief and it disappears altogether . . . If the symptoms remain unchanged . . . tell them they are dreaming, it is not as they think." She goes on to admonish the healer that he must try not to pity the sick or to feel anxious about them, since this would aggravate the difficulty. "If their belief of suffering is real to you it will be more difficult to make it unreal to them, which you must do in order to heal them."

The only new element distinguishing the second level is, it will be observed, the use of silent instead of audible arguments. But left unexplained is the mystery of how the practitioner's thought reaches into the consciousness of the patient. Is it by telepathy? The present-day Christian Scientist, wide inquiry shows, stoutly denies that telepathy is involved in treatment, and points out that the word *telepathy* occurs nowhere in all of Mrs. Eddy's writings. It is true she does not use it, but the word was not coined until 1884, by psychical researcher F. W. H. Meyers, after her vocabulary was pretty well fixed. She does, however, speak often of *thought transference*, which is the older expression for the same thing.

In orthodox circles it is maintained that Mrs. Eddy disposed of this troublesome question when she wrote, in *Science and Health* (p. 179), that the sick who are absent from their healers can be healed through Science as readily as those who are present, since space is no obstacle to Mind. The official explanation of this, as given in the church periodicals, is that "space is a false belief to which Mind is not subject."

Nevertheless, time and again Mrs. Eddy in the course of her instructions proposes what could only be called a telepathic procedure. Writing in the *Journal* (VI, pp. 559 ff.), she leaves little room for doubt about this when she writes of "a mind taught its power to touch other minds by the transference of thought, for the ends of restoration from sickness, or, grandest of all, the reformation and almost transformation into the living image and likeness of God . . ."

Not only is treatment designed to argue down the patient's beliefs in his consciousness, whether the practitioner is present on the immediate scene or absent from it, but the probing of the patient's consciousness is advocated. In her *Private Directions,* already mentioned, Mrs. Eddy writes: "The sick cannot always give the name of the disease that you are to argue against, so you should read the thought as much as you can and not wholly from their lips take your points to argue." This is not a unique instance of such instruction. The same point is made repeatedly in *Science and Health*, as where its author says that the practitioner attains the absolute Science of healing when he is able to read the human mind, so as to discern the error he would destroy. (p. 85)

The second level of treatment, then, postulates a personal communication between practitioner and patient by purely mental (silent) means, and this practice is known throughout the field as "addressing the thought." Among those operating at this level it is considered not only improper but unethical to address another's thought silently without first securing formal permission, except in the rarest of situations. In his article "Some Thoughts on Obtrusive Mental Healing" (*Sentinel*, XLIX, pp. 1075 ff.), editor John Randall Dunn presents the official view, declaring that in the vast majority of cases it is essential that patients be cognizant of the fact that they are being treated, and that they be fully in accord with the treatment. He quotes Mrs. Eddy's strictures against promiscuous mental treatment given without the knowledge or consent of the individuals being treated. (*Retrospection and Introspection*, p. 71) People who are unfamiliar with the signs of mental treatment and therefore unable to recognize what is affecting them, says Dunn, would be robbed of their right to individual freedom of choice. He asks how even a well-meaning Christian Scientist could pray for a friend, who he hears is suffering, without "willfully trespassing on his friend's mental precincts." This would be in keeping with Mrs. Eddy's statement that one should not enter mentally the personal precincts of human thought without first ascertaining that the person with whom he would hold communion desires it. (*Miscellaneous Writings*, p. 282)

To make possible absent treatment, the practitioner is here credited with imparting something specific to his patient, something in the way of thoughts designed to counteract the patient's erroneous beliefs. "The moral and spiritual facts of health, whispered

into thought, produce very direct and marked effects on the body."
(*Science and Health,* p. 370)

But there is an unfortunate corollary to this. If thought communicated, silently or audibly, can do good, it can also do evil; for
thought, whatever its origin, can produce a cancer as readily as a
flower if the belief is strong enough to manifest it. (*Christian
Healing,* p. 6) The use of thought for evil purposes is called "mental
malpractice," and Mrs. Eddy and her followers have had much to
say about this. In *Miscellaneous Writings* (p. 31), she says it is a
breach of the Golden Rule and a subversion of the scientific laws
of being to argue mentally in such a way as to affect disastrously
—morally, physically, and spiritually—one's fellows. Of course such
mental malpractice is unscientific, she continues, finding no place
in and receiving no support from the Principle or the rules of
Christian Science. Nevertheless it is consistently recognized as an
obtrusive factor, and one of the very troublesome factors with which
Christian Scientists are concerned. So potent is the danger that
disclosing the process of mental healing to frail mortals, when they
are uninstructed and unrestrained by Christian Science, is like
putting a sharp knife in the hands of a blind man or a violent
maniac and then turning him loose in a crowded city street. (*Science
and Health,* p. 459)

The deliberate employment of thought to evil ends is distinguished from its inadvertent use, and is referred to as "malicious
mental malpractice." There seems to be no clear-cut difference
between this and what is called "malicious animal magnetism,"
usually M.A.M., a power against which Mrs. Eddy herself felt the
necessity of almost continuous defense. Her letters and other writings show that she was sure Richard Kennedy and other disaffected
students were seeking to injure her by mental malpractice or
M.A.M. When Asa Gilbert Eddy died in 1882, she attributed his
death to the malpractice of a rebellious student, Edward J. Arens,
and summoned newspaper reporters to announce that her husband
had been mentally assassinated. How did she know this? In *Christian Science History* (1st ed., p. 16), she declared: "I possess a
spiritual sense of what the malicious mental malpractitioner is men-

tally arguing which cannot be deceived; I can discern in the human mind thoughts, motives, and purposes, and neither mental arguments nor psychic power can affect this spiritual insight." As late as 1908, she said to her chief secretary, Adam H. Dickey: "If I should ever leave here, will you promise me that you will write a history of what has transpired in your experience with me, and say that I was mentally murdered?" (Adam H. Dickey, *Memoirs of Mary Baker Eddy*) In her later years she was convinced that the physical difficulties which she suffered were the result of insidious mental malpractice.

How could such attacks be met? According to the diaries and memoirs of various followers who lived with Mrs. Eddy at different times, in her own case she had members of her household do mental "work" to offset such attacks. Dickey, who resided at her home from February, 1908, to the time of her passing in December, 1910, recorded much concerning the "watches" which were kept by various inmates to protect her against the malicious influence of mortal mind. One watch was from 9:00 to 11:00 P.M., the second from 3:00 to 5:00 A.M. Mrs. Eddy often commended the watcher who had succeeded in warding off the attacks during his or her watch, and rebuked those who had either failed to keep the watch, or had been unsuccessful in protecting her from the onslaughts of "the enemy." The one who kept the watch usually sat in the study outside Mrs. Eddy's sleeping-room door. Sometimes she gave instructions as to what they should take up in their watch. Mr. Dickey gives this as one example: "Mrs. Eddy's face is not deformed. Her eyes are large, natural; sight, hearing, and memory are never lost. Her finger joints are natural."

The author has been informed that M.A.M. is less emphasized in the present day than it was in Mrs. Eddy's time. But it has not disappeared by any means. One very persistent belief among Christian Scientists has been that Roman Catholicism is bent upon the destruction of Christian Science. The author has again and again come across a belief held that at certain times Roman Catholic monks deliberately work mentally for such destruction. Class notes of a number of well-known Christian Science teachers indicate that in church-sponsored classes they uniformly feel it necessary to discuss the matter of Roman Catholic opposition. The Catholic attacks are always seen as carried on by purely mental means, never through overt acts.

Little is found in Mrs. Eddy's writings on the subject. In *Miscellany* (p. 4) she asserts that a Christian Scientist loves Protestants and Catholics alike, as well as Doctors of Divinity and Doctors of Medicine. But in his *Memoirs* Dickey records that on a certain day he was given this for his watch period: "There is no psychology and no Roman Catholic prayers frightening this house. . . . Christian Scientists love the psychologists and the Roman Catholics and they love us. . . ." Evidently someone in the house believed that Catholics could be a source of harm; else why handle the claim?

Even in Kimball one finds not infrequent references to Catholicism. In the published outline (Boston, 1935), fully authenticated, prepared by Edward Kimball for teaching his first Normal class, will be found a section headed "Romanism," which reads: "Romanism claims to bestow a curse; also to furnish all the machinery through which the curse operates." Elsewhere Kimball is recorded as saying, in this same class, in reply to a question concerning proper defense against Roman Catholicism:

Know that it cannot touch you. . . . There is no wisdom, intelligence, etc., in the Roman Catholic faith. . . . It cannot oppose itself to Christian Science. This false claim cannot make use of beliefs to govern me, to hinder the progress of God's work. . . . True religion cannot be interfered with by anathema, condemnation, deceit. There is no mind through which it can act, nothing to act upon.

He goes on to say that the claim to be handled specifically is the fear Christian Scientists have of malpractice. In another place he is quoted as saying that there is no prenatal curse of Roman Catholicism called sexual poison; further, that there is no curse capable of causing diseased bones, or disintegration or dissolution of tissues, or of causing him or his patients to be mentally electrocuted, since Roman Catholicism is without reality or power and this uncovering of Truth constitutes its utter destruction.

Reputable persons have told the author that it is still a daily custom of perhaps the majority of class-taught Christian Scientists to "handle" Roman Catholicism. This statement is substantiated by two papers, copies of which are quietly circulated among practitioners, giving treatments, formulas, for combating the menace. One of these, running to three single-spaced typewritten pages, bears the signature of Willard S. Mattox, a Kimball student who taught in Denver. It is said to be a classic in its field. The other, ascribed to Dr. Francis J. Fluno, a leading lecturer and teacher under Mrs. Eddy's personal tutelage, runs to two single-spaced tyepwritten pages. A veteran practitioner says that he has repeatedly been shown copies of one or the other of these papers by various teachers and practitioners in the church, the copies in his file bearing the handwritten endorsement of a prominent Fluno student from whom he got them.

Arthur Corey, who is certainly a confirmed Christian Scientist though outside the church, writes that those Christian Scientists who think of their religion as a church rather than a science have lost their perspective in a preoccupation with what they must regard as deadly competition. They look with dismay upon the imposing organization of the Church of Rome, and then back at the comparatively negligible membership of the Church of Boston. Having accepted the proposition that everything is mental, they naturally then are inclined to attribute their every difficulty to what they term "R.C." If it is true, as Mrs. Eddy declares, that "the Christian Scientist is alone with his own being," then, he says, "the Scientist is going to have to purge his own consciousness rather than attributing power to external influences, and trying to offset the physical rosary with a set of rigid mental beads for morning counting." (*Christian Science Class Instruction,* p. 113)

With this observation we move up to a third level in the development of the idea of treatment of disease. It will be remembered that the earliest practice was in the Quimby line of frankly talking the patient out of his troubles. This is known throughout the field generally as "audible treatment," sometimes described as verbal, oral, or spoken. The second stage was reached in the mentalization of this same method, the practitioner now endeavoring to correct the patient's false belief through silent affirmation and denial. This has come to be known as "addressing the thought," and it is sometimes combined with the audible argument. The third stage is referred to in the church periodicals and elsewhere as "impersonal treatment," presumably because the practitioner at this stage does not address the patient personally, either silently or audibly. In this third, and radically new, concept of practice, the work of the practitioner is not directed at the patient, but is given over to self-correction. The practitioner really addresses himself, arguing away the false beliefs which plague his world.

In the before-mentioned *Sentinel* article, Dunn calls this "impersonal Christian Science work," and says that the Scientific Christian always has both the right and the duty to clear his own thought, or treat himself; that is, to refuse to grant power and reality to any picture of discord confronting him as human experience, whether it involves others or just himself. In this kind of treatment he is not addressing another's thought, but is remaining scrupulously inside his own mental precincts. But how does this reach the patient beneficially? Dunn says: "As he turns on the light of spiritual understanding in his own consciousness, and keeps his mental window shades up, is it surprising to hear that much darkness is dispelled?" That, of course, can only be regarded as a question and not an answer.

According to the Dunn editorial, the ethical requirements are satisfied and the scientific connection left to the patient, for "everyone touching his [the practitioner's] thought shares in and is blessed by the illumination." Even with this—which in the light of what follows will be seen to be a concession and a compromise—official Christian Science is still involved with the effect of one consciousness upon another, so far as treatment is concerned, for unless the patient personally responds to this "impersonal work," he still continues with his false beliefs after the practitioner has corrected them in his own thinking.

The origin of the third concept is to be found in *Science and Health,* and here and there in Mrs. Eddy's other writings; but it has not been recognized by all Christian Scientists, many of whom have never gone beyond the second stage. It is particularly thanks to Edward Kimball that it gained currency in Christian Science practice, and it has been chiefly through Kimball students and their offspring, so to speak, that the more advanced idea has been handed down within the church. There are those who have claimed that, indeed, the idea was not clear in Mrs. Eddy's own mind, though the germ of it was there, until Kimball took it up and began to emphasize it.

Authority for attributing the advanced view to Mrs. Eddy can be found in one of her best-known passages, in which, as we have seen, she declares that, through Science, Jesus saw the perfect man where mortals saw only sinning mortal man, and that this correct perception of God's likeness healed the sick. (*Science and Health,* pp. 476 ff.) It is noteworthy that she does not say that the sick mortal saw himself as perfect, and so was healed, but that Jesus was the one who saw man as God's likeness there. Clearly it was what Jesus thought or discerned, not what the sick man himself apprehended, which brought about the healing. In line with this, Mrs. Eddy writes, in *Miscellaneous Writings* (p. 62), that by holding in *her* mind the right idea of man, she is able to improve not only her own, but *others'* individuality, health, and morals.

This was something new. Quimby never saw it. Most early Christian Scientists had no grasp of it. Probably the majority of the practitioners have not yet grasped it. At least, they do not operate on this basis.

At this third level or stage of practice, the troublesome question of thought transference does not arise. Telepathy is neither postulated nor required in this mode of treatment. Here it makes no difference what the patient himself thinks, for if the practitioner, while mentally and silently pleading the case for Truth, is thoroughly persuaded in his own mind of the truth which he thinks, his patient is healed. (*Science and Health,* p. 412) Of course, if one is acting as his own practitioner, he must seek to see himself as God's likeness, hence perfect. (*Miscellany,* p. 242)

It must also be said that most of Mrs. Eddy's writings do not move on this so-called impersonal plane. In general, the theme is that only the patient's mind can produce results of any kind upon his body (*Christian Healing*, p. 6), so that it is the patient who must be instructed out of or awakened from *his* illusion, *his* belief of suffering destroyed, *his* consciousness changed. But we read in *Rudimental Divine Science* (p. 13) that a treatment is scientific which affirms the reality of harmony and denies the reality of discord, handling specifically what, according to belief, is diseased, "and if the *healer realizes* the truth, it will free his patient." The italics are Mrs. Eddy's own, and they are most significant. Not the patient, but the healer must realize the truth — yet the patient is restored. In a statement thought to have been recorded by Frank Mason, Mrs. Eddy once said, "Our *patients* manifest health after and in proportion to *our* consciousness of perfection," correlating this with the statement of Jesus, "And I, if I be lifted up from the earth, will draw all men unto me." (*Collectanea*, p. 145) A student in one of Mrs. Eddy's classes reports her as having said, "Treat yourself before you treat your patients," a statement that looks in the same direction though it does not go all the way.

Corey regards Mrs. Eddy's statement in her *Message of 1901* (p. 20), that the Christian Scientist is forever alone with his own being, as basic. From this, he writes,

it follows that all treatment would have to take place where the practitioner is thinking, not where someone else is thinking, and without any notion of pointing thoughts at people. . . . She left no shadow of doubt that, as she saw it, an erroneous belief can be corrected only at the threshold of consciousness—the practitioner's consciousness, if he is conscious of an erroneous belief. (*Personal Introduction to God*, pp. 151 ff.)

Kimball seemed quite clear in the matter. A review of his teaching concerning reality will reveal the foundation of his concept of treatment. Notes from some of his Normal classes report him as declaring that if one receives a telegram saying "I am sick," it is necessary neither to know the name of the patient nor the ailment from which he suffers, in order to treat the case successfully. "Abolish the claim on the ground that matter has no substantiality, that man is not a belief of life, [truth, intelligence or substance in matter], and that no evil belief has been impressed upon him. Mortal mind has not mesmerically imposed upon him evil or error. ...When you see that, you lift the claim"—that is, the patient is healed not when *he* sees the truth, but when *the practitioner* sees it. In other words, the practitioner must treat himself, not the patient. (Recorded by Rose E. Kent)

Kimball goes on, interestingly enough, to insist that it is not sufficient to make a general statement such as "God is All"; rather, the error must be analyzed and specific errors destroyed by specific handling. Thus it is that he makes particular denials.

The patient is under no mesmeric law and cannot be governed by any law of reaction; not subject to any law of climate, heat or cold, moisture, over-work or over-exertion. He cannot be subject to abnormal growth, vegetable or mineral poisons; not subject to death, anatomy, physiology, hygiene, hell, evil; he cannot be governed by many minds, etc.

Notes by another student state that, in order to have a treatment entirely effective, "there must not be left in the mind of the practitioner any sense of the reality of the claim he denies." Note again: in the *practitioner's* mind.

The clearest statement regarding this matter to come from Kimball is found in the Kratzer record, *Teaching and Addresses by Edward A. Kimball* (pp. 36 ff.) When you are required to accomplish a healing, have you got to heal a body? he asks. "No," he answers, "for the whole thing is mental, every bit of it. It has no relation whatever to time, place, matter, person or man, but is altogether a picture in mind. Now, in whose mind? I will say in the mind, so called, of the practitioner." This seems unequivocal. Kimball then elaborates. The practitioner

must first understand, when he has what he calls a patient, that the patient is purely a mental image, that the disease is purely a mental image, that the only thing to do is to meet it mentally; then, when he clears his own mentality, to know he will have nothing else to do, and that he never can do anything else. . . . He has nothing to do with matter— nothing to do with his patient, as far as that is concerned.

It is true that Kimball's daughter quoted this excerpt from his

Association address with a different twist, giving his answer to the question "In whose mind?" as being *Amongst others,* in the mind of the healer," instead of simply "In the mind of the practitioner." The inescapable significance of this latter version, which it is understood was given as a concession to officialdom, is that it swings back to the doctrine that the practitioner is dealing with a personal patient as a separate consciousness, into which he must somehow reach to correct false beliefs which he personally does not entertain. But the Kratzer version is in strict keeping with the other statements we have cited to verify the third level of practice.

The same idea is found running through the teachings of Bicknell Young. "Treat yourself, always start with yourself, and the patient is healed," Young said in one of his last classes. "It does not matter what someone else is thinking, but it does matter what I am thinking. What is going on is pure Mind—my Mind. And all that appears to be going on will undergo redemption if, called to a case, *I* know that the only man there is is already well."

George Shaw Cook said in his 1940 class that the first thing the practitioner learns is that he heals himself. A case might appear as person, place, or thing, but it is simply belief coming to the practitioner for acceptance or rejection. All we are ever dealing with is consciousness.

The author one day asked a State Committee on Publication, who is also a *Journal*-listed practitioner, about his method of healing. "Suppose I had a felon on my finger and asked you for treatment, how would you go about it?" Said he: "*I* would *know* that your finger was perfect. Seeing it as God sees it and so knowing it, it would be well."

"But suppose I go on thinking it is there, even when you know that it isn't, what then?"

"It doesn't make any difference what you think, when I know it is not there, it is healed. It is the knowing of the practitioner that determines the healing. It does not depend upon the belief or the faith of the patient."

This last remark is interesting in the light of what Kimball wrote on one occasion: "If I, as a practitioner, demand faith on the part of the patient, I limit my ability to heal him, for his sickness and his lack of faith are one." (Letter to Ira F. Adams, dated March 26, 1909)

Arthur Corey, quite the most vocal of the contemporary representatives of the Kimball school, writes at length of treatment in his *Christian Science Class Instruction.* Concerning the oft-heard statement that the practitioner treats only himself, he says, "This is quite true." In explanation, he writes: "But it must not be inferred that the practitioner has a private mind apart from his patients, which private mind must be corrected individually," for "mentation is one and indivisible, and this mentation is the universe. . . . In no sense do you ever treat 'another mind'. You correct belief through divine realization—a wholly impersonal operation. Where else could you correct it but where it is appearing—which is where you are and what you are thinking?" Where could you establish the truth of what you are conscious of except *here* at the point of awareness? You can never get outside of consciousness.

Argument is not what heals, Corey reasons, nor is it even indispensable to the healing process. It is no more than a human expedient for "sweeping away the mental smokescreens that Mind may unfold" in human experience. The goal of all metaphysical work, he maintains, is divine realization, the

attainment of that attitude of thought which is the altitude of God. *How* the practitioner arrives at this point, where nothing is left but divine Mind declaring its own divinity, is not however of any great importance, so that he may well bring anything into his treatment which seems to enable him to arrive more readily at his objective. Certainly the divine realization is hardly contained in the finite expressions he may have recourse to on the way, so they never need be lingered over.

If all this seems abstract and difficult to grasp, he makes it more concrete by using as illustration the treatment of a sick child by a practitioner working at the level of argument. What is to be done when he is called upon the case?

"Is the child," Corey asks,

someone or something out there in space apart from consciousness? How could I be aware of him if that were so? Whatever appears to me as the child must be consciously thought, and so is within consciousness. God's child is not sick, so it is not a sick child but the belief that the child is sick which requires handling. Whose belief? The child's? His mother's? Mine? What difference whose belief it appears to be? If it comes to me in the form of consciousness, as now, here is where it is to be taken care of.

Then Corey goes on to explore in great detail the analytical procedure of the practitioner in clearing his own thought by meeting the various arguments confronting him.

Corey makes it clear with the surrounding context that this treatment outline is no more than a passing illustration of the affirmation-and-denial method, rather than a criterion. "While examples of treatment are helpful in explaining the nature of treatment, no exemplary treatment can serve as a model, even temporarily. . . . Beware of the persistent tendency to pause at any particular level on a circumscribed concept." (p. 187) He recognizes no royal road into which the practitioner can settle, but asserts that the genuinely scientific attitude "implies a constant setting aside of cut-and-dried habits and devices of human mentation. Lifeless routine and unthinking orthodoxy must be abandoned in due course, or we lose the substance while glorifying the empty form." (p. 189) He deplores the substituting of stereotyped practices for ever-fresh thinking, and warns against intellectual and spiritual strait jackets.

He differentiates between treatment statements and teaching statements. "When one is speaking of perfection," he writes, "it should be evident that he is talking from the absolute or spiritual standpoint; while, on the other hand, any reference to the imperfect would have to be made from the comparative or human point of view. . . . When we say that man is as perfect as his Maker, we are not talking of man as mortal and material." (p. 9)

Arthur Corey is more consistently monistic in his teaching than any other the author has read. Most Christian Scientists, while theoretically excluding anything as real save Mind, at the same time practically concede a reality to something else, something called "mortal mind." Indeed, mortal mind all too frequently turns out to be their nemesis. Even Kimball falls into this difficulty. The outline of his teaching which he wrote out for Judge Hanna makes the tangible world a counterfeit obscuring the genuine creation of divine Mind. He follows Mrs. Eddy in declaring that "the starting-point of divine Science is that God, Spirit, is All-in-all" (*Science and Health*, p. 275), only to qualify this, as in his letter to Hinsdale, with the observation: "But in belief there is a suppositional claim of something else." With this mortal mind is set up as an opposing power and presence "in belief."

Corey's analysis of the same material tends to resolve the parallelism of the old school. He does not stop with Kimball's proposition that a lie is always a lie about something that is true; Corey concludes that "a misconception of *nothing* is impossible" so that "what you call reality is your current sense of reality." The so-called human concept would, accordingly, have to be the divine idea itself, as it appears humanly. Thus Kimball's process of "transformation" becomes one of spontaneous reinterpretation. "False sense" is another name for misinterpretation, and one "exchanges the objects of sense for the ideas of Soul" by understanding them. "Translating matter into Mind" is understanding substance to be Spirit. The visible universe is reality as you see it.

Unlike the so-called absolutists, Corey underscores the necessity for being practical. Merely calling a troublesome picture a lie does not dispose of the lie, but leaves it "a wrong sense of a right something," to use Kimball's expression. Corey reasons that matter is not a thing to be destroyed, but a misinterpretation to be corrected. "The twice-two-is-five must not be destroyed," says he, "but redeemed—through finding that it is really twice-two-is-four." There is neither destruction nor substitution in metaphysics applied, for Christian Science healing is Christian Science revealing. "What you are seeing as wrong is really right, but that does not imply that it is right in the way in which you are seeing it" (p. 194); so one must not resign one's self to the troublesome misapprehension, one must "handle" it. If, as Mrs. Eddy holds, "Evil and all its forms are inverted good," understanding applied must rectify this. "Good no longer appears negatively, then, but stands revealed in shining splendor. It is not merely retitled, but redeemed, by Truth. Knowing it as Spirit dispels its materiality and clothes it in the shimmering garments of light." (p. 174)

Corey's conclusion is that "you must always work from the basis of Spirit's allness. This that is Mind unfolding is God appearing, and so is the embodiment of all that is good and worthy and desirable. If this is God appearing, the recognition of that fact establishes the divinity of the appearing." (p. 150) "And where is all this taking place?" he asks. His answer is: "In the only place there is, the realm of thought. Yes, the demonstration of Christian Science is always subjective, even though it must appear to be external to pure consciousness. This that is Mind's communion meets your every need, for it necessarily unfolds in the language of your comprehension." (p. 174) Why necessarily? Because we think in the language of people-places-things, interpreting all experience in these terms. This is our mode of thinking, and so good is present to us only according to human standards of good.

Christian Science has passed through various stages in its development, all of which may be found in Mrs. Eddy's writings and in her practice. And all the stages are still evident today in the movement. Mrs. Eddy herself grew, but only a comparatively few grasped the meaning of her ultimate thought, her "revelation" as they call it. Edward Kimball did. And those who have accepted his lead, sometimes against great opposition, have continued to play down the older levels of her thinking and practice and to emphasize the higher reaches of her thought.

14

Developing Ideas Concerning
Mrs. Eddy

ONE OF THE notable features of the Christian Science movement is the extreme loyalty of the great majority of its members to its Founder and Leader, as Mary Baker Eddy is known among them. Has there been any change in this respect with the passing of time? Is this loyalty—indeed, this veneration—any different now than in her lifetime, or have the thought concerning her and attitudes toward her changed significantly? We have already observed that Mrs. Eddy had the quality of inspiring either very great devotion and regard or open hostility. Seldom have people been neutral toward her.

At her passing in December, 1910, there was a flood of newspaper comment on her life and her movement. Editorials appeared in most of the great newspapers praising her and her work. But most of these were by non–Christian Scientists. It is surprising how comparatively little concerning her appeared in the official publications of the church. Both the *Sentinel* and the *Journal* reprinted a fairly brief and almost wholly factual account of her funeral, taken from the *Monitor*. The *Sentinel* reprinted excerpts from scores of articles taken from the press of the country. Frederick Dixon had one long article about her in the first issue of the *Journal* published after her death. But aside from this, nothing was carried about her death and its impact upon the movement.

Does this mean any lack of respect or honor felt toward her? Not at all. Rather, the Christian Scientists' esteem for her seems to have grown with the years. The seeming neglect of that period may be explained on two grounds. First, in view of the Christian Science

idea of death, the passing of the Founder was necessarily something of an embarrassment. This fact is evidenced by the apologia
put out by the organization's chief public relations man, Alfred
Farlow, in the *Boston Journal* of December 30, 1910, and the *New
York Herald* of March 25, 1912. The movement, therefore, would
hardly be likely to give a prominent place to the event. Second,
Mrs. Eddy's many admonitions—however inconsistent with others
of her statements and with her acts—to keep Christian Science on
an impersonal plane rather than exalt personality would tend to
produce the same result.

While lip service has always been paid to "impersonalization"
by the Scientists, the practice has been throughout the whole history
of the movement to glorify Mrs. Eddy's person. Although Mrs. Eddy
more than once rebuked her editors for inordinate praise of her in
the periodicals, her letters seem to indicate that it was a question
neither of humility nor of impersonalization, but of strategy. On
December 13, 1891, she wrote her editor, Julia Field-King: "The
enemy gloat over any contribution which supports these charges—
Mrs. Eddy makes the *Journal* deify her personality." And while she
ultimately spoke of her withdrawal from Boston as intended to turn
her followers from personality to Principle, she never for a moment
permitted her spokesmen to neglect full credit to her on all scores.
It is a revealing fact that when she ruled that her name be named
whenever she was quoted, she required no such consideration for
other authors; and she herself quoted often without giving credit to
her sources. Many lines of self-laudation appear in her writings, and
her private correspondence went very much farther in this regard.
In setting up the Board of Lectureship, she gave the lecturers but
two specific duties, one of which was to tell about her life, the other
to answer attacks upon Christian Science. (*Manual*, Art. XXXI,
Sec. 2)

During her last class, taught in Concord in 1898, Mrs. Eddy
accepted without a word of protest the most fulsome personal
praise—as the authenticated account of an unimpeachable witness,
Sue Harper Mims, shows. In the presence of Mrs. Eddy, Mrs. Mims
told the assembled students that "our beloved Mother" had enabled

them to see all and more than the apostles had seen, emphasizing that they owed it all to her, "this beloved one who is God's messenger today." This set off a series of testimonials to their teacher, who sat through the scene with apparent humility and self-effacement. "Mother, how could we forget you!" said one student with tears in his eyes. Judge Hanna, one of the early "greats" in the movement, arose to say that in the post he held, all the machinations of evil conceivable bombarded him, that the world became night-black to him for days on end, and that it was only when he could contemplate her as the Revelator to this age that he got any light at all. Evil unremittingly whispered subtle suggestions aimed at hiding her from him, said the Judge, and he found relief, and safety, only as he could see her in that exalted role. Others spoke. At the height of her students' open adulation, Mrs. Eddy, addressing them as her dear children, declared that if they had not seen this for themselves she would have had to teach it to them, warning them that when her students became blinded to her as the one through whom Truth had come to this age, they always went straight down.

An interesting sidelight is cast upon the situation by the official version of Mrs. Mims's account published by the church authorities in *We Knew Mary Baker Eddy—Second Series* (pp. 35 ff.), which exhibits significant editing of the original document. Mrs. Mims's impressions emerge somewhat tempered by the editor, but not entirely erased is the picture of personal adoration given and accepted freely. A recently fixed taboo against quoting Mrs. Eddy directly is to be noted. As in the church's posthumous publication of the Tomlinson book, wherever Mrs. Eddy speaks in the witnesses' manuscripts, her words are preceded by such qualifying phrases as "She said, as I recall," "In substance she spoke as follows," and so on. Edna Kimball Wait was admonished for quoting Mrs. Eddy directly in her classes, even though she was repeating only what Mrs. Eddy had said in her personal presence.

Mrs. Mims said in 1898 that there was not a single day in which she did not declare at least once, sometimes more often, that malicious animal magnetism was powerless to blind her to Mrs. Eddy.

This attitude has been maintained and appears to have been formulated into a settled dogma, for Daisette McKenzie is allowed to say with official sponsorship: "The hostility of mortal mind endeavors to separate her [Mrs. Eddy] from her writings and so keep us from more intimate communion with her. Perhaps we sometimes read *Science and Health* without a thought of the author." Published in 1943, in *We Knew Mary Baker Eddy—First Series* (p. 41), this passage was considered important enough to be republished in the *Journal* of January, 1954.

If this were all, we might accept the official position that Mrs. Eddy sought no more than proper recognition for an "impersonal revelation"; but her voluminous correspondence does not sustain such a view. True, Mrs. Eddy once denounced as blasphemy the claim that she was "a Christ"; but it must be remembered that she did not teach that Christ was ever a person, defining *Christ* as something an individual in any age might embody. Thus she wrote Augusta Stetson, on December 17, 1900:

> I always explain Christ as the *invisible* and never corporeal. Jesus was a man corporeal, Christ was, is, and forever will be the Holy Ghost, or in scientific phrase, the spiritual idea of God. I am corporeal to the senses even as Paul was. But God has anointed me to do His work, to reveal His Word, to lead His people. And your faithful adherence to my directions and love for me has caused you to prosper in the field even as you have. . . . Jesus was called Christ only in the sense that you say a Godlike man. I am only a Godlike woman, God-anointed, and I have done a work that none others could do. As Paul was not understood and Jesus was not understood at the time they taught and demonstrated, so I am not. As following them and obeying them blessed all who did thus, so obeying me and following faithfully blesses all who do this.

It is not difficult to see from this statement why Mrs. Eddy was often spoken of by her followers in a way identifying her with Christ. Frequently she was bracketed in their remarks and writings with Jesus. Discussing the revelation of St. John as having "a special suggestiveness in connection with the nineteenth century," she explained that the spiritual idea was impersonated in the earthly life of Jesus, as the masculine representative, adding that the rule of Christ through divine Science was "represented first by man and, according to the Revelator, last by woman." (*Science and Health*, pp. 559 ff.)

Would this not place Mrs. Eddy at least on as high a level as the Master? Certainly it has been so interpreted both within and without the movement. Indeed, Mrs. Eddy's clear implication of the superiority of the feminine element over the masculine has led some of her followers to elevate her to a plane definitely above that of the Nazarene. One striking evidence of this appeared in 1949, when the church through its official spokesman told the public press that Mary Baker Eddy could not properly be depicted on stage or screen, yet offered no objection to the depiction of Jesus in the theater and before the cameras.

By the time the Leader retired to Concord, her physical absence, though it made little or no difference in the practical operation of the organization, introduced a new factor which proved to have far-reaching effects. Freed now from the necessity of adjusting their ideas concerning Mrs. Eddy to the facts of her physical life, her followers could think of her and idealize her person as they could not so well do while she was before them in the flesh. As we have said, she had already become a legend before her death. It was almost inevitable that, with her removal from the human scene, the myth-making tendency found in every personally founded religion should appear in Christian Science also.

Indeed, it had already appeared before her death. Some of her more zealous followers had come to think of her as more than human. Augusta Stetson, one of her very closest and most distinguished students, seems confidently to have believed that after her passing Mrs. Eddy would rise from the dead and confound the unbelievers. How many shared this view it is impossible to say, but that many did is proved by the fact that the church found it necessary to deny officially that Mrs. Eddy's return to this world was expected. (Bates-Dittemore, *Mary Baker Eddy*, p. 541) Still, Mary Baker Eddy's earthly experiences were and are often likened to those of Jesus, so that resurrection would seem a not unreasonable expectation.

All along language has been used concerning Mrs. Eddy which was first used with respect to Jesus of Nazareth. For example, Edward Everett Norwood once wrote: "She came that we might have Life and Truth and Love . . . and have them more abundantly." (*Miscellaneous Documents*, p. 133) Jesus said: "I am come that they might have life, and . . . have it more abundantly." (John 10:10)

Bancroft reports Mrs. Eddy as saying, on a special critical occasion, that she wished they were all awake to that particular hour of crucifixion, to the sense of the hour and the oil that they needed in their lamps at the coming of the Bridegroom. From such a saying one might be led to think she regarded herself as in some sense a second Christ.

In a letter written as early as January 20, 1882, she asked Julia Bartlett to stand ready to substitute for herself in leading the people. But she added, in almost a direct quotation from the Gospels, "not that you can unloose the sandals of my shoes," nor really "fill my place." But Julia seemed better fitted than anyone else. "Do not yield to temptation and say you cannot," she added, "but 'if you love me, keep my commandments.'" (*Miscellaneous Documents*, p. 179)

In his *Memoirs*, Adam H. Dickey writes that no one knew how much was owed her who offered herself as "a perpetual sacrifice for the good of humanity," and follows with a quotation from Isaiah 53: "He was wounded for our transgressions, he was bruised for our iniquities: the chastisement of our peace was upon him; and with his stripes we are healed." Dickey does not say *she* was wounded, and so on, but there is a clear parallelism between Mrs. Eddy and the suffering servant usually identified with Christ.

In his diary, another member of Mrs. Eddy's household writes that after he had been with her for three days, he felt an illumination. He asked her directly if he was correct in thinking that Isaiah 53 referred to Jesus and Isaiah 54 to her. Her answer was yes.

When Mrs. Eddy taught her famous Concord class and invited seventy people to attend, great emphasis was laid at the time and thereafter upon Luke 10:1: "After these things the Lord appointed other seventy also . . ." This emphasis has been frequently repeated in the church periodicals and elsewhere (e.g., *We Knew Mary Baker Eddy—Second Series*, p. 30).

The one certainty is that she was regarded as the fulfilment of Scripture. She was often held up, as was Jesus, as exemplar. A prominent teacher in an Association address exhorted her students to compare their present achievements with the works of Jesus or Mrs. Eddy in order that they might see how very far short they fell from measuring up to the dominion that was their rightful possession. It is an easily documented fact that this is by no means an uncommon exhortation among Christian Scientists.

Julia Bartlett relates that once Mrs. Eddy was talking to a group in an unusual manner, and then broke off with the statement that they could not understand what she had to give them. This led Miss Bartlett to the conclusion that many wonderful revelations were in store for them when they were ready to receive them from their Leader. She said that Mrs. Eddy like Christ might well say, "I have yet many things to say unto you, but ye cannot bear them now." (John 16:12) So far above the world was she that in it she was utterly alone, exclaimed Miss Bartlett, adding that sometimes Mrs. Eddy would express the wish for the coming of the time when she could give voice to the Truth she saw. (*Miscellaneous Documents*, pp. 188 ff.)

What was Mrs. Eddy's own feeling about such attitudes on the part of her students? On many occasions she heard from her followers the most flattering statements concerning herself. Adulation was common within the inner circles of the movement. Sometimes she seems to have rebuked it, but it is noteworthy that such rebukes were rare except in cases of *published* adulation. She openly rebuked Augusta Stetson for "allowing your students to deify you and me." (*Miscellany*, p. 359) But this came only after Mrs. Stetson's controversy with the authorities of the Mother Church had broken into print. Throughout the voluminous correspondence between the two for the many preceding years, Mrs. Eddy had no rebuke for Mrs. Stetson's consistently adulatory lines.

Of course, Mrs. Eddy did regard herself definitely as inspired of God to reveal the Truth. Statements to this effect are found all through her writings, some of which indicate that she regarded herself as the *exclusive* revelator.

James Gilman, the artist who provided the pictures illustrating her poem *Christ and Christmas*, relates in his *Diary Records* (p. 64) that on a certain morning in 1893 Mrs. Eddy said that the previous night she had had revelations which went beyond anything she had experienced before. In them she saw plainly "that all things were put under her feet, and the love of God was manifested in a way quite beyond her powers to describe." On another occasion the artist reports her as saying that Christian Science was a modern thought and should be expressed appropriately in modern surroundings. Trying to tell him what she wanted in the paintings he was doing for her, she said there was altogether too much looking backward two thousand years; people would find there was a way there in Concord as well as in Palestine. (*Diary Records*, p. 81)

Mrs. Eddy seems at times to have exhibited a high degree of humility. One of her followers, commenting on her gracious and cordial manner where she had expected to find serene aloofness, was particularly impressed with Mrs. Eddy's humility when speaking of herself as "the Discoverer and Founder of Christian Science." (Helen W. Bingham, *Miscellaneous Documents*, p. 146) In the same vein, Mrs. Eddy attributes the authorship of her textbook to God, rather than claiming any personal credit. (*Miscellany*, p. 115)

At other times, she takes quite a different tone. In her chapter on the Apocalypse, she becomes the final revelator of biblical prophecy, and her *Science and Health* is identified with the little book in the hand of the angel (pp. 558 ff.). Does this imply the divine choice of a scribe uniquely qualified? She definitely identifies herself as God's messenger (*Miscellaneous Writings*, p. 158), and when one looks up *messenger* in the official concordances one is referred back to *Mrs. Mary Baker Eddy*. Then she declares: "God selects for the highest service one who has grown into such a fitness for it as renders any abuse of the mission an impossibility. The All-wise does not bestow His highest trusts upon the unworthy. When He commissions a messenger, it is one who is spiritually near Himself." (*Science and Health*, p. 455)

Mrs. Eddy herself recounts stories of her childhood which seem to mark her as one who was destined to a great mission. Indeed, she told both Adam Dickey and Calvin Frye that her mother had often mentioned to a neighbor, Sarah Gault, strange thoughts she had concerning the child she was expecting. She could not help feeling that the child was holy and set apart for some wonderful work. She felt a sense of guilt at entertaining such thoughts but could not rid herself of them. (Dickey, *Memoirs,* pp. 133 ff.)

Then there was the story told by her in *Retrospection and Introspection* (pp. 8 ff.). As a child about eight years old she repeatedly heard a voice calling her by name, Mary, three times. She thought it was her mother's voice and sometimes ran to see what was wanted. Finally, she writes, the mother decided that this must be an experience like that of the child Samuel, so she bade her answer as did he: "Speak, Lord, for thy servant heareth." At last Mary did answer, after which the call never came again to her material senses.

Mrs. Eddy was seventy years old when this story was written. There is no known evidence that she had ever told the story before this recounting of it.

Adam Dickey relates a conversation he had with her concerning the voices. She told him of circumstances which followed the experience about which, she said, she had never spoken to anyone else. After she had made reply to the voice, she said, a most unusual event took place. Suddenly her body was raised off the bed, to the height of perhaps a foot. Then she was returned gently to the bed. Three times the phenomenon occurred. She was afraid to tell anyone about it, so kept it to herself. Later, as she was seeking to demonstrate the nothingness of matter and to prove the human body nothing more than a myth, it was to come back to her and she reflected deeply upon it. (*Memoirs,* p. 76)

Here is definitely the phenomenon of levitation—not to be her only experience of it, if Calvin Frye may be believed. In his diary Frye states that on one occasion, when he went into Mrs. Eddy's room suddenly, she was suspended in the air up near the ceiling. He was naturally astonished. She reassured him, bidding him not to be afraid, that she was quite all right. Then she quietly settled into her chair and all was normal. What would people think of one who experienced such things? (Frye Diaries, included in Dittemore collection, Book 3, p. 151)

Many cases of miracles, or what people would ordinarily regard as such, are told of her or by her. Several have to do with the control of weather. The Gilbert Carpenters, in their *Collectanea* (p. 14), include a note which they report was copied from a notebook by Mrs. Eddy in her own handwriting, to the effect that on September 24, 1907, "terrific" clouds filled all the sky but were changed instantaneously "by me" and only a gentle rain and rainbow followed. Adam Dickey avers that Mrs. Eddy described a number of cases in which she caused a thundercloud to disperse by simply looking on it and bringing to bear upon "mortal mind's concept of this manifestation of discord" what God had prepared for them. (*Memoirs*, p. 32)

To Dickey also we are indebted for the observation that Mrs. Eddy looked upon gentle rainfall as a delight, but abhorred thunderstorms, regarding them as evil and as a destroying agent of mortal mind; she assigned Laura Sargent to watch the weather and to keep it under control. He piously declares that, according to his recollection, there were fewer and fewer thunderstorms until they almost ceased altogether. (*Memoirs*, p. 31) Mrs. Eddy especially disliked snow, which she looked upon as a manifestation of error. According to Dickey, one set of directions to those of her household whose task it was to work mentally for her was to make a law that there should be no more snow that season.

Dickey says that a dying fruit tree on her grounds at Chestnut Hill was to be cut down, but that "she took the question up according to Christian Science" and almost at once "the tree began to grow and thrive." (*Memoirs*, p. 68)

Carpenter's *Spiritual Footsteps* (p. 59) carries a story about a sixty-day drought that affected the Concord region. One day the man who delivered milk to Pleasant View, Mrs. Eddy's home, told them that he could no longer make his deliveries since his well had gone dry and there was no water for his cows. However, he appeared the next day with the usual quantity of milk. Despite the fact that it had not rained, he said, there were two or three feet of water in his well. He asked the people of the household if they were witches or prophets.

Some of the stories of Mrs. Eddy's early healings read much like those of the Gospels. One follower asserts that her mother was told by Mrs. Eddy of one such. Walking along the street one day Mrs. Eddy saw a cripple at work piling wood. Pursuing him, she touched him on the shoulder, saying at the same time, "God loves you." Instantly the man was healed. (Abigail Dyer Thompson, *Miscellaneous Documents,* p. 145) Clifford P. Smith relates similar stories in his *Biographical Notes* series published by the church.

Norwood tells of an engineer whose eye had been put out by a hot cinder. Mrs. Eddy treated him and the eye was restored. But unfortunately it was smaller than the other. Mrs. Eddy said, "Can it be possible that I understand God so *little* as that?" She treated the man again, and the eye became perfect as to size. (*Miscellaneous Documents,* p. 137)

On still another occasion, relates Irving Tomlinson, Mrs. Eddy went into a furniture store to buy some chairs. She observed that the clerk had a bandage over one eye and was suffering. When she had looked over all their offerings and had left the shop, a student who had been with her reproached her for not giving close attention to the business at hand. To this she replied that she could not think of chairs when the man was suffering. Next day, when the student returned to the store to complete the business transaction, the clerk asked who the woman was who had been along the day before. "For," said he, "yesterday I was suffering from an abscess on the eye, but on removing the bandage last night it had quite disappeared." (*Twelve Years with Mary Baker Eddy,* p. 53)

Even as a child, we are told, she had the ability to heal. Julia Bartlett reports Mrs. Eddy told her she had learned as a child that if a playmate was sick or suffering and she went to her, the child would get well. So she often begged her mother to let her visit sick friends. (*Miscellaneous Documents,* p. 190)

As a child, she recalled in later years, she also had an unusual ability to find things that were hidden. In the game hide-the-thimble she could always go directly to the hidden thimble. Once the children hid it in the ashes of the stove, but Mary found it without the slightest difficulty. (*Miscellaneous Documents,* p. 190)

Adam Dickey tells how little Mary Baker learned that she could mentally address her pet dog and, without speaking aloud, get him to obey her directions. She had only to think, "Ben, go under the table and lie down," to get the dog to do so. And this happened many, many times. Dickey says she told him that this was one of the things from her childhood which she always kept to herself. (*Memoirs,* p. 74)

Dickey relates an interesting childhood healing experience. Once when Mary was very small, her elder brother was chopping wood. The ax slipped and he suffered a severe wound in the leg. When the wound refused to heal and the family had begun to despair of the brother's recovery, Mark Baker, their father, carried the little girl into her brother's room and had her gently touch the wound. From that very moment the wound began to heal and in a short time the leg was wholly restored. But as a result Mary suffered for days from a high fever. (*Memoirs,* p. 74) This sounds like the old Quimby idea of taking over the "grief" of the patient.

Gilbert Carpenter relates, presumably from his own observation while resident secretary to Mrs. Eddy, that one day while she was enjoying her daily carriage drive Mrs. Eddy noticed a piece of fur under a place on the harness. She was told it was to protect a chafed spot on the horse's shoulder. To this she said nothing. But when she returned and the animal was unharnessed the sore was entirely healed. She never permitted anything like this to go by, Carpenter asserts; as soon as it was brought to her attention it was promptly healed. (*Carpenter Notes,* Book 3, p. 124)

Tomlinson asserts that in Concord many were healed whom she happened to see as she drove through the streets and upon whom she centered her "illumined thought" even momentarily. The sick, the crippled, the helpless invalids, were, he declares, all made free by the love which she radiated. And it shone alike on poor and rich, friend and enemy. (*Twelve Years with Mary Baker Eddy*, p. 50)

Perhaps the climax in the matter of miracles is in her reported raising of the dead. Sue Harper Mims, writing at the time, states that Mrs. Eddy told the assembled students of the 1898 class of three times having raised the dead. This Mrs. Mims likened to the experience of Jesus who also raised three from the dead—the little maid, the young man, and Lazarus. (*We Knew Mary Baker Eddy— Second Series*, pp. 45 ff.) Here again is the parallel so frequently drawn between Jesus the Christ and Mary Baker Eddy.

Norwood reports Mrs. Eddy's having said that if they loved enough they could raise the dead. "I've done it!" she cried. (*Miscellaneous Documents*, p. 111) Again, Fanny L. Pierce relates that in her Primary class of 1888, Mrs. Eddy told of raising the dead and dying, through the realization of the allness of God. (*Miscellaneous Documents*, p. 87)

Irving Tomlinson, who was a resident in her home for a time, describes several cases in which persons who to all appearances had ceased to live were restored to life. One was a case told by Mrs. Eddy to Lord and Lady Dunmore of England. While living in Boston, she had become very fond of a small girl in the neighborhood. Not having seen the child about for a while, she went to the home and inquired concerning her. She was met at the door by the mother who, in tears, told her it was too late. The child was dead. Mrs. Eddy asked to see the little girl. Entering the sick room she took the lifeless body in her arms and requested the mother to leave her alone. Lost for a time in communion, wholly absorbed in the consciousness of Life, Truth, and Love, she was brought back to awareness of her surroundings by the child's asking to see her mother. When the mother entered the room, Mrs. Eddy put the child on her feet and bade her run to her mother. And, Mrs. Eddy told her guests from across the Atlantic, the little girl did so. Lady Dunmore later added to the account by telling Tomlinson that this was the first time the child had ever walked. (*Twelve Years with Mary Baker Eddy*, p. 57)

Dickey gives a dramatic account of the seeming death and

resurrection of Calvin Frye while he was residing in Mrs. Eddy's home. Dickey relates that Frye was found unconscious, in a contorted attitude, unbreathing, without pulse or other indication of life. When this was reported to Mrs. Eddy, she ordered Frye brought to her bedside. He was placed in a low rocking chair and the chair was then dragged with its burden into her bedroom. As the members of the household looked on, Dickey recalls, Mrs. Eddy shouted at Calvin to awake and return, to disappoint his enemies, that the Cause needed him. At last he raised his head, drew a deep breath, and said, "I don't want to stay." But he was commanded to awake and remain. Soon he was his old self, and remained on earth long after his Leader's passing. (*Memoirs*, p. 60)

Even inanimate objects seemed to enjoy some sort of divine protection if associated with Mrs. Eddy. Once the *Journal* related a story about a house burning down, with all its contents charred except a copy of *Science and Health* which had been left lying on a table.

More than a few times reference has been made by Mrs. Eddy's followers to clairvoyant powers which she seemed to exercise. Judge Ewing tells how once when he was going to lecture in Lynn certain rowdies were planning to break up the meeting. He started boldly with a tribute to Mrs. Eddy, and was surprised to discover that no outbreak followed. Next day, when he went to Concord to see her, before he could say anything Mrs. Eddy thanked him warmly for what he had said about her the night before. But, he cried, greatly surprised, "has someone been here before me and told you?" She replied simply that she had both seen and heard him.

Mrs. Eddy declared, in the first two editions of *Christian Science History* (p. 16), that she could detect whatever a malicious malpractitioner might be arguing mentally, and that she could not be deceived, in her reading of human thoughts, motives, and purposes, by either mental arguments or psychic power. Here is a definite claim to infallibility, to a personal omniscience.

Even unspoken references to her person seemed to work wonders. Mrs. Clifford P. Smith was very ill on one occasion, and her mental efforts at recovery were failing her. Suddenly she thought:

"Every word that Mary Baker Eddy ever wrote is true!" Instantly, she says, she was healed.

Is it any wonder that, with stories like these circulating about her, her followers might very well come to think of her in highly exalted terms? What kind of person is one who, from infancy upward, shows such remarkable healing powers and clairvoyance (if not omniscience), who can restore cripples with a momentary thought, who can raise the dead? And it is to be remembered that these stories were told by leaders in the movement.

Norwood tells of addressing a letter to her as "Mary Baker Eddy: Thou Who Art Favored Among Women"—the very salutation addressed to Mary, mother of Jesus, by the angel. (*Miscellaneous Documents*, p. 106) On another occasion Norwood described her as "the fairest among fifteen hundred million and altogether lovely," and said that although he had often seen her, she appeared on this occasion more "radiantly glorious" than ever before; in fact, that the glory of her face was "unutterable." (*Miscellaneous Documents*, p. 109)

In an address on the *Christian Science Monitor*, given at Sixteenth Church, Chicago, March 31, 1934, Algernon Harvey Bathhurst made some revealing statements on how Mrs. Eddy is regarded inside the movement. Bathhurst said he always kept on his desk a picture of the revered Leader which, whenever he looked at it, gave him a sense of love and peace. On a certain occasion he was facing a serious problem. What should he do? The picture was there before him. He reflected upon some things Mrs. Eddy stood for. Then he "handled" the matter. Immediately thereafter he got up and found himself doing the very thing he had before been unable to do. His problem was solved.

Certain of my Christian Scientist friends recall a characteristic experience they had while visiting Boston headquarters. In the meeting room of the Board of Directors hangs a painting of Mrs. Eddy. People entering the room spoke in hushed voices, as though entering a shrine, dropping almost to whispers as they stood beneath the Leader's portrait. The atmosphere was not unlike that ascribed to the Mother's Room, in the original Mother Church edifice, by Mark Twain in his book *Christian Science* (pp. 241 ff.).

Doubtless some of the demands made by Mrs. Eddy herself upon her followers contributed to this sense. For example, in 1895 she wrote this bylaw into the *Manual* (2nd ed., p. 15), where it remained for eight years through twenty-seven editions:

In 1895, loyal Christian Scientists had given to the author of their textbook, the Founder of Christian Science, the individual endearing term of Mother. Therefore if a student of Christian Science shall apply this title, either to herself or to others, except as the term for kinship according to the flesh, it shall be regarded by the Church as an indication of disrespect for their Pastor Emeritus, Mary Baker G. Eddy, and unfitness to be a member of The Mother Church.

Even when this title was relinquished with the 29th edition of the *Manual* in 1903, "owing to the public misunderstanding of this name," a substitute bylaw required that she, and she alone, be called "Leader." In the same *Manual* she ruled that she could summon any Christian Scientist to come to her home and serve her in any capacity she chose, under pain of excommunication, these latter provisions being maintained even into the final and present editions (pp. 64-69).

Official spokesmen for the church quite repudiate the idea that Christian Scientists deify Mary Baker Eddy. Nevertheless, there is a certain sense of awe and veneration felt for her which is clearly akin to that felt by peoples of other religions in the presence of their deities. While all "personalizing" is constantly deplored, in public testimonies, articles, and so on, much is made at the same time of Mrs. Eddy's person. Of course the word *worship* is never used in conjunction with her by her followers. But the practical difference does not seem to an outsider to be very great between the attitudes which many Christian Scientists exhibit toward her in speaking and writing, and the attitudes toward their deities held by representatives of some non-Christian faiths.

During her lifetime and ever since it has not been unusual for things to appear in the church periodicals lifting Mary Baker Eddy to a plane high above that of ordinary persons. At a time when the

Journal was admittedly under her close personal scrutiny, in 1885, it said:

What a triumphant career is this for a woman! Can it be anything less than the tabernacle of God with men—the fulfillment of the vision of the lonely seer on the isle of Patmos—the "wonder in heaven," delivering the child which shall rule all nations? How dare we say to the contrary, that she is God-sent to the world as much as any character of sacred writ? (III, 151)

Indeed, the early numbers of the *Journal* carry many, many such eulogies of Mrs. Eddy.

Certainly she is today regarded as the supreme and final Revelator. Tomlinson speaks of her "divine office" as Revelator, and proclaims her the fulfilment of Scripture. To be sure, there were occasions when she herself sought to turn her students' attention from her own corporeal personality. She has even written that those who seek her elsewhere than in her writings lose her instead of finding her. (*Miscellany*, p. 120) But such admonitions seem to be quite outweighed by much else that she has said and done, judging from the words and attitudes of her followers. Much is made of her "follow your Leader only so far as she follows Christ," but the official position, as set forth in the church publications, is that she follows Christ *all the way*.

To Irving Tomlinson, while Jesus was the first coming of the Christ, Mary Baker Eddy completely fulfils the second coming as prophesied in the Bible. Jesus, he says, revealed the Fatherhood of God; Mrs. Eddy, in the "second coming," revealed God's Motherhood. This seems to be her own view in *Science and Health* (pp. 562, 565). In her many works and her revelation of Christ to this age, Tomlinson thinks she stands before the world as the *one* in whom the prophecy of the second coming finds indisputable realization. (*Twelve Years with Mary Baker Eddy*, p. 215)

Mrs. Eddy herself wrote, in *Retrospection and Introspection* (p. 70), after stating that no one can ever take Jesus' place: "No person can take the place of the author of *Science and Health*, the Discoverer and Founder of Christian Science. Each individual must

DEVELOPING IDEAS CONCERNING MRS. EDDY

fill his own niche in time and eternity. The second appearing of *Jesus* is, unquestionably, the spiritual advent of the advancing idea of God, *as in* Christian Science." This passage is anything but obscure when taken in conjunction with relevant passages in her textbook. There she has defined the first coming as "the impersonation of the spiritual idea" by the man Jesus, "the masculine representative," and the second coming as the impersonation of the spiritual idea "last by woman," with "a special suggestiveness in connection with the nineteenth century." How could her followers escape the implication? Many obviously did not.

Bliss Knapp, in the biography of his parents, who were very influential Scientists in the pioneer period of the movement, says that when his father, Ira O. Knapp, first studied with Mrs. Eddy, her chapter on the Apocalypse had not yet appeared in the textbook. Mrs. Eddy orally explained the twelfth chapter, and as she did so, although he says she made no reference to herself personally, it was borne in upon him that she was herself "the woman clothed with the sun, and upon her head a crown of twelve stars." Ira Knapp wrote a long poem acclaiming her as such. He thought it just as essential that Christian Scientists today recognize the identity of the woman of the Apocalypse as that Jesus' disciples acknowledge Christ's living faith as exhibited nearly two thousand years ago.

Whether or not Ira Knapp was the first to get the idea, it is one that has been widely held in Christian Science circles since the early days. In a personal letter to Margaret Laird, William Lyman Johnson told of being commissioned by the Board of Directors during the Great Litigation to write a history of Christian Science. In it he had written about the Knapp idea of Mrs. Eddy as being literally the woman foretold by St. John. The book was never released, and Johnson withdrew under pressure. As late as 1928 the Directors would take no public stand on the issue. Some years later Johnson was able to impress Albert Field Gilmore, one of the influential leaders of that period, and a search was instituted for corroboratory evidence.

The venerable Irving Tomlinson, in his officially approved book, sets forth the belief that Mrs. Eddy recognized in her person the

fulfilment of the prophecy of St. John. He tells how pleased she was
to have a painting of the angel of the Apocalypse, with the "little
book" opened in hand, placed at the head of the stairs in her
Chestnut Hill house.

As far back as 1889, the *Journal* ran an unsigned editorial under
the title *Christian Science and Its Revelator*, which said: "Today
Truth has come through the person of a New England girl. . . .
From the cradle she gave indications of a divine mission and power
which caused her mother to 'ponder them in her heart.'" This
theme, which Mrs. Eddy did not disavow, has continued to be
played upon ever since, with increasing conviction and boldness.

After half a century or more of this sort of thing, it is hardly
surprising that this concept of Mary Baker Eddy should become
the dominating one within the organization. Neither is it surprising
that the unofficial concept should be made official and published to
the world. Under pressure of the overwhelming sentiment, the
Boston hierarchy finally instituted a procedure, not unlike that
used by the Roman Catholic church authorities in canonizing a
saint, to determine once and for all "Mrs. Eddy's place."

"In April, 1938," writes W. Stuart Booth, a member of the Board,
"the Christian Science Board of Directors, after fully considering
this important subject, appointed a committee of six to ascertain
what Mrs. Eddy considered herself to be in the light of Scriptural
prophecies." Besides her published works, the committee was
furnished from the Mother Church archives selected statements by
Mrs. Eddy "which she had decided should not be published." In
due course the committee members arrived at the unanimous
conclusion "that Mrs. Eddy, having chosen God above all else and
being spiritually prepared for her mission, was chosen of God to
reveal the Comforter to the world; that she regarded the twelfth
chapter of Revelation as pointing to her as the one who fulfilled
prophecy by giving the full and final revelation of Truth; that she
represents or symbolizes the spiritual idea of God typified by the
woman referred to in the Apocalypse." (*Sentinel*, XLVIII, 1895 ff.)

On June 5, 1943, five years after this procedure was started, the
Board of Directors issued a public proclamation certifying "the

position of The Mother Church as to Mary Baker Eddy's place in the fulfilment of Bible prophecy." Appearing first in the *Sentinel* (XLV, 985 ff.), it was republished in the *Journal* (LXI, 412 ff.). It declared: (1) that Mrs. Eddy understood herself to have been singled out by God as the Revelator of Christ to this age, bringing the foretold Comforter; (2) that, in giving the full and final revelation of Truth, she regarded herself the subject of St. John's vision, so that her work was actually "complementary to that of Christ Jesus"; (3) that she was literally the woman of the Apocalypse, exemplifying God's motherhood, while Jesus exemplified God's fatherhood; (4) that she understood herself to be "the God-appointed and God-anointed messenger to this age," being so closely identified with Christian Science, since the revelation and the revelator are inseparable, "that a true sense of her is essential to the understanding of Christian Science"; (5) that it was her very recognition of her status that empowered her to fight off "the dragon"—malicious animal magnetism; and (6) that this same recognition of her place and her mission by her followers is vital to the stability and growth of Christian Scientists "today and in succeeding generations."

Lest the full import of what they called "this great step forward" should be lost upon the field, the proclamation was followed by many articles and editorials fortifying and explaining it. In *Prophecy and Fulfillment,* Director Booth cites Scripture in support of his contention that both Isaiah and Moses foretold the coming of Jesus, just as both Jesus and John foretold the coming of Mrs. Eddy. (*Sentinel,* XLVIII, 1893 ff.)

This whole trend was epitomized and focused with the church's publication in 1946 of *Mary Baker Eddy: Her Mission and Triumph,* by Julia Michael Johnston. A singular and significant contribution, coming as it does with official sponsorship, this book is indispensable to the student who seeks to learn what the church authorities would like the world to accept as the correct view of Mary Baker Eddy.

Unhampered by the limitations suffered by the historian, Mrs. Johnston approaches her subject from the standpoint of the devout traditionalist. The result is that a character emerges from her pages who bears little resemblance to the Mrs. Eddy of authenticated record. Born of "a saintly mother" under peculiarly auspicious circumstances, little Mary conversed audibly with God, exhibited marvelous healing powers even as a little girl, and, above all, manifested a lifelong awareness of and consecration to her God-ordained mission. Time and again parallels are drawn between the experiences of Mary Baker Eddy and Jesus. Awkward facts are permitted at no point to mar the smooth flow of legend. Even Mrs. Eddy's own words, where incompatible, are not allowed to interfere with the picture Mrs. Johnston has undertaken to sketch.

In extenuation it might be observed that Mrs. Johnston writes from the point of view of a loyal convert, and it must be remembered that the Christian Scientist believes that "all that is good is true, and all that is evil and inharmonious is illusion." Mrs. Eddy's more ardent followers have always taken the position that anything derogatory to Mrs. Eddy, or inconsistent with her statement that "my history is a holy one," is to be dismissed without examination, on the ground that it is no more than the false testimony of mortal mind which, by its very nature, is bent upon misrepresenting the Revelator to overthrow the revelation. Indeed, Mrs. Eddy establishes this when she writes: "The human history needs to be revised, and the material record expunged." (*Retrospection and Introspection*, p. 22)

But whether or not Mary Baker Eddy is actually regarded as divine in so many words by the church, the lengths to which the official group will go to protect her memory against unfavorable disclosures or indignity is in fact strongly suggestive of a view of her person which is quite parallel to that of other religions with respect to their divinities. Many taboos are thrown around her person. As in the case of Studdert-Kennedy's sympathetic study of her life, the officials have seemed determined that nothing should appear which would in any way reflect upon her. She must not appear tired, or discouraged, or weak, or resentful, or angry, or nervous, or distressed, or sick. None of the very human qualities one expects to find in all human beings must be reported of her.

There is now a great deal of published material, and still more unpublished, in the diaries and notes of people who lived right in her home and had every chance to observe her. These relate in great detail that she actually did get cross, rebuking them strongly —that on a few occasions she behaved very badly indeed. Carolyn Foss Gyger's diary reports that Mrs. Eddy once scratched her face and, in another fit of temper, threw a shoe at her. This concurs with other testimony along the same lines. Mrs. Eddy was exacting in an extreme degree with those who attended her, as Dickey, Wilcox, Gyger, the Carpenters, and others testify. Episodes like those of the "in-case meals" make her seem downright contrary; but Eddy advocates like Gilbert Carpenter construe her behavior as being designed to benefit the members of her household, enabling them to learn and grow.

It is understandable that people as they grow older get childish and do childish things. It does not appreciably detract from Mrs. Eddy's greatness that she had a very human side. But official Christian Science will have none of it, and uses every device imaginable to prevent access to materials of this sort and to prevent their publication. Quite clearly an official view of Mrs. Eddy has developed, and nothing must be permitted to circulate that contravenes that view. This becomes a very, very difficult task, however, for there is at hand perhaps more detailed information, all authenticated, on her life public and private than on that of any other personage in recent history.

The author once suggested to a high official in the church that it would be a stroke of genuine strategy if the church would have a first-class motion picture made of the life of Mrs. Eddy. He pointed out the dramatic character of much of that life, and how it could be made a popular vehicle for the wide and favorable extension of her influence and that of her teaching. (The Martin Luther picture, which has had such a popular reception, had not yet been produced.) But the official's reaction was completely negative. It would be quite impossible to portray Mrs. Eddy on the screen, he asserted.

Why, ask many genuine Christian Scientists, may not Mrs. Eddy

be portrayed on the screen? God Himself walked the stage in Marc
Connelly's *Green Pastures*, smoking a "seegar." Jesus has been freely
dramatized on stage and screen again and again. Why not
Mrs. Eddy?

At one time word was received from a major producer that the
Boston interests, aroused by the widely publicized efforts of an
independent Christian Scientist to film Mrs. Eddy's story, had
sought to persuade a certain studio to undertake such a project for
them. A famous actress declared that she was offered a contract
to play Mrs. Eddy in this production. This particular venture was
balked when the owners of the script mentioned earlier (see p. 161)
stepped in, pointing to his own script already long on file in this
very studio. The studio apparently feared infringing certain basic
rights, at least to one feasible treatment of the difficult subject,
which he had acquired through priority under California law. A
conciliatory letter from one of the top executives ended the matter
for the moment.

Many, many loyal followers of Mary Baker Eddy believe that
the more the world knows of their revered Leader the better. What
is there to conceal? She herself declared: "Nothing has occurred in
my life's experience which, if correctly narrated and understood,
could injure me." (*Miscellany*, p. 298) These followers feel that it
is a disservice to the cause to suppress the facts, and point to Mrs.
Eddy's statement in the *Journal* (V, 117): "Alas for the future of
Mind-healing, if built upon the sand of falsehood." Neither she
nor her teaching needs protection at the hands of the church
authorities or anybody else, they contend, and they want the
protective measures relaxed. If she indeed brought Truth, this
Truth may be trusted to stand up under any attack that can be
made upon it.

15

The Dissenters

FROM THE BEGINNING of Christian Science history there have been those who found themselves in disagreement with some of the teachings or the policies of the Eddy organization. This was true in the founder's day. Person after person once close to Mrs. Eddy and enjoying her favor fell by the wayside. Most of them were expelled from the church and crippled by the stigma, but a few of them voluntarily withdrew. Names such as those of Richard Kennedy and Daniel Spofford come to mind at once from the earliest period. Later there were people like Clara Choate, Josephine Woodbury, Augusta Stetson, who though excluded from the organization continued in the faith. Most famous was Emma Curtis Hopkins, onetime editor of the *Christian Science Journal*, who proved himself to be an influential teacher and prolific writer outside the church.

Of all the dissenters only one was, however, to organize a countermovement on any notable scale. This was Annie C. Bill. True, Mrs. Stetson proved a formidable adversary after her excommunication, and Mrs. Hopkins won (and still has) a substantial unorganized following. While Mrs. Stetson's large personal following was to some extent unified by her writings, she never attempted to organize another church. She consistently maintained this position: "I am confident that I burst the bonds which held me to *material* organization when I finished my church edifice and taught Truth to those who were ready to assimilate it and rise higher and 'build on a wholly spiritual foundation.'" (*Reminiscences, Sermons and Correspondence*, p. 1180) As one of her students explained: "The Church Triumphant is a wholly spiritual state of consciousness to be attained by every individual. . . . This Church cannot be conceived of as limited to any individual or to any body of people." (Altman K. Swihart, *Since Mrs. Eddy,* p. 131)

Mrs. Bill, however, took the position that in essence the only thing wrong about the Christian Science church lay in its leadership after Mrs. Eddy's demise. At least, it was on this basis that she undertook to found a competitive church organization to take over or to displace the Mother Church with its branches. Her story has been told in considerable detail by Altman K. Swihart.

Mrs. Bill was born Annie Cecelia Bulmer, daughter of a Lincolnshire rector of the Anglican church, around 1865. She was a thoughtful, studious girl and read much in her father's library. She was not happy in the orthodox faith of her time, and when she first learned of Christian Science in 1904 she was very much attracted to it. A year later she took Class Instruction and joined the local branch church in London, as well as the Mother Church. There occurred soon after a split in the branch church, led by her teacher, whom she followed, becoming a member of the new Third Church. She became an active healer, although she did not seek listing in the *Journal.*

In Third Church Mrs. Bill found herself associated with Frederick L. Rawson, a very able engineer and scientist who, while a Christian Scientist, did not limit himself strictly to the officially approved views. Considering his influence pernicious, the Board of Third Church, in an order later sustained by the Board of Directors of the Mother Church, sought to prevent their members from discussing Christian Science with him. This ban, if submitted to, would have prevented all conversation on the subject with his wife and four sons, his six sisters-in-law, and his friends in the community.

Mrs. Bill, by now a close friend of Rawson, was unable to accept this decree; so in 1909 she resigned from both the branch church and the Mother Church. She did not, however, withdraw from the congregation, but continued to attend services and to speak at the Wednesday testimony meetings. Finding her a disturbing element, the Board of Third Church requested Mrs. Bill to refrain from speaking there. About three months before Mrs. Eddy's passing she appealed to the Leader to intercede, but nothing came of this. Undaunted, Mrs. Bill continued to speak at the public testimony meetings. Finally, in 1912, the Board of Third Church positively forbade her to enter the church building or its Reading Rooms.

After Mrs. Eddy's death, Mrs. Bill saw the difficulty the Mother Church officials faced in trying to operate according to the *Manual*, with so many of its vital provisions requiring its author's specific approval at the time of any action under them. It finally occurred to her—and she thought of herself as the first to make the discovery—that the church must be formally dissolved and reconstructed under a new constitution. She regarded herself as the natural successor to Mrs. Eddy, on the authority of her presumably unique discovery of the *Manual* impasse and of what she regarded as the only legitimate way around it.

Mrs. Bill accordingly felt duty-bound to form the new organization. Into it the Mother Church and other churches might, when they saw the light, come as branch churches. After her exclusion from Third Church in 1912, she organized in London "The Central and Universal Church of Christ, Scientist." Letters of invitation to Third Church and to the Mother Church brought no response. In 1913 she first presented to her little congregation her new *Manual*, under which the model church was to be governed. Mrs. Eddy's *Manual* was the prototype and, as it provided in its first article for a Pastor Emeritus, the new *Manual* had to make a similar provision. Annie Bill, of course, became Pastor Emeritus by right of her revolutionary discovery.

Mrs. Bill maintained that the Boston Board could not inherit Mrs. Eddy's mantle, that the leadership had been clearly reserved for woman. True, Mrs. Eddy had said in a newspaper interview, in answer to the question as to whether her successor would be a man or a woman, "I can answer that it will be a man." But here the word *man* could only be taken in the generic sense, for Mrs. Eddy had always in her writings emphasized the spiritual superiority of woman over man. In a letter to the Pope at Rome, Mrs. Bill declared: "I have learned and proved that spiritual discovery comes in these latter days through woman, and that man is necessarily kept waiting until she has accomplished her task..." (*Since Mrs. Eddy,* p. 202)

In her bylaws she provided that nothing new should be added without the assent in writing of Mrs. Bill herself. Assuming the prerogatives of Mrs. Eddy's office, Mrs. Bill declared hers the only legitimate Christian Science church, boldly asserted the right of her organization to the title of Mother Church, and contended that she had the sole right to appoint the trustees of the Christian Science Publishing Society, together with all rights to the *Journal, Sentinel, Herald, Monitor,* and *Quarterly Bible Lessons.* Her group actually began to publish a *Journal,* etc., essentially replicas of the Boston periodicals. In addition she declared her London group the only legitimate executors and administrators of Mary Baker G. Eddy's will. At the same time she began pressing her claims in the American press through paid advertisements.

Now she got action from the Board of Directors of the Mother Church in Boston, who sought a legal injunction forbidding further use of the official titles for her publications. Mrs. Bill forthwith dropped her use of these titles and designs, declaring that she yielded "upon the ground that we do not wish to contest a purely commercial issue which, however it might end, could not fail to injure the cause of Christian Science." (*Since Mrs. Eddy,* p. 210)

The name of the church was changed, as it was to be changed again and again in succeeding years. Her own title of "Pastor Emeritus" she changed to that of "Leader."

In 1920, at the height of the Great Litigation, she came to Boston to push her movement. There were many dissatisfied elements in the late Mrs. Eddy's church. It was a propitious moment. Among the more important malcontents was John Valentine Dittemore, senior member of the Board of Directors of the Christian Science Church, Boston, who had been dismissed from the Board by his fellow-Directors for incompatibility but was fighting their action in the courts. He readily granted Mrs. Bill an interview and she found little difficulty in interesting him in her crusade.

Healed through Christian Science in 1903 of a chronic ailment, Dittemore had embraced the faith and gone through Class under Martha Harris Bogue of Detroit. A prosperous businessman, he was vice-president of the Van Camp Packing Company and president of the Federal Packing Company, both in Indianapolis, when Mrs. Eddy was under widespread attack in 1907. As a national advertiser he was in a position to exert some influence on the press of the country, and he volunteered to come to Mrs. Eddy's aid in the matter of the Milmine articles in *McClure's* and the Next Friends' Suit. On invitation he went east to work with the church officials. His services must have been effective, for in 1908 he was made Committee on Publication for the important state of New York. In 1909 he was summoned to Boston to become a Director. He remained in that post until he was dismissed in 1919.

Dittemore did not always enjoy the most amicable relations with his fellow-Directors. Indeed he had, by his own admission, opposed his colleagues on no fewer than thirty issues in two years. Moreover, he sought through outside contacts to influence their decisions. The growing friction reached its climax when the decision was taken to subdue the Trustees of the Publishing Society by removing one Trustee at a time. Dittemore had urged their wholesale dismissal, regarding them as traitors to the cause, but his colleagues overruled him on the ground that such a drastic move would be hazardous strategy. He denounced this as an unprincipled compromise. His own removal followed. This was the anomalous position in which Mrs. Bill found him in 1920.

In 1921 Dittemore went to England to study the new movement, now known as "The Parent Church." He was soon made "Deputy Leader" and delegated the necessary authority to take over its organizational work.

His lawsuit was still pending in 1924 when, in anticipation of winning back his seat on the Mother Church Board, Dittemore prepared a resolution to be presented at the Board's first meeting thereafter. In it he asserted that at Mrs. Eddy's death the Mother Church should automatically have been dissolved; that the church should have but one leader, and that Annie C. Bill and the Parent

Church were the logical and legitimate successors to the old organization; and that all real estate and other properties under the control of the Directors should therefore be turned over to the Parent Church.

Meanwhile Dittemore remained also a Trustee under the will of Mrs. Eddy, and it was in this capacity that he wrote his fellow-officers proposing the withdrawal of the Eddy *Manual* from circulation as outmoded, useful only as a model in future developments. At once the trustees under the will petitioned the court to remove Dittemore from his post, contending that he was no longer a follower of Mrs. Eddy, but had become the follower of one Mrs. Bill, "who is attempting to displace Mary Baker G. Eddy and usurp her positions in relation to Christian Science." At this juncture Dittemore submitted his resignation as trustee for the estate, thus forestalling a court decision in the matter.

A letter written by C. Augustus Norwood, general counsel for the Mother Church, indicates that an out-of-court settlement of Dittemore's claims against the Board of Directors was effected, in which Dittemore received a sum of money and acceded to certain agreements relative to his own future actions. Now dissociated from the Mother Church, he was still a force to be reckoned with.

Back in 1907 Dittemore had financed and published the official Sibyl Wilbur biography of Mary Baker Eddy. Afterward, when he had become a Director, he enjoyed the approval of his fellow-Directors in his industrious search over many years for materials bearing upon the life of Mrs. Eddy and the development of her church. He had kept in his personal files copies of a vast number of documents which had gone into the archives of the Mother Church. He was eventually to permit access to some of this material by Dakin, for publication in his book, and to use it himself in his collaboration with Ernest Sutherland Bates in the writing of *Mary Baker Eddy: The Truth and the Tradition,* a book which stirred the church and its officials to the very depths. The essential accuracy of its factual materials was, as we have noted, certified by the church's chief authority in such matters, Judge Clifford P. Smith. So seriously did the Directors regard the Bates-Dittemore book that they finally bought its copyright and plates from the publisher, Alfred A. Knopf, thus suppressing a valuable source work.

John Dittemore's industry and organizational ability were a great asset to the Bill movement. He edited the church magazine, the *Christian Science Watchman,* lectured widely, and taught classes in England and America. Many of his friends followed him into the new movement.

At first Annie Bill was profoundly loyal to Mrs. Eddy and her writings. But then, in 1928, a stunning blow fell which was to change the whole picture for her. Among those who followed Dittemore to her side was the Boston bookseller and publisher, A. A. Beauchamp. Employed by the Mother Church Directors back in 1916-17 to do research in and index the Eddy correspondence and other manuscripts in the official archives, Beauchamp had come across the letter of a New England woman to Mrs. Eddy, calling attention to the fact that "The Man of Integrity," which Mrs. Eddy had published as her own in 1896 (*Miscellaneous Writings,* pp. 147 ff.), had actually been written by the Rev. Hugh Blair, who had died in 1800. The article had been published in 1835 by Lindley Murray in his *English Reader* (pp. 118 ff.), and the correspondent had enclosed the pages torn from the *Reader.* Also, Beauchamp learned that at the time of her death there was found in Mrs. Eddy's private library the little book *Philosophic Nuggets,* containing other passages which she had borrowed and presented as her own. When Mrs. Bill saw Beauchamp reading a copy of this latter book, she asked him about it, only to discover the incontrovertible evidence of her heroine's plagiarisms. "I thought Mrs. Bill would lose her reason, the shock was so great," relates Beauchamp in a letter dated February 21, 1944. Beauchamp says that he tried to minimize it all, "but no, she said it was too basic," and the episode proved to have "a far-reaching effect."

It was more and more difficult for Annie Bill to defend Mary Baker Eddy as these disclosures followed one upon the other, for Mrs. Eddy had all through the years denounced with unremitting vigor everything in the way of literary pirating. Plagiarism, she had written, was a growing evil which would undermine the very foundations of Christian Science if not stamped out. Meanwhile to this was added the publication of the Frye diaries and other supporting evidence testifying to Mrs. Eddy's use of drugs on occasion and recourse to physicians. Inevitably there came a break with the Eddy tradition. Mrs. Bill continued to believe in Christian Science, but she no longer attributed its origin to Mrs. Eddy. From the published letters of Mrs. Eddy to Phineas Parkhurst Quimby, which had appeared in *The Quimby Manuscripts* in 1921, and other materials made accessible by Dittemore, she concluded that Mrs. Eddy had gotten it from Quimby and had served only as a bridge over which it had come to herself.

This was hard for the old-school Christian Scientists to take, even those who had followed Mrs. Bill out of the Boston organization; but as it came to be accepted, her own position grew stronger than ever. Logically, she felt that she must withdraw her own books in which she had extolled Mary Baker Eddy and attributed Christian Science to her. She did this, and in 1930 came out with a new textbook, *The Science of Reality: Its Universal Design and Practical Application.* Shortly afterward she ordered the discontinuance of the use of Mrs. Eddy's *Science and Health.* In the public worship services of the Parent Church she decreed that instead her own new book be used, along with the Bible. Since the term *Christian Science* had suffered by reason of the exposure of Mrs. Eddy's shortcomings, it seemed best to discontinue the use of it. So the name of the church was once more changed. Henceforth it was to be called "The Church of the Universal Design."

Annie C. Bill had now quite displaced Mary Baker Eddy, and her *Science of Reality* had superseded *Science and Health.* Along with this went substantial changes of essential belief and practice. The sectarian Christian reference of Mrs. Eddy gives way to a more universal outlook, limited to no particular religious sect or denomination. There seems to be less emphasis on strictly individual healing, more on the condition of the community and of mankind as a whole. Here is involved a cardinal principle of Mrs. Bill's teaching—namely, "common consent."

Much of the illness of the world depends upon general acquiescence in erroneous belief, and the practicing metaphysician must take this into account. So far this represented no radical departure from Mrs. Eddy's teachings. *Science and Health* (pp. 177 ff.) asserted that when a poison victim dies even while both patient and physician are anticipating his recovery, "the result is controlled by the majority of opinions, not by the infinitesimal minority of opinions in the sick-chamber." Mrs. Bill argues that healing consists properly in treating not the individual alone, but the thought of the world. Even death may thus eventually be overcome. Overcoming death has in the past been accepted by common consent as impossible. But change this idea in the thought of the world and immortality is demonstrated as a natural consequence. The unreality of death will be shown when common consent to the idea of the inevitability of death is changed. By direction of common consent, Mrs. Bill hoped she could change the whole world.

Common consent, then, has potentialities for good or evil. Why not make use of it? Had not Mrs. Eddy done so when she advised her followers to leave surgery and bone-setting to the fingers of a surgeon "until the advancing age admits the efficacy and supremacy of Mind"? (*Science and Health,* p. 401) Indeed, she had gone farther when she wrote: "I have always instructed students in Christian Science to be wise and discreet, conforming, where conscience is not offended, to the usages of men." (*Sentinel,* III, 217 ff.) In this same article she explained that she herself had submitted to dental surgery, being careful not to turn the dentist's mental protest against herself by opposing his methods. If such care is not exercised, she observed, "his mental force weighs against a painless operation, whereas it should be put into the same scale as mine, thus producing a painless operation as a result."

Following this argument, Mrs. Bill reasoned that the metaphysician who worked with, rather than against, common consent in medical and surgical matters benefited from the weight of world opinion on his side. This shift of emphasis culminated in an open break with the stand of orthodox Christian Scientists against all recourse to medical aid (except, of course, in the case of anesthetics for relief of extreme pain).

Curiously enough, Mrs. Bill, like Mrs. Eddy, was impressed by the Anglo-Israel theory, which regards the Anglo-Saxon people as the descendants and spiritual heirs of the Lost Tribes of Israel. In this she was probably influenced by Dittemore, who had long been an Anglo-Israel enthusiast. But Mrs. Bill openly espoused the theory, incorporating it into her teaching. Identifying Ephraim with Britain and Manasseh with America, she concluded that only as Britain and America co-operated could the highest spiritual development be achieved.

She tends to a different view of marriage, in some respects, from that of Mrs. Eddy. The Eddy teaching is that "the nuptial vow is never annulled so long as the animus of the contract is preserved intact." (*Miscellaneous Writings*, p. 290) Mrs. Bill thought the marriage contract might be limited to a specific term of years, renewable by mutual agreement. She was inclined to believe nine years would be a good maximum limit for people to have to live together without a reappraisal of the contract. In the matter of the physical relationship, she agreed with Mrs. Eddy that celibacy is nearer right than marriage. (*Miscellaneous Writings*, p. 288)

Throughout the twenties the Parent Church and the Mother Church often clashed in the public press. One controversy had to do with Mrs. Bill's charge that the policy of the Mother Church in opposing medical help for patients while under the care of practitioners was a perilous one. The Bill-Dittemore forces cited the death of Walter J. Kline of Lockport, New York, in November, 1928, which the coroner reported as due to "criminal negligence" on the part of the attending Christian Scientists. The Parent Church offered statistics to show that the death rate in the Mother Church exceeded that of any other group. Mother Church spokesman Judge Smith retorted that the "appalling mortality" alleged among Mrs. Eddy's leading students, to be specific, could be explained by the fact that the death rate is greater in old age than in youth, and that these particular people were elderly. Then the Frye diaries were produced to prove that Mrs. Eddy had availed herself of physicians in her later years. The Board responded to this with an editorial in the *Journal* (XLVI, 669), asserting that Mrs. Eddy used drugs in but a few instances and then only for relief from extreme pain.

The Mother Church was accused repeatedly of interfering with freedom of speech, press, and religion in the affairs of the Parent Church, whose members found it difficult to secure halls for lectures and services and had to buy advertising space in the newspapers to get their views before the public. They even found it difficult to get their advertisements inserted. On February 17, 1929, Sir Henry Japp was booked to speak over the Columbia Broadcasting System for the Parent Church; but when he arrived with Dittemore at the studio a few minutes before he was scheduled to go on the air, he ran into difficulties. The CBS management had been prevailed upon to bar his speech unless he would agree to open it with a disavowal of any connection with the Mother Church in Boston. When Sir Henry refused this last-minute change in his script, he was barred from broadcasting. The Parent Church then sued for damages, but the suit was eventually dropped.

The early growth of Mrs. Bill's movement was very slow. Until the time when Dittemore joined her, she never had more than a handful of people at any one point. But after that growth was for a while phenomenal. In only a few years there were branch churches scattered over the globe, though concentrated chiefly in America and England. As late as 1928 forty-four churches were listed. Swihart estimates that there were eighty branches in 1931, though the total membership was small, possibly only a thousand or twelve hundred. (*Since Mrs. Eddy*, p. 233)

So far as the author has been able to discover, there is not now active a single church representing the Bill movement. It would appear, therefore, that the movement has all but vanished in the last quarter-century.

Why did the Parent Church fade out? Some Mother Church members say the Parent Church was foredoomed because its leaders were disloyal to the teachings of the Founder of true Christian Science, that it died out because Truth triumphed, as it always will eventually. Others feel that the loss of its leaders was really respon-

sible. Annie Bill was the first to die. Dittemore followed her from
the scene on May 10, 1937. A few weeks previously, when he lay
dying, he had recanted. He was under the care of a Mother
Church practitioner when he wrote from his Gramercy Park apart-
ment in New York to the Board of Directors that he had concluded
his former course had been prompted by disaffection. He declared
that he now felt he had made a mistake "in letting personal opinion
and matters of policy" induce him to renounce Mrs. Eddy and fight
her organization. (*Christian Science Monitor,* May 11, 1937)

Frederick Rawson, whom Mrs. Bill had assisted in the editing of
his *Life Understood,* continued to practice healing and to teach
classes with considerable success in England and America up until
the day of his death in the middle twenties. Many of his followers
continue independently in the practice and teaching work today.
His association with Mrs. Bill terminated with the publication of
his book in 1912, and he never promoted opposition to the Mother
Church after leaving it.

Aside from the Bill movement, there has been no notable
attempt to set up a Christian Science church in competition with
the one Mrs. Eddy founded. What, then, becomes of the dissenters?
There have been many, and some of those who have gone out of
the Eddy organization had been outstanding leaders in it.

In general, dissent has expressed itself chiefly in three ways.
First, there has always been the comparatively large class of individuals, including not a few practitioners and teachers, who are
dissatisfied with the church as presently controlled but stay in it
with the hope of "healing it from the inside." Most of these members
avoid voicing their discontent. Otherwise they would invite dismissal. They continue to go to church while quietly disregarding
the official rulings. They read other than approved books; they
sometimes make use of the medical skills of physicians in certain
cases without a sense of guilt; they doubt and even disapprove
some aspects of the church belief and practice. But they do not
break with the church, being disposed to remain within the organization so long as they can do so without too great sacrifice of
conviction.

Then there are those who do not or cannot hide their discontent but still seek to remain in the church. When their insubordination is discovered, they are soon brought to book. As a rule they are first admonished, or threatened, and finally put on probation for a period of years. This has proved a more effective form of control than excommunication, inasmuch as excommunication puts them quite beyond the reach of authority, whereas probationers can be kept silent and submissive in the hope of winning their way back into official favor, a prerequisite to regaining their former privileges. But this hope more often than not proves vain. Eventually the ax falls, and they are pronounced unworthy to continue in the church. By that time the stigma of censure has largely alienated their personal following, so that their banishment produces no untoward disturbance in the ranks.

Among the many who have suffered this fate was the late Peter V. Ross. In 1943 Ross was deprived of his teaching franchise and placed under a three-year probation on a charge of immorality. His friends contend that this was only a pretext, that he was never proved guilty; and they point to the fact that he was allowed to continue as a *Journal*-registered practitioner for another year. How could the Board thus endorse him in the healing work, which involves the most intimate of professional relationships, while finding him, as they state in a letter to the Committee on Publication dated April 14, 1944, unfit to teach "after careful consideration of all the testimony" in connection with "serious complaints concerning his personal conduct"?

Ross, who had written several innocuous books on Christian Science, had been asked to withdraw from the lecture platform several years before any such charges had been raised. The complaint at that time was that he had been speaking extemporaneously. Later he was to regret not leaving the organization while he still enjoyed the prestige of a greatly beloved teacher and lecturer and practitioner. Referring to this, he once wrote: "Everyone knows that he should quit when going strong but few have the courage to do it."

In any event, he had hung on, continuing in the practice even after his name was removed from the *Journal* registry of practitioners in 1944, advising his students: "You and I have only to go on quietly and sensibly with our affairs, which in these turbulent days is quite enough." If there was any hope for reinstatement, his prospects were certainly not improved when it became known that he was openly approving Arthur Corey's anathematized activities. In a letter dated October 27, 1945, Ross wrote a Chicago correspondent that he considered Corey "a great chap" whom he knew personally, that he was "much impressed by his sincerity and ability." In this, as in other letters to comparative strangers, he wrote: "His [Corey's] opponents are giving him and his book a publicity which of course will redound to his advantage. Except for this opposition the sale of the volume could have been negligible. Now it will be very considerable, and it should be because the book is very stimulating and enlightening."

In 1947, Ross wrote his students and friends: "It has now become clear that Boston has no intention of reinstating me." The forced dissolution of his Association meant no more, he ventured, than the end of "the outward formalities of material organization." But many of his followers had drifted away after he was disciplined and failed to fight back. His most prominent pupil, John J. Selover, Committee on Publication for Southern California, had repudiated him by going through Class with another teacher. Selover was later elevated to the lecture platform and then to teachership. Ross, now shorn of all standing in the church and deserted by many upon whose allegiance he had counted, was finally excommunicated. In 1947 he passed on, a broken man.

Alice L. Orgain was another in this category. In 1929 Mrs. Orgain, a veteran practitioner, undertook to write and publish independently a book called *As It Is*. To her amazement and consternation, before the book was off the press she received a telegram from the Board in Boston, saying, "We have seen thirty-three pages of a book attributed to you," charging copyright infringement as well as *Manual* violation, and asking that the book be held up. Mrs. Orgain discovered that someone in the printing establishment had surreptitiously removed sections from the book as it was being made up, sending them on to the Board. (Incidentally, she had to replace at great cost the mutilated copies unwittingly sent out to purchasers later.) The usual routine was followed—admonitions, hearings, disciplinary rulings, and so on—with many additional charges thrown in as the case moved along. The Board also took other steps against Mrs. Orgain, such as sending telegrams and letters out into the field. For example, they wrote one First Reader in a New York church that Mrs. Orgain's writings were "objectionable," that she was guilty of violating the *Manual,* and that her membership in the Mother Church was awaiting action by them, adding that they felt it was helpful to let him know of the above situation, and through him the members of his church. A practitioner who wrote the Board objecting that one of these telegrams was not true found her name subsequently dropped from the *Journal.* Finally Mrs. Orgain was excommunicated. (Personal letter to the author, July 21, 1944) She continued in the practice, however, and has since gone on publishing her own prolific writings on Christian Science.

The Rev. Glenn A. Kratzer, after falling from official grace, continued his work in Chicago as a practitioner, teacher, writer, and publisher for many years, enjoying a not inconsiderable success. He left a very definite mark on the movement, partly through his own writings, but mostly because he released to the field the collected *Teaching and Addresses of Edward A. Kimball.*

There were many others. William W. Walter was asked to retire from the *Journal* registry on the ground that publishing his own books disqualified him from being listed as a practitioner. He had written *The Pastor's Son,* an innocuous novel in which Christian Science healing was featured. (Walter, *Five Years in Christian Science,* pp. 91 ff.) Undaunted, Walter continued in his practicing, teaching, and writing from Aurora, Illinois. His principal work, *The Sickle,* a modified version of Christian Science ideas, remains the textbook for several thousand students even today, years after Walter's passing.

Lillian de Waters, of Stamford, Connecticut, is another Christian Science practitioner to win distinction after leaving the church.

From her prolific pen have flowed many, many books since near the turn of the century.

Some who belong in this second category leave the church after probation has been imposed upon them or disciplinary action threatened. These escape the greater stigma of outright expulsion, a stigma which has been known to handicap some of those who have sought to continue as Christian Scientists outside the Boston organization. Margaret Ledward Laird and John Lawrence Sinton resigned while in controversy with the Board of Directors. Mrs. Laird, a very popular leader, continued uninterruptedly in the practice, of course, and has written a small book called *Government Is Self-Government*. Since January, 1954, she has been issuing from Los Angeles a monthly subscription letter "on world events and individual experiences analyzed from the standpoint of Christian Science."

Finally, there is the category of dissenters who have no personal quarrel with the authorities, yet leave the church voluntarily, while in good standing, as a matter of principle. They are convinced that organization per se is incompatible with Christian Science. The argument is that organization could not exist without some measure of conformity on the part of all its members, and that this necessarily violates the freedom of thought and conscience essential to science and/or religion. They cite Mrs. Eddy's observation that whatever of value organization may have, it is fraught with peril, and that, beyond a point, "continued organization retards spiritual growth and should be laid off . . ." (*Retrospection and Introspection,* p. 45)

Most vocal of this group is Arthur Corey, who severed his connections with the church while enjoying unusual success in the organization, on the conviction that Christian Science must be liberated from institutional confinement. Since his resignation in 1945 he has gone on practicing, teaching, and writing. Also he has converted the Farallon Press, which was founded in 1930 by the Studdert-Kennedys as an outlet for independent Christian Science literature, into a foundation for "fostering public interest in and the progress of a scientific approach to God." The Farallon Foundation is a nonprofit public service, operating under state regulations and

duly recognized as such by the United States government. Its offi-
cers—Arthur Corey, Clarissa Hale Corey, and attorney Maurice J.
Rankin—all serve without remuneration. Farallon headquarters, in
Los Gatos, California, are under the able management of Helene
Hood, a class-taught student of Edna Kimball Wait and Arthur
Corey, who gave up an executive post with the Scott, Foresman
publishing house in Chicago to devote her full time to the cause of
a free press in Christian Science.

Frederick Dixon, most distinguished of all the Christian Science
editors, was European chief of Publication Committees and also a
Christian Science teacher. He was summoned from London at Mrs.
Eddy's request to become editor of the *Monitor* at Boston, and later
became editor-in-chief of all the church periodicals. When the
Great Litigation opened in 1919, Dixon proposed to the Board of
Directors of the Mother Church that he stay out of the controversy
and confine himself to keeping the *Monitor* strictly unbiased and
nonpartisan in the factional dispute. The Directors readily agreed.
Before long, however, they notified Dixon that he would have to
come out publicly on their side. This he declined to do, declaring
that he had not become a Christian Scientist for the purpose of
yielding personal support to any body of men, or to commit himself
to any form of personal ecclesiastical support. (Swan News Service,
November 28, 1923) Under the Publishing Society Trustees he
remained the editor, and there is no question that he did maintain
a policy of complete impartiality in the church publications.

After the court action terminated, Dixon declared that the
controversy never would have arisen had Christian Scientists heeded
Mrs. Eddy's guidance. She left the *Manual* in such a condition that
the church could not operate under it after her demise, and he
was convinced that she did nothing that was not deliberate.
Accordingly, he wrote the Directors, "obedience to Mrs. Eddy can
only be achieved by dissolving the material organization; the
spiritual reality is, of course, indestructible." Nothing remained for
the obedient follower but "to devote his energies to demonstrating
the truth of Mrs. Eddy's teaching as Principle may direct."
(*Christian Science and Organized Religion,* pp. 138 ff.) Resigning

from the Mother Church, Dixon launched in New York the *International Interpreter*, a monthly periodical given over to world affairs. His death, three years later, put an end to this publication.

Hugh A. Studdert-Kennedy, long-time foreign editor of the *Christian Science Monitor*, renounced the organization on the same grounds following the Great Litigation, although he was not himself directly involved in that controversy. He was to write the classic work on this question, *Christian Science and Organized Religion*, in which he declared that material organization has no permanent place in the outlook of ascending man, equating this with Mrs. Eddy's declaration that "organization and time have nothing to do with Life." (*Science and Health*, p. 249) Studdert-Kennedy remained a public practitioner of Christian Science to the end of his days in 1943, meanwhile turning out quite a few successful books on the faith.

Other prominent Scientists to withdraw were Clarissa Hale, Henry M. Newmark, and Gustavus Swift Paine. Miss Hale, who was eventually to become Mrs. Arthur Corey, was a writer for the periodicals and a consultant to Clifford P. Smith and Frederick Dixon. Newmark was secretary to Dixon. Paine, a popular Christian Science teacher and an editor of the *Journal* and *Sentinel*, has continued activity in New York as a practitioner all these years.

Of all the dissenters since the Bill-Dittemore enterprise, John Doorly comes the nearest to having founded an organization. But it is no church; just a loose association. It really cannot be called an organization at all. It is simply the body of his followers drawn together by their loyalty to Doorly and the fact that a publishing house in London, the Foundational Book Company, is maintained to continue the printing and circulation of his books and those of some of his followers. During the Litigation Doorly had fought on the side of the Directors when they were seeking to subdue the Trustees of the Publishing Society. But when, two decades later, he ran into conflict with their authority he took a militant stand against their dictatorial powers. This brought about his excommunication, but his bold stand served to stiffen his followers and to rally them for a general exodus.

Why have no rival organizations developed?

While many factors are no doubt involved, there are apparently just two main reasons for this. First, the majority of the dissenters remain loyal to Mrs. Eddy and will not oppose anything she is known to have founded. The other reason is that most of the dissenters who do not fall in with this view are those who believe that organization itself is the enemy of Christian Science, and many say of all religions. The former cling to the organization, even while refusing to conform, until they are forced out. The latter are basically not interested in the organization; they do not fight it, and feel that it will disappear with the further progress of Christian Science.

Most prominent among the outspoken dissenters who sought to stay in the church and reform it after their own ideas was Herbert Willoughby Eustace. Eustace, it will be recalled, led the struggle against the Board of Directors in the Great Litigation. He continued an active leader in the field until his death in 1957. Not long before his passing he flew from his home in Los Angeles all the way to London to hold a class, and held others at New York and San Francisco on the return trip. The title of his book, *Christian Science: Its Clear, Correct Teaching,* indicates that he considered his teachings true Christian Science. For many years after his expulsion he taught large and frequent classes, so that his pupils today run into the thousands. As such they have, of course, no standing in the church. But many within the church study his writings, which he could never have published had he remained in the organization. Yet he never attempted to found a rival church. Nowhere is there a Christian Scientist with greater reverence than he had for Mrs. Eddy, and he maintained that what Mrs. Eddy established must be supported. Like Augusta Stetson, he believed that it was spiritual progress, "demonstration," which forced him out of the material organization and into a more spiritualized sense of church. Nevertheless he disapproved voluntary withdrawal, and always subscribed to the view that whatever is wrong with the human organization can be corrected from within. All through the bitter conflict with the Directors and afterward, he confidently believed that in what he was doing he was serving best the cause of Christian Science, to which he gave his whole life.

Another outstanding example of Christian Scientists who revere the church as Mrs. Eddy's sacred demonstration, yet seek to reform its administration, is furnished by the Gilbert Carpenters, father and son, whose story we have already told.

A striking example of the extremes to which dissenters will go in clinging to the organization while disagreeing with its leadership is the case of Alexander Swan II. Swan, a popular Los Angeles practitioner, wrote a book called *God on Main Street,* presenting traditional Christian Science in popular style. When its preparation took time from his practice, he asked that his name be temporarily withdrawn from the *Journal* registry, as it has long been the rule that those listed be full-time practitioners. When the book was completed, Swan sought to reinsert his name but was refused listing. On September 27, 1951, Swan sued in federal court to compel reinstatement, at the same time claiming damages amounting to around $250,000. He maintained that his action was taken solely in the interests of the Christian Science movement, which he conceived to be embraced in the church. "I find there are those who are perfectly content to pursue Christian Science without organization," he said; but he added that "for reasons which may not be even clearly apparent to me, I am cherishing my membership in the Mother Church." Alexander Swan died on October 12, 1955, while his case was still pending.

And so the pattern continues. A more recent case is that of Hendrick J. De Lange, prominent practitioner, lecturer, and teacher, who, according to a lengthy statement released by him under date of October 15, 1957, was forced out of the church organization after many years of devoted service.

Undoubtedly there are types of dissenters who do not fall into any of the three major categories described above, but they evidently constitute a negligible minority. There are bound to be some malcontents, for instance, who would organize an opposition if they had the ability, the means, or the prestige to do so. Then there must be those who have suffered so at the hands of organizations that once out of the one which they had come to know, in this case the Christian Science church, they desire to have nothing to do with organizations of any kind. The number of such individuals, however, could not be great, for one seldom encounters them in the field. Certainly Arthur Corey does not belong to any of these categories, for his personal experiences with the church were not unhappy ones. Nor does Corey lack the means, the ability, and the opportunity to organize. Again and again some of his more zealous followers have urged him to form a church, create an organization. His files contain letters showing that some have even tried to force him to do so. But he is adamant. Christian Science belongs to the world. It must be as free as the air. He will take no risks of limiting its outreach by confining it within any organization, however ideally constructed. This feeling is shared by many.

Most of those who depart the church, at least the lay dissenters generally, simply continue to be Christian Scientists without benefit of organization membership. Many of them do not bother to resign formally. Some continue to attend church services, either regularly or sporadically. Those who feel the need of organizational ties find many congenial groups at hand into which they can go and upon which they can lean. The New Thought groups, while differing substantially in theory, do nevertheless engage in practices which closely resemble those of Christian Science.

Have the leaders who were excluded or withdrew from the church found, as one might expect, a place of leadership in these kindred movements today? During Mrs. Eddy's time Emma Curtis Hopkins became associated with the New Thought wing of mental healing, and Charles Fillmore came out of Christian Science to found Unity. But the author's extended questionnaire study of the religious backgrounds of several hundred leaders of such groups as Unity, Religious Science, Divine Science, etc., revealed that almost none of these leaders had come out of Christian Science. More of them had been Methodists, Presbyterians, Baptists, and Catholics than Scientists. The only prominent former Scientist was Elizabeth Carrick Cook, head of the Church of Absolute Science, who had been a class-taught student of Dr. Fluno, close disciple of Mrs. Eddy.

What of the future? No one knows, of course, what will happen. Can an organization so strongly authoritarian as the Christian Science church continue to exist in a democratic society without revolt sooner or later occurring? There are those who think that the outlook for democracy itself is not too good. With the rise of the strong dictatorships, whether of the fascist-nazi or the communist type, democracy is certainly threatened. Not a few persons are convinced that democracy has simply had its day and will pass. If it does, then the contrast between the controls of the authoritarian state and the authoritarian church will be slight. There may be a clash of authorities. This has occurred before, as between the Roman Catholic church and the state. The choice will not be between authority and freedom, but between authorities. Shall the state or the church have the authority over the individual at this or that particular point? Freedom will have vanished.

This is a gloomy view, but, many hold, a realistic one. Given the new techniques of control of mass communication, it is asserted, men's minds can and will be shaped so that George Orwell's fantasy *1984* may come true. They may well cry "war is peace" and think that it is. We may be only on the threshold of an era in which the old Judeo-Christian view of the worth of the individual will disappear. The feeble efforts of the occasional individuals who may rebel against centralized control will then be no match for the powerful forces which have at their command all the means of compelling uniformity of thought and action.

In such a case freedom of thought and action within the field of religion would of course be completely lost. There would be precious little reason for the existence of religious freedom when there was no freedom in any other area of life.

But the author does not believe that the wave of the future is totalitarianism. He believes that the rise of totalitarian systems is but a passing phase of our human scene.

This is, of course, frankly a faith and quite undemonstrable, but there is a good deal in past history to justify it. It is allied too to another faith, that there is a moral order in the universe which must soon or late bring to naught the totalitarianism built upon a disregard for moral values, as all totalitarianisms essentially are. They carry within themselves the seeds of their own destruction. They rise and flourish for a time, but ultimately tyrannies fail; they must fail, if there is a moral order in the universe. If this faith is well founded, if freedom is a value which persists in man's relationships, if our democracy maintains itself, then soon or late totalitarianisms in religion will break down, and among them that of Christian Science. The author does not know how soon this breakdown will come; but come it will, he believes, and there will be either an enforced reform from within or a radical break with the church of at least a substantial minority who may seek to form a newer, freer branch of the faith, which will permit the essential liberties which already many dissenters within the church are longing for, if not openly demanding.

Highly placed leaders of the Christian Science church speak of the monolithic strength of the church, and glory in the fact that no significant break with the church has ever occurred. They look with complacence upon the dissatisfaction voiced by the few dissenters who are vocal. Maybe they are right. But there is slowly building up a degree of disagreement with the present leadership and policies of the church which may, one day, and sooner than one might now be inclined to think, eventuate in an explosion that will rock the church.

But this is to deal in prophecy, and the author is neither prophet nor son of a prophet, but only a reporter of what he has observed in the life of the great Christian Science movement since the death of its great founder. He only hopes that the undoubted values which the movement has imported into the life of human society will not be lost or obscured by whatever occurs in the future.

Bibliography

THE LIST of books offered here is by no means a complete bibliography of Christian Science. It does, however, contain the major items upon the basis of which a history of Christian Science must at present be written. In the archives of the Mother Church there is of course a vast mass of original material: letters of Mrs. Eddy as yet unpublished, as well as much of the correspondence of early leaders of the movement; detailed reports of all kinds to the Boards of Directors and the Trustees of the Publishing Society; and all sorts of important documents. But this extremely valuable source material is not available as yet to historical scholars. It is to be hoped that some day free access to the archives will be given to interested research scholars. Only then can the complete, the definitive, history of Christian Science be written.

Included here are many books of little value to the historian, but useful to one who wants to see the total outreach of the movement. There are, for example, a number of books of fiction written by Christian Scientists from the point of view of that faith. There are also a great many by believers in Christian Science who are no longer included in the membership of the church, in which they set forth their variant interpretations of the faith.

The author has not by any means made use of all the titles in this list, particularly those which are fictional; but it seemed worth while to include them as they, too, are studied seriously by many Christian Scientists. Many of the books listed, and most of the manuscripts, are difficult of access, being found chiefly in the rare book sections of the greater libraries or in private libraries. The author will be glad to give information to interested scholars concerning books which they are unable to find.

ADAMS, KENNETH B. *Christian Science Association Addresses*. Berkeley: Lederer, Street & Zeus, 1948.

ADAMS, WILLIAM. *The Elements of Christian Science*. Hooker Press, 1850.

Advance of Prohibition, The. Boston: Christian Science Publishing Society, 1920.

ARMSTRONG, JOSEPH. *The Mother Church*. Boston: Christian Science Publishing Society, 1897.

AUSTIN, B. F. *New Thought, Christian Science and Spiritualism*.

BACH, MARCUS. *Report to Protestants*. Indianapolis: Bobbs-Merrill, 1948.

BAKER, ALFRED E. *Class Notes*. Boston: J. Raymond Cornell, 1935.

———. *Metaphysical Obstetrics*. Providence: Cornell Book Co., 1935.

———. *Private Metaphysical Work Performed for Mary Baker Eddy*. Providence: Cornell Book Co., 1936.

BANCROFT, SAMUEL PUTNAM. *Mrs. Eddy as I Knew Her in 1870*. Boston: Geo. H. Ellis Press, 1923.

BARRETT, WILLIAM. *The Religion of Health*. London: J. M. Dent & Sons, 1925.

BATES, ERNEST SUTHERLAND, and DITTEMORE, JOHN VALENTINE. *Mary Baker Eddy: The Truth and the Tradition*. New York: Alfred A. Knopf, 1932.

BEASLEY, NORMAN. *The Continuing Spirit*. New York: Duell, Sloan & Pearce, 1956.

———. *The Cross and the Crown*. New York: Duell, Sloan & Pearce, 1952.

BEECHER, MARGARET. *Some Truths and Wisdom of Christian Science*. New York: Pulpit Press, 1904.

Bible and Christian Science, The. Boston: Davis & Bond, 1905.

BILL, ANNIE C. *Christian Science versus Plagiarism*. London and Washington: A. A. Beauchamp, 1929.

———. *Science, Evolution and Immortality*. Washington: A. A. Beauchamp, 1927.

BLAVATSKY, H. P. *Some of the Errors of Christian Science*. Point Loma, Calif.: Theosophical Publishing Co., 1907.

Blight That Failed, The. New York: Blue Ribbon Books, 1930.

BLOME, ARNOLD. *A Voice Is Calling*. New York: G. P. Putnam's Sons, 1926.

BOOKER, RICHARD. *Dominion through Mind Power* and *The Magic of Knowing*. Los Gatos, Calif.: Farallon Foundation, 1955.

Boone, J. Allen. *Letters to Strongheart.* New York: Prentice-Hall, 1941.
———. *You Are the Adventurer.* New York: Prentice-Hall, 1943.
Braden, Charles S. *The Scriptures of Mankind.* New York: Macmillan, 1952.
———. *These Also Believe.* New York: Macmillan, 1949.
———. *The World's Religions.* Nashville: Abingdon-Cokesbury, 1939.
Brinkley, William. *Marblehead.* Westwood, N. J.: Revell Co., 1953.
Brisbane, Arthur. *What Mrs. Eddy Said to Arthur Brisbane.* New York: M. E. Paige, 1905.
Brown, Charles Reynolds. *Faith and Health.* New York: Thomas Y. Crowell Co., 1910.
Buckley, J. M. *Faith Healing and Christian Science.* New York: Century Co., 1892.
Burton, Edmund F. *Why I Became a Christian Scientist.* Des Moines: The Midwestern, 1908.
Carpenter, Gilbert C., Sr. and Carpenter, Gilbert C., Jr. *Brown University Address.* Tiverton, R. I.: Newport County Sentinel Press, 1931.
———. *Mary Baker Eddy: Her Spiritual Footsteps.* Providence: Privately printed, 1934.
———. *Visions of Mary Baker Eddy.* Providence: Privately printed, 1937.
Cary, Beth. *Individual Completeness.* Los Angeles: Metaphysical Science Association, 1916.
Channing, George. "What Is a Christian Scientist?" *Look,* November 18, 1952.
Chaudet, Louis William. *The Common Sense of God.* Los Angeles: Times-Mirror Press, 1941.
Christian Science or Ecclesiasticism: Which? New York, 1922.
Christian Science Journal. Monthly. Boston: Christian Science Publishing Society, 1883 ———.
Christian Science and Legislation. Boston: Christian Science Publishing Society, 1905.
Christian Science Monitor. Daily newspaper. Boston: Christian Science Publishing Society, 1908 ———.
Christian Science Quarterly. Boston: Christian Science Publishing Society, 1890 ———.
Christian Science Sentinel. Weekly. Boston: Christian Science Publishing Society, 1898 ———.
Christian Science Series. Bimonthly. Boston: Christian Science Publishing Society, May 1, 1889–May 1, 1891.
Christian Science War Time Activities. Boston: Christian Science Publishing Society, 1922.

406   CHRISTIAN SCIENCE TODAY

CHUTE, MARCHETTE. *The End of the Search*. New York: North River Press, 1947.

———. *The Search for God*. New York: E. P. Dutton & Co., 1941.

Committee on General Welfare of The Mother Church, Report of. New York: Federal Press, 1922.

COOK, JAY W. *Lectures on Absolute Science*. San Francisco: California Press, 1927.

COREY, ARTHUR. *Christian Science Class Instruction*. San Francisco: Farallon Press, 1945; now pub. by Farallon Foundation, Los Gatos, Calif.

———. *Personal Introduction to God*. New York: Exposition Press, 1952; now published by Farallon Foundation, Los Gatos, Calif.

Correlatives, Scriptural Readings, Benedictions. Jamaica, N.Y.: Helpful Books Co., 1939.

CRELLEN, JOHN SAMUEL (comp.). *Shakespeare, Christian Science and the Bible*. New York, 1904.

CUNRADI, CHARLES. *Elucidative Thought on Animal Magnetism*. London: Privately printed, 1952.

CUTTEN, GEORGE B. *Three Thousand Years of Mental Healing*. New York: Charles Scribner's Sons, 1911.

DAKIN, EDWIN FRANDEN. *Mrs. Eddy: The Biography of a Virginal Mind*. New York: Charles Scribner's Sons, 1929.

DAVIS, ALICE PITMAN. *From a Boundless Basis*. Seymour, Iowa: Herald Publishing Co., 1952.

DAY, GEORGE B. *The New Interpretation*. Chicago: Privately printed, 1889.

———. *The Platform*. Chicago: Privately printed, 1890.

DE LANGE, HENDRICK J. *Daycroft Address*. Stamford, Conn., 1940.

DE WATERS, LILLIAN. *The Voice of Revelation*. Stamford, Conn.: Hycliff Publishing Co., 1950.

D'HUMY, FERNAND E. *Mary Baker Eddy Fulfills Prophecy*. New York: Library Publishers, 1954.

———. *Mary Baker Eddy in a New Light*. New York: Library Publishers, 1952.

———. *Women Who Influenced the World*. New York: Library Publishers, 1955.

DICKEY, ADAM H. *Memoirs of Mary Baker Eddy*. Boston: Merrymount Press, 1927.

DOORLY, JOHN W. *Christian Science Practice*. London: Foundational Book Co., 1950.

———. *God and Science*. London: Frederick Muller Ltd., 1949.

———. *The Pure Science of Christian Science*. London: Foundational Book Co., 1946.

————. *Science of the Bible: Talks Given Weekly in London, 1947-1950.* 9 vols. London: Foundational Book Co., n.d.

DRESSER, HORATIO W. *The Quimby Manuscripts.* New York: Thomas Y. Crowell Co., 1921. The suppressed first edition contains the Mary Baker Patterson (Eddy) correspondence with Phineas Parkhurst Quimby.

EDDY, MARY BAKER. "Address by Mrs. Eddy," in *World's Parliament of Religions,* ed. JOHN HENRY BARROWS, II, 1419 ff. Chicago: Parliament Publishing Co., 1893.

————. *Christ and Christmas.* Illustrated by JAMES F. GILMAN. Edward N. Pearson Press, 1893; now pub. by Christian Science Publishing Society, Boston.

————. *Collectanea.* Comp. by GILBERT C. CARPENTER, SR. and GILBERT C. CARPENTER, JR. Providence: Privately printed, n.d.

————. *Correspondence Between Mrs. Eddy and the Christian Science Board of Directors.* 2 vols. Comp. by GILBERT C. CARPENTER, SR. and GILBERT C. CARPENTER, JR. Providence: Privately printed, 1944.

————. *Essays on Christian Science.* Comp. by GILBERT C. CARPENTER, SR. and GILBERT C. CARPENTER, JR. Providence: Privately printed, n.d.

————. *Footprints Fadeless.* Boston: Joseph Armstrong, 1902.

————. *Historical Sketch of Metaphysical Healing.* Boston, 1885.

————. "Life," *Christian Science Journal,* XXXVI, 1 ff.

————. Miscellaneous writings: Many articles and statements unpublished elsewhere are to be found in the *Christian Science Journal,* 1883-1910, and the *Christian Science Sentinel,* 1898-1910. In addition, short excerpts from Mrs. Eddy's writings held in the Mother Church archives have appeared in these periodicals and are listed in their indexes.

————. *Notes on the Course in Divinity.* Comp. by GILBERT C. CARPENTER, SR. and GILBERT C. CARPENTER, JR. Providence: Privately printed, 1933.

————. "Principle and Practice," *Christian Science Sentinel,* XX, 10.

————. *Private Directions for Metaphysical Healing.* Boston: Privately printed, 1881; now pub. by Rare Book Co., New York.

————. *Prose Works.* Boston: Christian Science Publishing Society, 1925.

————. *Repaid Pages.* Copyright 1896, but not published at that time. Providence: Privately printed, n.d.

————. *Science and Health.* 1st ed., Boston: Christian Scientist Publishing Co., 1875; now pub. by Rare Book Co., New York. 2nd ed., Lynn: Asa G. Eddy, 1878; now pub. by Rare Book Co., New York. 3rd ed., Lynn: Asa G. Eddy, 1881; now pub. by Rare Book Co., New York.

6th ed., Boston: Privately printed, 1883; now pub. by Rare Book Co., New York. 16th ed., ed. JAMES HENRY WIGGIN. Boston: Privately printed, 1886; now pub. by Rare Book Co., New York.

————. *Science and Health with Key to the Scriptures: Authorized Edition.* Boston: Christian Science Publishing Society, 1906.

————. *The Science of Man.* Lynn: Thos. P. Nichols Press, 1876; now pub. by Rare Book Co., New York.

————. *The Science of Man—Revised.* Boston: Privately printed, 1883; now pub. by Rare Book Co., New York.

————. "Science and the Senses, Address," *Chicago Christian Scientist,* July, 1888.

Editorial Comments on the Life and Work of Mary Baker Eddy. Boston: Christian Science Publishing Society, 1911.

EUSTACE, HERBERT W. *Christian Science: Its Clear, Correct Teaching.* Berkeley: Lederer, Street & Zeus, c. 1934.

FARLOW, ALFRED. "Christian Science versus Superstition: Reply to Prof. Jastrow," *Milwaukee Medical Journal,* 1911.

————. "The Relations of Government to the Practice of Christian Science," *Government Magazine,* 1907.

————. *Replies to Clergymen.* Boston, 1908.

FARNSWORTH, E. C. *The Passing of Mary Baker Eddy.* Portland, Ore.: Smith & Sale, 1911.

————. *Sophistries of Christian Science.* Portland, Ore.: Smith & Sale, 1909.

FAUNCE, W. H. P. *Searchlights on Christian Science.* New York: Revell · Co., 1899.

FIELD-KING, JULIA. "The Genealogy of Mary Baker Eddy." Unpublished (1882).

FIREBRACE, AYLMER. *If Thou Criest After Knowledge.* London: Allen & Unwin, 1952.

FISHER, H. A. L. *Our New Religion.* London: Ernest Benn, 1929.

FLOWER, B. W. *Christian Science as a Religious Belief and a Therapeutic Agent.* Boston: Twentieth Century Co., 1909.

FOX, EMMETT. *The Sermon on the Mount.* New York: Grosset & Dunlap, 1934.

GARSTANG, HAZEL JANE. *Thy Kingdom Come.* Coral Gables, Fla., 1950.

GESTEFELD, URSULA N. *Jesuitism in Christian Science.* Chicago, 1888.

————. *The Science of the Christ.* Chicago, 1889.

————. *A Statement of Christian Science.* Chicago, 1888.

GILLENSON, LEWIS W. "The Story of Christian Science," *Look,* April 12, 1950.

GILLESPIE, JOHN. *Scriptural References Sustaining the Doctrines of*

Christian Science. Boston: Christian Science Publishing Society, 1901.

GILMAN, JAMES F. *Diary Records and Recollections of Mrs. Eddy.* Providence: Privately printed, n.d.

GILMORE, ALBERT FIELD. *Christ at the Peace Table.* New York: Prentice-Hall, 1943.

————. "Christian Science," in *Varieties of American Religion,* ed. CHARLES S. BRADEN. Chicago: Willett Clark & Co., 1936.

GLUCK, CARL. *Divine Science with Key to "Christ and Christmas."* Los Angeles: Times-Mirror Press, 1923.

GOLDSMITH, JOEL S. *The Infinite Way.* Los Angeles: Willing Publishing Co., 1947.

GOODWIN, WILLIAM M. *The Christian Science Church.* Washington, D.C.: Privately printed, 1916.

GRAHAM, ANDREW J. *Biographical Notes.* Charles River, Mass.: Runnymeade Co., 1936.

GRANT, RICHARD SOUTHALL. *Landmarks for Christian Scientists.* Boston: Rand Avery Co., 1934.

GREENBAUM, LEON. *Follow Christ.* St. Louis: Primitive Publishing Co., 1916.

GREENWOOD, SAMUEL. *Footsteps of Israel.* Boston: A. A. Beauchamp, 1922.

GREY, ELMER. *The Planning of Christian Science Church Edifices.* Los Angeles: Kingsley, Mason & Collins Co., 1916.

GRIFFITH, DEAN. *Peace, Health, Plenty.* Los Angeles, 1948.

GRINDROD, ALFRED H. *For Christian Scientists.* Sheffield, England, 1947.

HALDEMAN, I. M. *Christian Science in the Light of Holy Scripture.* New York: Revell Co., 1909.

HALDEMAN-JULIUS, E. *Christian Science Explained.* Joplin, Mo., 1930.

HAMLIN (WILKINSON), GEOFFREY. *Notes on the Manual and Trust Deed.* Boston, 1922.

HANNA, SEPTIMUS J. *The Christian Science Case.* Boston, 1899.

————. *Christian Science History.* Boston, 1899.

————. *Civil and Religious Liberty.* Boston: Christian Science Publishing Society, 1905, 1909.

HARDY, E. R. *Is Christian Science Quackery and Anti-Christian?* Buffalo, 1889.

HARRIS, SARA. *Father Divine: Holy Husband.* New York: Doubleday & Co., 1953.

HART, H. MARTYN. *An Examination of Christian Science.* New York: James Pott & Co., 1897.

HAUSHALTER, WALTER M. *Mrs. Eddy Purloins from Hegel.* Boston: A. A. Beauchamp, 1936.

410 CHRISTIAN SCIENCE TODAY

HAY, ELLA H. *A Child's Life of Mary Baker Eddy.* Boston: Christian Science Publishing Society, 1942.

Hearings on Proposed Medical Bills. Boston: Christian Science Publishing Society, 1898.

HIGGINS, MARVIN RANDOLPH. *The Pacific Coast Sanatorium.* San Francisco: John Henry Nash, 1937.

Him Only Shalt Thou Serve. Owings' Mills, Maryland: Published for the Peace Association of Christian Scientists by Evelyn Owings, n.d.

HOPKINS, EMMA CURTIS. *Christian Science Lessons.* Chicago, 1894; now pub. by High Watch Fellowship, Cornwall Bridge, Conn.

HORWOOD, HAROLD. *Mary Baker Eddy: Her Communications from Beyond the Grave.* London: Psychic Press, 1948.

HUBBARD, ELBERT. *Little Journeys to the Homes of Great Teachers.* East Aurora, N. Y.: Roycrofters, 1908.

HUSE, SIBYL MARVIN. *Essays on Divine Metaphysics.* New York: G. P. Putnam's Sons, 1930.

———. *Offspring or Spiritual Generation.* New York: G. P. Putnam's Sons, 1922.

JENKINS, ANNE ELIZABETH. *Principia Addresses.* Elsah, Ill., 1946.

Jesuitism Secretly at Work. New York: The American Standard, 1924.

JOHNSON, WILLIAM LYMAN. *History of the Christian Science Movement.* 2 vols. Boston, 1920.

JOHNSTON, JULIA MICHAEL. *Mary Baker Eddy: Her Mission and Triumph.* Boston: Christian Science Publishing Society, 1946.

———. *Principia Addresses.* Elsah, Ill., 1945.

KAPPELER, MAX. *Christian Government: Its Scientific Evolution.* London: Foundational Book Co., 1946.

———. *The Structure of the Christian Science Textbook.* London: Foundational Book Co., 1954.

KERSEYMER, VIOLET. *Principia Addresses.* Elsah, Ill., 1936.

KILPATRICK, WILLIAM D. *Principia Addresses.* Elsah, Ill., 1941.

KIMBALL, EDWARD A. *The Endeavor to Handicap Truth.* Boston: Christian Science Publishing Society, 1905.

———. *Lectures and Articles on Christian Science.* Chesterton, Ind.: Privately printed, 1921 and 1938.

———. *Normal Class Notes.* Boston: J. Raymond Cornell, 1935.

———. *Teaching and Addresses.* Chicago: Kratzer, 1917; now pub. by Metaphysical Science Association, Los Angeles.

KNAPP, BLISS. *Ira Oscar Knapp and Flavia Stickney Knapp.* Norwood, Mass.: Plimpton Press, 1925.

KRAFT, F. A. *Christian Science.*

KRAMER, EDWARD L. *How to Demonstrate Christian Science.* St. Louis: Kimball Press, 1948.

KRATZER, GLENN A. *Dominion Within.* Chicago: Central Christian Science Institute, 1913.

———. *Revelation Interpreted.* Chicago: Central Christian Science Institute, 1913.

———. *Spiritual Man.* Chicago: Metaphysical Science Association, 1914.

LAIRD, MARGARET LEDWARD. *Government Is Self-Government.* Evanston, Ill.: Portal Press, 1952.

LARSON, C. D. *The Good Side of Christian Science.* New York: E. J. Clode, 1916.

LEA, CHARLES HERMAN. *A Plea for Christian Science.* London: J. M. Dent & Sons, 1915.

LEAKE, SAM. *The Healing of Sam Leake.* San Francisco, 1923.

———. *Letters on Right Thinking and Self-Healing.* San Francisco Metaphysical Publishing Co., 1925.

LEE, CHARLES H. *Divine Direction or Chaos.* New York: Philosophical Library, 1952.

LEE, MARY SANDS. *Principia Addresses.* Elsah, Ill., 1944.

Legal Aspects of Christian Science. Boston: Christian Science Publishing Society, 1899.

Legal Rights and Obligations of Christian Scientists. Boston: Committee on Publication. Issued under slightly differing titles without date; frequently revised.

LICHTENSTEIN, MORRIS. *Jewish Science and Health.* New York: Jewish Science Publishing Co., 1925.

LOMAXE, PAUL M. *Mary Baker Eddy: Spiritualist Medium.* 1946.

LONGYEAR, MARY BEECHER. *Hear, O Israel!* Boston: Geo. H. Ellis Press, 1922.

———. *The History of a House.* Brookline, Mass.: Zion Research Foundation, 1925.

LORD, FRANCES. *Christian Science Healing: Its Principles and Practice.* Chicago: Lily Publishing House, 1888.

LORD, MYRA B. *Mary Baker Eddy: A Concise Story of Her Life and Work.* Boston: Davis & Bond, 1918.

LUTZ, ALMA. *Mary Baker Eddy Historical House.* Brookline, Mass.: Longyear Foundation, 1940.

McCABE, JOSEPH. *The Absurdities of Christian Science.*

McCRACKEN, WILLIAM D. *Mary Baker Eddy and Her Book.* Tamworth, N.H.: M. W. Starr, 1925.

McNICKLE, FLOYD M. *Absolute Christian Science.* Chicago, 1942.

MANN, ALBERT C. *Principia Addresses.* Elsah, Ill., 1942.

MARCOSSON, ISAAC F. "The Girlhood of Mary Baker Eddy," *Munsey's Magazine,* April, 1911.

MARS, GERHARDT C. *The Interpretation of Life.* New York: D. Appleton & Co., 1908.

MATTERS, MARGARET MURNEY G. *Principia Addresses.* Elsah, Ill., 1939.

MATTOX, WILLARD S. *Conservation of Public Health.* Boston, 1914.

MEEHAN, MICHAEL. *Mrs. Eddy and the Late Suit in Equity.* Cambridge, Mass.: University Press, 1908.

MILMINE, GEORGINE. *The Life of Mary Baker G. Eddy and the History of Christian Science.* New York: Doubleday, Page & Co., 1909.

———. "Mary Baker G. Eddy," *McClure's Magazine,* XXVIII-XXX (1907-8).

Miscellaneous Documents Relating to Christian Science and to Its Discoverer and Founder, Mary Baker Eddy. Providence: Privately printed, n.d.

MOEHLMAN, CONRAD HENRY. *Ordeal by Concordance.* New York: Longmans, Green & Co., 1955.

MOLL, ALBERT. *Christian Science, Medicine and Occultism.* 1902.

MURRAY, C. A. (EARL OF DUNMORE). *The Revelation of Christianus.* Cambridge, Mass.: University Press, 1901.

MURRAY, LINDLEY. *English Reader.* Claremont, N. H.: Claremont Manufacturing Co., 1834.

MURRAY, S. VAN ALEN. *Christian Science.* New York, 1908.

———. *Flesh and Matter.* New York, 1910.

MUSSEY, HENRY RAYMOND. *The Christian Science Censor.* New York: The Nation, 1930

NORTON, CAROL. *The Christian Science Church: Its Organization and Polity.* Boston: Christian Science Publishing Society, 1904.

———. *The Christian Science Movement.* Boston: Christian Science Publishing Society, 1904.

———. *Studies in Character.* Boston: Page Co., 1906.

———. *Woman's Cause.* Boston: Dana Estes & Co., 1895.

OAKES, RICHARD. *The Chicago Addresses of Mary Baker Eddy.* Aldershot, England: W. & L. Hunt, 1950.

ORCUTT, WILLIAM DANA. *Mary Baker Eddy and Her Books.* Boston: Christian Science Publishing Society, 1950.

ORGAIN, ALICE L. *Angelic Overtures of Christ and Christmas.* New York: H. Wolff Co., 1941.

———. *As It Is.* Cincinnati: Johnson & Hardin, 1932.

———. *The Detached Branch.* New York: Lenz & Riecker, 1931.

———. *Footsteps of Prayer.* New York: Privately printed, 1944.

———. *Progressive Revisions.* New York: Rare Book Co., 1933.

————. *The Story of the Christian Science Church Manual.* New York: Rare Book Co., 1934.

OVERBURY, ARTHUR E. *Mary Baker Eddy's Challenge Answered.* Monrovia, 1937.

PARTINGTON, BLANCHE, et al. *Francis J. Fluno, C.S.B.* Oakland, Calif.: Wm. J. Marnell, 1933.

PEABODY, FREDERICK W. *The Religio-Medical Masquerade.* Boston: Hancock Press, 1910; New York: Revell Co., 1915.

PENNINGTON, JEANNE G. *Philosophic Nuggets.* New York: Ford, Howard & Hulbert, 1899.

Permanency of The Mother Church, The. Boston: Christian Science Publishing Society, 1954.

PICKFORD, MARY. *Why Not Try God?* New York: H. C. Kinsey & Co., 1934.

PITTMAN, ALFRED. *Principia Addresses.* Elsah, Ill., 1943.

PODMORE, FRANK. *Mesmerism and Christian Science.* London: Methuen, 1909.

POWELL, LYMAN P. *Christian Science: The Faith and Its Founder.* New York: G. P. Putnam's Sons, 1908.

————. *Mary Baker Eddy: A Life Size Portrait.* New York: Macmillan, 1930; now pub. by Christian Science Publishing Society, Boston.

Proceedings in Equity 1919-1921 Concerning Deed of Trust of January 25, 1898 Constituting the Christian Science Publishing Society; also *Supplement.* Limited subscription ed. Boston: Christian Science Publishing Society, 1922.

PURRINGTON, W. M. A. *Christian Science: A Plea for Children and Other Helpless Sick.* New York: E. B. Treat & Co., 1900.

RAMSAY, MARY E. *Christian Science and Its Discoverer.* Cambridge, England: Heffer & Sons, 1923; now pub. by Christian Science Publishing Society, Boston.

RAWSON, FREDERICK L. *Life Understood.* London: Crystal Press, 1912.

REVERE, PAUL (WALTER H. WILSON and KARL N. SMITH). *Support for the Christian Science Board of Directors.* Washington, D.C., 1945.

RILEY, FRANK L. *Spiritual Healing.* Los Angeles: Phillips Press, 1917.

RILEY, W. B. *Eddyism.*

ROBINSON, HENRY. *Biographical Sketch of Rev. Mary Baker G. Eddy.* Concord, N.H.: People & Patriot Co., 1901.

ROBINSON, JOSEPH S. *Waymarks in the Life of Mary Baker Eddy.* Springfield, Mass.: Pond-Ekberg Co., 1942.

ROSS, PETER V. *If a Man Die He Shall Live Again.* New York: Hobson Book Press, 1945.

————. *Leaves of Healing.* New York: Hobson Book Press, 1946.

————. *Lectures on Christian Science.* New York: Hobson Book Press, 1945.

————. *Letters of a Traveler.* New York: Hobson Book Press, 1945.

RUBENSTEIN, I. H. *Contemporary Religious Jurisprudence.* Chicago: Waldain Press, 1948.

SCHROEDER, THEODORE. *Christian Science and Sex.* 1920.

SEAL, FRANCES THURBER. *Christian Science in Germany.* Philadelphia: John C. Winston Co., 1931.

SEITZ, DON C. *Uncommon Americans.* Indianapolis: Bobbs-Merrill, 1925.

SELLERS, CHARLES W. *The Private Life of Mary Baker Eddy.* Detroit: Privately printed, 1935.

SHELDON, HENRY C. *Christian Science So-Called.* New York: Eaton & Mains, 1913.

SHERMAN, BRADFORD. *Historical Sketch of the Introduction of Christian Science in Chicago and the West.* Chicago: Privately printed, 1912.

————. *The Mystery of Life, or What Is Mind?* Chicago, 1915.

SHORT, WILLIAM. *Christian Science: What It Is.* New York: Thomas Whitaker, 1899.

SIMONSEN, SEVERIN E. *From Methodist Pulpit into Christian Science.* Los Angeles: Haynes Corp., 1928.

SMITH, CLIFFORD P. *Christian Science: Its Legal Status.* Boston: Christian Science Publishing Society, 1914.

————. *Christian Science and Legislation.* Boston: Christian Science Publishing Society, 1905-9.

————. *Historical Sketches.* Boston: Christian Science Publishing Society, 1941.

————. *Judge Jones and the Manual as Applied to Kentucky.* Boston, n.d.

SMITH, CUSHING. *Behold Genesis.* New York: Pageant Press, 1957.

SMITH, FRANCES W. *Mrs. Eddy's Writings Made Comprehensible.* San Francisco, 1949.

SNOWDEN, JAMES H. *The Truth About Christian Science.* Philadelphia: Westminster Press, 1920.

SPRAGUE, FRANK H. *Spiritual Consciousness.* Boston: Lee & Shepard, 1900.

SPRINGER, FLETA CAMPBELL. *According to the Flesh.* New York: Coward-McCann, 1930.

STEIGER, HENRY W. *Christian Science and Philosophy.* New York: Philosophical Library, 1948.

STETSON, AUGUSTA E. *Give God the Glory.* New York: Privately printed, 1911.

————. *Reminiscences, Sermons and Correspondence.* New York: G. P. Putnam's Sons, 1926.

——. *Sermons and Other Writings*. New York: G. P. Putnam's Sons, 1926.

——. *Vital Issues in Christian Science*. New York: G. P. Putnam's Sons, 1914.

STEWART, IRMA. *Job: His Spiritual Value*. New York: North River Press, 1943.

Story of Christian Science War Time Activities 1939-1946, The. Boston: Christian Science Publishing Society, 1947.

STRANG, LEWIS C. *Freedom through Right Thinking*. New York: Roland Publishing Co., 1925.

——. *The Master and the Modern Spirit*. New York: Roland Publishing Co., 1925.

STUDDERT-KENNEDY, HUGH A. *And I Will Give Him the Morning Star*. London: G. P. Putnam's Sons, 1936.

——. *Arise Shine*. London: G. P. Putnam's Sons, 1938; San Francisco: Farallon Press, 1945.

——. *Christian Science and Organized Religion*. San Francisco: Farallon Press, 1930.

——. *The Impatience of a Layman*. New York and London: Century Co., 1926.

——. *Mrs. Eddy: Her Life, Her Work, Her Place in History*. San Francisco: Farallon Press, 1947; now pub. by Farallon Foundation, Los Gatos, Calif.

——. *The Visitor*. San Francisco: John Henry Nash, 1930; New York: G. P. Putnam's Sons, 1930; London: G. P. Putnam's Sons, 1934; now pub. by Farallon Foundation, Los Gatos, Calif.

STIRLING, JAMES HUTCHISON. *The Secret of Hegel*. Edinburgh: Oliver & Boyd, 1866, and New York: G. P. Putnam's Sons; rev. ed., 1898.

SWAN, ALEXANDER. *God on Main Street*. New York: Greenberg, 1951.

SWIHART, ALTMAN K., II. *Since Mrs. Eddy*. New York: Henry Holt & Co., 1931.

TAYLOR, NEMBHARD. *The Analysis of Man*. Berkeley: Privately printed, 1953.

TODD, ARTHUR J. *Principia Addresses*. Elsah, Ill., 1940.

TOMLINSON, IRVING C. *The Revelation of St. John an Open Book*. Boston: Privately printed, 1935.

——. *Twelve Years with Mary Baker Eddy*. Boston: Christian Science Publishing Society, 1945.

TWAIN, MARK (SAMUEL CLEMENS). *Christian Science*. New York and London: Harper & Bros., 1907.

UNDERHILL, ANDREW F. *Valid Objections to Christian Science*. New York: E. S. Gorham, 1902.

WALTER, WILLIAM F. *Five Years in Christian Science.* Aurora, Ill.: Privately printed, 1910.

———. *The Sickle* and *The Sharp Sickle.* Aurora, Ill.: Privately printed, 1918.

We Knew Mary Baker Eddy. Boston: Christian Science Publishing Society, First Series, 1943; Second Series, 1950; Third Series, 1953.

WEAVER, EDWARD E. *Mind and Health.* New York: Macmillan, 1913.

WEILL, ELLA. *The Progress of Pilgrim from Material Sense to the Spiritual Sense of God, Man and the Universe.* New York: G. P. Putnam's Sons, 1922.

WHARTON, JEAN PAGE. *Blueprints for Living.* San Gabriel, Calif.: Willing Publishing Co., 1951, 1954.

WHITESIDE, CHARLES WATSON. *A Viewpoint on the World Situation.* Berkeley: Lederer, Street & Zeus, 1937.

WIGGIN, JAMES HENRY ("PHARE PLEIGH"). *Christian Science and the Bible.* 1886.

WILBUR, SIBYL. *The Life of Mary Baker Eddy.* New York: Concord Publishing Co., n.d.; now pub. by Christian Science Publishing Society, Boston.

WILBY, THOMAS W. *What Is Christian Science?* New York: John Lane Co., 1915.

WILDING, W. F. W. *Christian Science and the Healing Art.* New York, 1890.

WILLIAMSON, MARGARET. *The Mother Church Extension.* Boston: Christian Science Publishing Society, 1939.

WINSLOW, WENTWORTH BYRON. *Let God Do It.* New York: Dodge Publishing Co., 1937.

WOLCOTT, P. C. *What Is Chirstian Science?* New York: Revell Co., 1896.

WOOD, CLEMENT. *The Real Mary Baker Eddy.* Kansas City: Haldeman-Julius, 1925.

———. *The Truth About Christian Science.* Kansas City: Haldeman-Julius, 1925.

WOODBURY, JOSEPHINE CURTIS. *Quimbyism, Or the Paternity of Christian Science.* Letchworth: Garden City Press, 1909.

———. *War in Heaven.* Boston: S. Usher Press, 1897.

WOODWARD, CLIFFORD A. "Recent Growth of Christian Science in New England," *New England Magazine,* April, 1914.

WORKS, JOHN D. *U.S. Senate Speeches of July 6, 1911, and April 29-30, 1912.* Reprinted from *Congressional Record.*

WORMLEY, A. E. *Israel Yesterday and Today.* Boston: A. A. Beauchamp, 1918.

WYNNE-TYSON, ESME. *The Unity of Being*. London: Andrew Dakers, 1949.

YOUNG, HELEN L. *Scriptural Healing*. New York: Oxford University Press, 1907.

YOUNG, VASH. *A Fortune to Share* and *Let's Start Over Again*. Cleveland: World Publishing Co., 1931.

ZAHN, FRANKLIN. *We State Our Case: Some Questions Answered by Christian Scientist Conscientious Objectors*. Portland, Ore.: Willamette Press, 1945.

ZWEIG, STEFAN. *Mental Healers*. New York: Viking Press, 1932.

CHRISTIAN SCIENCE NOVELS

BURNHAM, CLARA LOUISE. *The Right Princess*. Boston: Houghton Mifflin Co., 1904.

BUTLER, MAUDE M. *Violette*. Boston: Davis & Bond, 1917.

CARY, BETH. *Complete in Him*. Chicago, 1915.

CORELLI, MARIE. *The Master Christian*. New York: Dodd, Mead & Co., 1900.

CUMMINS, MARY HORNIBROOK. *The Awakening*. Boston: Davis & Bond, 1905.

DE WATERS, LILLIAN. *Glad Tidings*. Boston: Davis & Bond, 1909.

HAYES, HIRAM W. *Paul Anthony: Christian*. Boston: Davis & Bond, 1904.

JOHNSON, WILLIAM LYMAN. *From Hawthorne Hall*. Boston: Homewood Press, 1922.

STOCKING, CHARLES FRANCIS. *Carmen Ariza*. Chicago: Maestro Co., 1915.

STOCKING-TOTHEROH. *A Businessman of Syria*. Chicago: Maestro Co., 1923.

WALTER, WILLIAM W. *The Pastor's Son*. Aurora, Ill.: Privately printed, 1908.

YATES, CATHERINE M. *On the Way There*. Boston: Davis & Bond, 1904.

UNPUBLISHED MATERIAL

A vast quantity of authenticated transcriptions of class instruction, addresses, diaries, memoirs, studies, correspondence, etc., of an authoritative nature, has been preserved, mostly in private libraries, though some of this material is in the Library of Congress, some in the Huntington Library, some in the Boston Public Library, and some in various theological libraries such as those of the Union Theological Seminary, Princeton Theological Seminary, and Perkins School of Theology, Southern Methodist University.

Index

109, 110, 113, 116, 122, 127, 147, 148, 207, 212, 213, 223, 231, 240, 246, 250, 285, 298, 309, 365; affirms Mary Baker Eddy "woman of the Apocalypse," 374; alleges fraud in Lieber document, 33; approves publication of Kimball *Lectures and Addresses*, 315; authority of, 240; and Annie C. Bill, 382; and the Carpenters, 213; considers Eddy script for movies, 378; control of Class Instruction, 99; control of doctrine, 99; control of lecturers, 120; control of literature, 99, 124 ff., 206; control of property, 99; control of public statements, 123; control of reading, 99; control of source materials, 203; control of teachers, 207 ff.; defends Mrs. Eddy's use of anesthetics, 38; defends Mrs. Eddy's use of drugs, 389; final authority, 110; first session of, 104; and Fourth Church, Rochester, 247; important statement of, 280; and Glenn Kratzer, 313-14; and *Mary Baker Eddy: The Truth and the Tradition*, 132, 150; and *Memoirs of Mary Baker Eddy*, 164 ff.; and *Mrs. Eddy: The Biography of a Virginal Mind*, 203; and *Mrs. Eddy as I Knew Her in 1870*, 131; offers to answer specific questions, 204; opposes fluoridation of water, 262; and pacifism, 289; policy concerning medical indoctrination, 261; protects official view of Mrs. Eddy, 167; regimentation by, 198; responsibilities of, 73; and *Science and Health*, 278; self-perpetuating, 66; set up, 51; succeeds Mrs. Eddy in authority, 62; supreme authority, 90; wins battle, 91; withdraws recognition of Watford, England, church, 248. *See also* Corey, Arthur; Doorly, John W.; Great Litigation; Laird, Margaret Ledward; Sinton, John L.; Studdert-Kennedy, Hugh A.; Wilson, Walter H.

Board of Education, 103, 104, 318
Board of Lectureship, 120, 357
Body, 301, 302, 311, 319, 327

Boise Public Library, 188
Booda, Esther Harris, 192
Booker, Richard, 184, 185
Books: approved, 120, 125; interference with circulation of, 198; obnoxious, 127; safe, 126
Booksellers, intimidation of, 189
Boothe, Stuart, 149, 375
Boston, 8, 11, 34, 43, 44, 45, 46, 53, 87, 115, 122, 126, 147, 151, 154, 176, 198, 199, 207, 222, 228, 237, 276, 357; trouble in, 47
Boston "dictatorship," 173
Boston Globe, 69, 290
Boston Herald, 37, 48
Boston hierarchy, 160, 374
Boston Journal, 357
Boston Post, 23
Boston Public Library, 164, 188
Boston Traveler, 45
Boycott, 127, 202; of periodicals, 87; of publications, 87
Braden, Charles S.: experience with Christian Science officials, 204 ff.
Braden-Channing letters, 196 ff.
Bradshaw, Sue, 46
Braley, Judge, 81
Branch churches, 43, 66, 88, 98, 122, 237, 238, 244, 249, 282, 380
Breymann, William H., 329
Brook, Mrs. Peggy, 232
Buck, Kate, 175
Bureau of History and Records, 131, 132, 140
Bütikofer, Emily, 236
Bylaws, 39, 55, 85, 89, 104, 117, 122, 222, 225, 238, 239; amendment impossible, 62; codified, 54; personal, 85; versus Trust Deed, 76

California, 160, 260, 274, 275; growth of Christian Science in, 270-71; rural growth, 273
California Metaphysical College, 46, 102
Calvinism, 13, 14
Camp Welfare Committee, 287, 291, 293
Canada, 268, 291
Carpenter, Gilbert C., Sr., 168, 208 ff., 365, 377, 398; excommunicated, 213

We Knew Mary Baker Eddy, 359
Welfare centers, 292
Wentworth, Rae, 180
Wentworth, Mrs. Sally, 26
Wesley, John, 116
West Coast, growth of Christian Science on, 270
Whipple, Sherman L., 76
Wiggin, James H., 14, 100
Wilbur, Sibyl, 12, 21, 34, 338, 384
Wilcox, Martha, 332, 334, 377
Willis, John B., 69
Wilson, Walter H., 241; excommunicated, 242; theory of church government, 244. *See also* Paul Revere
Wilson, Mrs. Walter H., 244

Woodbury, Josephine, 40, 139, 156, 283, 308, 379
"Work," preventive, 293
World War I, 286-88
World War II, 291
Worship, 119; public, 57; service, 284

Yoga, 32
Young, Bicknell, 113, 114, 173, 174, 175, 215, 229, 233, 323, 326, 327, 328, 330, 331, 332, 351; and Edward Kimball, 328; permitted note-taking, 113; Normal class of, 328
Young people, 71; clubs for, 284

Zurich, 236

r

Date Due